Governance and
Politics in Africa

Governance and Politics in Africa

edited by
Goran Hyden
Michael Bratton

Lynne Rienner Publishers — Boulder & London

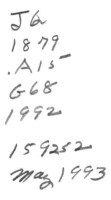

Published in the United States of America in 1992 by
Lynne Rienner Publishers, Inc.
1800 30th Street, Boulder, Colorado 80301

and in the United Kingdom by
Lynne Rienner Publishers, Inc.
3 Henrietta Street, Covent Garden, London WC2E 8LU

Library of Congress Cataloging-in-Publication Data
Governance and politics in Africa / edited by Göran Hydén and Michael
Bratton.
    p. cm.
Includes bibliographical references and index.
ISBN 1-55587-234-4 (alk. paper)
ISBN 1-55587-285-9 (pbk. : alk. paper)
    1. Africa—Politics and government—1960- 2. Political
participation—Africa. I. Hydén, Göran, 1938- . II. Bratton,
Michael.
JQ1879.A15G68 1991
323'.042'096—dc20
                                                        91-25811
                                                        CIP

British Cataloguing in Publication Data
A Cataloguing in Publication record for this book
is available from the British Library.

Printed and bound in the United States of America

The paper used in this publication meets the requirements
of the American National Standard for Permanence of
Paper for Printed Library Materials Z39.48-1984.

Contents

Illustrations

TABLES

FIGURES

MAP

Preface

Nineteen ninety was a benchmark year for Africa in much the same way that 1960 was. For the first time since independence, African government leaders took initiatives to share power with others in society. Thus, in over half of the continent's states, political reforms were debated and, in some countries, officially implemented. Africa took the first steps toward what many Africans are inclined to call "the second liberation."

The significance of 1990 is that African leaders acknowledged that the conduct of politics matters—and that there is scope for improvement. In this respect, there is a resemblance to 1960, when the primacy of politics was regarded as a prerequisite for development. Through reform of the structural legacies inherited from the colonial powers, as well as through mobilization of the masses, politics was seen to serve national development. This conceptualization of politics, however, also served as an invitation for leaders to concentrate political power. Development became a top-down affair, and politics increasingly an activity confined to a small clique of people. The latter ran away with politics, so to speak, turning public matters into private and making a mockery of political accountability.

Not only did individual political leaders lose legitimacy in the process, but so did politics as a public concern. By the 1980s, as they continued to see political leaders use their public positions to foster their own personal interests, people in most African countries had developed a cynical view of politics. This alienation of leaders from followers, we believe, was at the root of Africa's economic and social ills. Political will had been crippled and social energy exhausted. In short, the political formula adopted by the vast majority of African states at independence of "one leader, one ideology, and one political party" had run its course.

This disillusionment with political autocracy began to translate itself into demands for reform in the 1980s, as intellectuals and wage earners expressed concern about the decline that their countries were experiencing in literally all sectors of life. Yet it was only in 1990 that this trickle of demand turned into a flood and forced the incumbent political leadership to respond.

For much of the 1980s these leaders had been able to blame economic hardship on the International Monetary Fund and the World Bank, using the apparent failure of proposed structural reforms as their principal ammunition. The rapid turn of events in Eastern Europe in 1989 and the downfall of its Communist regimes, however, prompted African leaders to reconsider their position. What had to many of them been a model of rule had disintegrated. If autocracy was no longer tolerable in Eastern Europe, why should it be tolerated in Africa?

Africa has come full circle. The rediscovery of politics as an independent variable in development is reminiscent of the early part of the 1960s when Kwame Nkrumah's advice to his fellow nationalists, "seek ye first the political kingdom, and everything else will be added unto ye," was heeded across the continent. The big difference between now and then is that the first liberation was based on political victory over external powers, while the call for a second liberation stems from the oppressiveness and inadequacies of domestic forces. The latter implies the need for liberalization and, in the long run, democratization: the right of Africans to criticize their fellow Africans in public without fear of being harassed or thrown in jail; the right to form associations that are not controlled by official appointees; and the right to a fair trial before independent judges. For countries accustomed to treating all evils as having an external source, the social and political transformation implied in the second liberation is no mean agenda. Many observers rightly ask themselves if Africa is capable of such broad reforms, particularly at a time when the continent also suffers from economic decline. Yet Africa in the 1990s has little choice but to embark upon reforms that create political conditions in which latent social energy can be mobilized for progressive purposes. At the core of such reform efforts are new styles and forms of governance.

Drawing on Africa's postindependence political experience, we attempt to place current reform programs in perspective and to develop a conceptualization that enables us to think of these in a comparative fashion. More specifically, we try to examine the way a cross section of African countries have been governed since independence; to bring the reader up to date on the political reforms initiated in various African countries in the past few years, and especially in 1990; and to develop the concept of governance for use in comparative political analysis.

We believe that all these objectives are important, but we wish particularly to emphasize the last one. Governance, as used in this book, refers to the management of regime relations; that is, the rules that set the framework for the conduct of politics. Political actors differ in terms of how much attention they pay to these rules, but they tend to become especially attentive at times when society demands reform, and old rules need replacement. We believe that such demands are currently being raised in many parts of the world. It is important, therefore, to develop a conceptual scheme that permits cross-country comparisons. This is particularly important for us as Africanists, because much of the literature on African politics in recent years has treated it as unique or exceptional. While we do not disagree completely with this assertion, the winds of change in Africa and elsewhere provide an ideal opportunity for breaking the trend toward area insulation.

In Chapter 1, Hyden deals with this challenge, providing the basic parameters of a new approach to the study of politics that offers the basis for comparison across regions or areas. Hyden acknowledges the need for sensitivity to variations in the empirical realm. His analysis is not meant to provide a tight framework for the remaining chapters but stands as a contribution of its own to the conceptual and theoretical debate that the ongoing political reform efforts in various parts of the world give rise to. Other contributors to this book, however, address in various detail several of the points raised in the introductory chapter.

Chapter 2 is a continentwide review of political protests and reforms in recent years. More importantly, Bratton and van de Walle provide markers to enable us to understand the extent to which a second liberation is under way. We realize that things continue to change, and the empirical information provided will need constant updating. But this chapter has its place in our volume because it provides a sense of the range and depth of change attempted in African countries.

The next nine chapters provide empirical illustrations of three types of regimes. The first of these (on Senegal, Botswana, and Nigeria) includes countries where experimentation with democratic governance has been a consistent feature of the postindependence period. While respecting the efforts that political actors in these countries have made to institutionalize democratic governance, the authors of these chapters also emphasize the difficulties and challenges. Thus, Young and Kante, in Chapter 3, point to Senegal's problem of gaining popular acceptance of the principle of fairness in the election of popular representatives. In Chapter 4, on Botswana, Holm and Molutsi discuss the socioeconomic conditions that may sustain such processes as political liberalization and democratization. Williams, in Chapter 5, concentrates his analysis on the problems of creating a constitutional framework in Nigeria that is strong enough to withstand the centrifugal pressures of ethnic and religious forces.

The second regime type (illustrated here by Ghana, Burkina Faso, and Niger) is populist but also military. Of particular interest are the efforts by young and radical army officers to bring about popular participation in national affairs without using political parties. Chazan, in Chapter 6, devotes her attention to the political space created in Ghana under Flight Lieutenant Jerry Rawlings's rule since the early 1980s. In Chapter 7, focusing on the problems of building grassroots legitimacy of military governance in Burkina Faso and Niger, Robinson concludes on a rather pessimistic note: military rulers may be instrumental in bringing about a social transformation and thus open the door for more-democratic governance, but they are not very likely to succeed in institutionalizing such practice.

The third regime type is made up of one-party states (Kenya, Rwanda, Tanzania, and Zaire) all of which have faced growing pressure for change in the last few years. In Chapter 8, Barkan argues that Kenya under Jomo Kenyatta was in the process of building democratic forms of governance, but that his successor, Daniel arap Moi, has destroyed the fragile base for such a political practice that was built in the 1960s and 1970s. Rwanda has been a remarkably successful country as far as rural development goes, but in recent years dissatisfaction has grown with the skewed way in which public resources have been allocated within the country. Newbury, in Chapter 9, traces the experience with different forms of governance in that country and how the debates in recent years are pointing toward greater openness and tolerance. Tanzania has been unusually stable and peaceful for over thirty years in spite of being ruled in an autocratic, albeit benign, fashion by one of the continent's strongest political organizations. Tripp, in Chapter 10, examines the prospect for the rise of popular organizations in the shadow of a dominant party-state, particularly in the light of the deteriorating economic conditions for which much blame must be laid on the country's socialist policies. The importance of the parallel economy is at the center of MacGaffey's study of Zaire in Chapter 11. She believes that the ineffectiveness of the Mobutu state in serving the people has encouraged or forced both opponents and sympathizers of the present regime to engage in entrepreneurial activities that have further reduced the power of the state but have given rise to new social forces that demand more democratic governance.

The concluding chapter, by Bratton and Rothchild, pulls together the discussion in previous chapters by focusing on the institutional bases for more accountable and legitimate forms of governance in Africa. Their discussion is also an assessment of the usefulness of the concept of governance, and thus a further look at how we can improve the comparative study of political reforms in Africa and elsewhere.

This volume lends itself to use in courses both in African politics and in comparative politics. For the more conceptually and theoretically interested student, it raises fresh ideas on how to study politics comparatively. For the more empirically oriented person, it provides not only a broad range of detailed case studies but also an up-to-date analysis of ongoing political protests and governance reforms.

Goran Hyden
Michael Bratton

1

Governance and the Study of Politics

Goran Hyden

The subject matter of political science is by definition a moving target. Politics is dynamic. So are its underlying economic and social variables. For political scientists, therefore, it should be only in the nature of things to accept that their theories are not forever. The explanatory power of a particular theory shifts with changes in the empirical realm over which neither the theory nor the theorist has much, if any, control. Such self-recognition does not always come easily. After all, as researchers we invest not only reason but also values in what we do. Scientific explanation is also a means to "conquer" the minds of others. We strive to institutionalize our ideas, at least within fields of the discipline. The result is that we are often slow in adapting to empirical changes. We overlook the need to change, or at least adjust, our conceptual lenses.

Every now and then, however, history throws us out of our notions of conventional wisdom. One such jolt took place in the wake of World War II, when two related trends served as impetus for redefining the subject matter of political science. The first was the polarization of the world into two ideological blocs—the East and the West. The second was the emergence of the "Third World," that is, former colonies that became politically independent. Together, they once and for all forced political science out of its narrow concern with constitutions, law, and formal government institutions as we knew them in Europe and North America. And this led to the birth of the field of comparative politics, as it is now known.

COMPARATIVE POLITICS AT THIRTY

By developing a theory and a conceptual apparatus that responded to these twin challenges, books like *The Politics of Developing Areas* (Almond & Coleman 1960) had a tremendous influence on what was still an innocent and wide-eyed discipline. They triggered off several more theoretical volumes (e.g., Almond & Powell 1966; Binder et al. 1971) as well as many empirical studies, some of which, notably *The Civic Culture* (Almond & Verba 1963),

1

have become classic works in the field. Even though the structural-functional approach associated with this first effort at real comparative analysis produced very few doctoral dissertations, and its notion of modernization as a more or less linear historical process soon came under fire (Zolberg 1966; Huntington 1968), we are forever indebted to the intellectually stimulating work by these comparativist pioneers.

For some, the trend for comparative politics since the 1960s has been only downhill. For instance, Wiarda, in an edited volume assessing the state of the field (1985), laments the proliferation of theories and perspectives and thus its lack of a core, the assumption being that one dominant theory is both necessary and desirable for intellectual development. I disagree. Theoretical and conceptual diversity rather than unity is the mark of progress, at least in the social sciences, where the empirical realm by definition sets the terms for our studies. For example, the many political economy studies that grew out of the dependency approach of the 1970s, as well as the spurt of a liberal political economy literature in the 1980s, drawing its inspiration from rational choice theory, were both adequate responses to new socioeconomic and political circumstances, and as such theoretical and conceptual advances.

The fact that we are captives of the very circumstances that we try to study means that history more than anything else serves as the catalyst of progress in political science. When history moves only gently forward, reigning paradigms continue to dominate our minds. When significant events occur, new paradigms or theoretical perspectives arise. For example, 1968 marked the end of the modernization approach with its emphasis on political culture, and its replacement by, first, a radical and, subsequently, a conservative political economy approach. This does not mean that we typically throw all the intellectual goods of the previous era overboard. Much of it stays as legacy within the field and is kept alive, at least in most departments, by courses and seminars devoted to the evolution of the comparative study of politics.

The challenge here, really, is to avoid two pitfalls to which we all are easily prone. The first is our nostalgic inclination. We all have our intellectual heroes and we do want to pay them respect. These figures easily become all that matters when it comes to teaching or designing research. This may be a safe approach, but it often makes teaching and research not only dull but also increasingly outdated. With due respect to the individual scholars who have contributed to recent volumes on comparative politics (e.g., that edited by Weiner and Huntington [1987]), the collective product appears déjà vu.

The second pitfall is our concern with logical consistency. It is only natural that we try to refine our models or theories by making them logically more consistent. By pressing in such a direction, however, we also typically end up making our perspective on reality even more partial than it has to be.

For example, in recent years it has been commonplace to embrace rational choice theory, because its epistemological and methodological premises permit a degree of logical consistency in assumptions about human behavior that competing approaches are not seen to do. The result is that we produce images of politics that are very one-sided and often emphasize the extreme—for example, in terms of how power is being used by some merely to control others. Although such an interpretation corresponds to much political reality—and therefore easily becomes dominant—it is not necessarily descriptive of all politics. Critics of our discipline have a point when, for example, they portray us as being excessively cynical and pessimistic in interpreting the core of our subject matter.

Comparative politics at thirty years of age may not quite yet have reached its midlife crisis, but it is clear that it could benefit from conceptual renewal. At thirty, there ought to be more to scholarship than testing what to many are increasingly outdated concepts and propositions derived therefrom. Fortunately, history in recent years has been benign to political science by redefining relations both among and within nations. In all modesty, we wish to seize that window of opportunity to rethink the comparative study of politics. The exercise here is not meant to be exhaustive, but at least indicative of where we might be going and how.

NEW CHALLENGES

Nineteen eighty-nine has often been compared with 1789, a watershed year in European history that marked the victory of secular rationalism and the gradual emergence of bourgeois values of progress. These values were to set the pace for Europe and much of the rest of the world for the next two centuries. But 1789 also gave rise to its opposites: the search for totalitarian control, the quest for the romantic and emotional, as well as the demand for equality of all.

If the storming of the Bastille in Paris stands out as the key event of 1789, the fall of the Berlin Wall may be its equivalent for 1989. More than anything else, it symbolized the demise of the totalitarian Communist regimes in the Soviet Union and Eastern Europe. Although the rapid change in that part of Europe would never have been possible without Mikhail Gorbachev's decision to engage in economic and political liberalization at home and, above all, to refrain from military interventions in the former Soviet satellite states, it was the visual impression of the demolition of the Wall that expressed the euphoria for political reform both in Europe and elsewhere. It helped enhance pressures for such reforms first in Eastern Europe and subsequently in other parts of the world where the legacy of one-party control had taken root. Nowhere was the vigor of this reform effort better tested than in the Soviet Union itself when, in August 1991, the military—called out in an apparent move to restore autocracy—retreated in the face of massive popular support for the advocates of glasnost and perestroika.

If 1989 was Europe's year, it may be no exaggeration to suggest that 1990 was Africa's. It witnessed the definite cracking up, if not complete fall, of one of its own most hated walls: apartheid. Combined with the release of Nelson Mandela, this chain of events in South Africa has occupied a prominent position in public media throughout the world. What is even more important here, however, is that, together with the reforms in Eastern Europe, it has been instrumental in reinforcing demands for political changes in other African countries. These changes have received little, if any, coverage in the world's media; yet they are both widespread and potentially far-reaching, as Bratton and van de Walle document in the next chapter.

It is not surprising that these and other global events have generated a renewed interest in democracy among political scientists. As a respected longtime analyst of democratic theory, Giovanni Sartori, argued with elation on a panel at the 1990 American Political Science Association meeting in San Francisco, democracy now finds itself without enemies or viable alternatives. It is imperative, therefore, that we focus on how countries can avoid "bad" politics, what Sartori identifies as "a self-aggravating management of the public realm, the end result of which is parasitic encroachment, waste and overall impoverishment." What he is echoing here is a point that was made a long time ago by George Catlin (1930)—then a mainstream view—that interest in power does not a priori translate into irresponsible behavior. It also reiterates the message in Lucian Pye's presidential address from 1989, when he challenged fellow political scientists to "go beyond delineating 'political man' as the exceptional power seeker and try to unearth the personal qualities essential for the civilized activity that is true politics" (Pye 1990:16). Certainly, most of the political reform leaders in Eastern Europe and Africa are neither selfish nor dictatorial. The notion that political structures and institutions can be reformed so as to make individual actors expend their energy in the labor of the public interest therefore makes sense.

I find myself in agreement with much of this. We can adequately grasp the current political changes in many parts of the world only by treating politics as an independent variable. Unlike political economists, who tend to regard it as a reflection of underlying material forces, we should recognize that values and norms shape the world. Politics is creative and, as the recent reform efforts indicate, it has been responsible for a reorganization of relations among groups in society as well as a redefinition of worldviews. This shift in explanation from economic to cultural variables is discernible also in the field of international relations, where in recent years regime studies are increasingly becoming more popular than rational choice–based accounts of bureaucratic politics or investigations of global economic structures and their impact on relations among nations.

What I am less certain about is the usefulness of democracy as the organizing concept for comparative studies in the 1990s. First, there is the problem of what the concept stands for. In spite of efforts by its chief theorists, such as Robert Dahl (1971), to define it so as to make it potentially useful to settings other than Western multiparty systems, there is always a tendency both to view democracy in such Western terms and to assume an inevitable trend in such a direction. Second, there is a question of what is empirically going on in the countries attempting a transition to democracy. Is it succeeding or is it stalling? At this point, we do not know, but it seems prudent to choose concepts that are less loaded at a time when the empirical facts are still pointing in many directions. Third, there is the assumption that already democratic countries are somehow free from threats of bad politics. This seems highly questionable not only in reference to newly democratic countries such as those in Latin America but also to older democracies in both Western Europe and North America. Is the political system in the United States capable of dealing with the economic and social challenges that are likely to arise in the 1990s? Is Canada going to remain an operational democracy in the light of growing pressures for provincial autonomy? Can the West European welfare states make the transition to leaner times without losing their democratic ideals? Can the European nations retain their democratic traditions within the context of a large European Community?

We raise these questions, not because a certain answer is anticipated, but to point to the challenges that these countries face as democracies. Furthermore, and equally important, we wish to identify a set of concepts that are potentially applicable not only to countries in transition to democracy but also for those already democratic. We propose that it may be particularly valuable to explore the usefulness of governance and related concepts for the study of comparative politics in the 1990s.

GOVERNANCE AND RELATED CONCEPTS

The concept of governance is not new. It has been around in both political and academic discourse for a long time, referring in a generic sense to the task of running a government or any other appropriate entity, for example, an organization. More recently, it has gained particular significance in the literature on African development as a result, among other things, of the World Bank's (1989) identifying the crisis on the continent as one of governance. More specifically, the Bank refers to such phenomena as the extensive personalization of power, the denial of fundamental human rights, widespread corruption, and the prevalence of unelected and unaccountable government. Implicit, if not explicit, in this perspective, is a call for liberalization and democratization. Development will take place only if political leaders abandon their authoritarian practices.

Richard Joseph at the Carter Center of Emory University in Atlanta has also been very instrumental in helping to popularize the concept among Africanists by conducting annual seminars under the auspices of the Center's African Governance Program. Much of the time at the first such seminar in 1989 (Carter Center 1989a, b) was devoted to trying to define what is meant by governance. Many participants accepted that it is a more useful concept than government or leadership mainly because it does not prejudge the locus or character of real decisionmaking, as Michael Lofchie (1989) put it. For example, it does not imply, as *government* does, that real political authority is vested somewhere within the formal-legal institutions of the state. Nor does it imply, as the term *leadership* does, that political control necessarily rests with the head of state or official political elites. It enables us to suspend judgment about the exact relationship between political authority and formal institutions in society.

This is not a definition but a useful take-off point for further specification of the meaning of the concept. Much literature in recent years has focused on state-society relations (e.g., Callaghy 1984; Migdal 1988; Rothchild & Chazan 1988). This approach has helped us understand such issues as why state capabilities are limited and why people often find ways around state-initiated legislation. This literature, however, has also raised problems in the use of the state/society dichotomy. First, the state is rarely the sole harbinger of political power. Second, it is often the public realm, not just the state, that is weak. Individuals see nothing wrong in using public resources for private or communal purposes. This attitude extends to a wider set of institutions than those we officially call the state.

The notion of a public realm encompasses both state and society and draws the line instead between private and public. What is of interest here is the extent to which there is a civic public realm (Ekeh 1975) and how it is being managed and sustained by political actors, some in the state, others in civil society. Do civic institutions, like government departments, political parties, or the media, all of which participate in the public realm, enjoy respect and legitimacy? Such questions point to the significance of respect for rules that protect the public realm. Such rules (or the absence thereof) have been the subject of recent studies on both Africa (Jackson & Rosberg 1982; Joseph 1987) and Latin America (e.g., O'Donnell, Schmitter & Whitehead 1986). O'Donnell and his colleagues use regime as a shorthand for the explicit or implicit rules that define who the relevant political actors are and through which channels and with which resources they actively seek political positions (O'Donnell, Schmitter & Whitehead 1986:73). This definition may be redefined for the purpose of this study to refer to the formal and informal organization of the center of political power, and its relations with the broader political community. A regime, then, determines who has access to political power, and how those who are in power deal with those who are not (Fishman 1990:428).

Regime is distinct from both government and state. It is a more permanent form of political organization than a specific government, but a regime is typically less permanent than a state. The state is an institutionalized structure of domination and coordination of both law-and-order and development types of activities. To be sure, the two phenomena are empirically intertwined, but it makes sense to keep them analytically distinct. A state, for instance, may remain in place as regimes come and go, something that we have witnessed in many countries of Africa. It is less common that a regime survives a state, but one could argue that this is what happened in Iran, for example, when the army as well as the civil bureaucracy refused to carry out state functions in the last phase of the shah's days in power. Such a breakdown of state functions destabilizes the regime as well, as the case of the Belgian Congo (Zaire) at independence in 1960 illustrates. But where the state does not break down, it often proves capable of serving subsequent regimes—tyrannical or democratic—as well as it served any previous regime.

A regime is not a set of political actors (although regimes often get associated with specific leaders), but rather a set of fundamental rules about the organization of the public realm. A regime provides the structural framework within which resources are authoritatively allocated (Easton 1965). It is like the house you live in: you want it to be both durable and pleasant but you also want to be able to rebuild or refurbish it as circumstances change.

Governance, as defined here, is the conscious management of regime structures with a view to enhancing the legitimacy of the public realm. In this definition regime and governance structure is the same, and structures, as discussed further below, are rule-based. Legitimacy is the dependent variable produced by effective governance, but it also translates into what Coleman (1988) and Ostrom (1990) call social capital. Ostrom translates this into "rules-in-use," that is, those that keep people motivated in actively contributing to public causes. Generating social capital, or social energy, as Hirschman (1984) prefers to call it, is an important part of progress, both in a socioeconomic and political sense.

Governance and policymaking are separate conceptual entities, yet in practice often affect each other. The principal difference is that governance deals with "metapolicies," or what Kiser and Ostrom (1982) call constitutional choices. One can ask: but to whom do questions about the organization of the public realm matter? The answer is that they matter to most people, but not all the time. Rules are typically stable, and as long as they serve their purpose, people, including politicians, do not care much about them. But if circumstances in society change, and rules get interpreted as constraining or outdated, they become targets of political mobilization. Since much of the legitimacy of those in power rests with how well they make use of existing rules, they have a vested interest in paying attention to them. If they overlook them, however, civil society responds through the activation of organized groups demanding change. The recent changes in Eastern Europe provide illustrations of both: in some cases (e.g., the Soviet Union and Hungary), the Communist leadership adjusted the rules in a preemptive fashion, thereby gaining legitimacy for themselves. In Poland, Czechoslovakia, and Romania, by contrast, the incumbent political leaders were too slow or uninterested in responding, and as a result had to yield to growing activation of civil society. Authority had shifted from those holding power in the state to those in society. Governance structures and their management make a difference. In particular, governance has a bearing on the elasticity of regimes facing major challenges to their stability.

Having established the rationale for a concern with governance and how it relates to other relevant concepts, it is now time to examine more closely the basic dimensions of the concept, its corresponding empirical dimensions, its relation to regime types, its link to political development, and its applicability to the study of African politics.

BASIC DIMENSIONS OF THE CONCEPT OF GOVERNANCE

Governance, as I have tried to show, implies human agency, but it transcends the narrow horizons of rational choice theory by insisting, like Etzioni (1988), that politics is more than the satisfaction of short-term individual interests. Methodological individualism, with its stress on incremental changes, fails to acknowledge the full scope of politics. The approach proposed here also differs from the more pessimistic perspective of structuralist theories, both Marxist and non-Marxist, according to which change is possible only by some apocalyptic intervention. The governance approach sits somewhere between these two extremes by assuming that human beings make their own history but not in circumstances of their own choice, and that political culture is an independent and superordinate factor in the study of development. I shall explore its basic dimensions in further detail.

The Actor Dimension

Much of the theorizing about politics has centered on the concepts of power and exchange. The usual treatment of these concepts is to set them apart as polar opposites, one dealing with asymmetrical, the other with symmetrical relationships. Power, in Max Weber's classic definition (1947:152), "is the probability that one actor within a social relationship will be in a position to carry out his own will despite resistance, regardless of the basis on which this probability rests." Within this perspective, which has been very influential in political science writing, power relations are characterized by conflict and compulsion.

The concept of exchange refers to a mutually rewarding and beneficial relationship (Blau 1964:91–92). A person enters such a relationship of his free will. Both parties to an exchange are perceived as winners. Exchange relations, however, are opportunistic and need regulation by law. In economics, for example, contracts and formal agreements are an integral part of the exchange model (Arrow 1963). Political scientists have increasingly borrowed this model for extending their understanding of political decisions and relations (e.g., Olson 1965; Niskanen 1971). In the 1980s rational choice theory made a significant inroad into the study of politics, comparative as well as international relations. Its simple methodology and stable assumptions about a utilitarian human behavior attracted many converts, for whom the efficiency of the model was decisive. Although few Africanists have adopted this approach, those, like Bates (1981), who have done so with sensitivity to African data have been influential.

The problem with these dominant conceptualizations is that they provide one-sided views of politics. They tend to assume that its extreme manifestations are also the most typical. There are good reasons to question that premise. If we are concerned with capturing dimensions of politics that these approaches overlook, it is necessary to bring in the concepts of reciprocity and authority as intermediate stations between power and exchange.

Reciprocity has much in common with exchange (Oakerson 1983). Both are mutually productive transfers. Both increase welfare. Reciprocity, however, is distinct from exchange in that it lacks discreteness. Reciprocity characterizes a continuing relationship between or among persons. It is based fundamentally upon expectations of behavior, not immediately contingent, on the part of others. In a reciprocal relationship each contributes to the welfare of others with an expectation that others will do likewise. The considerations relevant to the establishment and maintenance of reciprocal relationships also differ significantly from those relevant to simple exchange. The language and precepts of moral reasoning are fundamental to reciprocity. While it is possible for exchange to occur on a quite narrow base of agreement, reciprocity requires broader agreement and consensus on the basic norms of social action. While contract is the typical instrument of sealing an exchange, covenant may be the appropriate concept to characterize what takes place in confirming a reciprocal relationship. There is no immediate quid pro quo. Reciprocal relationships, therefore, are typically based on an underlying normative consensus. They may also be described as socially embedded exchanges.

Exchange is the core of economic thought, including development economics. It is the fundamental economic nexus, the basic relationship in any market-based model. It is a productive relationship in the Pareto-superior sense that both parties are better off, while nobody is left worse off. It is not surprising, therefore, that economic development is associated with an increasing range of opportunities for exchange. In a similar vein, it can be argued that political development is associated with an increasing range of opportunities for reciprocal relationships. But how can reciprocity be combined with power? I suggest that in order to grasp the essence of governance, the concept of authority be brought into the framework as the missing link between power and exchange, as illustrated in Figure 1.1.

Authority means legitimate power, that is, the voluntary acceptance of an asymmetrical relationship. In this sense, it comes close to being a reciprocal relationship. Both imply an underlying normative consensus on the rules for the exercise of power, although one is symmetrical, the other asymmetrical. Analysis of authority in these terms is hardly new. Social contract theorists, such as John Locke, placed reciprocity at the heart of their explanations of authority. They envisioned the public as giving political leaders obedience and legitimacy in return for effective performance of governmental duties. Moreover, should political leaders prove unable or unwilling to perform such services, the public had the right to withdraw its allegiance and stop obeying. Contemporary theoretical treatment of authority (e.g., Blau 1964:209) is remarkably consistent with the traditional social contract explanations.

Figure 1.1 The Actor Dimension of the Governance Concept

| Power | Authority | Reciprocity | Exchange |

By introducing reciprocity and authority as intermediate concepts, it becomes possible to overcome the dichotomization of power and exchange as irreconcilable concepts (Baldwin 1978). Power is not necessarily unilateral— that is, a zero-sum game, where A is the victor and B is the victim. Nor is it merely an opportunistic game played by utilitarian actors without regard for the consequences to others. There is a middle ground, where politics is a positive-sum game; where reciprocal behavior and legitimate relations of power between governors and governed prevail; and where everybody is a winner not only in the short run but also in the long run. This is the ground occupied by the concept of governance. Our delineation of this concept, however, is incomplete without a discussion also of its structural dimension.

The Structural Dimension

The concept of social-political structure has variable meanings. For the purpose of understanding governance, structures may be viewed as constituting the normative framework created by human beings to pursue social, economic, and political ends. A structure is the product of persons living together and engaged, competitively or cooperatively, in the pursuit of similar objectives. Thus, structures manifest themselves in basic laws or rules within which decisions or policies are made and implemented. Structural change is tantamount to a change in the rules of the game (cf. Kiser & Ostrom 1982).

Structures, however, may be of two different kinds. The first is often referred to as ascriptive and forms part of the natural world over which human beings have limited control. These structures are sometimes also called primordial (Ekeh 1975). I prefer the term *god-given*, indicating that they have a character that does not lend itself to alteration by human beings at will. In much of the development literature, this kind of structure has typically been described as standing in the way of progress. To be sure, these structures are problematic in that they are not so easily subject to change. They breed compliance rather than innovation. Yet it is important to acknowledge that it is within this type of structure, for example, family and community, that such traits as trust are developed and fostered more effectively than anywhere else. Their importance in contemporary politics is clearly beyond doubt as secular structures fail to hold societies together. Examples from the Soviet Union, Europe, Africa, and Asia abound. In the same way, therefore, as power and authority or exchange and reciprocity are two sides of the same coin, compliance and trust are integral parts of god-given structures.

The second type of structure is usually called civil and refers to those that are spontaneously created with a view to regulating political behavior and interactions. These structures may be brought about by fiat by a central authority or by agreement between governors and governed. They differ from the first type in that they are not merely subject to constant affirmation but also to frequent amendment. For this reason, I prefer to call them *man-made*. These structures are sometimes seen as modern, and were presumed, in much of the earlier political development literature (Almond & Coleman 1960; Binder et al. 1971; Tilly 1975), to be superior to their ascriptive or traditional counterparts. Such structures have typically been more adaptable, but, as modern history tells us, they have not always been used for noble ends. Human hubris, if not evil, has often colored the desire for change and led to political repression and social misery. As a result, modern societies have realized the need to hold their political leaders in check.

While, as societies develop, man-made civic structures become necessary to transcend the limitations of community, there is always the risk that leaders using such structures fail to be responsive to rank-and-file members. As consensus about the validity of basic norms can no longer be taken for granted, trust is insufficient to sustain effective social action. That is why in this context accountability becomes particularly important. The two concepts, however, are not contradictory but complementary. Trust without accountability is blind trust. Accountability without trust gives rise to suspicions of inquisition (Oakerson 1983).

If compliance and trust are the hallmarks of god-given structures, innovation and accountability may best describe the two sides of man-made structures. For the purpose of understanding governance, I suggest that trust and accountability constitute intermediate stations on a continuum between compliance and innovation (see Figure 1.2).

If we see structures as rules and rules-in-use as social capital, I wish to take this point a step further by suggesting that this social capital is made up of both fixed and movable components. Rather than assuming that structures are either wholly man-made, as rational choice theorists do, or institutionalized so as to live a life of their own (March & Olsen 1984), the premise here is that every society is made up of both, although the particular mix obviously varies. The implication of this point is that some structures are like fixed capital, that is, both costly and difficult to alter. People prefer the house the way it is, even if circumstances may call for alteration. Other structures are like the furniture or other interior features of the house. They can be more easily changed. The occupants take the initiative without hesitation and often with joy.

The Governance Realm

With the help of the discussion above, it is now possible to suggest the existence of a governance realm that is bounded by the four properties that we have identified as particularly important to good politics: (1) authority; (2) reciprocity; (3) trust; and (4) accountability. The governance realm should be seen in relation to the public realm in the way management is to organization: as a means to an end. As suggested by Figure 1.3, they form part of what may be described as an often overlooked aspect of politics. At a time when there is growing interest in the ways politics can be used to strengthen the public realm and its role in social and economic progress, the notion of a governance realm takes on particular significance. My general proposition is that the more regime management is characterized by the qualities associated with the governance realm, the more it generates legitimacy for the political system and the more, therefore, people will participate in the public realm with enthusiasm. These qualities are of course likely to be present in different degrees at any one time, but they all bear on key organizational dimensions in any given political system.

Trust refers to a normative consensus on the limits of action present in a political community. The most important thing about this variable is that it is not based on an expectation of its justification (March & Olsen 1989:27). It is sustained by socialization into the rules and is not a contract. Indicators of trust in a political community are the extent to which individuals and groups in society cooperate in associations that cut across basic divisions such as ethnicity, race, religion, and class.

Reciprocity refers to the quality of the social interaction among members of a political community. Reciprocal action—as opposed to mere exchange

Figure 1.2 The Structural Dimension of the Governance Concept

Compliance	Trust	Accountability	Innovation

Figure 1.3 The Conceptual Boundaries of the Governance Realm

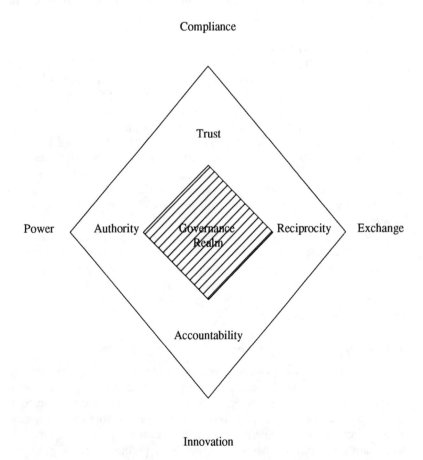

Compliance

Trust

Power | Authority | Governance Realm | Reciprocity | Exchange

Accountability

Innovation

relations—tends to have the effect of generating new forms of consensus about the basic rules of politics. As such, consensus is stored away, so to speak, enabling the political community to transcend existing boundaries of trust. An important indicator of reciprocity in politics is the extent to which individuals are free to form associations to defend and promote their interests in the public realm.

Accountability refers to the effectiveness with which the governed can exercise influence over their governors. This variable becomes politically significant particularly in societies that are socially and economically differentiated. Trust and reciprocity are not easily sustained in such contexts without specific rules for holding political leaders accountable to civil society. In other words, while trust and reciprocity typically generate the conditions in which rules of accountability get accepted, these rules take on a role of their own by filling a vacuum that neither of the other two variables fills. Indicators of accountability consist of various forms of holding elected and appointed officials responsible for their decisions and actions.

Authority is largely facilitated by the presence of the other variables, but it goes beyond these in stressing the significance of effective political leadership. Citizens judge political decisions along two lines: (1) how effective they are in solving specific problems affecting them; and (2) how these decisions are carried out. Effective problem solving may be autocratic and as such lack legitimacy. Such naked exercise of power does not lead to an interest in and a respect for the public realm. Instead, people are likely to withdraw or go underground in opposition to the regime. Indicators of authority, therefore, consist of compliance with not only given policies but also the process by which they are arrived at, that is, the extent to which leaders respect rules or change them in ways that are acceptable to the governed.

The four variables discussed above may be seen as prerequisites for *effective* governance, as measured in terms of legitimacy generated for a regime. The more of them that are present, the stronger the probability of effective governance; the less of them, the stronger the possibility of regime collapse. But how does the study of governance get translated into more-concrete empirical dimensions?

The Empirical Dimensions of Governance

Defined as regime management, governance is concerned with how rules (or structures) affect political action and the prospect of solving given societal problems. For much of the time, governance means the mere sustenance of the regime, but the real test of governance comes in situations where regime changes are needed to meet new demands or deal with new problems. The uncertainty or conflict that such demands or problems create generates pressures among governors or governed, or both, to change the rules of the game. Regime changes are more difficult, and often more painful, than ordinary policy alterations. The former imply more or less far-reaching shifts in the basic rules of how society conducts its public affairs or how governors and governed relate to each other. The study of governance, then, involves the identification of the conditions that facilitate good governance and, by implication, effective problem solving. I suggest that these conditions can be identified along three separate axes, as illustrated in Figure 1.4.

Citizen influence and oversight refers to the means by which individual citizens can participate in the political process and thereby express their preferences about public policy; how well these preferences are aggregated for effective policymaking; and what means exist of holding governors accountable for their decisions and actions. These empirical dimensions may be summarized as follows:

1. Degree of political participation;
2. Means of preference aggregation; and
3. Methods of public accountability.

Responsive and responsible leadership refers to the attitudes of political leaders toward their role as public trustees. In particular, it covers their orientation toward the sanctity of the civic public realm; their readiness to share information with citizens; and their adherence to the rule of law. This second set of empirical dimensions, therefore, are:

1. Degree of respect for civic public realm;
2. Degree of openness of public policymaking; and
3. Degree of adherence to rule of law.

Figure 1.4 The Three Principal Empirical Dimensions of Governance

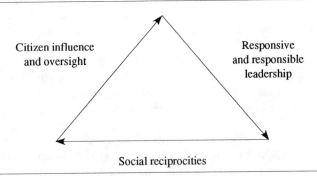

Social reciprocities refers to the extent to which citizens or groups of citizens treat each other in an equal fashion; how far such groups demonstrate tolerance of each other in the pursuit of politics; and how far voluntary associations are capable of transcending the boundaries of such primary social organizations as kinship, ethnicity, or race. In sum, this third set of empirical dimensions are:

1. Degree of political equality;
2. Degree of intergroup tolerance; and
3. Degree of inclusiveness in associational membership.

Space does not permit a further elaboration of the specific empirical indicators that help in assessing or measuring these dimensions, but, depending on the circumstances from country to country, it is possible to develop such indicators (or their proxies, if necessary). Instead we will turn to a discussion of governance in relation to different regime types.

GOVERNANCE AND REGIME TYPES

Polities and regimes can be divided up many different ways. One such way that is common in comparative politics is to distinguish between market-based and state-based regimes, indicating the extent to which the market or the state serves as the primary mechanism for resource allocation. A basic distinction can be made, therefore, between a "statist" and a market-based "libertarian" regime, the latter indicating the extent to which individuals perceive themselves as autonomous actors. In recent years, some authors— for example, Streeck and Schmitter (1985)—studying advanced industrial societies, have added another, "associative" regime type. This applies to societies that have evolved neocorporatist tendencies in the past two decades and where, therefore, associations, and especially their leaders, become entrenched in some form of political "concertation" with government. This term refers to mediated negotiations between a fixed set of interest organizations, each of which mutually recognizes the status and expected entitlements of all. From these emerge relatively stable compromises through the pursuit of group interests. This body of literature, which has two branches—one on "societal" corporatism, a second on "state" corporatism— marks the recognition of institutions other than the state and market as contributing factors to political order and political choice. This theorizing is also evident in the "New Institutionalism" literature that emerged in US political science following the original contribution by March and Olsen (1984).

These three regime types, however, do not necessarily exhaust the varieties that can be found in the empirical universe of political systems. For instance, they do not cover those regimes in Africa and elsewhere in the world where community loyalties are still very strong and override other factors. This type has grown in significance in recent years as countries formerly under Communist rule have found themselves overwhelmed by reemerging ethnic loyalties. It is important, therefore, to add to this list a "communitarian" regime type. Such a regime is based on the simultaneous participation of a great variety of primary social organizations (more god-given than man-made), which clamor for equal access to centrally controlled resources. Community-specific values are encouraged at the expense of others, and governance structures are socially embedded in multifunctional relations.

With the help of these four regime types, it may be useful to try to locate different polities. In Figure 1.5 we suggest such a location of polities in relation to these four regime types. Problems of governance are not unique to any particular regime, but the challenges each regime typically encounters are different. I shall now try to make a preliminary assessment of which are the strong and weak points in each regime type so as better to indicate what the challenges to effective governance are. For the purpose of developing hypotheses on this topic, I suggest that each regime type be placed according to an ordinal scale of one to three in relation to each of the nine empirical dimensions identified in Figure 1.4, where one stands for regime strength, three for regime weakness, and two for an in-between quality (see Table 1.1).

These classifications are meant to be tentative and subject to empirical testing. Some interesting propositions emerge from this exercise. One is that communitarian regimes are most likely to face problems of governance, with statist regimes coming in second. Neither libertarian nor corporatist regimes, however, escape the risk of governance crises, although they may not be as deep and serious as those facing the other two types. On the basis of this tentative identification of the governance structures in different regime types, it is possible to suggest that the most probable cause of a governance crisis can be attributed to the factors set out in Table 1.2. Communitarian regimes are likely to encounter more fundamental problems because of their lack of autonomy from other structures in society. The notion of a civic public realm is hard to develop and institutionalize. Governance structures tend to be informal, and formal associational life weak. As a result, community interests are typically articulated in a "raw" fashion, making the task of aggregating preferences particularly hard. Governance crises tend to occur because of the incompatability of unprocessed community demands on the one hand, and limited public resources on the other. In the light of a weak social capital base, regimes find it hard to cope with these pressures, thus making effective governance hard, if not impossible.

Libertarian regimes are most likely to suffer a governance crisis for either of two reasons. The first is the inability of the those in leadership

Figure 1.5 Indicative Location of Regional Political
Systems in Relation to Types of Regime

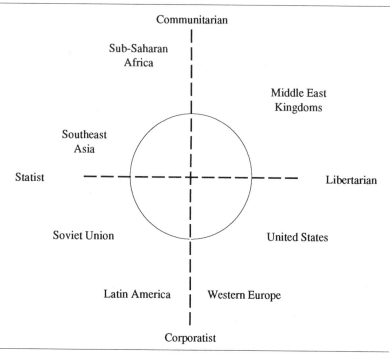

Table 1.1 Indicative Locations of Possible Governance Crises by Regime Type

	Dimension	Communitarian	Libertarian	Corporatist	Statist
Citizen influence	Participation	2	2	1	2
	Aggregation	3	1	2	3
	Accountability	2	3	1	3
Responsive leadership	Civic respect	3	2	1	2
	Policy openness	3	1	2	3
	Rule of law	3	1	2	3
Social reciprocities	Political equality	2	1	1	2
	Group tolerance	3	2	2	2
	Associational inclusiveness	3	1	1	3

Table 1.2 Regime Types and Likely Causes of Governance Crises

Regime Type	Main Cause
Communitarian	structural embeddedness
Libertarian	structural fragmentation
Corporatist	structural patronage
Statist	structural monopoly

positions to aggregate citizen preferences in an effective manner so as to deliver authoritative decisions. The United States comes closest to being an illustration of this regime type. While opportunities for citizen control are plenty, and local-level governance structures are very responsive to citizens' demands, the institutional fragmentation that characterizes this type makes it very inefficient in aggregating and overcoming the influence of special interests at higher levels in the system. The second reason is the tendency for the utilitarian values to get entrenched in such a way that citizen interest in politics wanes. A case in point is cost-benefit analysis, which elevates a quasi-scientific method to such a level of prestige that politics in the sense of conflict over scarce resources is discredited and replaced by the ideal of the "administrative state."

The corporatist regimes face a different problem. Here power is shared among interest organizations representing different groups in society. By getting entrenched in the political establishment, these organizations contribute to making the regime "top-heavy." Rank-and-file members become dependent on the ability of such organizations to deliver benefits, and as long as their leaders ensure such delivery there is no immediate problem. Difficulties are likely to arise, however, when belts have to be tightened. In these circumstances a governance crisis is not unlikely because leaders have to make compromises with their counterparts in other organizations and in government—often at the expense of the interests of the rank and file. Although these regimes typically prove more elastic than their statist counterparts, this patronizing approach tends to produce alienation or revolt, and thus a governance crisis. The welfare states in Scandinavia are a case in point as they struggle to adjust to leaner economic times and the legacy of the longtime dominance by mass organizations in politics.

Where power is concentrated to the state, the most probable cause of a governance crisis stems from the alienating effects of such a monopolization of power. The long-term detrimental effects of such a regime on development have been most dramatically illustrated in recent years by events in the Soviet Union and Eastern Europe. By ignoring the citizen control dimension, leaders become increasingly arrogant and unresponsive, thus seriously depreciating available social capital.

One of the implications of this analysis is that no regime is necessarily superior to the others. Governance crises are integral parts of all. I suggest, therefore, that it is time to abandon the idea of stages in political development —with regimes placed in a ladderlike fashion, with Western democracies at the top.

GOVERNANCE AND POLITICAL DEVELOPMENT

The most ambitious attempt to define political development was the structural-functional approach of the 1960s in which the concept was viewed as the increase in structural capabilities of a given political system to cope with predefined crises—state building, nation building, resource distribution, and participation—that societies encounter as they modernize (Almond & Powell 1966). The problem with this approach derives primarily from its epistemological assumption that systems exist in an almost reified fashion, with objective functional needs, and that objective comparisons can be made along such lines. Efforts to operationalize this approach proved very frustrating. In the 1970s, therefore, it lost its attraction.

In the last fifteen years the concept of political development has received little attention. As noted in one of the recent overviews, political development has become a generic term applied to a whole range of approaches, regardless of whether they view politics in developmental terms or not (Weiner & Huntington 1987). Political economists, whether of the Marxist or liberal persuasion, who—as we have seen—have been influential in the field since the 1970s, have done little to rehabilitate the concept. In fact, to them politics is a dependent variable, reflecting material conditions (Marxists) or an exogenous normative preference—self-interest (liberals).

Working in the periphery of these mainstream traditions, Stephen Chilton (1988) has more recently attempted to give political development a fresh content by drawing on the generic epistemology of psychologists such as Jean Piaget and Lawrence Kohlberg. Here the prime indicators of progress are moral and cognitive. Development occurs as political actors within a given society are able to resolve moral and cognitive ambiguities and contradictions. Drawing on empirical test results from studies of individuals, the assumptions of this approach are that moral reasoning varies in its structures (the logical relationships of the concept) among at least six possible stages; the stages can be hierarchically organized such that each stage represents an integration and differentiation of the previous stage; stages are acquired in a hierarchical order, with no skipping of stages and no retrogression to lower stages; and these assumptions apply uniformly to all cultures. In this perspective, political development is an inevitable progress toward greater civility and equality in interpersonal and intergroup relations.

Chilton's work is the most stimulating effort in recent years at getting a new handle on the concept of political development. His approach has the advantage of acknowledging the role of individual political actors by stressing the importance of critical thinking and discourse as mechanisms for achieving change. The problem, however, is that it deals with "big" variables that really show up only in a longer-term historical perspective. It does not help us very much when it comes to understanding the more immediate challenges that political systems face on a day-to-day basis. If we wish to bring political development back in, therefore, we have to seek inspiration also from other sources.

I suggest that it is possible to assess political development with the help of the governance approach discussed here. To elaborate on that point, it may be useful to borrow a few leaves from the literature on organization development and from the critical theory in social philosophy that has been significant to European scholars for at least two decades and that is now receiving a hearing also among social scientists elsewhere (for a recent important contribution by US political scientists, see Thompson, Ellis & Wildavsky 1990).

The governance approach brings back to life the Aristotelian distinction between praxis and theoria, that is, the need to establish a meaningful relationship between the abstract world that researchers create with their theories and models on the one hand, and the empirical political world in which day-to-day action takes place on the other. It is important to remember, as Hannah Arendt (1958) reminds us, that in Aristotle's original scheme the purpose of praxis was to generate good judgment (*phronesis*) based on the particular challenge facing the polis. Ever since praxis was incorporated into modern theory by Marx, however, its meaning changed, referring instead to work as the critical link between theory and practice. Much theorizing in the last hundred years has been based on that premise: it is in work that individuals realize their inner self and full potential; work expresses at one and the same time both the freedom of human beings and their bond with nature. This is the nexus for generating social consciousness not only in Marxists' work but also in that of many others.

This link between social consciousness and the enhancement of the productive forces has met with increasing criticism in recent years. Leading the attack, Habermas (1971, 1973) pointed to the difficulties of combining praxis and techne. Rationally organized work can do no more than generate products that are better or worse in relation to existing premises. It does not, however, produce truth or intersubjectively valid norms. Only what Habermas calls "communicative action" is capable of producing such awareness. Critical theory, then, commends a continuous interchange of ideas, interpretations, and criticisms between theorists (such as social scientists) and political actors. The purpose of theory is to become practical, to make a difference. As such, it must be intelligble in terms of the felt needs of the individuals to whom it is addressed.[1]

In emphasizing that actors do not necessarily have to be helpless victims of institutional and structural arrangements, the approach proposed here also borrows from literature in business administration. There scholars have already drawn the conclusion that pushing rational-purposive action too far without consideration of the human factor is detrimental to the cause of business. The principal message of a series of influential books, beginning with those of Ouchi (1981) and Peters and Waterman (1982), is that a company, in order to be successful, must develop a strong sense of self-motivation and loyalty among its employees. The key to real excellence is to instil a sense of purpose in the employees and thereby get them to put in the extra amount of effort that sets a company apart from its competitors. This often implies changes in governance structures, as the authors of landmark books (e.g., Burns & Stalker 1962) and more-recent contributions (e.g., March & Olsen 1989; Hult & Walcott 1990) suggest. The positive consequences of such changes for development have also been traced by Uphoff (1991), who shows how in Sri Lanka multiplicative outcomes are reached by stressing the importance of generating new social capital to augment limited material inputs.

In its assumption that what matters today, and in the future, is whether politics is good or bad, the governance approach is cast in a postmaterialist and postpositivist vein similar to that discussed above. Although it does not deny the possibility that societies or polities evolve along a similar historical track, the governance approach, for example, does not assume that political development implies that polities increasingly take on more pluralist features. This is where it departs from the literature trying to measure democracy (Bollen 1980) or freedom (Gastil 1989). While that literature is important in its own right and obviously overlaps to some extent with the concerns of this approach, the study of governance is performance-oriented. It examines how well a polity is capable of mobilizing and managing social capital—both fixed and movable—so as to strengthen the civic public realm. In this respect, it comes closer to the literature on business management. In the same way as business management theory treats the organization as crucial to business success, the governance approach treats regime—the organization of political relations—as essential for social and economic progress.

In the light of the frustrations and limitations encountered in generating a single grand theory of political development, I suggest that the most productive and rewarding approach to the study of political development is to evolve more-concrete indicators to highlight the three principal empirical dimensions of governance identified above: (1) citizen influence and oversight; (2) responsive and responsible leadership; and (3) social reciprocities. It involves the use of a similar set of concepts that provides a basis for common discourse and some comparison, but it recognizes that, as cultural entities, political regimes are always bound to differ. In the same way as business management styles will differ and the literature will keep referring to American or Japanese versions of such styles, regime management will reflect cultural peculiarities that can be grouped together and compared with a set of types, as indicated in Figure 1.5 above. This is a lower level of ambition than that of previous efforts to define the concept of political development, but it has the advantage of being less ethnocentric and more oriented toward answering the questions of practical politics.

GOVERNANCE AND AFRICAN POLITICS

These advantages ought to be obvious to any comparativist but become particularly important for Africans and Africanists who have found themselves gliding into what I, at least, see as growing area insulation. The governance approach provides a means of conceptually linking up more closely with the broader field of comparative politics, yet offers a meaningful way of relating to the ongoing efforts in the continent to reverse autocracy and build democracy. In doing so, it also recognizes that progress in the field of Comparative Politics is ultimately dependent on the reconnaissance work done by area specialists. Without this work the study of comparative politics would be reduced to a meaningless exercise in theoretical involution.

In recent literature on African politics it is clear that the prime contemporary challenge is how to restore a civic public realm. The trend of postindependence politics in most African countries has been to disintegrate the civic public realm inherited from the colonial powers and replace it with rivaling communal or primordial realms, all following their own informal rules. The result has been at least four shortcomings that researchers have identified as major and the cause of the prevalence of "bad" politics in Africa:

1. The personalized nature of rule;
2. The frequent violations of human rights;
3. The lack of delegation by central authorities; and
4. The tendency for individuals to withdraw from politics.

The personalized nature of rule in so many African countries means not only that public policymaking lacks the logic and empirical content that typically characterizes such an activity in other contexts but also that governance structures are largely informal and subject to arbitrary change. The patrimonial or prebendal character of such governance has featured prominently in the literature in the 1980s (e.g., Jackson & Rosberg 1982; Callaghy 1984; Joseph 1987). This writing provides ample evidence of the dire consequences that this type of rule has for the development of Africa. For example, it encourages clientelist relations that may generate trust on a dyadic (two-person) basis but that discourage the growth of new forms of trust and reciprocity that transcend such rudimentary and narrow relations.

Human rights was for a long time a nonissue for Africans. In the 1970s, however, a debate began about such rights: are they the same in Africa as elsewhere (see, e.g., Pollis & Schwab 1979)? The majority of African writers on the subject came out in defense of a difference: individual human rights are a Western concept; in Africa, rights are communitarian or group-based. Following the widespread abuses of civil and political rights by such rulers as Idi Amin, Emperor Bokassa, and Macias Nguema in the late 1970s, however, Africans gradually began to recognize their significance. Particularly important was the role played by African lawyers in lobbying for the adoption of an African human rights charter by the Organization of African Unity. Following the adoption of the African Charter of Human and Peoples' Rights in 1981, a more open debate began about the importance of civil and political rights for development in Africa. Although it has continued to be dominated by non-Africans (e.g., Donnelly 1982; Welch & Meltzer 1984; Howard 1986; Forsythe 1989), Africans have gradually taken a more prominent role on these issues and independently published their contributions (e.g., An-na'im & Deng 1990). One of the most important messages coming out of this literature is that African governments can no longer and at will, by invoking the demand for national unity, violate civil and political rights of their citizens. Respect for this type of governance structure is a prerequisite for turning politics into a positive-sum game.

The reluctance to delegate authority to institutions outside the political center has two dimensions. The first is the unwillingness to decentralize authority to independent institutions of local governance. The reasons for such unwillingness as well as the costs associated with it are examined by several authors in a recent volume edited by Wunsch and Olowu (1990). Their point is that much of the continent's social energy is wasted because of the inadequate linkages between an omnipotent center and peripheral communities searching for ways of making progress on their own. The second reason refers to the marginalization of civil society. A prominent feature of African postindependence rule—regardless of ideological color—has been the tendency to curb any independent political activities outside an institutional network controlled by a ruling party-state. These issues were well covered in a volume edited by Chabal (1986) and have continued to move closer to the top of the research agenda in Africa, as confirmed by an edited volume by Anyang'Nyong'o (1987) and the discussions at the two Carter Center workshops (Carter Center 1989a, b, 1990). By curbing associational life, African regimes have fostered blind compliance and a lack of concern for a strong civic public realm.

The final implication of Africa's "bad" postindependence politics is the tendency for individuals to evade rather than engage the political authorities.

The shrinking of the civic public realm has limited the opportunities for citizens to use what Hirschman (1970) calls their "voice" option: they have been reluctant to speak out for fear of being locked up in jail or maltreated in other ways. Instead, they have become increasingly dependent on their "exit" option: their ability to vote with their feet by escaping political control. This topic has become an increasingly prominent feature of the literature on African politics in the last decade, as Hyden (1980), Chazan (1983), and MacGaffey (1987) indicate. The phenomenon has gained even greater significance more recently, as African governments, for budgetary reasons, have been forced to contract their activities. The state simply does not reach out into society as it used to do. Whether this is a positive or negative trend is still subject to debate, but some writers, such as Diamond (1988), Bratton (1989a), and Barkan (forthcoming), believe that this vacuum creates opportunities for civil society to grow. In this respect, state contraction may pave the way for stronger governance structures.

These four shortcomings have come under increasing attack throughout the continent since 1990, as Bratton and van de Walle clearly indicate in Chapter 2. As they also suggest, however, the big question is not only how new governance structures can be brought about but also how they can be sustained so as to help generate new social capital. Attempts to democratize African countries may lead to more pluralism along lines that are familiar to Westerners, but they may also prove to be a redefinition of the trend toward indigenizing relations of political authority that has been evident ever since political independence in these countries. The consequences of such a redefinition could be very different from those anticipated, certainly by those striving to introduce democracy along Western lines. In fact, the apparent paradox is that the ongoing efforts to privatize Africa's economies are likely to enhance stable forms of pluralist democracy only to the extent to which this process also strengthens the civic public realm. Is that going to happen? That is the big question before the students of African politics in the 1990s.

CONCLUSION

Governance may be the comparative politics equivalent of policy analysis. In the same way as the latter is concerned with improving policymaking, governance is the study of how to improve politics and the conditions determining that effort. The question of how regimes can be altered to strengthen the contribution that politics makes to development is of special significance in the post–cold war period when the Leninist-Stalinist mastodon has been largely abandoned and societies are looking for alternative governance structures. This book is meant to demonstrate the significance of this topic to Africa.

I have also intended to show in this chapter how this concern with improving the quality of politics bears on the way we study it in a comparative fashion. By suggesting that governance constitutes a new focus in comparative politics, I have tried to evolve a framework of analysis that lends itself to the twin objectives of being both comparative and relevant to practical concerns. Many issues need more-elaborate discussion than has been possible here, but it is, I hope, adequate to provide the basis for further discussion. My colleagues, Michael Bratton and Donald Rothchild, make an initial contribution in this direction in the final chapter of this book.

Let me conclude by suggesting that future studies in comparative politics are best served by recognizing the significance of cultural variables and therefore also the importance of diversity and flux characterizing all political regimes. The positivist assumptions that have guided so much of the social sciences in the past three decades—and still continue to have a considerable influence—are no longer very helpful guideposts for research, particularly in the field of comparative studies. As Uphoff (1990) stresses, there is no single tangible reality out there, fragmentable into independent variables that can be studied in isolation and then predicted and controlled. There are no objective laws that we can take refuge in or unearth for future use. As I suggested in the opening of this chapter, our subject matter is a moving target and, what is more, we are captives of it. It is a historical irony, to say the least, that it is not the social sciences but the physical sciences that in the 1990s seem most ready to recognize the relativity of their subject matter. As Guba (1985) argues, much of the social sciences continues to stick with a Newtonian paradigm while the hard sciences have abandoned it in favor of one that acknowledges relativity and related issues. At thirty years of age, comparative politics can hardly be presented with a better birthday present than an invitation to explore more systematically and intensively its future direction. This chapter is written in all modesty as a contribution to that present.

NOTES

I am grateful to Michael Bratton and Valerie Asseto for helpful comments on a first draft of this chapter.

1. This emancipatory orientation echoes the writings of at least one of the fathers of modern political science, Harold Lasswell, who once wrote: "No democracy is even approximately genuine until men realize that men can be free" (Lasswell & McDougal 1943:225).

2

Toward Governance in Africa: Popular Demands and State Responses

Michael Bratton & Nicolas van de Walle

For scholars of comparative politics, the current era presents fascinating and uplifting challenges. How can we explain the worldwide trend of breakdown in authoritarian regimes and assess the prospects for their sustainable replacement with legitimate forms of governance? By what precise struggles and accommodations is power divided and redistributed in monopolistic political systems? Interest in these questions has arisen as a direct response to political events, most notably the ground-shaking collapse of Communist regimes in Eastern Europe (Bulgaria, Czechoslovakia, East Germany, Hungary, Poland, Romania, and Yugoslavia) at the dawn of the 1990s. In retrospect, this cataclysm was presaged by a rumble of democratic transitions in southern Europe (Portugal, Spain, Greece, and Turkey) in the 1970s and in Latin America (Argentina, Brazil, and Chile among several others) during the 1980s.

In Africa, too, authoritarian regimes are under siege. Across the continent African governments face pressures for political change on a scale unprecedented since the dissolution of colonial rule a generation ago. During 1990 citizens took to the streets of capital cities in some fourteen African countries to express discontent with economic hardship and political repression and to demand democratic reform. During the same period at least twenty-one governments launched seemingly significant reform efforts to permit greater pluralism and competition within the polity (see map). Richard Sklar's (1983) bold prediction that Africans would come to prefer the unpredictable vicissitudes of democracy to the stifling abuse of "developmental dictatorships" has begun to be brilliantly vindicated.

The dynamic process of popular protest and political reform has only just started in Africa, and its future course and outcomes in a range of diverse countries is highly uncertain. But the moment is opportune to attempt a preliminary assessment of recent events. While the terrain of transitions from authoritarian rule in Africa is shifting, we hope to identify at least a few emergent landmarks. In this chapter we take on three tasks. First, we catalog the characteristics of recent popular protests in sub-Saharan African countries,

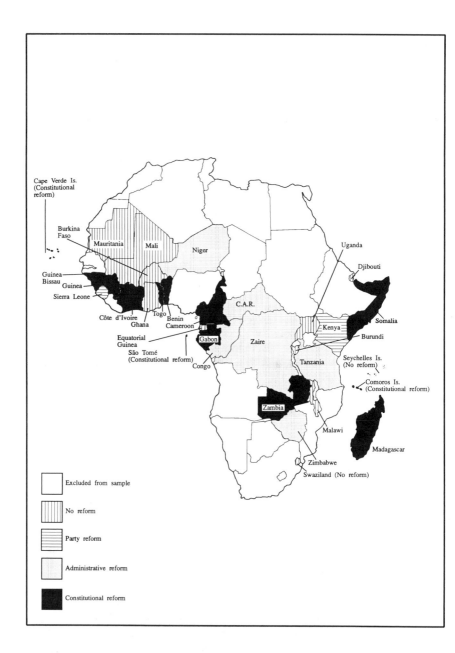

Cape Verde Is.
(Constitutional
reform)

Burkina
Faso

Mauritania   Mali   Niger

Guinea
Bissau
    Guinea
Sierra Leone

Côte d'Ivoire   Togo
        Ghana   Benin
Equatorial   Cameroon
Guinea
São Tomé
(Constitutional reform)
        Congo

C.A.R.

Gabon

Zaire

Uganda

Djibouti

Kenya

Somalia

Burundi

Seychelles Is.
(No reform)

Comoros Is.
(Constitutional reform)

Tanzania

Zambia

Malawi

Madagascar

Zimbabwe
Swaziland (No reform)

Excluded from sample

No reform

Party reform

Administrative reform

Constitutional reform

Governance Reform in Africa
November 1989–November 1990

focusing attention on the turbulent spring of 1990. Second, we review the nature of government responses, noting the range of governance initiatives undertaken by African leaders during 1990, and recording backlashes, crackdowns, and reversals where they occurred.

Finally, and most importantly, we seek to explain why the political firmament is now shifting in Africa after thirty years of institutional stasis. The comparative literature on democratization suggests that openings in authoritarian rule are forged by a complex array of forces, some structural and some contingent, some external and some internal.[1] We acknowledge that, in sub-Saharan Africa, the protests and reforms of 1990 were shaped by the crippling effects of a structural economic crisis and precipitated by democratic initiatives in Eastern Europe, China, and South Africa. We nonetheless argue that African governments introduce governance reforms primarily in response to indigenous political demands.[2] Our analysis focuses on the emergence of a loose multiclass assemblage of domestic protest groups, and explains the extent of governance reforms with reference to the political resources, skills, and styles of opposition and government leaders.

Lest we are misunderstood, we should emphasize that the current transformations of authoritarian regimes in Africa are incipient. Cracks in the edifice of autocracy should not be mistaken for fully fledged transitions to democracy. As leading theorists have admonished, political liberalization and democratization are simultaneous, complementary, but ultimately autonomous processes: the former refers to the disassembly of authoritarian regimes, whereas the latter requires the deliberate construction of democratic institutions (O'Donnell & Schmitter 1986). It is entirely possible that liberalization can occur without democratization, and in some parts of Africa the disintegration of authoritarian rule may be followed by anarchy or intensified corruption, rather than by stable and accountable governance. Previous transitory episodes of democracy following multiparty elections in Ghana (1979), Nigeria (1979), Uganda (1980) or Sudan (1986), provide inauspicious precedents in this regard.

Constitutional reform mandated from above is thus insufficient for regime transition; much also depends on the intentions of existing and emerging political leaders and the sincerity of their commitment to open and responsive politics. Commonly, incumbent elites regard political liberalization as an unpalatable but unavoidable step to salvage central political control within a destabilized state. And contenders for power often perceive multiparty competition as a chance for access to rent-seeking opportunities so long denied to them as political outsiders. We therefore conclude our analysis by raising questions that can be answered only in the fullness of time. Are political protests sustainable? Do they portend a transition to democracy anywhere in Africa? In the absence of true democracy, can citizens take advantage of openings in authoritarian regimes to move toward more-liberal and accountable modes of governance?

APPROACH AND METHOD

In this chapter we attempt to generalize inductively from observation of two types of events—popular protests and political reforms. We wish to understand the frequency and nature of these events, and the causal relationships, if any, between them. To gather data, we systematically scanned news sources[3] for reported incidents of protest and reform in African countries over a one-year period following the opening of the Berlin Wall on November 9, 1989.[4] The scope of the study was limited to authoritarian regimes in which there was an unrealized potential for peaceful governance reform. Certain countries were therefore excluded: those embroiled in civil war; countries undergoing a planned transition from military to civilian rule; and countries already multiparty democracies.[5] Within the forty-five states in sub-Saharan Africa we therefore studied thirty-one "reformable" regimes.

Like Hyden, we view governance as an interactive process by which state and social actors reciprocally probe for a consensus on the rules of the political game. Because protest and reform are intertwined, these two sets of events are difficult to separate analytically. For example, state elites often meet the initial occurrence of a minor popular demonstration with a token concession or a vicious crackdown. The very inadequacy or inappropriateness of the government's response, however, fuels more-widespread and insistent unrest. In turn, governments are willing to embark on meaningful constitutional reforms only after protesters have proved a determination to continue to press, and escalate, their demands.

We therefore conceive of protest and reform as a series of dynamic exchanges in which strategic actors take their cues from the behavior of adversaries. From this perspective, political change can be seen to have a life of its own that is beyond the direction of any protagonist. As Naomi Chazan notes in Chapter 6, there is no grand design to the reform process; instead, "individuals, groups, and government leaders constantly [alter] their course of action in light of specific events and conditions in other sectors."

Because the promulgation of governance reforms is the most important turning point in the process of political change, a word is in order about the definition of reform. A wide variety of government actions can plausibly be labeled political reform measures, from adjustments in party or administrative regulations to the revision of national constitutions. In this study we use a pragmatic, behavioral, and broadly inclusive definition: reform is any measure taken by a ruling elite to increase political competition. Where elite concessions grant mass political rights, such as freedom of political expression and freedom of political association, reform amounts to political liberalization. Only where holders of national political office are elected freely and fairly can a transition to democracy be said to be under way (Karl & Schmitter, private communication, 1990.)

In practice, the prospects for regime change depend importantly on the balance of power and cohesion among competing political coalitions. Defections may often be fatal to the state elite. As Adam Przeworski (1986:56) has argued, "the first critical threshold in the transition to democracy is the move by some group within the ruling bloc to obtain support from forces external to it." Actual reform outcomes also depend on the ability of opposition forces to aggregate primary associations in civil society into a cohesive social movement or political party. This makes possible "the emergence of a new elite that arouses a depressed and previously leaderless social group into concerted action" as Dankwart Rustow (1970:354) presciently observed two decades ago. We therefore assess the prospects for sustainable change of regime in terms of the fragmentation of the incumbent elite and the emergence of an alternative ruling coalition.

THE DYNAMIC OF PROTEST AND REFORM

In different African countries there is a rich variety of issues, positions, clashes, adjustments, and outcomes in the movement toward governance. Despite such diversity, we propose below a rough sequence of stages of protest and response that is common to many African countries, while noting that some have advanced farther than others through the sequence.

The Birth of Economic Protests

As indicated on Table 2.1, there were important popular protests in fourteen African countries during 1990. Pinpointing the genesis of these events is difficult, since there is no logical place to start a chronology. African populations have not been passive in the face of declining living standards and government malfeasance; students, civil servants, workers, and professionals have regularly voiced their opinions in strikes, demonstrations, marches, and boycotts. For example, Zambia witnessed violent riots in December 1986 when the price of maize-meal was doubled as a result of subsidy cuts under an International Monetary Fund (IMF)–sponsored economic adjustment plan. Benin's capital, Cotonou, was the scene of public sector strikes throughout 1989, as civil servants protested against accumulated arrears in their salaries. And, over the years, university campuses have been the scene for periodic outbreaks of dissent in many African countries. Thus the unrest of 1990 followed a series of precedents (see Foltz, 1973; Wiseman, 1986).

The protests usually began with corporate demands by interest groups seeking to improve material conditions within their own sector of the urban economy. Typically, unrest originated on a university campus with students demonstrating against a government decision to impose austerity measures that affected them directly. In Gabon in January 1990, for example, students took strike action over teaching shortages and poor study facilities; in Côte

Table 2.1 Popular Protests in Selected African Countries
(November 1989–November 1990)

	Date of First Outbreak	Role of Students	Role of Civil Service	Role of Unions	Role of Churches	Defections from State Elite
Benin	11/89	L	H	M	M	H
Cameroon	2/90	M	L	L	M	M
Comoros	1/90	L	L	L	M	L
Côte d'Ivoire	2/90	H	H	M	L	L
Gabon	11/89	M	H	M	M	L
Togo	9/90	H	H	L	L	L
Zaire	5/90	H	M	L	H	M
Zambia	6/90	M	L	H	H	H
Mali	10/90	M	M	H	L	M
Congo	4/90	M	M	H	M	H
Central African Republic	3/90	L	H	L	L	M
Kenya	2/90	H	L	L	H	L
Niger	2/90	M	M	H	L	L
Sierra Leone	5/90	H	L	L	M	L
Zimbabwe	10/89	H	L	H	M	M

Sources: See note 4.
Key: L = Low or Absent; M = Moderate; H = High
Note: The table refers to the one-year period from November 9, 1989, to November 8, 1990, only. Protests before or after these dates are excluded. In the case of Benin, protests lasted throughout 1989, and in the case of Zimbabwe, began in October 1989. In the case of Mali, protests did not get under way until 1991. Mozambique and Senegal, countries outside of our sample, also witnessed significant protests during this period.

d'Ivoire in February 1990 several inopportune electricity cuts before midterm exams sparked the first significant protests.

Student demands, however, did not always address parochial and material concerns. In Zimbabwe in October 1989 campus troubles broke out over an attempt to hold a seminar marking the first anniversary of student anticorruption riots and quickly escalated into a critique of the government's use of state of emergency powers to quell dissent. In Kenya, where students had long complained about overcrowded educational facilities and soaring unemployment rates, they protested in February 1990 the alleged implication of government security forces in the murder of Foreign Minister Robert Ouko.

The protests gathered momentum by appealing to a coalition of diverse corporate interests. Students were joined by faculty and civil servants complaining about salary arrears, subsidy cuts, or—as in Côte d'Ivoire—the possibility of a salary reduction. In Benin, public denouncements by students and civil servants had become endemic in late 1989, as payment arrears reached seven months. And in Zambia, Zimbabwe, and Kenya, students attracted workers and the self-employed to join in condemning the corrosive effects of inflation on living standards.

Initial Government Responses

Governments responded to these initial protests with a familiar formula of threats, repression, and selective compromise. Where protests concerned bread-and-butter issues, national leaders generally tried to placate protesters by going partway to meet their demands. Piecemeal concessions were the norm: in the Côte d'Ivoire, for example, President Félix Houphouët-Boigny reduced student room-and-board costs by half and delayed, before eventually renouncing, the civil service pay cuts; in Gabon, President Omar Bongo similarly announced a new public sector salary scale as well as health and social security reforms.

Where protests had clear political overtones from the outset the government tended to resort directly to repression. President Daniel arap Moi of Kenya ordered paramilitary units to open fire on mourners at the Ouko funeral and imposed bans on public demonstrations and "rumor-mongering." The Zimbabwean government closed the university and briefly detained without trial student leaders and the head of the national congress of trade unions. In northwestern Cameroon, the police killed at least six protesters while trying to disperse an illegal rally by a banned political party, the Social Democratic Front.

Some leaders quickly ran out of economic options and had no choice but to begin making major political concessions. This happened first in Benin where the lamentable state of the economy, the withdrawal of French support, and the government's nearly complete loss of credibility led to an implosion of the regime in the waning months of 1989. President Mathieu Kérékou made several efforts to contain the unrest with concessions; he allowed several independent civilian ministers into his government in August 1989 before pronouncing a general amnesty in September and renouncing Marxism-Leninism and the leading role of the party in December. By then, Kérékou's own allies in the government had begun to desert him. Leading army officers distanced themselves from the regime, while part of the government-controlled trade union, the UNSTB, jumped to join the opposition.

Yet few countries were in the dire economic straits of Benin. Most governments were able to rally their supporters as a tactic to undergird the ruling coalition and to isolate and weaken the opposition. Official marches in favor of the single-party state were organized, for example, in Cameroon (March 1990), Côte d'Ivoire (April), and Togo (May). Some regimes resorted to more-extreme methods of intimidation: opposition leaders were arrested in Kenya, Côte d'Ivoire, and Cameroon; and in Gabon, Joseph Renjambé, secretary-general of the leading opposition party, was assassinated.

The Politicization of Demands

In previous years such time-honored government tactics had usually served to quell unrest. Not so in 1990; instead, popular demands escalated. The question of why will be considered below; for the moment, suffice it to record that protesters were emboldened to broaden and politicize their claims.

Government responses of evasion, threat, and violence fueled a second round of popular rage. Spurred on by deepening economic hardship and reacting against heavy-handed regime responses, protesters began to call for systemic political change. For the first time particularistic interests took a back seat to general calls for the ejection of national political leaders. Protesters began by linking their economic grievances to official corruption and mismanagement, which they blamed for the depressed condition of the economy. Slogans explicitly attributed the national debt to the ill-gotten gains of state elites. In Côte d'Ivoire, for example, a target of the protests was the Basilica of Yamoussoukro, the gilded replica of Saint Peter's of Rome for which President Houphouët-Boigny personally paid an "official" cost of some US $145 million. In Zaire, President Mobutu Sese Seko—who had initiated a political opening by eliciting public comment on his rule— was apparently shocked to receive frank and bitter criticism from churches, students, unions, business groups, and individuals accusing him and his cronies of monopolizing power and raiding the national treasury. Striking civil servants openly displayed the slogan "Mobutu voleur!" (Mobutu thief!).

Opposition figures, whose courageous and underpublicized dissidence had previously seemed quixotic, now acquired a new audience. In Cameroon, the rearrest and trial of the anglophone writer Albert Mukong for "subversive acts" in February 1990 attracted international attention and led to a lawyer's strike. In the Côte d'Ivoire, as student unrest escalated, the media turned university Professor Laurent Gbagbo into the leader of the opposition despite the fact that his party, the Front Populaire Ivoirien (FPI), initially had only a minuscule following. In Kenya, when Bishops Henry Okullo and Alexander Muge and the Reverend Timothy Njoya spoke from the pulpit against corruption and human rights violations, they found themselves feted as leaders of an incipient social movement. In other countries as well, the church hierarchy weighed in on behalf of reform (see Table 2.1).

In this atmosphere opposition politicians found it opportune to give voice to the idea of multiparty competition. In Zambia, Frederick Chiluba, chairman of the Zambia Congress of Trade Unions (ZCTU), paved the way for a multiparty debate by publicly asking, in reference to Eastern Europe, "if the owners of socialism have withdrawn from the one party system, who are the Africans to continue with it?" (*Times of Zambia*, December 31, 1989). In March, Chiluba called for a referendum on party pluralism, announcing that "the ZCTU believes that the one-party system is open to abuse; it is not the people in power who should direct political change, but the ordinary masses" (*Africa Confidential*, April 1990). In Cameroon, Yondo Black, the ex-head of the national bar, was arrested in February for attempting to form an opposition political party; his arrest lead to an open call for multiparty elections by his successor at the bar, Bernard Muna. And in May 1990 in Kenya, two former cabinet ministers, Kenneth Matiba and Charles Rubia, called a press conference to demand the restoration of a multiparty constitution.

Following these initiatives, it was not long before the multiparty cause was adopted by protesters in the streets. At this stage, popular demonstrations commonly escalated into the worst public violence since independence. In Zambia in June 1990 crowds led by students chanted multiparty slogans at riots in Lusaka in which a monument commemorating Kenneth Kaunda's role in the nationalist struggle was set ablaze. In Kenya, the arrest of Matiba and Rubia and the announcement of a government ban on a multiparty rally led to four days of looting in several urban centers in July 1990. Crowds throughout Nairobi flashed a two-finger sign indicating support for political pluralism and called for the release of political detainees. In Gabon, riots in Port-Gentil turned into open support for the Parti Gabonais du Progrès, a newly created opposition party. Still, in countries as diverse as Cameroon, Sierra Leone, and Congo, the democracy protests never gained a wide popular audience, remaining circumscribed to groups within the civil service and university (see Table 2.1).

Wherever multiparty sentiment raised its head, state leaders mounted an ideological campaign in defense of the status quo. Their rhetoric, often betraying a panicky overreaction to mass events, revived old arguments about the supposed advantages of unipartism. In November 1989 President Kaunda of Zambia warned that party competition would constitute a return to "stone-age politics" by inciting ethnic loyalties and electoral violence. In a televised speech in April 1990 Cameroon's president, Paul Biya, argued that the one-party state was the best way to deal with the country's socioeconomic problems. Moi of Kenya and Robert Mugabe of Zimbabwe were vociferous in rejecting efforts by Western governments to promote multiparty competition as interference in the sovereign rights of African states. Implicit in all such arguments was the notion, as General Kolingba of the Central African Republic put it, that "the country is not ready for [multiparty democracy]" (*Marchés Tropicaux et Méditerranéens*, May 18, 1990). Ironically, this was precisely the argument used by colonial officials to delay granting political independence to Africans.

The Onset of Governance Reforms

Nonetheless, at some time during 1990, and usually after protest demands became politicized, a substantial number of African heads of state bowed to popular pressure and embarked upon a course of political liberalization. The content and extent of governance reforms varied widely among countries, but all cases involved concession of rights to political expression, association, or contestation. We discern three types of governance reforms (see the map on page 28, and Table 2.2): (1) party reforms, permitting greater political competition within the ruling single party, usually through amendments in party structures and procedures; (2) administrative reforms, involving changes in bureaucratic practice implementable within the existing framework of law; and (3) constitutional reforms, to check the powers of the party or state.

Constitutional reform was the most sweeping and commonly occurred after the other two; on the other hand, party and administrative reforms followed no obvious chronological sequence. Leaders often began to liberalize the institutions over which they were most confident of control. After the July riots in Kenya, for example, President Moi instigated a commission of party members to review the structure and operations of the ruling Kenya African National Union (KANU). In public hearings held countrywide, citizens raised broad political concerns, especially elite corruption, ethnic favoritism, and the need for limitations on the executive powers of the presidency. But Moi was willing to permit reforms only within KANU itself, for example by agreeing to restore secret balloting in party primaries and pledging to end the expulsion of dissidents from the party. Similar moves to liberalize the operations of the single party—both as a prelude to multiparty competition, and in an effort to prevent it—occurred in Gabon, Togo, Cameroon, Madagascar, Sierra Leone, Burkina Faso, Mali, Mauritania, and Congo. In Gabon and Zaire the party was renamed. While reforms within ruling parties were genuine reforms that increased the scope for political competition, they were partial and in many instances appeared to be little more than attempts to preempt more serious change. They rarely satisfied popular demands for political pluralism.

In several countries, on the other hand, the onset of governance reform was marked by the lifting of administrative restrictions on political activity by journalists, intellectuals, and opposition leaders. In Tanzania, restrictions on press freedom were eased, new political publications emerged, and the government-controlled media began to carry a broader range of opinion, including relatively open debates on the merits of the single-party state.[6] In July 1990 in Zimbabwe, the government released all 250 political prisoners then in custody and lifted the state of emergency that had been in place since independence.

Some states did not proceed beyond party and administrative reform, whereas other states passed through such reforms en route to more-sweeping dispensations (see Table 2.2). In Cape Verde, for example, constitutional

Table 2.2 Governance Reform in Selected African Countries
(November 1989–November 1990)

	Governance Reform			Multiparty Election Scheduled
	Party	Admin.	Constit.	
Protest and Major Reform				
Benin	o	x	x	February/March 1991
Cameroon	x	x	x	
Comoros	o	o	x	March 1990
Côte d'Ivoire	o	o	x	October/November 1990
Gabon	x	x	x	September/October 1990
Togo	o	x	x	
Zaire	x	x	o	1992
Zambia	o	x	x	October 1991
Protest and Minor Reform				
Congo	x	x	o	
Central African Republic	o	x	o	
Niger	o	x	o	
Zaire	x	x	o	1992
Zimbabwe	o	x	o	
Kenya	x	o	o	
Sierra Leone	x	o	o	
No Protest but Reform				
Cape Verde	o	o	x	January/February 1991
Guinea	o	o	x	1995
Guinea-Bissau	o	o	x	
Madagascar	o	o	x	1996
Sao Tome and Principe	o	o	x	January 1991
Somalia	o	o	x	February 1991
Tanzania	o	x	o	

Sources: See note 4.

Key: x = occurrence of reform; o = absence of reform

Note: The table refers to the one-year period from November 9, 1989, to November 8, 1990, only. Any political reforms initiated before or after these dates are excluded. Governments in several countries outside our sample also undertook party reform (Ethiopia) and constitutional reform (Angola, Mozambique, Rwanda) during 1990. The residual countries in our sample, that is, for which we found no evidence of either popular protest or political reform during 1990, are Burkina Faso, Burundi, Djibouti, Equatorial Guinea, Ghana, Mali, Malawi, Mauritania, Seychelles, Swaziland, and Uganda.

reform ending single-party rule and legalizing opposition parties was a first step toward the convening of parliamentary elections in January 1991.

Two Steps Forward, One Step Back

As well as being partial, the reform process in sub-Saharan Africa also proved to be halting and contradictory. While granting minor political concessions with one hand, some leaders cracked down with the other. Concurrently with launching the party reform commission in Kenya, President Moi sought to stamp out the political debate by detaining his opponents and decreeing a halt to public discussion of multipartyism. At the same time as granting salaries and benefits to striking workers, President Bongo in Gabon banned all strikes and demonstrations and imposed a limited curfew. And, in perhaps the most flagrant case of perverse reform, Mobutu of Zaire unleashed his presidential guard in a massacre of students at the University of Lubumbashi, just two weeks after announcing a return to political pluralism.

Other leaders tried to sidestep the need for meaningful reform by revolving the ranks of the political elite. They used cabinet reshuffles in an effort to prevent rivals from taking advantage of popular discontent and instigated "party restructuring" campaigns in order to ensure that local officials were correctly transmitting the official party line. In January 1990 in Togo, for example, President Eyadema announced an invigoration of the ruling Rassemblement du peuple togolais in preparation for national elections. And in June 1990 in Zambia, President Kaunda dismissed cabinet ministers and transferred provincial governors in an attempt to isolate dissidents and solidify political loyalty within the United National Independence Party. Such measures did not amount to progress toward governance because they simply rotated members of the old guard among existing political offices. At this stage, there was no structural change in political institutions and no broadening of political competition.

Even where leaders were forced to back down, the end result did not necessarily alter the status quo. Swimming against the reform tide, President Mugabe of Zimbabwe campaigned for most of 1990 as a self-proclaimed apostle of the one-party state. He took his party's overwhelming victory in March 1990 national elections as a mandate to convert Zimbabwe into a de jure single-party entity. Ultimately he was faced with a revolt within the Zimbabwe African National Union–Patriotic Front, whose Politburo and Central Committee refused to grant the necessary authority. In September 1990 Mugabe announced a revocation of plans to legalize the one-party state, at the same time reconfirming his preference for party dominance at the polls.

At the extreme, a significant subset of Africa's "strongmen" continued to insist on the maintenance of authoritarian rule. In Ghana, Jerry Rawlings implemented a tightly controlled, top-down program of decentralized state-building dressed in the ideological garb of guided democracy. And in Malawi, life-President Hastings Banda continued to flatly deny opportunities for political dissent outside—or even within—the governing Malawi Congress Party. This no-reform strategy worked most effectively in those African states—such as Ghana and Malawi—that did not experience significant protest during 1990.

Toward Constitutional Reforms

In many African countries, however, the reform momentum carried far and fast during 1990. Confronted with continuing dissent, state elites began to recognize that they had lost the capacity to govern without a renewal of legitimacy. Citizens began to entertain the possibility, unthinkable just one year earlier, that some single-party regimes would expose themselves to multiparty elections of indeterminate outcome.

In many places the inception of meaningful reform began when top leaders agreed to convene extraordinary national conventions to address the crisis of governance. In Benin and Gabon, these fora were especially created for the occasion and drew upon a cross section of major organized social interests. In Benin, for example, the commission contained seven cabinet ministers and invited participation from political, religious, and trade union organizations. This National Conference of Active Forces emerged with a mandate to develop a new national constitution. In Mali, Cameroon, Burkina Faso, and Congo, constitutional discussions were similarly held but contained within the structures of the single party. In Zambia, constitutional proposals were developed simultaneously by a Presidential Commission and in the National Assembly, although both were shunned by the opposition as being too heavily weighted toward the ruling party.

Such fora devised important constitutional innovations. Proposals were made to curb the powers of the executive branch of government, for example by limiting the number of terms served by the national president. In São Tomé and Principe in March 1990, President Pinto da Costa approved a limitation on the duration of the presidency of two terms, and in April 1990, President Bongo announced the reduction of the presidential term in Gabon to a five-year term, renewable only once. At the same time reforms adjusted the balance of power between party and state, usually by ending the constitutional supremacy of the former. In Benin and Congo, the leading role of the party within the state was officially abandoned in December 1989 and July 1990 respectively.

The most startling and far-reaching constitutional innovations, however, concerned multiparty competition. Several countries took the step of legalizing opposition political parties where they were previously prohibited. For example, in Madagascar, a March 1990 law allowing independent political parties was followed rapidly by the formation of four such parties. In Zaire in April 1990 President Mobutu resigned as head of the Popular Movement of the Revolution and ended its monopoly by lifting a twenty-year ban on opposition parties. And in Niger in June 1990 the Higher Council for National Orientation decided to legalize three clandestine political parties.

In perhaps the most remarkable turnabout of an eventful year in Africa, President Kaunda of Zambia was forced to accept a popular call for multiparty elections. Initially dead set against party pluralism, Kaunda first began to back down in April 1990 by agreeing to a referendum on the matter. His ploys to delay the referendum were soon overtaken by events because, by September, Zambian towns were witnessing unprecedented mass rallies, including one that may have involved up to 100,000 people, in favor of a multiparty constitution. In that same month the UNIP National Council, the party's main policymaking body, capitulated to demands to abandon the referendum and move directly to a multiparty constitution and election.

By November 1990 eight African states—Benin, Cape Verde, Gabon, Côte d'Ivoire, Guinea, Madagascar, Zaire, and Zambia—had scheduled multiparty elections (see Table 2.2). Two countries—Gabon and Côte d'Ivoire—had already held elections. In the last section we ask whether these elections mark a transition to democracy.

ANALYTICAL ISSUES

We now turn from description to analysis, by probing the causes, nature, and implications of governance initiatives in Africa.

How Did the Protests Evolve?

It is tempting to attribute the eruption of political protest and governmental responses of tentative liberalization to structural causes: crippling economic crisis and a related loss of political legitimacy. From the onset of nationalist politics in Africa, leaders entered a more or less explicit covenant with followers to distribute the material benefits of development. Especially after the suspension of meaningful competitive elections with the advent of single-party and military rule, African governments possessed few other means of renewing legitimacy than ensuring economic growth and distributive justice.

Yet, far from being "developmental dictatorships," African regimes faced a twenty-year economic crisis occasioned by falling export revenues, rising import prices, and the mismanagement of centrally planned economies. Far from stimulating growth through new investments and distributing benefits through social programs, state elites drained wealth from state-managed economies through self-serving, rent-seeking behavior (Bayart 1985; Sandbrook 1985; Joseph 1987). During the 1980s economic decline necessitated drastic austerity measures to curb imports and reduce government spending, often under conditions set by foreign donor institutions.

Politically, austerity and corruption violated the covenant that underpinned the right to rule of African leaders and estranged them from the social base of their own ruling coalitions. Powerful urban constituencies such as civil servants and employees of public corporations faced an inexorable decline in living standards. University students, a privileged and volatile group, saw employment opportunities dwindle as automatic access to civil service jobs was eliminated. The self-employed and the unemployed sank into acute poverty.

The economic crisis and the bitter adjustment pill are thus a ubiquitous background to the current unrest; political protests signal the rejection by African populations of developmental dictatorship as a model of governance. Nonetheless, it is ultimately misleading to interpret political protest in strictly economic terms. First, there is little or no correlation between the intensity of political unrest on one hand and the severity of economic crisis or austerity measures on the other. Some countries, with very deep economic problems, such as Tanzania, Guinea, or Guinea-Bissau, witnessed little or no unrest during 1990; yet riots and strikes shook relatively wealthy countries such as Kenya, Cameroon, Gabon, and Zimbabwe. Second, a purely economic argument fails to explain why the unrest happened when it did. Some governments had imposed austerity measures in the context of donor-monitored economic reform programs as early as the first oil crisis in 1973, and any account of the unrest has to explain why it did not occur before the spring of 1990. Last, economic protests previously occurred without destabilizing the incumbent regime, yet analysis must explain why governments were no longer easily able to isolate and contain disaffected groups by 1990. Thus the economic crisis provides the context in which the political protests began but cannot fully explain them.

Indeed, protesters in 1990 were galvanized in an explicitly political direction. Commonly, the issue of elite corruption served as a vehicle for transforming narrow economic grievances into broad political demands. Protesters began to draw a connection between economic failures and the lack of political accountability in single-party states. They blamed patronage and nepotism for the economic crisis, rather than condemning Western protectionism or the decline in commodity prices. Implicit in such an attribution of blame was the notion that sounder and more-honest management would make the present austerity measures unnecessary .[7]

Corruption by state elites proved to be a convenient target for the mobilization of broad popular antagonism, but the issue did not lend itself readily to a systematic political program. Accusations of malfeasance led inexorably to demands to expel political leaders, but little more; how to change rulers and establish more-accountable forms of governance was less clear.

In this ideological and programmatic vacuum, opposition leaders raised multiparty democracy as a convenient banner under which to gather inchoate demands for political change. The notion of political pluralism sparked popular support insofar as it was the antithesis of the discredited system that had led to the present mess. Yet, as articulated by protesters in African countries, the call for multiparty democracy seemed to signify little more than a general discontent with the political status quo and an urge to try something—anything—different. As one news analysis remarked, "many Africans are now so poor that they are prepared to back virtually any demand as long as it implies change. More political parties? Fine, as long as something changes. This may not be sophisticated but it is natural that the poor should reason thus and that opposition politicians, hungry for power should exploit it" (*Africa Confidential*, July 27, 1990).

Were There Diffusion Effects?

Many Africans long harbored deep-seated dissatisfactions with the single-party system as a device for arbitrary rule and private enrichment. Yet only a few intellectuals were willing to speak out on the need for political reform because of the danger of imprisonment or exile, even death. Although the African state was in decline, its internal security apparatus retained a residual capacity to instil fear, discourage open debate, and prevent popular mobilization. Under these circumstances, we argue that there was pent-up pressure for political change within African countries that was the principal raison d'être of the popular protests.

We recognize, however, that events outside sub-Saharan Africa were responsible for helping to release this pressure during 1990. The international environment for political protest changed during 1989 as a consequence of democracy movements in countries as varied as the Soviet Union, East Germany, China, Algeria, and South Africa. While external events were not the main causal factor, they did shape the politicization and timing of protests in sub-Saharan Africa. African politics were influenced in several ways, albeit with key regional distinctions and variations. The liberalization of authoritarian regimes elsewhere served to further delegitimize the African one-party state by helping to confirm the place of democracy on the political agenda and providing opposition groups with a potent new theme for protest. And the fall of strongmen in Eastern Europe gave pause to African leaders and limited their room for maneuver.

Political changes in Eastern Europe appear to have influenced both elite and mass behavior in Africa. At the elite level, the ouster and summary execution of Nicolae Ceausescu in Romania in December 1989 had a sobering effect on his African peers and allies. For example, Mobutu's announcement of political reform and Kaunda's turnabout on multiparty elections seemed to be attempts to forestall their own violent overthrow. Ex-President Julius Nyerere's influential speech of February 1990, in which he pronounced that the single-party state was no longer sancrosanct, followed directly on the heels of a visit to East Germany to terminate formal relations between Tanzania's Chama cha Mapinduzi and the East German Communist Party. And events in the Communist world seemed to have greatest impact in such countries as Ethiopia and Mozambique with Marxist-Leninist regimes and dependence on Eastern-bloc aid. At the mass level, access to information on the democracy movements in Eastern Europe was often restricted in government-controlled media. But in Kenya, where the Cable News Network beamed satellite pictures of mass protest from Leipzig and Prague, the government could not prevent the spread of popular sentiment in favor of political resistance.

Other external events closer to home probably had an even greater meaning for Africans. The independence of Namibia in April 1990, under a liberal constitution and a multiparty electoral system, was celebrated across the continent. The prospect of meaningful political reform in South Africa—which suddenly arose with the release of Nelson Mandela in February 1990, the "unbanning" of the African National Congress, and the preparations for constitutional negotiations—led to a review of domestic policies, especially in the Southern African frontline states. For example, the lifting of emergency regulations and the release of political prisoners in Zimbabwe in July 1990 followed close on the heels of similar measures in South Africa.[8]

In West Africa, the Algerian experience was influential; riots in October 1988 led to the legalization of opposition parties and the defeat of the ruling FLN at the hands of Islamic fundamentalists in local elections in March 1990. The francophone countries were particularly influenced by a cultural unity forged over the years by a shared media and the pull of French intellectual life. The events in Algeria were featured prominently in such prestigious, international media as the weekly magazine *Jeune Afrique* and Radio France Internationale. The national constitutional conference in Benin in February 1990, which turned into a devastating indictment of President Kérékou's regime, was carried live on the national radio to neighboring Togo, Burkina Faso, and Côte d'Ivoire. Kérékou's progressive loss of control to a civilian government of neutral technocrats provided opposition groups in these countries with an appealing scenario to emulate at home. While impossible to prove, the birth of a protest movement in Togo seemed to be a direct result of liberalization in Benin. And in the Central African Republic, the two hundred intellectuals and former government officials who fruitlessly submitted an open letter to General Kolingba in May 1990 calling for a national conference on a transition to multipartyism specifically invoked the prodemocracy movements in the rest of Africa.

What Is the Relationship Between Protest and Reform?

We now move beyond the partial explanations offered by structural and diffusionist interpretations of events to integrate into analysis the contingent effects of popular demands on governance reforms. As can be seen in Table

2.2, there is a clear, positive relationship between popular protest and political reform in contemporary Africa. In all fourteen countries in which demonstrators made demands for political change during 1990, governments made at least a nominal reform response.

But the extent of reform initiatives—whether party, administrative, or constitutional measures—varied considerably from country to country. In seven African countries (Benin, Cameroon, Comoros, Côte d'Ivoire, Gabon, Togo, and Zambia; see Table 2.2) mass demonstrations were followed by major constitutional initiatives. Zaire is in a class by itself insofar as Mobutu's initial promise of reform occurred before the first wave of protest: his announcements sent thousands of jubilant citizens racing into downtown Kinshasa waving branches and blocking streets; and his failure to follow through incurred strikes by doctors, nurses, and other public workers.

In practice, the beginning of a constitutional reform process was marked when leaders took one or more decisive steps: to convene a national forum to revise the constitution; to permit outlawed political parties to operate; or to schedule multiparty elections. While these reforms usually occurred sequentially, certain countries skipped stages or reversed parts of the sequence. For example, Côte d'Ivoire went directly to multiparty elections without a constitutional assembly, and Zambia announced multiparty elections before parties were legalized. And in most of these countries the constitutional reform process was incomplete at the time of writing (November 1990), with debates ongoing about the precise legal arrangements for a new political order.

But the main point is that several African political leaders crossed the Rubicon by allowing regime opponents to become involved in debates about the constitutional future of the country. They set in motion a process leading inexorably to a revision of the formal rules by which national politics are played. The reform debate addressed fundamental questions about the balance of power between the state executive and other institutions in polity and society. Heads of state, especially those faced with a crisis of legitimacy, calculated that their best chance of survival in office was to take into account the views of others. For the first time, state elites had little choice but to surrender a degree of control and to allow a measure of uncertainty to enter the reform process.

The distance that a government traveled down the road to major constitutional reform also depended on the prevailing depth of repression. In Zaire, for example, where arbitrary and patrimonial dictatorship was well entrenched, the announcement of multiparty competition amounted to a major break with the existing rules of the political game. By contrast, in Zimbabwe, which had been bound by its independence constitution to allow freedom of political association, the decision to forgo unipartism did not require constitutional reform and did not mark a departure from the previous regime.

The extent of reform also depended critically on the willingness of top political leaders to loosen their grip on power. Thus, in five countries where there was protest-induced change (Central African Republic, Congo, Niger, Zaire, and Zimbabwe) leaders relaxed administrative restrictions on opponents but withheld the prospect of constitutional change. By releasing dissidents from jail and restoring a degree of press freedom, leaders created openings in the otherwise blank façade of authoritarian rule. While relatively minor, sparingly applied, and always reversible, these reform measures did amount to a liberalization of existing political regimes. The most reluctant leaders (as in Kenya and Sierra Leone) tried to satisfy protesters by limiting political debate and competition within the confines of the ruling single party. Because such leaders conceded as little as they could get away with and appeared to lack a sincere commitment to political liberalization we judged their reforms to be merely nominal.

Are there patterns to the extent of reform? Interestingly, the data do not support either a structural or diffusionist interpretation. One might argue, for example, that governments with relatively strong economies were able to avoid major constitutional reform by undercutting political protest through economic concessions. But, whereas the state elites of Kenya and Zimbabwe were able to employ this strategy, those of Cameroon and Gabon were apparently unable to do so. One also might note that major constitutional reform occurred disproportionately in the francophone countries of West Africa, lending credence to the notion of a diffusion effect in this region, perhaps reinforced by consistent donor pressures from France. And yet, more than half of the governments that responded to protest with mock or minor reforms also originated in this same region of Africa.

We therefore place the weight of our interpretation on contingent factors such as the skill of state elites at using available political resources, the coherence of opposition coalitions, and the relative strengths of elite and opposition groups. We argue that major political reform at the constitutional level of politics was most likely to occur when two circumstances combined: a state elite ran out of political resources; and an alternative ruling coalition emerged with an articulate political program. We discuss these factors in the next two sections of this chapter.

For the moment, let us close with a comment on the odd category of African countries in which elites dispensed political reforms in the absence of significant domestic protest. We found seven countries in this category (Cape Verde, Guinea, Guinea-Bissau, Madagascar, São Tomé and Principe, Somalia, and Tanzania). As most were small or remote countries, they followed rather than led international trends, with the lusophone countries probably imitating Mozambique in abandoning Marxism-Leninism and allowing multiparty competition. In Somalia's case, President Siad Barre's declaration of multiparty reforms appeared to be a particularly cynical attempt to convince the United States to restore cuts in foreign aid. These were the only African cases in which diffusion effects appeared to work alone in prompting reform.

Why Do Leaders Give In?

What explains the decision to undertake political reform, and the subsequent speed and extent of implementation? We start with the premise that leaders are motivated primarily by the desire to remain in power. They respond to the circumstances at each stage of the reform process by assessing the political resources at their disposal and the best way to wield them for political survival. Such calculations are necessarily imperfect, given the climate of great uncertainty during periods of ferment.

The momentous decisions of African leaders in 1990 have to be understood through this prism. In almost all cases, political reform occurred incrementally, in a series of stops and starts, with grudging elite concessions interspersed with pressures from citizens and donors, and sometimes interrupted by official retrenchment. Openings in authoritarian rule often occurred without the express intent of incumbent elites but, depending on the strength of opposition forces, was slowed, sidetracked, or even halted by recalcitrant leaders. We assume that leaders attempt to make the most out of each successive phase in the reform process. Thus, they almost invariably prefer the status quo to the unknown, until they believe that it is not sustainable and that they must instead attempt to manage an inevitable change. This logic explains the efforts by leaders in Burkina Faso, Togo, and Zaire, among others, to preempt the outbreak of protest in their countries by promoting limited reform.

Leaders bring different levels of skill to these tasks. Kérékou and Kaunda clearly lost the initiative by underestimating the strength of their opponents, resisting every demand, and having to back down in stages. Mobutu, the consummate tactician, was able to retain a measure of initiative by surprising his countrymen with a package of sweeping reforms of his own design. Similarly, leaders vary in their values and styles. It is widely believed that Biya would sincerely like to quicken the pace of liberalization in Cameroon, but that he is held back by hard-liners in the army and party. On the other hand, Moi's instinctive response to dissent appears to be repression.

Other African leaders proved to be constrained by past commitments to an ideology of democracy, which baggage proves difficult to discard. Such leaders as Biya or Kaunda, who had always legitimized their rule with the rhetoric of participation, found it more difficult to resist the sirens of multiparty elections than such leaders as Rawlings, Blaise Compaoré, or Banda, who had based their right to rule on revolutionary purity or paternalism.

These differences in style, commitments, and skill mediate the uses that leaders make of the political resources at their disposal. The availability of political resources does not allow one to predict the strategies leaders pursue once political reform is on the national agenda; instead, resource availability tends to determine whether leaders can successfully pursue a chosen survival strategy. One must remember that leaders may decide that political longevity is best enhanced by pursuing political reform.

A key political resource is effective control over powerful institutions such as the army, the party, and the trade union movement. Rumored unhappiness in the army seems to have helped convince Houphouët-Boigny of the need for accommodation in Côte d'Ivoire, for example, while Kérékou's fate was sealed when key elements of Benin's army began advocating a return to the barracks. A competent single party and the support of official unions is also important in helping state leaders contain unrest and spread the official line. Whereas ruling parties remained loyal to national leaders in Kenya and Tanzania, UNIP support wavered in Zambia. State unions became a force for reform in countries such as Congo or Côte d'Ivoire, while continuing to toe the line in other countries. Cohesion among elites in the face of unrest proved to be a critical variable in explaining which leaders were able to ride out the storm.[9]

Elite cohesion also depends on a second type of political resource: the discretionary revenues that derive from control of the state apparatus. African leaders have based their power on clientelist or prebendal networks fueled by access to state resources. In recent years both economic austerity and market reforms undermined patronage politics by starving its participants of resources. In turn, this has made the regimes more vulnerable to unrest and less able to buy support and co-opt opposition. We conclude that leaders of resource-poor states in agrarian economies such as Mali and Burkina Faso steadfastly resisted reform precisely because they lacked the wherewithal to manage the reform process. By contrast, state leaders in richer countries—such as Zaire, Gabon, and Cameroon—enjoyed a steady flow of revenues from oil and mineral exports and may have calculated that they could still dominate the political game, even after reform. Such strategies are not without risk for state leaders, and we do not mean to belittle the liberating impact of political openings. Reform initiatives, especially at the constitutional level, significantly reconfigure the rules of political competition. A modicum of space emerges for independent political activity that skilled opponents can exploit and expand. Nonetheless, incumbent leaders continue to exercise executive power that can be used to impede opposition by limiting opportunities for expression and electioneering. Thus, some leaders come to prefer a reform process they believe they can control.

Foreign aid is a third type of resource of significant political importance to African state elites, particularly in the poorer countries of the continent. How influential is the recent talk of political conditionality by Western donor agencies? The ability of donors to influence reform politics in Africa is related to the dependence of state leaders on aid resources. Leaders with independent discretionary resources at their disposal are more likely to reject donor pressures to pursue inimical policies. Bongo, in oil-rich Gabon, for example, could afford to ridicule French pressure for political reform; in Benin, on the other hand, the desperate need to pay civil service arrears obliged Kérékou to accept all the conditions—including the nomination of a technocrat, Nicéphore Soglo, as prime minister—that the French imposed on him.

The end of the cold war changed the permissive attitude of Western governments toward autocracy and malfeasance among strategic allies and allowed the expression of more-idealistic foreign policy goals. The United States acted first, when Assistant Secretary of State for Africa Herman Cohen spoke in April 1990 of the need for African countries to move toward democracy. The United States subsequently reduced or eliminated military aid to strategic allies such as Kenya, Somalia, and Zaire largely in response to these governments' violations of political rights. Even while the United States was still refining its goals and methods for promoting democratization, some African governments began to behave as if political conditionality were already in place (Brent 1990). France also reversed its long-standing attitude of intervening to support incumbent leaders against political threats in its former colonies (Chipman 1989). The refusal of Paris to send troops to Abidjan in May, when Houphouët invoked the notorious secret clause of the 1961 bilateral military cooperation agreements, sent shock waves throughout French West Africa. France's open support for democratization at the Franco-African Summit of La Baule in June 1990 only encouraged opposition groups and convinced governments of the virtues of accommodation and compromise.

Political conditionality is a highly imperfect instrument, however, and its impact on events should not be overestimated. In Kenya, the US ambassador's outspoken statements in favor of multipartyism encouraged the opposition but surely also contributed to the hardening of the government's position. In other countries token gestures made to please the foreign funders did not result in significant political changes: Mobutu's promises of democratization originated in a bid to placate donors, as well as outmaneuver his internal opposition.[10] In the absence of strong domestic forces pushing for reform, state leaders are unlikely to succumb to international pressures. Indeed, it is time now to focus on the other side of the equation, the role of forces in civil society in bringing about political reform.

Has an Alternative Ruling Coalition Emerged?

Earlier, we discussed the resources that state leaders use to modulate the pace of political reform. Yet mass protesters also bring to the struggle a range of political resources that can shape outcomes. We assume that a strong and cohesive opposition—what we call an alternative ruling coalition—is necessary to move toward governance.

We use the term *coalition* advisedly in the African context. Broad-based social coalitions of the kind that mark politics in Western countries do not fully exist in sub-Saharan Africa, where formal political participation has long been restricted to a small minority. Rather, power is based on loose alliances of elite factions with narrow social bases usually grounded in clientelism (Bayart 1989; Lemarchand 1972). In the past these regimes found grudging and passive support from an urban coalition of civil servants, unionized labor, the import trade sector, and the military rank and file. This narrow constituency, and its dependence on patronage, explains the inability of state elites to make tough economic choices. It also explains why, when patrimonial resources begin to dry up, previously cohesive regimes incur elite defections.

We argue that the political protests of 1990 sowed the seeds of an alternative ruling coalition in African countries, even though those seeds did not everywhere sprout and grow. The opposition initially emerged on university campuses and in church congregations, and drew moral and political leadership from individuals outside of state patronage networks. The movement gradually attracted mass support from populations who suffered directly from cutbacks in services, subsidies, and employment. Whether the opposition movement turned into a coalition capable of seeking political power depended on two critical factors: (1) the emergence of professional political leaders, either from "exile" outside single-party politics or from defections within the existing regime; and (2) the creation of organizational linkages among the diverse social components of the opposition movement.

What is the nature of the opposition? First, the social composition of the protesters was almost exclusively urban; we found no evidence of rural unrest in any of the countries in our sample.[11] This reflects the fact that recent economic adjustment measures have tended to benefit the countryside, at least in relative terms. Even in the West African franc zone—where the strong appreciation of the real effective exchange rate required cuts in official prices for export crops—the countryside remained quiet. In Côte d'Ivoire, opposition leader Laurent Gbagbo appealed to cocoa farmers by promising to increase and stabilize producer prices, but this did not stop farmers from granting electoral support to Houphouët.

Second, the protests were sustained politically by the middle classes. Of course the urban poor expressed their desperation by engaging in looting once riots broke out; but the students, teachers, miners, and civil servants who led the protests en masse were relatively privileged elements in African countries. The bourgeoisie is a weakly developed class in African countries, being highly dependent on the state and crippled by economic crisis. One must therefore question whether it can sustain efforts to win economic and political freedoms and to lead a political coalition that includes lower classes with whom it does not share basic interests.

Third, the protests took on a regional or ethnic cast in several countries. Groups who were unhappy with their share of the existing economic pie played a prominent role in fomenting and spreading protest in several countries. In Kenya, for example, the July 1990 riots diffused from Nairobi to towns in the heartland of the Kikuyu, the ethnic group who have lost most power and prestige under the Moi regime. The protests in Cameroon did not mobilize widespread support except in North West Province, where the provincial anglophone elites perceived neglect of their region by francophone leaders in the capital. Similarly, the unrest in Gabon is said to have fed off the northern Fang people's unhappiness with the prominence of Bongo's own Batéké group in positions of power.

Who were the leaders? As the protests turned explicitly political, professional politicians began to replace student and church activists in leadership positions. Associations or parties formed around exiled dissidents and sought to register or gain recognition, sometimes from a base in a European capital. Familiar faces reappeared as former cabinet members and senior officials who had fallen out of official favor clambered to return to active politics. Thus in Benin, previous state presidents—Justin-Tometin Ahomadégbé, Emile-Derlin Zinzou, and Hubert Maga—were among the first to begin campaigning for the presidency. And in Zambia, the ruling party began to split as UNIP soft-liners like Humphrey Mulemba defected to join veteran politicians such as Arthur Wina who had long been in the political wilderness. Whatever their political base, ambitious politicians tended to see mass protest as an opportunity to gain or recapture positions of power.

The capacity of opposition leaders to mount a credible bid against incumbent elites hinged in part on organizational resources, such as the strength and independence of associations in civil society. Where civic organizations were officially sanctioned by the state or single party, they did not lead the protests so much as scramble to keep up with an increasingly radicalized rank and file. Trade unions, torn between the economic aspirations of their members and cozy corporatist arrangements with the state, are illustrative in this respect (Sandbrook & Cohen 1975). Some union leaders, for example, were wary of losing the handsome membership dues and tax revenues collected under law and threatened by political pluralism.[12] Others maintained a measure of independence from the state, notably in Zambia, where the 1990 unrest marked the coming of age of a union movement with few parallels on the continent. The head of the Zambia Congress of Trade Unions vaulted to leadership of the opposition movement by refusing to accept appointment to the Central Committee of the governing party.[13]

Much also depended on the ability of leaders to aggregate the parochial interests of the diverse elements in the opposition into a coherent front. In Kenya, where churchmen and lawyers had taken strong independent initiatives to oppose state repression, the opposition movement lacked the coordinating hand of a unified leadership. In Zambia, however, a new alliance among workers, businessmen, and churchgoers began to take shape under the organizational umbrella of a Movement for Multiparty Democracy.

For the most part, however, the political structures born in the 1990 protests were fragmented and sectionalized. A dizzying number of new political parties registered with the national authorities: some seventy-five in Gabon; over forty in Zaire; and more than twenty in Côte d'Ivoire. Some were parties in name only, made up merely of a leader and a handful of followers. Mobutu initially tried to limit registration to three parties with controlled composition and platforms; he later recanted, apparently calculating that fragmentation of the opposition was to his electoral advantage. The Gabonese government went so far as to promise 20 million CFA francs to every registered party, and then stood back and watched while internal squabbling and accusations of financial improprieties discredited several leading contenders. By the end of 1990 an alternative ruling coalition, with a credible leadership and coherent program, had yet to emerge in most African countries.

A TRANSITION TO DEMOCRACY?

From our foreshortened vantage point close to the drama of unfinished events, we hazard a guess that the year 1990 is a watershed in African politics. We suggest that this turn of decade will be recorded retrospectively as a moment as portentous for the direction of political change on the continent as 1960 (the year of political independence) and 1966 (the year of the military coup). In 1990 African citizens stood up and insisted on political accountability from their rulers. Partly to accommodate demands and partly to preempt them, a sizable proportion of Africa's authoritarian regimes (twenty-one out of our sample of thirty-one) adopted more-liberal and competitive practices of governance (see Table 2.2).[14] The thirty-year trend in African politics toward political centralization began to reverse, with political elites embarking on cautious experiments to divide and distribute political power.

But we argue that the partial liberalization of authoritarian regimes does not amount to a transition to democracy. By the criterion of free and fair elections, we cannot say that any of the African regimes studied is indisputably embarked on a democratic route. By November 1990 multiparty elections were held or scheduled in eleven countries (Benin, Cape Verde, Comoros, Côte d'Ivoire, Gabon, Guinea, Madagascar, São Tomé and Principe, Somalia, Zaire, and Zambia; see Table 2.2). But the ruling elite was often careful to defer the polling until a date in the distant future (Guinea and Madagascar) or to be vague about the precise timing in 1991 when the elections would be held (Zaire and Zambia). In two cases (Côte d'Ivoire and Gabon) multiparty elections actually took place, but irregularities in campaign and polling procedures called into question the legitimacy of the electoral process.

Hence, the struggle between state elites and opposition movements is likely to unfold along lines that are already discernible. From the moment that multiparty elections are announced, incumbent leaders will place obstacles in the path of opposition parties. The ruling party will harass opponents on the campaign trail, for example by preventing them from holding public meetings or restricting access to advertising and media coverage. Incumbents will make full use of state resources to further their own campaigns, for example by using government transport to ferry supporters to rallies and the polls. Governments can also be expected to turn a blind eye to violent intimidation when it emanates from among their own supporters.

Even when elections are held, state elites will not concede easily to indeterminate outcomes. In the elections in Côte d'Ivoire and Gabon in October 1990, the first multiparty contests in either country since independence, the accuracy of election results was hotly contested. In Côte d'Ivoire, incumbent Houphouët-Boigny claimed a landslide victory in presidential elections with 81.7 percent of the vote; but challenger Gbagbo, without disputing the election outcome, retorted that the ruling party had massaged results to inflate Houphouët's margin of victory. In Gabon, the Gabonese Democratic Party was returned to power with a narrow parliamentary majority amid allegations of fraud, ballot rigging, and intimidation. President Bongo immediately called for the formation of a national unity government with the six other political parties who won seats, thus rekindling the ideology of unity associated with single-party regimes, rather than encouraging pluralism, diversity, and contestation.

It would be wrong to see the Ivoirien or Gabonese election results as a mandate for the political status quo, or as automatically replicable in countries with less-formidable national leaders. But we have several reasons for concluding that authoritarian regimes in Africa do not stand on the brink of a transition to democracy. These reasons harken back to the structuralist, diffusionist, and contingent explanations of political liberalization in Africa that we have explored.

First, we note the underlying structural constraint of Africa's economic crisis on the prospect for democratic transitions. As one trenchant commentator has observed, "the effort to promote democracy in the midst of acute economic distress is historically unprecedented" (Young 1990:89; see also Sandbrook 1990).[15] Whether or not current authoritarian leaders survive, the need for economic adjustment will remain. Whoever is in power will face macroeconomic disequilibria and have little choice but to proceed with administering some formula of economic austerity. Because the social costs of adjustment fall disproportionately on urban and bureaucratic interests, these groups are likely to become alienated from any government, even a democratically elected one.

It is therefore somewhat puzzling that the demands of African protesters combine corporatist claims on the public purse with calls for multipartyism and democracy. This can be attributed in part to a self-serving need to justify particularist demands. Perhaps African populations will accept austerity policies more readily once they are openly debated and carried out by an elected government. But the demands of the protesters may also be contradictory and irreconcilable. If so, for the foreseeable future, any African government will confront the unenviable task of choosing between economic and political reform, between growth and democracy.

Second, we doubt the sort of democratic outcomes recently achieved in parts of Eastern Europe will automatically diffuse to Africa. The breath of freedom blowing from this region is undoubtedly a source of inspiration to the educated middle and working classes in Africa's capital cities. But these classes in Africa are a social minority sitting atop agrarian societies composed mainly of poorly educated, self-provisioning peasants. In terms of social structure and (lack of) democratic experience, African countries resemble less the industrial societies of Poland, (East) Germany, and Czechoslovakia than the agrarian backwaters of Romania, China, or North Korea. It is sobering to recall that in the latter group of countries, political protest either did not arise at all (North Korea), was ruthlessly crushed with state power (China), or was hijacked by an ambitious faction from within the governing clique (Romania). In none of these countries was the mass of the agrarian population sufficiently attached to democratic values, or aware of events in the capital and the world, to demystify the regime's account of events or to counter its crackdowns.

Finally, our analysis of the contingent dynamics of protest and reform in sub-Saharan Africa leads us to conclude that political elites continue to enjoy an important advantage over mass protesters. However weakened their political legitimacy and economic base, top political leaders can still mobilize the coercive resources of the state against nongovernmental opponents. By contrast, opposition movements in Africa are spontaneous assemblages of diverse urban interests, ranging from privileged public servants to the *lumpenproletariat* of the shantytowns. Occasionally these elements are organized into formal associations—such as churches, trade unions, and professional associations—with an independent resource base and a policy voice to pursue specific interests. Only rarely, however, are these elements aggregated across the breadth of civil society into an alternative ruling coalition with a sustainable multiclass social base and a coherent platform for governing.

It is extremely difficult to gauge the effectiveness of the new opposition movements in Africa. The incomplete evidence to date suggests that civic forces lack the support and organization to unseat ruling parties, especially given the tremendous advantages incumbency brings to the latter. More critically, we see little sign that the opposition can promote an alternative set of political values that would result in immediate changes in governance. The roots of protest in efforts to protect corporate privilege, and its narrow base among the urban bourgeoisie bespeak a conservative reaction against economic austerity. The opportunism of opposition political leaders, their patronage followings, and their links with current state elites, all suggest that a change of leaders would probably perpetuate a clientelistic pattern of politics as usual.

Nonetheless, opposition groups did prompt the 1990 protests and in so doing put new issues on the political agenda in Africa. These include the recognition of basic civil and political liberties, the end of arbitrary regulation and state exaction, and greater transparency and accountability in public decisionmaking. The projection of these governance issues into open public debate may in the end be the most significant aspect of the 1990 protests. Although an alternative ruling coalition did not fully emerge everywhere, the political ideas to support such a coalition did make an important first appearance.

NOTES

The authors wish to thank Diane Tchudziak and Jeffrey Coupe for research assistance.

1. As far as external forces are concerned, some analysts attribute democratic reform to the modernizing impact of an expanding global economy (Pye 1990) or to the diffusion effects of successful democratic revolutions elsewhere in the world (Klingman 1980; Hill & Rothchild 1987). For Africa, there is an emerging literature on aid as an instrument of governance reform (Brent 1990; Lancaster 1990; USAID 1990; *Africa Confidential*, July 15, 1990). Reform pressures from within domestic society are addressed more directly in the recent literature on democracy in Africa (Chabal 1986; Diamond, Linz & Lipset 1988a; Fatton 1990; Hayward 1987; Ronen 1986; Wiseman 1990), but few studies have yet taken explicit account of the upsurge in popular protests in 1990 and its relationship with prodemocracy movements in the rest of the world. One exception is *Africa Demos*, a quarterly bulletin of the African Governance Program of the Carter Center, which tracks and evaluates political reforms in Africa.

2. Because African states are weaker than states in these other regions, they are unusually exposed to influence by international forces. But we think that Lowenthal's (1986:ix) assessment for Latin America and southern Europe is relevant to Africa: "although international factors may condition the course of [regime] transition, the major participants and dominant influences in every case have been national."

3. The main sources were *AFPress Clips, Africa Confidential, Africa International, Africa News, Africa Research Bulletin* (Political Series), Economist Intelligence Unit *Country Report*, Foreign Broadcast Information Service *Daily Report, Jeune Afrique, Le Monde, Libération, Marchés Tropicaux et Méditerranéens, New African, The New York Times, News From Zambia, Politique Africaine, Weekly Review*, and *West Africa*.

4. This starting date is justified by the opening of the Berlin Wall as a historical watershed, and the increased number, tempo, and scale of protest and reform events in Africa in the following months. Our somewhat arbitrary one-year

study period should not be taken as implying that such events did not occur before November 1989 or after November 1990.

5. We excluded, as countries embroiled in civil war, Ethiopia, Sudan, Angola, Mozambique, Rwanda, Chad, and Liberia. The immediate political task in these countries was to establish a cease-fire and initiate peace talks before constitutional questions on the structure of governance could be addressed. Nigeria and Lesotho we excluded as countries undergoing a planned transition from military to civilian rule. A managed process of political reform was already under way from above, with a phased series of steps including constitution writing and elections, but disallowing unplanned popular interventions. We excluded, as countries that are multiparty democracies, Senegal, Gambia, Botswana, Mauritius, and Namibia. While protesters may sometimes still demand further political liberalization (e.g., in Senegal, following the 1988 elections), the political reform process was essentially complete. We did include Zimbabwe in our sample, however, because the recent protests there probably slowed or prevented the regime's slide toward authoritarianism.

6. As Tripp notes in Chapter 10, leaders also set in motion steps to make the trade union and cooperative movements independent of the party.

7. As an Ivoirien trade union leader explained, the 1990 budgetary shortfall was equivalent to the previous year's capital flight of 125 billion CFA francs. The inescapable conclusion? "The rich just have to repatriate their money." Quoted in "La cour du vieux roi Houphouët-Boigny," in *Libération*, April 13, 1990.

8. Nonetheless, the impact of the South African example was notably reduced by Mandela's visits to African capitals where he lent prestige to government leaders, notably in Kenya where he refused to be drawn into supportive comments about opposition protests.

9. Joan Nelson (1984) emphasizes the importance of elite cohesion with reference to the political management of economic reform.

10. See Chapter 11.

11. The reader is reminded that we excluded from consideration countries in the throes of civil war; organized political opposition clearly originates from rural areas in Angola, Ethiopia, Mozambique, and Sudan.

12. In the Congo, for example, the support of the official trade union, the Confédération Syndicale du Congo, for the movement toward multipartyism cooled considerably when it became clear that such reform also implied pluralism in the union movement and the end of the mandatory employee union contribution that financed all of its operations. See "Les apparatchiks règlent leurs comptes: Congo, reconversions tous azimuts," *Jeune Afrique*, October 17–23, 1990, p. 30.

13. At the same time, in April 1990, the rank and file of the Mineworkers Union of Zambia voted out of office its chair, who had accepted a UNIP Central Committee post.

14. If countries beyond our sample are included (i.e., those embroiled in civil war or undergoing a planned transition to civilian rule), then political reforms occurred in twenty-six out of forty-one countries during 1990.

15. The view that there is a contradiction between economic and political reform is disputed elsewhere in the literature: Larry Diamond (1988:26) considers that economic reform will help create "a more authentic and autonomous bourgeoisie in the informal economy" whose members will press for a further loosening of state controls on economic and political activity.

3

Governance, Democracy, and the 1988 Senegalese Elections

Crawford Young & Babacar Kante

The 1988 Senegalese elections were a moment of high drama in the political evolution of Africa. Four presidential candidates and six party lists for National Assembly seats participated in a contest marked by increasingly heated debate. During the three-week period of official campaigning, citizens watched transfixed as nightly television coverage reproduced the escalating intensity of opposition denunciation of the Parti Socialiste (PS) regime of Abdou Diouf, to which the PS and Diouf responded in kind. The accumulated tensions exploded into serious disorders, particularly in the capital city of Dakar, in the wake of the voting, as the opposition disputed the proclaimed triumph of Diouf and his party as fraudulent. Security forces blanketed Dakar for nearly three months, as a state of emergency was invoked to contain a wave of disaffection, especially among the youth. Only gradually did a relative calm return to the capital.

Not only Senegalese were intent observers of this electoral melodrama. This was much more than a minor episode in the political history of one country; at issue was the broader question of the viability of a transition to democracy in Africa more generally. Beyond this lay an even more fundamental problematic: can the contemporary African state be transformed from a parasitic patrimonial autocracy into a genuine institution of governance?

Here we draw on the valuable concepts of Goran Hyden, in proposing the governance notion as orienting focus for political inquiry that transcends the dismal science of documenting decay and despair (Hyden 1988, 1989). In the Hyden delineation of governance, core aspects are legitimacy of the exercise of power, construction of solidary reciprocities, development of trust in state–civil society relationships, and institutionalization of accountability (Hyden 1988: 31). Governance, for Hyden, involves much more than simply the pluralization of politics and acceptance of political competition that constitute democratization. We believe, however, that the accumulated instruction of postcolonial African political history suggests that democratization of the political process is an indispensable requisite to

57

making possible "the deliberate acts of political leaders to overcome structural constraints to the realization of productive reciprocities," by which Hyden (1988, 24) defines governance. Equally necessary is to enlarge opportunities for creative initiative by political actors and ordinary citizens located at the base of society, in turn linked to liberalization.

The forlorn condition of the contemporary African state is not in dispute (Rothchild & Chazan 1988; Bayart 1989; Mbembe 1988; Sandbrook 1985). Battered by the economic crisis of the 1980s, African polities were beset by a growing disaffection of civil society and a deepening dependency on external economic and political forces. A reweaving of the frayed relationship with the populace appeared an urgent remedy; legitimacy lost had to be regained. Revival of the trust of the citizenry had as its ransom some mechanisms for accountability. Democratization, broadly conceived, appeared an indispensable element in this transaction. In turn, the electoral process was a core component of democracy operationalized. The 1988 Senegalese presidential and parliamentary elections—with unrestricted entry rules for the competition—fell in the midst of a growing consensus that African recovery required "getting politics right," and thus assumed singular importance as a test case for the perils and promise of democratization as remedy. In this chapter, we wish to locate the Senegalese case in the broader African context of political opening, then examine the electoral drama itself, reflecting on its implications for the notion of governance.

PRESSURES FOR DEMOCRATIZATION IN AFRICA

Perhaps no more eloquent measure of the scope of consensus that African revival has political as well as economic prerequisites is the common endorsement of democratization in the sharp, even polemical documentary combat between the United Nations Economic Commission for Africa (ECA) and the World Bank in 1989. The ECA in its stinging attack on the structural adjustment programs nurtured by the World Bank declares that an "African alternative framework" must be grounded in "democratization of the decision-making process at national, local and grassroots levels so as to generate the necessary consensus and people's support" (ECA 1989:50). The World Bank, noting the derelictions of "coercive and arbitrary states" where officials "have served their own interests without fear of being called to account" summoned African states to political renewal, labeled "governance" but redolent of democratic theory: "a systematic effort to build a pluralistic institutional structure, a determination to respect the rule of law, and vigorous protection of the freedom of the press and human rights" (World Bank 1989:60–61). When economists, wont to view reason of state as a branch of econometrics, prescribe democracy and governance as therapy for disabled economies, the time has come for all to take notice.

The 1988 elections in Senegal provoked a sustained, often passionate debate about the nature and essence of democracy, and its links to change and recovery. The term *governance* is of course known mainly to academics, and recently the external development community, but its themes resonated in this collective exercise in political reflection. Such debates, as we will show in our examination of the elections themselves, are not new in Senegal, although their intensity has deepened. What has altered the discussion is the newly globalized context in which it is situated. In recent years there has been what Afrifa Gitonga (1988:5) labels "a progressive sanctification of the democratic ideal," a "quasi-universal acceptance and adoration of democracy as a system."

This, in turn, reflected a transformation of political discourse and practice throughout the world. The tides of change began to flow in the mid-1970s in Western Europe, where the last outposts of authoritarian rule fell (Spain, Portugal, Greece). In Latin America, where so recently the bureaucratic-authoritarian state model appeared ascendant (O'Donnell 1973; Malloy 1977; Collier 1979), the empirical underpinning for the paradigm vanished as Argentina, Brazil, Uruguay, and Chile evolved away from this mode of domination. To general astonishment in 1990, the Sandinista revolution was voted out of office. Most extraordinary of all was the overnight collapse of state socialism and its ossified Leninist structures in Eastern Europe in late 1989.[1] Islands of autocracy remained: the Middle East; China; parts of Southeast Asia; Cuba. But the currents of democratic change flowed powerfully, indeed seemingly irresistibly. Scholars who had barely completed major collective inquiries into breakdown of democratic regimes (Linz & Stepan 1978) redirected their intellectual energies to the examination of transitions from authoritarian rule (O'Donnell, Schmitter & Whitehead 1986).

The cumulative impact of these events—especially the stunning extinction of Leninist regimes in Eastern Europe—placed intense pressure on African states by the end of the 1980s. Such respected theoreticians of the single party as Julius Nyerere began to equivocate. And the earth began to move in that most redoubtable fortress of exclusionary politics, South Africa.

The winds of liberalization shaping the present conjuncture in global affairs have—for the moment, at least—silenced the once-vocal partisans of the powerful unitary state as political monopolist. Default speaks powerfully for democratization; no credible substitutes now stand. As President Dawda Jawara of Gambia recently responded to a query from a British scholar as to why democracy was important, "if you look at the alternatives, I think you can see why" (Wiseman 1990:182). This conclusion had been reached by Senegal's leaders and intelligentsia by the 1970s, but elsewhere it was far newer. Leninism became extinct in Africa with the May 1991 destruction of his giant statue in Addis Ababa, Ethiopia, as final symbolic requiem. The illusion of the democratic single party had equally vanished. The premise that rapid development required the ransom of autocracy—"developmental dictatorship," as Sklar (1987) put it—has lost all credibility.

If authoritarian formulas are currently on the defensive everywhere and in many areas in retreat, the quest for clarification of democracy becomes more urgent. Regimes that embark on a path of democratic opening confront at once fundamental issues as to what conditions must be fulfilled to reach this objective. Vast confusion exists as to precisely what democracy is, in theoretical terms, and what empirical requisites must be observed for a state to lay convincing claim to this legitimation. Naturally we have no ambition to resolve a debate that has engaged some of the most fertile philosophical minds for two and a half millennia. Rather we wish to take note of some of the major themes that have emerged in recent passages from authoritarian to democratic forms, particularly in Africa, and relate these to the 1988 Senegalese elections (Sartori 1987; Dahl 1956).

The first temptation is recourse to the etymological meaning, rule by the people. This proves to be the beginning rather than the end of the discussion in the empirical world of contemporary states; what is crucial is identifying the nature and limits of rule, defining the people, and delineating the mechanisms through which the former is carried out by the latter. The Greek derivation of the word *democracy* is nonetheless helpful as a start, suggesting as it does that the critical elements are the state (rule), civil society (people), and the nexus between them: productive reciprocities, if we join democracy to the concept of governance.

The historical evolution of the Western state illustrates this dimension of the democratic concept. The rise of the modern state occurred in tandem with elaboration of an absolutist form, whose philosophers constructed the doctrine of sovereignty as a creed of potentially unlimited state power. These pretensions evoked a long struggle by civil society, following different trajectories in different countries, but whose common object was to constrain state authority. The paramount institutional arenas of combat were the legislative bodies, and sometimes the judicial system. At issue above all was the transfer of sovereignty from the rulers to the people. From this emerged modern constitutionalism, or the contractualization of state–civil society relationships. A constitutional state (or *état de droit*) became bound by its own public law; the great debates pivoted about structuring of the state, so that the constitutional compact between state and civil society was self-enforcing. Thus one major component of the idea of democracy lies in structural questions concerning the institutions of rule: embedding the representational principle; enforcing accountability; ensuring responsiveness; averting concentrations of power permitting the state to shed its constitutional shackles.

Another set of elements in the concept of democracy hinges on the processes by which civil society ensures that state action is responsive to its voice. The central institutional devices have been elections, and political parties to organize and structure the competition. The integrity of these processes in turn requires guarantees of freedom of expression, diffusion of opinion, and association.

Beyond structural and processual elements in democracy, we encounter core values, above all liberty and equality. Human freedom is not simply a means to the goal of a constitutional state; it is rather an end in itself. Whether this notion is rooted in religious doctrine, as in older ideas of natural law, or is of more-secular origin, the consequence for the idea of democracy is the same: preservation of the inviolable integrity of the individual human being. An unbreachable wall of civil liberty guarantees, protecting the citizen from arbitrary state action, is thus indispensable not only to assure fair political competition, but also to uphold human liberty as an ultimate end.

Equality has similar standing as intrinsic to the concept of democracy. All members of civil society merit equal valuation both in institutional processes in the public realm, and in the application of rule by the state. More closely viewed, equality as norm has innumerable ambiguities and dilemmas. The power of the norm is in no way eroded by the empirical inability of the state to deliver equal goods to all, or of the constitutional system to apportion influence or efficacious participation in equal segments to all citizens (Rae 1979).

Equality constitutionally empowers individuals as citizens and opens to them the institutions of access: political parties and other associations; representative bodies. The vitality of citizen involvement serves as one operative measure of democracy; participation wins frequent mention as a core value. In the major recent collective work on Third World democracy directed by Diamond, Linz, and Lipset (1988b:xvi–xvii), participation is listed as one of the three defining characteristics of democracy (along with competition and civil liberties).

We are very far from exhausting the topic of defining democracy; however, some of the main dimensions have been considered. We may note the important overlap (although not identity) of the governance concept elaborated in Chapter 1; both democracy and governance are embodied in structures, values, and norms. The complexity of democracy as concept is clear enough; from this it follows that there may be competing visions that stress different aspects. Dahl (1956:4–60) has argued, in the US case, the sharp contrast between the Madisonian views of democracy, which dominated the framers of the Constitution and focused on dividing and limiting the power of the state, and also on constraining the plebiscitary power of a momentary majority, and a more Jacobinic, populist theory whose central thrust is securing the enforcement of the sovereign will of the majority. A parallel divergence is found in Brazilian public opinion, in the judgments rendered on the recent transition to democracy (Rochon & Mitchell 1989); one segment of the Brazilian citizenry valued especially the procedural dimensions (rule of law, respect of civil liberties, open multiparty competition), while another focused on substantive aspects (mass participation, responsiveness to popular demands). Dilemmas of this nature suggest that the translation of democracy from normative theory into empirical formula governing state–civil society relations will vary substantially, depending on historical, situational, and regional circumstance.

From this perspective, we can appreciate the specificity of the current debate on democracy in Africa. While drawing on a discourse that is universal, the debate is located in the particular circumstances of contemporary Africa. Critical historical determinants are the singularly authoritarian legacy of the colonial era; the patrimonial political monopolies under single-party or military auspices (or both) that swiftly became the predominant political formula after independence; the frequently predatory use of power for accumulation of wealth by the political class; the growing disaffection and withdrawal of civil society, culminating in a widespread sense of "failure" of the African state.

The pervasive sense of crisis and impasse, political as well as economic and social, provides the context for the intense contemporary debate on democracy in Africa. The profoundly dispiriting circumstances confronted by most African civil societies are measured against two yardsticks. At all levels of society, a somber present, which older generations find diminished in comparison with a remembered past, and younger cohorts perceive as offering no future, is set against the extravagant promises of a more abundant life advanced by the independence generation of political leaders three decades ago. Sharpening the contrast is the dramatic difference between the economic boom times of the 1950s and the deep depression of African economies in the 1980s. A second measure comes from the growing divergence between African development trends and those of some other regions, especially East and Southeast Asia with which Africa has frequently been analytically associated in notions of Afro-Asia or the Third World.

Recourse to democratic theory in the reconstruction of the African state was thus indispensable both to remoralization of the public realm and reincorporation of civil society. Accountability, which arises from an ongoing state–civil society dynamic, is the crucial element in democracy and governance. Operationally, its achievement above all requires a process guaranteeing that rulers must answer to the ruled; the ultimate sanction of civil society is the prerogative of ousting the incumbents. From this follows the central concern with elections as the empirical mechanism for democracy. Elections, as a formal ritual, had usually remained an integral part of the legitimating ceremonies of public life in single-party states (Hayward 1987). But their reduction in a number of countries to mere plebiscitary exercises diminished the credibility of the practice, although not the ideal; the sharp decline in turnout exhibited in the single national list one-party contests in Senegal (and elsewhere in Africa) illustrates this trend (Coulon 1988). Thus the debate on democracy in Senegal and elsewhere centered on elections, and details of their conduct that could enforce accountability and empower civil society; party system, rules of competition; rights of association and expression; equitable procedures in electoral organization.

The prolonged utilization of the electoral process as mere ritualization of the grip on power by an incumbent regime and ruler brought an important new issue to the fore—alternation, a cry heard with particular insistence in Senegal. The tendency of single-party or military regimes to become in practice systems of personal rule, whose natural disposition to perpetuate the hold on power translated political monopoly into the life-presidency, injected into African contemporary politics the classical crisis of historical states: legitimate succession. The electoral principle had to incorporate the possibility of peaceful accession to power by a challenger, if an alternative to the coup or anointment of a crown prince by the incumbent were to be discovered. Axiomatically, the life-president is beyond the reach of meaningful accountability. Alternation—or at least its real possibility—as an integral component of the electoral path to democracy thus entered the debate.

In sum, the summons to democracy is heard everywhere in Africa. Effective use of the electoral mechanism to institutionalize pluralized politics through meaningful competition, by which accountability and responsiveness in governance can be enforced, is a crucial element. Herein lies the singular importance of the 1988 Senegalese elections, in their revelation of both the possibilities of political opening, and the intimidating obstacles to full democratization.

THE SENEGALESE 1988 ELECTIONS
AS A TEST OF DEMOCRACY

In certain respects, Senegal is an unusual case, marked by its own unique colonial history and long electoral tradition. Certainly the trend toward democratization started precociously in Senegal, with the restoration of multipartyism in 1976, and has advanced further than in most countries. But important barriers remain, highlighted by the angry reaction of many to the announced 1988 election results, especially in Dakar.

Competitive elections have a long and rich history in Senegal; they first occurred in St. Louis in 1848, and from the 1870s were a regular feature of political life in the four coastal communes (Dakar, Gorée, Rufisque, St. Louis). Participation was extended into the Senegalese hinterland from 1945 on, and intense political competition characterized the terminal colonial period. However, following the political crises attending achievement of independence, the 1963 Constitution—while theoretically tolerating opposition parties—created an electoral regime institutionalizing de facto a single-party system (Fall 1977:21).[2] Meaningful political competition was restored in 1976, by a limited multiparty system with two opposition formations assigned political space to the left and right respectively of the ruling party. Presidential and legislative elections occurred under this formula in 1978. In 1981, after Léopold Senghor ceded the presidency to Abdou Diouf, all limits on the number of parties were removed. The electoral code governing the conduct of the two national elections carried out under unrestricted multipartyism (1983 and 1988) dates from this moment (Diagne 1986).

These new arrangements, combined with a disposition to factional politics with long historical roots, produced a rapid proliferation of parties; by the time of the 1983 campaign sixteen were already officially recognized, most representing minuscule clusters of intellectuals, and at least six (depending on one's definition) claiming doctrinal guidance from Marxism-Leninism. Seventeen were in existence in 1988. In the 1983 elections most of these parties were newly created; thus the 1988 balloting offered the first real occasion to measure the electoral potential of these diverse formations.

The electoral system, however, made participation by the smaller parties difficult. For the legislature, a formula inspired by the West German system was utilized; half the seats were allocated by proportional representation on a national basis, with the other half contested by department. To compete, parties had to offer full candidate lists, a difficult requirement for the small formations. Further, parties were not permitted to form electoral coalitions, an additional handicap for the small groups.

In the event, only four parties put forward presidential candidates, and six entered legislative lists. At the presidential level, incumbent President Diouf faced as principal contender Abdoulaye Wade, of the Parti Démocratique Sénégalais (PDS). Wade, a perennial contender, was an economist who once headed the Dakar law faculty; his party combined a radical, populist rhetorical style with an underlying liberal ideology (Wade 1989).[3] Two minor candidates rounded out the list: Babacar Niang, of the Parti pour la Libération du Peuple (PLP), and Landing Savane (And-Jef/Mouvement Révolutionnaire pour la Démocratie Nouvelle). Niang was an erstwhile follower of the late Cheikh Anta Diop, a widely revered cultural nationalist, while Savane spoke for the far left, with a revolutionary antiimperialist language.

Diouf entered the campaign with important advantages, beyond that of incumbency itself. The most important marabouts from the major brotherhoods that structure much of Senegalese religious life offered their support, explicit or discreet. The ruling PS was a well-oiled patronage machine, closely tied to the state apparatus, organized throughout the country and enjoying substantially greater resources than the opposition.

At the legislative level, six parties entered the race (as compared to eight in 1983).[4] In addition to the PS, the PDS, and the PLP, these included the Ligue Démocratique/Mouvement pour la Parti du Travail (LD/MPT), the Parti de l'Indépendance et du Travail (PIT), both Marxist-Leninist, and the Parti Démocratique du Sénégal/Rénovation (PDS/R), a liberal formation. The two Marxist-Leninist parties had a significant audience among intellectuals, teachers, and students, although this did not translate into electoral strength. The other two were inconsequential.

The conduct of the campaign and the balloting was governed by an electoral code sharply contested by the opposition parties since its enactment in 1982. The most controversial provisions were those allocating half of the time on state media to the ruling party, with opposition parties equally sharing the balance for the parliamentary elections (although presidential candidates received equal time); the impossibility of verifying the identity of those appearing at the voting stations; and the absence of obligatory secrecy of the ballot. In addition, the government had a substantial advantage in its control of the state-financed daily, *Le Soleil*, which published exhaustive accounts of the PS campaign but gave little space to the opposition. In the words of the minister of information, "this newspaper is not affected by the legal texts governing the state media coverage of the campaign, particularly with respect to printing the declarations of the candidates" (*Le Soleil*, February 18, 1983).

Although officially the campaign was limited to a three-week period preceding the elections, in reality it began well before the stipulated date in February 1988. President Diouf arranged elaborate and extended official visits to three important regions, replete with pledges of local amenities. The opposition adopted a strategy of systematic harassment of the government in the months before the campaign, through a series of court suits challenging aspects of the electoral code, and other devices. Social agitation multiplied on various fronts (students, teachers, police) in 1987, as groups sensed that before the voting the government might by electoral calculus make concessions certain to be refused once Diouf was secure in a new mandate.

From the outset the government was placed on the defensive. Acutely conscious of the social malaise provoked by growing youth unemployment, a crisis in the school system, and declining purchasing power of urban populations, the PS found peddling its purported successes in structural adjustment a tough sell to a deeply skeptical electorate. In showcasing its leader, the party fell back on such limp slogans as "Abdou l'utile," "Abdou le batisseur," "Monsieur Moulin," and the like.

The opposition was unconstrained by any share in the responsibility for current discontents. As the campaign wore on, the PDS in particular focused its efforts on huge rallies in the urban centers, with scathing denunciation of PS rule as directly responsible for declining public well-being. Most effective of all was its simple and shopworn yet profoundly evocative slogan of "sopi" (change), unencumbered by any specification of its content. Although the first part of the campaign was peaceful, tensions mounted rapidly in the final days, with serious disorders in Thies three days before the voting.

The actual voting took place on a single day, in three thousand polling stations scattered through the country. Upon presentation of a voting card, the citizen was provided two ballot papers, one for the presidency and one for the legislature. These were to be deposited in separate boxes for each presidential candidate, and for each party competing in the legislative elections. A curtained area where this could be done secretly was available, but most voters used the open voting area. Staffing the polling stations were civil servants; the opposition parties were entitled to have observers present at the polling stations, but only the PDS had the organizational resources to cover many stations. In most rural areas only the PS was represented. The ballots were tallied at the voting stations; the polling station head then had to sign and forward a report of the conduct of the voting and the results. The Supreme Court was charged with monitoring the entire process; however, it had a surveillance team of only twenty available to cover the three thousand polling stations (Ngom 1989). In most places the voting itself occurred without incident, although 156 polling stations submitted flawed reports (lacking the signature of the chief administrator, for example), which led to the disqualification of the 46,141 votes recorded at these precincts.

The official procedure for counting the ballots was complex, and the law prescribed a five-day delay before announcement of the results. However, the government chose to release on election night what it characterized as a sample of the returns, showing a decisive victory for Diouf and the PS; rioting began at once, starting at the university in Dakar, then spreading to many areas of the city the following day. The opposition claimed widespread fraud had robbed them of victory.

The results, as published, confirmed the PS triumph. Of those registered (1,932,265, of a population of approximately 6 million), some 1,135,501 cast votes. Registration is neither automatic nor obligatory; probably several hundred thousand potentially eligible citizens had not taken the trouble to register. The announced results are shown in Table 3.1.

Diouf lost about 10 percent of his 1983 majority to Wade.[5] In the parliament the PDS contingent increased from eight to seventeen seats (compared to 103 for the PS).

The abstention rate was relatively high, as in the preceding elections; although 59 percent of those actually registered voted (as compared to 58 percent in 1978 and 63 percent in 1983), fewer than half the potentially eligible voters turned out (roughly the same as the 1990 Zimbabwe elections, or Second Republic Nigerian balloting).[6] The minimum voting age (twenty-one) removed from the balloting (although not from militant street action) a generation (eighteen to twenty) particularly affected by unemployment and enthusiastically receptive to the "sopi" slogan. Registration was an arduous requirement for rural populations some distance from an administrative center; so also was the required appearance at this state outpost to obtain a voting card, then again to actually vote. Fear may have played some part; the climate of tension and threats in the final campaign days may have discouraged some from voting. Others may have believed the results

Table 3.1 Results of the 1988 Senegalese Presidential and
Parliamentary Elections (in percentages)

Presidency		Legislature	
Diouf	73.2	PS	71.3
Wade	25.8	PDS	24.7
Niang	0.8	PLP	1.2
Savane	0.3	LD/MPT	1.4
		PIT	0.8
		PDS/R	0.4

preordained, and the nuisance of traveling to the polling station not repaid by the utility of the act.

The actual impact of the marabouts' support for Diouf is difficult to measure. Their instructions were not unanimously followed. However, if one examines the results at Djourbel, stronghold of the Mouride order whose leader had gone furthest in giving a religious instruction (*ndigel*) to disciples of this brotherhood to vote for Diouf, one finds clear evidence of its impact. Diouf in this region received 88 percent of the votes. Opposition politicians denounced the marabouts' intervention in the voting, although they were swift to throw themselves at the feet of the marabouts whenever a possibility existed of securing their support. Closely inspected, the brotherhoods themselves are divided into tendencies, and not all maraboutic factions have supported the PS (Magassouba 1985).

The 1988 elections clearly marked an eruption of youth into the political scene. Although many were unable to vote, their weight was felt in the campaign, and especially in the disorders surrounding its final phases and outcome. Although Senegalese youth has long been highly politicized, it had never been so thoroughly aligned with the opposition campaign. Whether its electoral mobilization signified a deep-seated adhesion to the projects of the opposition is much less certain.

The PDS tried hard to bring about an alliance of small opposition parties in support of its presidential candidate; in the end, only the PIT and LD/MPT responded to its solicitation, with the PIT defecting soon after the elections. Wade did, however, succeed in establishing himself as the prime spokesperson for the opposition and an indispensable interlocutor for the government in restoring social peace.

One may note the hostile public reaction toward two small parties that supported Diouf, the PDS/R and the Parti Africain pour l'Indépendance des Masses (PAIM). In the collective consciousness, opposition—it would seem—must be total to be credible, a troubling inference if correct, given the importance of tolerance to the democratic process. In 1983 Cheikh Anta Diop—notwithstanding his immense intellectual prestige—suffered in public esteem for his reluctance to openly oppose Diouf.

The rioting that greeted the electoral results was fueled by an opposition claim—widely believed among youth and in some other quarters—that Wade had really won the elections, but that massive fraud had denied him the victory. That some degree of fraud existed is beyond dispute; indeed, electoral irregularities are a traditional feature of Senegalese balloting, extending back far into the colonial period (Sylla 1983–1985). Probably the largest source of dishonesty was the possession by some PS local luminaries of bundles of electoral cards, distributed to their clientele. Thus, the opposition alleged, some ruling party supporters were able to vote, in classical Chicago style, "early and often." In rural polling stations, where opposition parties could not station observers, illiterate citizens voting in full view of local administrators and the PS agent faced undoubted psychological pressures to vote for the government. In a number of Dakar and Thies voting stations, with highly vocal and visible PDS support, the polling station head refused to sign the voting report, which had the effect of disqualifying all votes cast at this precinct. However, although such malpractices clearly existed, their exact magnitude and their impact on the results are difficult to determine.

Certainly the ruling party exploited various weaknesses of the electoral code. But the opposition allegations that the election was stolen really boiled down to the assertion that popular discontent was so transparent and so massive that the PS could not conceivably have won. Cited as evidence was the size and enthusiasm of the election rallies of the PDS, particularly in the final phases. But here one must carefully distinguish between crowds at Wade electoral harangues and the electorate; many of the exuberant rally participants were youth too young to vote. Further, the electoral effervescence was limited to the cities, especially Dakar, where strong opposition support was clear. But PDS ability to penetrate the interior of the country was far more circumscribed; its limited organizational and communication resources did not suffice to effectively challenge the rural PS machine. Thus, in our judgment, fraud and other electoral handicaps of the opposition doubtless enlarged the size of the PS majority but did not change the results. The precise balance of forces is difficult to calculate, but Senegal appears to remain a dominant party system without alternation.

In the aftermath of the elections Senegal offers the spectacle of a fractionalized opposition confronting a victorious but crisis-ridden ruling party. The corrosion of its long tenure in office and resistance of its cadres to any rejuvenation of its leading ranks weaken the PS from within. Yet its continued control of the state and long political experience permit Diouf to retain the initiative, reflected in his success in securing the participation of Wade and three other PDS and PIT leaders in a coalition cabinet in early

1991. The opposition parties have not yet begun a conquest of public opinion in anticipation of the 1993 elections; a number continue to fight the battle of 1988, claiming that Diouf lacks legal standing as president because of unresolved allegations of election fraud.

The opposition sought to challenge the results on two fronts—judicial appeal and social agitation. The juridical objections were surprisingly weak and ineffectual. They called for annulment of the entire elections, on such grounds as the claim that irregularities had occurred in distribution of voting cards, that underage individuals had voted, that an excessive number of votes had been disqualified because of improperly certified returns, and that some returns had been transmitted to the Supreme Court in procedurally flawed ways. The Court rejected these challenges, either because they were introduced too late or because the appellants failed to document their charges.

The fury of the streets was far more serious. Although confined to Dakar, outbreaks of disorder occurred in several parts of the city; municipal buses were attacked, cars overturned and burned, gasoline stations besieged in the hope of acquiring Molotov cocktail fuel, and neighborhood state offices ransacked. A state of emergency and early curfew were imposed, and the army brought in to occupy the capital. Although the first outburst of anger subsided, Dakar remained tense (and the curfew in effect) for nearly three months, with sporadic incidents of violence and vandalism. The security forces exhibited exemplary discipline; the disorders, remarkably, brought no fatalities.

However, one possible casualty of the electoral tensions was the credibility of the Supreme Court. The electoral code was amended after the 1983 elections to invest the Supreme Court with responsibility for supervising the elections and verifying the results. Although this change was welcomed across the board when introduced, one may fear that the recourse primarily to mass action rather than court process to challenge the results begins to cast doubt on the neutrality and objectivity of the Supreme Court. In evaluating the Court decision to reject all the appeals, either on technical grounds or on their merits, one must recollect that, in electoral jurisprudence, a judge will always hesitate to invalidate an entire electoral result, and generally only will do so when fraud is clearly proved and the outcome close enough so that the violations in question might have altered the decision. In general, the gap between the scope of Supreme Court responsibilities and the modesty of its means risked compromising its prestige by placing the judiciary in the position of certifying the regularity of a process that it lacked the capacity to truly verify.

Beyond these difficulties, those charged with assuring the integrity of the electoral process confronted an opposition that appeared convinced that, after its defeats in 1978 and 1983, it was certain to win, but that the PS would cheat the PDS of its triumph by fraud. The visible strength of the opposition in the capital provided a misleading prism for gauging the elections; in

Dakar, official returns showed Diouf obtaining only 54.93 percent compared to 40.67 percent for Wade. It is thus perhaps unsurprising that the wave of violence following the elections was limited to Dakar. With little confidence in its legal challenges, the opposition drew up a two-stage plan for protesting the anticipated fraud. On the eve of the elections its followers were urged to monitor the balloting themselves, resisting the police if need be. In the event that these measures failed, PDS militants were directed to undertake peaceful occupations of some ministries (*Wal Fadjri*, January 2, 1988). This served as trigger for a wave of uncontrollable vandalism, in the context of a student strike covering schools from the primary through university levels. In response, the government declared a state of emergency on the day following the elections, and arrested several opposition leaders, including Wade, Abdoulaye Bathily of LD/MPT, and Amath Dansoko of PIT. As soon as these opposition figures were tried and convicted, President Diouf called on the National Assembly to vote an amnesty law, covering all infractions relating to the elections, as well as freeing some jailed Casamance separatists. Even before the trials, Diouf ordered a price reduction for some key commodities. He followed up by inviting Wade to join him in a round table bringing together all political formations to discuss the problems facing Senegal.

Although these gestures of appeasement momentarily lowered the political temperature, the round table and other secret conversations with the PDS failed to reach agreement. Tensions remained strong, as the opposition persisted in its demand for new elections or a coalition government. Finally, the 1989 crisis with Mauritania created internal unity and helped to bring about a truce on the domestic front.[7]

In retrospect, one could say that the polarization between ruling party and opposition really began in 1981/82, with the drafting of the electoral code, unanimously repudiated by opposition formations. About the same time, unemployment began to afflict university graduates for the first time, and a downward spiral on the economic front set in. Despite this hostile environment, the PS set out to organize the 1988 elections on exactly the same bases as in 1983. It did not foresee that the opposition would escalate the militancy of its challenge of the electoral procedures and results. In turn, the opposition was to some degree a prisoner of the intensity of social discontents on which its campaign fed; mass pressures pushed, in part, toward greater aggressiveness.

Within the opposition the PDS was the clear winner, emerging with enough seats to officially constitute a legislative opposition with some procedural rights; in 1983 its contingent was too small to enjoy these prerogatives. But its success derived solely from its posture of systematic criticism, rather than any real alternative program. For the productive reciprocities of governance and accountability of democracy to be achieved, the opposition parties must face the challenge of moving beyond seduction of the electorate by articulation of its manifold discontents, to reassuring it through demonstrating its capacity to provide an alternative model of governmental action.

Worthy of mention is the virtually complete absence of ethnic tension in a bitterly contested election campaign. Three of the four presidential candidates were Wolof, and the fourth (Savane) from the Diola group in Casamance. Although some Diola are dissident, even separatist, Savane made no appeal to regional sentiment in his campaign (and received almost no votes in Casamance). The reasons for the low valence of ethnicity in Senegalese politics are too complex to examine in detail; among other factors are long-standing close historical interactions of Senegambian populations (Barry 1988), crosscutting ties of common religious affiliation, and the role of Wolof as lingua franca. The absence of ethnic mobilization in the Senegalese elections suggests that political competition does not necessarily and inexorably politicize ethnic cleavages in sub-Saharan Africa.

CONCLUSION

What then are the lessons of the 1988 elections for liberal democracy more broadly in Senegal? Here we wish to relink the challenge of deepening and consolidating democratization in Senegal to the larger concepts of governance and the empowerment of civil society. We believe that "the creative potential of politics," suggested by Hyden (1988:16) as the key to governance, can be best realized through this avenue. In contemporary Senegal, civil society's trust of the state—compromised by the flaws in the 1988 elections—can best be recaptured by further movement toward democracy. At the same time the condition of both democracy and governance in Senegal needs to be located in historical and comparative context. The shortcomings of the 1988 elections were not a wholly novel development in Senegalese politics, but a recurrent refrain. Allegations of fraud and irregularity have marked all the competitive postindependence elections (1963, 1978, 1983) and many during colonial times. In our judgment, the outcry was somewhat greater on this occasion, and the skepticism concerning the results rather more widespread; thus— while not new—imperfections of the electoral process were more damaging.

Set against the three decades of Senegalese independence, present preoccupations with alternation and the integrity of the electoral process can be seen as a further step in a dialectic of democratization that began in the mid-1970s. Until then, the dominant goal appeared to be the construction of what Coulon (1981) termed the "integral state," whose political, administrative, economic, and ideological apparatus exercised comprehensive hegemony over peasantry and urban mass. The de facto (although never de jure) political monopoly of the PS predecessor, Union Progressiste Sénégalaise, centralized administrative control over local institutions, parastatalization of the economy (seventy-five state corporations were created from 1970 to 1975), and power concentration in presidential hands were elements in this dynamic of state expansion and civil society subordination. Beneath this apparently hard hegemonical structure lay networks of clientelistic linkages joining president and party to civil society through the intermediation of a host of marabouts and local patrons.

However, even at the peak of this state-building moment, civil liberties were not extinguished. While effective organization of political opposition was made impossible, freedom of speech remained intact, and the state remained generally subject to its own law. By 1975 this state-aggrandizing scheme had reached its outer limits, and a tide of liberalization—political and economic—began to set in. The reintroduction of limited (1978), then unlimited (1983) party competition in national elections was only the most visible and spectacular manifestation of this trend. Also important were such measures as the partial dismantling of the parastatal economy, especially the hated peanut-marketing monopoly.

In the Diouf vision, the liberalization of the state and political process were to be accompanied by its rationalization ("moins d'état, mieux d'état" was the slogan). Technocracy was to replace clientelism as daily operative ethos in state transactions: slimmer, more transparent and thus accountable, also more competent, even tougher in its more-circumscribed domain (Coulon 1988). The productive reciprocities of governance were to supplant the venal reciprocities of clan politics.

These goals are only imperfectly realized. A shrinkage of the state has occurred, opening more space—economic, social, and political—to civil society, whose autonomy has increased in consequence. But the imperatives of retaining power for Diouf and the PS have placed sharp limits on efforts to democratize the ruling party internally, to displace the old generation of "barons" with a reformist generation, much less to dispense with the maraboutic support system. Indeed, the PS still exhibits a number of reflexes dating from its years as a de facto single party. Its patrimonial conception of governance means that any democratization of structures can come only as an act of grace by the ruling party. This condescending attitude carries a presumption that opposition formations should be considered only as minor parties. A broader concept of the role of opposition in the constitutional order is one requisite for strengthened democracy and governance.

If we view democracy in terms of the three broad criteria identified earlier (constitutionalization of power, integrity of electoral process and political competition, preservation of freedom and equality), we may suggest that some extension of democratization has occurred in all three domains, in comparison with 1975. The existence of a forceful opposition voice, and the discipline of even limited electoral competition, has reinforced the accountability of the state and circumscribed its autonomy. Even with the flaws in the electoral code and the element of fraud, the degree of political competition now embedded in the Senegalese political system is important, although, as we argued above, further reform is indispensable. Finally, although the record is not unblemished,[8] the scope of civil liberties has increased. Freedom of speech, press, and association are not only respected by the state, but now deeply rooted in Senegalese political culture as basic values.

Governance is an even more elusive attribute of a state than democracy, and broad judgments are difficult and debatable. Here we would stress that the Senegalese polity, even during the days of the "integral state," never fell victim to the extravagances and excesses of such states as Guinea, Zaire, or Uganda. Thus, while afflicted with a difficult economic and social crisis, Senegal never experienced a period of broad-front state decay, or corrosion of the basic physical infrastructure. Thus the environment of governance is very different from that in more-derelict polities.

Yet we are convinced that more-effectual governance—greater legitimacy, higher trust in state–civil society relationships, strengthened accountability— will require further expansion of democracy. In the particular sphere of elections fairness in process is crucial. More-equitable rules of the game are a prerequisite for the "enabling environment" in which the full potential of governance in its broadest sense, as elaborated by Hyden, may be fulfilled.

NOTES

1. The impact of occurrences in Eastern Europe is interesting evidence of the extraordinary global repercussion of political events. While no systematic empirical evidence is known to us of the scope of diffusion of this information to all segments of the African populace, we are convinced that the reach of communication media, formal and informal, ensured a broad awareness of these changes. The demonstration of the surprising vulnerability of such one-party regimes, the new revelations of their incompetence and corruption in the wake of their demise, and subsequent demonstration of the narrowness of their support, all served to embolden opponents of African single-party autocracies and to supply new ammunition for their critique.

2. The mechanism was creation of a single national constituency, with the majority party winning all seats.

3. Three different candidates (in addition to Wade) had challenged Diouf in 1983: Mamadou Dia, a grand old figure of the independence struggle, leading the Mouvement Démocratique Africain; the old champion of Marxism-Leninism, Majhemout Diop; and Omar Wone, heading the tiny Parti Populaire Sénégalaise.

4. Disappearing from the presidential roster were the Parti Africain de l'Indépendance, the Parti Populaire Sénégalais, the Mouvement Démocratique Progressiste, and the Rassemblement National Démocratique.

5. It is striking to note that the Diouf margin was closely similar to that of Robert Mugabe (78 percent) over Edgar Tekere in the 1990 Zimbabwe elections.

6. It is impossible to know the precise turnout figure because no certain number of citizens aged twenty-one or over is known. Census age profiles show that well over half the total population is under twenty-one. Thus, even though 59 percent of those registered voted, clearly fewer than half those potentially eligible took part.

7. The hostilities between Senegal and Mauritania suddenly flared up in April 1989. The initial trigger was the shooting of two Senegalese cultivators on the border; Senegal charged the culprits were Mauritanian border guards, an allegation denied by Mauritania. News of the incident brought a wave of attacks on Mauritanian shops in Dakar. In response, murderous assaults on Senegalese residents of Nouakchott took place, apparently with the complicity of some officials. This in turn sparked a far more violent rampage in Dakar and some other towns against Mauritanian traders. More than 100,000 had to be repatriated to their respective country of origin following this violence. Tension between the countries has remained strong; the emotions stirred by the crisis engendered a *union sacrée* psychosis in Senegal and dampened the militancy of opposition challenges to the legitimacy of President Diouf.

8. In 1990 Amnesty International alleged that prisoners linked to the resurgent Casamance separatist movement were subjected to torture.

4

State-Society Relations in
Botswana: Beginning Liberalization

John D. Holm & Patrick P. Molutsi

Governance is the study of the management of a regime's relations with its populace. Analysts of governance, who examine the effectiveness of elites in working with social groups to set and implement policy on the basis of agreed values, can approach African politics from a choice of two perspectives.

One is the liberalization approach in which the degree of reciprocity and accountability in state-society relations are the primary concern. The expectation is that political leaders share power with civil society by establishing a set of rules that restrain and channel conflict among themselves and among groups and citizens seeking to influence decisions. The public comes to obey policies because those policies are perceived as fairly enacted. At the other pole is the developmentalist school, which focuses on building an authority structure with the capacity and will to give direction to society. From this perspective it is necessary that a small elite direct the energies of various social groupings toward a collective goal such as economic growth or national security. Because of the wisdom of those in authority, the public accepts their leaders' right to limit debate and otherwise restrict persons or groups who reject or hinder the realization of priority goals. The prevailing policy issue is how each sector of society can best serve development objectives or the state.

Most analysts of the African state have until recently supported, albeit reluctantly, the developmentalist approach at the expense of group autonomy so long as the appropriate "progressive," "mobilizing," or "stabilizing" objectives were sought by those in charge.[1] Lately, studies of governance have switched to advocating political liberalization (Carter Center 1989a). This change reflects a recognition that enhancement of state authority for a variety of purposes has caused a common fault: arbitrary decisions benefiting leaders rather than mobilizing the public.

The central question of the current liberalization approach is under what conditions African states can move toward greater reciprocity and accountability in their relations with society. We respond to this question by analyzing the experience of Botswana, one of a few countries in Africa in which a multiparty system has existed for over two decades, and in which elements of civil society have forced the political elite to begin restraining a dominant bureaucracy in a liberal direction.

Our argument is that liberalization in developing countries such as Botswana entails creating social organizations capable of influencing political institutions and elites. It is societal weakness that slows this process. The oppressive character of the state, which is inherent in its modern form in both the developed and developing worlds, is not countered in Botswana and other developing countries with a myriad of organized social groups capable of influencing political elites. In effect, the modern state has been imported to countries such as Botswana in the absence of structures of accountability and a normative consensus able to restrain and channel its vast power resources.[2]

LIBERALIZATION HYPOTHESES

Our analysis will focus on five hypotheses that have guided most comparative politics research on political liberalization.[3] In summary these are that:

1. Capital accumulation for economic development leads to authoritarian government.
2. States dependent on major social groups are more likely to liberalize.
3. The more the state operates by universalist norms, the more likely liberalization will take place.
4. Communal (religious, ethnic or racial) conflict frustrates the growth of autonomous social groups.
5. Economic liberalization precedes and forces political liberalization.

The basic logic involved in these hypotheses is laid out in more detail at the beginning of our discussion of each. Generally these hypotheses assume an underlying modernization process that includes political liberalization. The one reservation we have to this assumption is that political culture makes a difference. The more there are pluralistic and liberal values in the premodern culture, particularly among the ruling elite, the more likely will be political liberalization. We will argue at various points in the subsequent discussion that Botswana's illiberal political culture has slowed liberalization.

Since we are examining only one country, our conclusions do not represent a definitive test of the above five hypotheses. Such a test requires that similar analyses be done on a number of African countries that have both undertaken and failed to undertake liberalization of their political system. In addition, as Sklar (1987) argues, other forms of liberalization should be considered; for example, establishment of the rule of law, independent local governments, and local participatory institutions ranging from unions to agricultural cooperatives.

POLITICAL LIBERALIZATION IN BOTSWANA

The Traditional Polity

Botswana's politicians, supported by some scholars (Ngcongco 1989), contend that their democracy arises from a precolonial culture that was democratic. The institutional basis for this argument rests with the Tswana *kgotla*. Since the early part of the nineteenth century the kgotla was a gathering place for adult commoner males to consider issues raised by the chief, or his headman in the case of tribal subdivisions. Women, young people (up to thirty), and minority groups (i.e., non-Tswana) might attend but had to remain silent.

The chief set the agenda at kgotla. He decided on the issues to be discussed after consulting with his advisors who were headmen and close relatives. Whenever possible the chief forged an alliance of this advisory group on the course of action to be adopted. At the kgotla meeting his advisors would speak first and specify the desired solution. Other members of the community might oppose the chief's advisors when public opinion was decidedly resistant to proposed courses of action. This meant that the kgotla was a source of effective popular control when the chief abused his power, and he was willing to put the issue on the agenda for a public discussion. This was not a likely occurrence. Otherwise, a narrow political elite used the kgotla as a means for mobilizing public support for its policies (Schapera 1970).

Colonial Rule

British colonial rule in Botswana was minimal in its administrative presence, even by African standards. As a result colonial officials had so little power that they found the kgotla attractive as a means of mobilizing popular support for programs they sought to implement. In some very critical instances the result was a struggle between the chiefs and the colonial bureaucrats to manipulate kgotla decisions. In the process, the people came to view some form of kgotla consultation, manipulative as it might be, as necessary for implementation of the new state's programs at the local level (Mgadla & Campbell 1989).

The extent of public accountability arising from this form of policymaking was quite limited. The kgotla prior to independence was a place where a community could air its objections to a particular policy, providing at least a segment of the public was sufficiently disaffected. The people did not propose policies or vote on their acceptability.

The New Botswana State

Independence brought a radically new form of government based on elections, some political rights associated with liberal democracy, and a powerful bureaucracy promoting rapid social change. Among the first actions of Seretse Khama's Botswana Democratic Party government in the late 1960s was to abolish all formal powers of the chief except his right to chair the kgotla and preside over traditional law courts. The Constitution made the National Assembly supreme at the national level, with the House of Chiefs having only advisory functions. At the local level, elected councils replaced the chiefs as the top political authorities.

The first generation of elected officials were generally lacking in sufficient education to understand many policy questions. Moreover, they had no motivation to learn. There were striking exceptions, such as Khama himself and Quett Masire, his vice-president, who both admired and supported the development of a skilled civil service. As a result, after independence the civil service continued to follow the colonial model in which a highly educated and politically sophisticated bureaucratic elite set the basic policy directions (Picard 1987). This elite was led by expatriates hired at first from Great Britain but gradually from North America and a number of European countries as well.

During the middle 1970s a Tswana educated class began to take over the top civil service leadership. The politicians were only too willing to allow their more educated countrymen to continue to make the critical policy choices. This new bureaucratic elite assumed that they could make fundamental policy decisions without reference to outside social and political organizations. They had earned the right to rule through their schooling and apprenticeship under experienced European civil servants. Localization thus had no significant liberalization effect.

The 1980s brought the first serious challenges to this bureaucratic state in terms of issues of political liberalization. Opposition politicians took over a number of local councils and started to criticize government policies much more aggressively than their BDP predecessors had. Interest groups including teachers, trade unions, civil servants, environmentalists, businessmen, farmers, women, journalists, and lawyers began articulating proposals for policies to serve their interests. Assisting this burgeoning of groups was the emergence of five weekly private newspapers that published information critical of government programs and politicians' behavior.

Party primaries, which began in 1984, served to bring a new and more educated group of politicians into Parliament and the councils. In Parliament this new breed began to raise many questions about cabinet decisions and the behavior of ministers. The cabinet itself is increasingly made up of persons with bachelors' and masters' degrees who are capable of analyzing policies and concerned about the effect of government decisions on electoral chances. As a result cabinet debates are becoming more intense, and ministers are setting policies in their ministries or forcing their subordinates to think of additional alternatives.

Botswana's liberalization has not been radical. It has been a gradual process wherein criticism and modest proposals are followed by a slow reordering of influence and priorities. At times there are regressions. In 1983 the government enacted a labor relations law that greatly limited the freedom of unions to organize and negotiate (Molokomme 1989). BDP officials intimidate newspaper editors from time to time with threats and condemnations (Grant & Egner 1989). In response to the South African destabilization campaign, the 1986 Parliament passed a security act that government has used to keep secret almost all information related to the Botswana Defense Force, including all appropriation data except the total budget figure. In 1987 the cabinet closed the university for several months when students took to the streets to protest peacefully against harsh police actions in a politically inflamed kidnapping case. However, each of these illiberal measures, as well as others, has been subject to varying degrees of public debate.

Having outlined Botswana's tradition of governance in this century and the increasing liberalization that has taken place since the beginning of the 1980s, we now examine the conditions associated with the government's turn toward this new approach.

LIBERALIZATION AND CAPITAL ACCUMULATION

Gerschenkron (1962) hypothesized that in countries having backward economies political elites centralize the capital accumulation process in state institutions in order to force the pace of economic growth. This concentration of economic power necessitates authoritarian rule to protect the expropriation of private resources. Gerschenkron developed his ideas on the basis of the experience of nineteenth-century France, Germany, and Russia. Many African leaders have concluded that a similar necessity exists if they are to bring about modernization of their economies.

Since independence the Botswana state has centralized the direction of economic development in institutions that it controls. At first the source of its economic power was foreign aid. Over the last twenty years foreign investment in copper, nickel, and diamonds has created a mining sector that generates government income covering over half of its expenditures. Overseeing all major decisions on economic growth is the Ministry of Finance and Development Planning. The ministry channels much of the state's income back into the economy for infrastructure development and joint ventures with foreign private capital (Harvey & Lewis 1990).

The state's management of these resources has been based on a number of criteria. It has invested primarily in large mining projects with the idea that future income from this source would be used to promote social equality. With regard to foreign exchange, the government has an explicit policy of not allowing the real exchange rate to appreciate, as huge surpluses have accumulated.[4] The net effect is that urban consumer groups have not been advantaged, as in many other African states (Bates 1981). The objective is to protect local entrepreneurs against cheap foreign products and keep inflation down. A sizable portion of mining income is increasingly being put into various public welfare programs designed to take care of basic needs, specifically health, education, housing, and drought relief.

During the latter part of the 1980s there was a rising demand for government to finance and otherwise promote private Tswana entrepreneurs. The government has responded very hesitantly because of a fear that local Tswana businessmen will turn government aid into a permanent subsidy. There is a grant program that provides short-term aid for up to five years if there is employment creation. Also government has financed large cattle owners to transform their poorly managed cattle posts into more-productive ranches. Finally, ministries have provided various forms of protective regulation to local private entrepreneurs in various sectors ranging from horticulture to manufacturing and transport.

Several characteristics of the Botswana approach to the financing of economic development are important to the hypothesis of centralized capital accumulation. First, the state has not expropriated the wealth of certain groups in society. It has huge income surpluses because of the rapid expansion of the diamond mines. This means that there is no need for an authoritarian political structure to extract investment funds from society. Nevertheless, with its great income and effective economic planning, government gives strong direction to the economy.

Second, the ruling BDP represents rural property interests and is consequently not afraid to restrain the income demands from the urban sector. Their urban opposition came originally from the cities of South Africa where the struggle for liberation was defined in terms of race. When these activists returned to Botswana in 1960 after the Sharpeville massacre, they failed to win much support in this almost entirely rural nation where the reactionary ways of the chiefs were of more concern than the racial biases of the British. Thus, Botswana came to independence with political leaders who thought in terms of transforming the rural areas rather than attending to the needs of its new towns. Able to retain their electoral support subsequently, these leaders have repeatedly rejected urban demands to consume rather than to reinvest the country's expanding national income.

Third, these rural-based leaders allied themselves with expatriates who held most of the top civil service positions through the first decade after independence (1966–1976). This alliance began as a way to satisfy foreign donors who were financing a significant portion of the state's budget in the late 1960s and early 1970s. Of long termer-significance, the BDP politicians did not look to the state for income and status. They had large herds of cattle for this purpose and could thus afford to leave government to foreign technicians. The founding BDP politicians began a tradition of allowing the bureaucracy to make most of the important policy decisions on technical and bureaucratic grounds.[5] As the new Tswana civil service leaders arrived in the 1970s they militantly guarded this tradition. When the massive profits of the mining sector flowed into state coffers in the 1980s the result was not economic inflation or the pervasive political corruption that has alienated the public in such countries as Nigeria and led to military rule. Rather, economic growth augmented the power of the civil service.

Our argument with regard to the Gerschenkron hypothesis is that when the state depends on sources other than peasants to obtain investment capital there is less pressure for an authoritarian approach, especially if critical political conditions have a congruent effect.[6] In Botswana's case, one congruent condition is that the political elite sought income and status from a rural social structure rather than government. Thus it has not burdened the government budget with graft or the need to augment urban income. Another condition is that the rapid pace of Botswana's economic growth allowed government to provide significant returns to all social strata plus make the necessary capital investments. As a result, economic issues do not have the potential to threaten the democratic regime, let alone cause serious electoral problems for the BDP.

LIBERALIZATION AND
STATE DEPENDENCE ON SOCIAL GROUPS

According to many analysts, the colonial powers in Africa created states dependent on foreign support (Hyden 1980; Callaghy 1984; Cohen & Daniel 1982; Rothchild & Chazan 1988). This state in its postcolonial incarnations, now dependent on foreign aid and capital, has thus been isolated from indigenous social structures. It has not felt compelled to build a normative consensus for its authority, particularly with the vast peasant population, and consequently has felt little pressure to liberalize.

In Botswana during the colonial period the state organization was very isolated from society. Usually the British officials would contact the chiefs only when seeking to persuade them to carry out directives or to move on development projects. No national economic program existed. Only in the last decade of British rule did the government launch its first major development project, an abattoir to facilitate the commercial cattle sector.

After independence state–society linkages grew massively. The central government took over all governmental functions, allocating some, such as primary education, water, and roads, to district and town councils. It then steadily stepped up the services it delivered at both the local and national levels. Paved or improved dirt roads were built to all population centers and the school system expanded to include free education for all elementary-age children. In 1989 free secondary education became a reality in the form of both technical and traditional academic programs. Investments in the economy, most with a government component, have continually driven up employment by an average of over 11 percent a year since the late 1960s (Harvey & Lewis 1990:275). Health clinics provide curative and preventive medicine to almost the entire population on a regular basis. Government water projects bring reliable sources of water to all but the smallest of settlements. Agricultural programs offer farmers payments for clearing their fields, free plowing if they do not have draft power, free seeds, and financial assistance in drilling private boreholes, among other things. During the drought from 1982 to 1987 government programs provided all needy groups in the population (probably around 65 percent in the rural areas), no matter how remote, sufficient food to insure that there was only a marginal increase in malnutrition during the entire period.

These services are delivered in a context of a noticeable elite-mass interaction. Top officials, heavily influenced by their expatriate allies, have come to believe that government programs work better if the public can be induced to participate, even in a token form, in governing processes. The result has been the spread of various forms of participation developed in the industrial democracies of Europe and North America.

Most important for the politicians has been attention to elections as a means to retain power. BDP leaders spend much time maintaining and improving their party as a campaign organization.[7] In addition, they insist that before each election a sizable portion of government programs have a grassroots payoff, regardless of the efficiency effects, so that they can point in every village to something that resulted from their rule. In the 1980s, as the opposition Botswana National Front (BNF) began to take over politically in the new towns, the size of these election-oriented programs dramatically increased.

The government has also sought to obtain popular consent for specific programs through public consultations. Elected councilors are asked to approve projects in their districts, and no village development takes place without a village kgotla meeting where government presents its proposals and listens to public reactions. Major economic initiatives, outside of mining and roads, are not undertaken without national conferences where public servants and interested members of public debate the problem and the proposed plan of action.

Government has retained traditional chiefs and headmen largely to legitimize local programs with their support and to handle many civil matters in their courts. However, the cost is that these leaders sometimes mobilize their public in kgotla meetings when discontent exists. Thus, government officials keep an eye on possibilities of such discontent and occasionally retreat when one or more chiefs seem to be marshaling support through criticism in kgotla.

All of the above points of contact between the Botswana state and various publics have insured that the political elite is much less isolated from citizen thinking than was its colonial predecessor. This is not to say that the participation taking place gives civil society much influence over the direction of government. Botswana's political elite aggressively manipulates public thinking. There are public works and drought relief programs to win votes at election time. The constant consultations in kgotlas, councils, and national conferences are remarkably similar, in their attempts to co-opt leadership groups and to limit the agenda, to the leadership approaches of colonial and precolonial times.

There is one positive effect of all this participation. A belief is developing among the educated citizens and the elites that they have or should have open state-society relations (Somolekae 1989). They look down on not only South Africa for this reason but also their African neighbors to the north. Among top politicians, there is not a hint of support for a one-party state, even in private discussions.

LIBERALIZATION AND UNIVERSALISTIC BUREAUCRACY

A common theme in the study of African politics is that the state has yet to capture its citizens, that is, to have effective administrative control in terms of keeping order, collecting taxes, and implementing social and economic change. Rather, communally oriented norms (religious, ethnic, and familial) dominate citizen thinking and subvert state directives. The polity is thus immobilized and unable to respond to social problems or promote economic growth. Those not benefiting from this particularism seek exit options, such as migration, bribery, second jobs, and nonpayment of taxes (Hyden 1983; Callaghy, 1984).

In this context, excluded social groups, and particularly those which would promote various forms of modernization, have no reason to organize and demand government action. Only when a universalistic state begins to take shape must citizens seek means of being included in the policymaking process; for example, forming interest groups, electing leaders, and being informed as to why and how government decisions are made (Jackson & Rosberg 1982).

The Botswana experience supports this argument. The multiplicity of programs mentioned in the previous section operate according to relatively universalistic norms. Personnel procedures are regularized, with merit criteria playing an important role. Budget controls are pervasive and effective.

National economic plans set the agenda for government investment to the extent that projects can obtain funding only after they have been incorporated in the plan. In spite of the resulting red tape, policy approval and implementation take place. Civil servants look upon their positions as their primary sources of employment and income and generally perform their duties during office hours. It is rare to find a government employee who is primarily concerned with a second job, a situation that Tripp (1988a) indicates is typical in countries such as Tanzania.

The first two presidents of Botswana emphasized the universalism of their leadership. For many of the more traditionally oriented citizenry, regardless of their ethnic identity, Seretse Khama after his election in 1966 became the rightful "chief" of all of Botswana. But President Khama took pains to emphasize the universal character of his role by reaching out to all segments of society in his travel, speeches, and government programs. He made a point of excluding chiefs, headmen, and elders from all political processes, and governing through civil servants, with the district Commissioner as his principal spokesman in each district. Ethnic politics seldom played a major role in appointments. His successor, Quett Masire, has continued this approach.

Party politics also reflect this universalistic quality. Both Khama and Masire have insisted that the BDP campaign throughout the country, regardless of the party's ethnic support in any one area. In the 1989 election this persistence paid off with BDP victories in three constituencies long considered ethnically safe for the opposition. The main opposition party, the BNF, survived through the 1979 election on ethnic voting. However, in the 1980s it has increasingly mobilized a working-class constituency through bread-and-butter appeals on such issues as the need for housing subsidies, the absence of public transport, and the restrictive character of the government's incomes policy.[8]

Important to the hypothesis of citizen participation is that citizens do not exit the state's authority. Rather, they challenge the universalistic state by seeking to liberalize state-society linkages. In the first decade after Botswana's independence exit options were important to many in the population in terms of subsistence agriculture and labor migration to South Africa. This all changed by the middle 1980s. A vastly expanded and very effective universalistic state made the exit option not only difficult but unattractive for its populace of 1.2 million. Government itself had expanded from fifteen thousand employees in 1971 to approximately fifty thousand in 1985. As we mentioned in the previous section, its range of programs had become considerable. Even more important, the first five economic plans created a booming private economy, where formal sector jobs went from thirty-seven thousand to over 121,000 between 1971 and 1985. The fact that government also set overall compensation levels in the private sector and carefully regulated union activity insured its presence was felt by many in the population.[9] Finally, exit to South Africa took a considerable slide by the mid-1980s, going from as much as 25 percent of the working-age population in 1970 to around 6 percent by 1985 (Colclough & McCarthy 1980:171, 267; Botswana, MFD 1985:30).[10]

The public has reacted to the state's massive penetration of their lives by attempting to influence the policy process. However, the result is not a model pluralistic democracy.

The less educated, particularly in the rural areas, have looked to community structures for help. Some ask the chief or headman to intervene with government officials. Some have used kgotla meetings to articulate demands for community improvement and to remind politicians and civil servants of their problems. A few have used party caucuses in their community to nominate new persons to the local council or Parliament. The problem with all these community-based approaches is that they have an impact only on policy implementation in individual communities, while top national leaders remain unaffected (Molutsi & Holm 1990).

Among the more educated strata, citizens began in the 1980s to develop interest groups. Professional associations have taken root among lawyers, teachers, and accountants. Both foreign and domestic entrepreneurs have created organizations to represent their interests. They are countered by a rapidly spreading union movement, which is increasingly using strikes as a tool in its negotiations. A women's liberation movement has begun to take form, protesting the sexist bias of many Tswana cultural practices. Farmers' associations have started lobbying government relative to its loan policies. Five weekly private newspapers emerged during the 1980s to give coverage to the meetings and other activities of these new groups.[11]

All of this organizational activity has the primary purpose of influencing government in its policymaking. Graft is of little avail because of the Tswana moralistic culture. Even political connections have little impact because elected officials cannot approach civil servants except through their permanent secretaries, who are very protective of authority. And, because of its massive income, government has so much to offer in funding and services that citizens cannot afford to take an exit option.

Thus far, most of the new groups have little impact on government policy. They are poorly organized, with only a handful of people doing most of the work. Members see little need to pay sufficient dues to sustain an effective staff. For periods of time some groups do not function at all, then a new leadership comes along to revive them.

A classic example of this ineffectiveness is the Botswana Federation of Secondary School Teachers (BOFESETE), an organization established in 1986 by secondary school teachers to represent their interests. The core leadership consists of four or five activists, who generally are from one or two schools. Its dues of $0.50 a month will not support a full-time staff or even a leaders' tour of the country. The organization has largely manifested itself through a few newsletters and an annual meeting, to which representatives from around the country pay their own way to attend. BOFESETE has conducted several work stoppages. One in 1988 was effective in delaying the grading of Junior Certificate exams.

Politicians and civil servants tend to look at most new interest groups as nuisances that should be marginalized rather than recognized. They define the state as a universalistic entity that is above negotiating with selfish interests. Their models in this regard are the colonial and traditional governments, which did not consider vertical organization within society to be legitimate. Thus for four years the Ministry of Education refused to recognize BOFESETE for any purpose, even though it clearly expressed the deep resentment of the secondary school teachers with their work environment. Then, in 1990, a new minister of education did agree to recognition; however, he has not yet specified the purposes for which BOFESETE is recognized.

The resulting lack of dialog is striking. The BOFESETE leaders had no serious discussion with political leaders during its first four years of existence. Even interest groups that government recognizes receive little chance to discuss policy issues with government officials except at advisory councils where civil servants set the agenda. The degree of interest group isolation from the political process is highlighted by the trade unions. Through the 1980s their leaders had no formal interactions with the leading opposition party, the BNF, even though it sought to represent the working class in its election programs.

In sum, the universalistic state bureaucracy in Botswana has inspired the organization of a good number of interest groups, but they have yet to institutionalize themselves in a way which insures any significant control of public policy. There are no clear norms that induce the public to support these groups. Many in the less educated and the rural population have preferred a community-based approach, which truncates citizen influence at the local level. Politicians and civil servants reject the idea that interest groups represent society. Group leaders themselves have yet to find a way to force political elites to give them any significant role in policymaking. Thus the rise of a universalistic state in Botswana has stimulated the formation of groups, but it has not led to organized social groups having effective influence in top-level decisions.

The fact that a political culture that sanctions societal influences on the Botswana state is only beginning to be established is not unusual. Most preindustrial and industrializing societies in Europe, Asia, and Latin America have had a similar problem (Almond & Verba 1963). The political elites fear or overlook the need to incorporate interest groups in state decisionmaking. Change comes from a series of confrontations in which interest groups insist that they have a permanent voice in the regime.

ETHNIC CONFLICT AND
AUTONOMOUS SOCIAL ORGANIZATIONS

A persistent concern of Africanist social scientists (e.g., Kasfir 1976a; Jackson & Rosberg 1982; Diamond, Linz & Lipset 1988a) is the extent to which ethnic politics stifles the growth and effectiveness of autonomous organizations that can demand influence in national and local government decision bodies. This stifling derives from several bases. At the grass roots, ethnic polarization means that citizens give special interest organizations (e.g., youth, unions, and trade associations) lower priority than ethnic concerns (Horowitz 1985). At the national level, Huntington (1968) and others argue that an authoritarian approach is required to overcome the resistance of ethnic elites to national integration, particularly in economic and political terms.

Ethnic politics in Botswana is conditioned by three factors. First, the Tswana culture pervades most of the country in that an overwhelming majority (around 80 percent) belong to one of the eight major Tswana ethnic groups. Even more speak Setswana or a close variant as their first or second language. The government reinforces this relative cultural homogeneity by pursuing an aggressive assimilation policy that includes a refusal to use the non-Tswana languages in the schools, over the radio, or in government records.

Second, many in the non-Tswana population[12] bitterly resent the strong pressure to assimilate to the Tswana culture but recognize that they must work within the existing political structure. For this reason opposition political parties have not succeeded in mobilizing this resentment into a broad political coalition.

Third, members of the eight major Tswana groups tend to see other Tswana groups as having relatively equal status to their own. Horowitz (1985) refers to this as an system of unranked groups. As a result, ethnic struggle has always been limited in that members of each group perceive the others as having a right to exist, and alliances among groups have shifted so that there are no permanent enemies or friends. In contemporary politics the two main political parties (the BDP and the BNF) represent specific ethnic groups, particularly in the rural areas. But there are still shifts. For example, the Bangwaketse vote for the BDP has increased since 1979 at the expense of the BNF. And in 1989 the Bakgatla in Mochudi switched their vote from the BDP to the BNF.[13]

Botswana's rapid economic development since independence has taken place largely in new towns that are outside of neighboring ethnic societies, both physically and socially. It is possible that this could lead ethnic competition, as Epstein (1958) noted on the copperbelt of Zambia, and Young (1965) found in Zaire. In point of fact, leadership goes to those who transcend ethnic diversity and effectively mobilize specific interests. Several factors at least are involved. One is cultural homogeneity. The facts that all the political elites speak Setswana and that the Tswana population is so large means that leaders can be understood without translation. Also important is that non-Tswana groups, as we have mentioned, recognize that they cannot achieve much politically without going into coalition with the Tswana population.

Both the political and civil service elites seek to keep ethnic conflict dispersed (Horowitz 1985). At the national government level there is a conscious attempt to deemphasize ethnic politics. When there was even the perception that an ethnic clique may have formed at the top of the civil service, Seretse Khama would have the persons involved reassigned. At Khama's death in 1980, the BDP reaffirmed his rejection of ethnic politics by electing Quett Masire who was from the Bangwaketse, a group that had long supported the BNF. Masire became president because he had been without question the leading organizer in the BDP since its founding in 1962.

Civil service socialization policies also seek to frustrate the development of ethnic identities. Staff are routinely rotated around the country without regard to ethnic identity. Promotions are not governed by concern for ethnic balance. To further combat parochialism, the Ministry of Education places the better secondary students, most of whom will enter the civil service, at residential schools outside of their home districts.

Ethnic politics is allowed to flourish only in elected local councils and through traditional authorities, both of which regularly seek to protect their people and culture against the national government. The chief of the Bakgatla has rejected centrally devised land-use plans, fostered tribal age regiments, and promoted opposition parties in his area. The chief of the Bangwaketse verbally abuses national government civil servants in kgotla and other meetings, much to the joy of his followers. The district council in the Bamangwato has dragged its feet as far as implementing the national government's private ranching scheme, going so far in one case as to hire its own consultant to review proposed ranching areas (Hitchcock 1978). All councils have fought national programs that would give tribal land to Batswana from other areas or lead to developments that would employ such "foreign" elements. The ethnic dimension in all these struggles gives those identifying with each group at least a symbolic sense that their interests are being preserved in the postcolonial state.

This show of ethnicity is not allowed to get out of hand. The minister of local government and the president have reprimanded the two chiefs just mentioned on several occasions. The Banawaketse chief was even suspended for a time. The Ministry of Local Government and Lands (MLGL) also brings local councils into line through financial inducements, appointing strong-willed civil servants to administer councils that become too independent and, when necessary, abrogating council motions. On some issues national ministries persist in countering a local council for years until the local body agrees to an acceptable compromise. For instance, a program to set up large private cattle ranches on tribal communal lands has moved forward for fifteen years in fits and starts as MLGL badgered local councils and land boards into giving up particular blocks of land. The same is beginning to happen with the establishment of wildlife management areas.

Thus far the BDP government has been successful in its strategy of controlled dispersion of ethnic conflict. However, the three major opposition parties (the BNF; the Botswana People's Party [BPP], which is strong among the Kalanga; and the Botswana Independence Party, which has a following among the Bayei) are talking seriously about forming an electoral coalition that would seek to unite most minority ethnic groups, the working class in the cities, and at least one Tswana group. This alliance could render ethnic politics in Botswana much more state-centered, and thus potentially more threatening to political stability. The BDP has thus far countered this possibility by incorporating elites from almost all non-Tswana groups in its organization. For instance, at present three Kalanga are members of the cabinet, out of a total of ten persons. The party has several Bakalagadi on its delegation in Parliament, one of whom was in the cabinet for a number of years. Two Bushmen were elected to the Ghanzi council on the BDP ticket in the 1989 election. The result of this multiethnic approach is that many non-Tswana perceive that in spite of the BDP's assimilation approach it provides opportunities for members of their group.

The hypothesis of this section is that ethnic conflict reduces the possibilities for liberalization. We have argued that the political elite in Botswana have effectively dispersed ethnic struggle to institutions of local government. While ethnic identification does provide a basis for much partisan conflict, it has not developed into a form of state-centered conflict that could threaten political stability, and ethnic conflict has not undermined liberalization. On the other hand, the fact that the central government has refused to give local governments any significant independence—for example, allowing the councils part of their budget as block grants that they can spend as they wish—reflects in part a fear that ethnic conflict could get out of hand. In this sense, ethnic conflict has limited liberalization at the local level in Botswana, thus confirming in part the Huntington argument.

ECONOMIC LIBERALIZATION
AND POLITICAL LIBERALIZATION

A classic hypothesis of the political development literature is that the growth of a market-oriented bourgeois class leads to social inclusiveness in politics and the liberalization of the state. Moore (1966), Huntington (1968), Lindblom (1977), and Powell (1982) among others have made this point. The bourgeoisie has both the necessary independence from government and the resources to organize itself in pursuit of its own interests. The rapid political liberalization of Eastern Europe and the Soviet Union raises serious questions about this hypothesis in that no market-based bourgeoisie existed to push the process forward. Rather, organizations of the intelligentsia, the working class, and the church mobilized the masses within a context of increasing nationalism to confront the Communist elites and force political liberalization.

In some respects, African polities are similar to these Communist regimes in that a bureaucratic rather than an entrepreneurial bourgeoisie has played the dominant role in policymaking. This bureaucratic class has promoted itself and the state at the expense of economic development, particularly in the private sector. The result has been a very weak economic bourgeoisie and thus the absence of a major social force pushing for political freedoms vis-à-vis the state.

When the BDP came to power in Botswana in 1965, it did so as a party of large cattle owners, an agricultural bourgeoisie. As we have mentioned, this group wanted to commercialize its holdings with the help of the state. As a tradeoff it allowed the gradually expanding bureaucratic class to gain control over the policymaking process. The state bureaucrats attempted through their Tribal Grazing Land Policy, launched in the early 1970s, to force the large cattle owners to develop more-productive operations. While the politicians frustrated this bureaucratic power play at critical points, the civil servants have otherwise molded the outlines of economic growth through the planning process.

As the 1980s proceeded, market-oriented Tswana entrepreneurs began to emerge, particularly in the urban areas. Most came from government occupations. Some were retirees (the retirement age is forty-five), but others quit early because they saw great opportunity in the fast-growing private sector. Most invested in commerce and real estate, although there was some interest in manufacturing. In a number of cases, this new class sought out opportunities in the rural areas, particularly their home villages. To facilitate this transition of civil servants to the private sector, policies governing investment by government officials were loosened to allow officials to invest in private enterprises as long as they were not majority partners.

This new economic bourgeoisie has increasingly been seeking to obtain political power. In part, it has been easy to work with former colleagues in government who have provided a sympathetic ear regarding contracts and preferential regulations. But as a group this class has lacked the numbers, wealth, and ideological coherence to take control of any of the political parties. Without a party clearly sympathetic to its interests, the new bourgeoisie has split among the three major parties (BDP, BNF, and BPP).

Also compounding the emergence of the new Tswana bourgeoisie has been the dominant position of Asians in Botswana's commerce. For most Tswana businessmen, the Asians are competition that prevents their obtaining their fair share of the market. There are almost no grounds for cooperation, even on the political level. The consequence is that government officials and the new bourgeoisie are ambivalent about moving ahead with wholesale privatization because it might end up mostly benefiting the Asians.

The major impact of the Tswana bourgeoisie thus far has been to liberalize Botswana's political parties. As outsiders to prevailing power groups, they have sought to loosen the control of the top leaders by siding with dissidents in intraparty debates. They have promoted primaries as a means of selecting party candidates and have themselves furnished most of the candidates in the primaries, often going back to their home constituencies in the rural areas to run. Also increasing their influence is that members of the bourgeoisie have contested and won many party offices. In the 1990s they are likely to dominate the central committees of both the BDP and the BNF. The bourgeoisie is already critical to the financing of all the major parties. Besides money, they have provided extensive contribution in kind in the form of transportation for members to attend rallies and political meetings.

The degree of influence the bourgeoisie has over the parties is not yet decisive because of a number of considerations. Particularly critical is that the major parties are still led by persons whose policy agendas harken back to the 1960s and early 1970s. For the BDP leaders, this has meant protecting cattle owners. The BNF has rallied around anticolonial and socialist themes. And the other parties have played to ethnic concerns. Further limiting bourgeois influence is that its contributions have been countered by other influences. While the BDP draws on the affluent section of the urban bourgeoisie, the party obtains most of its income from foreign governments, foreign investors, and the local Asian community. The BNF looks to the petite bourgeoisie for most of its funds, but this group's influence is opposed by a sizable activist contingent that is committed to radical socialist politics.

The new Tswana bourgeoisie has also been important to the emergence of organized social groups, particularly in the urban areas. Besides founding professional associations, they are involved in human rights groups, chambers of commerce, trade groups (e.g., for builders and owners of trucks), sports societies, and several women's associations. While the bureaucratic bourgeoisie can also be found in some of these groups, the market bourgeoisie provides the financing and the prestige necessary to insure some autonomy from government so that the leaders can speak for particular interests in civil society.

In sum, the Tswana economic bourgeoisie has grown slowly and divided its influence between government and opposition. The economic bourgeoisie has promoted liberalization within the parties and through the growth of special interest groups. It has yet to take a dominant leadership role in politics either organizationally or intellectually. With more privatization, which is advocated by both top civil service and BDP leaders, the old-guard, rural-based party leaders will fall. Even if the new bourgeoisie takes over the

BDP, and it remains in power, these new political leaders will have to struggle with the civil service leaders for control of the policy processes, which we noted the latter have dominated for the last twenty-five years.

CONCLUSION

What does our examination of Botswana tell us about the five liberalization hypotheses that have been considered? Clearly, some aspects of each generalization receive support. The Tswana state used its enormous income to minimize the participation of civil society in the economic development process. In this sense the first hypothesis, that capital accumulation works against liberalization, is confirmed.

With regard to hypothesis two, the country's lack of social pluralism has allowed the political elite to establish participatory structures giving the appearance rather than the reality of bottom-up influence. Government can do this because civil society lacks both the organization and the culture to demand influence in politics.

The third hypothesis is confirmed in the sense that an expanding universalistic state has stimulated a growing array of autonomous associations. Because corruption is minimized, groups have few other options. Even villages are turning to communal structures such as the kgotla to influence the all-powerful state bureaucracy.

The fourth hypothesis is that communalism retards the emergence of liberal political structures. At the local level in Botswana, council politics, party organizations, and traditional authorities function to suppress public debate by promoting ethnic concerns. Also, the central ministries keep local elected councils on a short leash in part because of the councils' ethnic chauvinism.

Finally, in accordance with hypothesis five, economic liberalization has provided a basis for political liberalization. The new market-oriented bourgeoisie has promoted the opening of political parties and the growth of interest groups. Within the decade it will be challenging the presently dominant civil servants.

In the case of each of the liberalization hypotheses Botswana has deviated from some expected outcomes. These exceptional aspects of the country's experience provide evidence of the potential for flexibility in the liberalization process. Most important, leaders who are both politically shrewd and committed to democracy have made a difference. The BDP under Khama's and Masire's direction has set up a wide range of participatory structures to legitimize its rule. While these structures are in many respects manipulative, they have also democratized the heretofore authoritarian Tswana culture. The Khama-Masire leadership consistently worked to disperse ethnic conflict rather than allowing it to become state-centered.

Another factor fostering Botswana's exceptionalism is that the unranked character of the eight major Tswana ethnic groups has muted the impact of ethnicity on political conflict. This ethnicity of mutual respect has certainly allowed more of an opening for experimentation with liberal practices. In particular, it has allowed for the emergence in the last decade of interest groups in national politics, even if they do not yet set the agenda for political decisions.

The heavy involvement of foreign investment and aid has also been important in Botswana's liberalization. The initial investments for the mines came from outside in the form of private capital. These projects in turn have been so successful that government now has adequate income for future development, thus abrogating any need to oppress the peasants in order to obtain savings for capital investment. In addition, foreign aid organizations have enhanced the influence of lower-income groups by successfully insisting on highly participatory development projects (Molutsi 1991).

Another condition for Botswana's exceptionalism is the country's political stability, in spite of the rapid economic development internally and the racial civil war in South Africa. This stability has allowed considerable space and time for institutional learning and experimentation. There has thus been opportunity for various state-society linkages, ranging from the kgotla and local primaries to newspapers and interest groups, to be tested on a sustained basis so that those seeking liberalization could begin to think of ways to open each of these institutions more to the public. In contrast, many other African states have periodically abolished all sorts of major government structures, particularly as they enable state-society relations. In the process, there has been little time to contemplate the utility of a given set of structures, let alone the kind of reforms that might improve them.

One aspect of Botswana politics is not exceptional with respect to the rest of Africa. Botswana has no tradition of group politics. This has meant that interest groups have been relatively slow to gain much influence over government, even with the growth of a bureaucratic state and a market-oriented bourgeois class. Some forms of community-based participation have begun to give those in the rural areas a sense that they have a right to influence the policy process, if only at the stage of implementation.

The amount of liberalization taking place in Botswana should not be overestimated. Most politicians and top civil servants still have the developmentalist orientation we mentioned at the beginning of this chapter. They believe they know the public's problems and the best solutions. The liberalization approach to governance remains nascent in the sense that a number of liberal structures exist, but their influence on government decisions is minimal. Most important in this regard is that elections have not resulted in a change of the ruling political party or more than a few major changes in policy. Interest groups are beginning to make a lot of noise, but civil servants almost always marginalize their influence to advisory councils.

Political freedoms are not abridged, but important policy debates are still conducted mostly among the ministries.

The Botswana polity has begun to transform its developmentalist structures. It will become a liberal regime only when various elements of civil society organize effectively enough to challenge civil service domination. The foundations for such a challenge were laid in the 1980s. It is possible that with the rise of interest group power and the market-based bourgeoisie in the 1990s liberal forms of governance will become more of a reality.

NOTES

The authors most appreciate the helpful advice that the editors, the reviewer, and Richard Weisfelder provided us for redrafting this chapter. We also are indebted to our colleagues on the Democracy Research Project, with whom we worked in gathering much of the data on which this chapter is based. The Democracy Research Project was assisted in the collection of its data by funds received from the following organizations: the Social Science Research Council of New York; Swedish International Development Agency; Friedrich Ebert Stiftung; the Human Rights Fund of the US State Department; British Council; US Information Agency; University of Botswana; Cleveland State University; National Democratic Institute for International Affairs; and the Swedish Agency for Research Cooperation with Developing Countries.

1. This is a long tradition that covers many perspectives. See, e.g., Apter 1965; Huntington 1968; Saul 1985; Amin, Chitala & Mandaza 1987; Wilmsen 1989. All see the government's primary responsibility being to promote a particular type of development.

2. For a contrasting point of view, which sees the state in the Third World as weak and society as strong, see Migdal 1988.

3. Goran Hyden (1989) developed these hypotheses with particular reference to the Tanzanian experience. We have reformulated them for purposes of examining Botswana.

4. Botswana's foreign exchange surplus in 1990 was approximately two and one-half times the gross national product.

5. The only major exception in terms of civil service domination of government's policies was with respect to cattle holding and ranching. The cabinet regularly intervened to assure that the Tribal Grazing Land Policy and programs related to conservation did not affect traditional holdings and practices.

6. David Becker (1982) makes a similar point with respect to Peru in a very different context of military rule. The military leaders used the income from mining to carry out a land reform benefiting the peasants, thereby helping to consolidate the dominance of an emerging bourgeois class.

7. There are many aspects of the BDP in its present form that parallel the US urban political machine with its constituency service concerns.

8. During 1990 and 1991 the major opposition parties held several meetings in an attempt to form a united opposition front against the BDP.

9. Government allowed real wages to rise by only 13 percent from 1974 to 1979, and by 20 percent from 1979 to 1985 (Harvey & Lewis 1990:171).

10. Labor migration to South Africa did not decline simply because of expanding employment in Botswana, although this was a factor. Also important

was that the South African government and mining companies cut back on the opportunities for migrant labor.

11. These organizations are not simply a response to the presence of the universalistic state. They would not have been possible without the growth of the a middle class that had the skills to run them and the resources to fund them.

12. Most numerous are the Kalanga, who could be as much as 10 percent of the total population and live in the northeastern part of the country near the Zimbabwean border. The Bakalagadi and the Bushmen may be another 3–4 percent each. They live in the central and western Kalahari areas.

13. On the ethnic basis of party attachments, see Holm 1988.

5

Accommodation in the Midst of Crisis?
Assessing Governance in Nigeria

Donald C. Williams

Improving the quality of democracy in the pursuit of governance has been an elusive goal over the last four decades of Nigerian history. Although successive military governments shared a cynical view of democratic rule, they nonetheless invested an enormous amount of time and resources in reestablishing its framework in 1978 and again in 1989. Stimulated in part through vociferous public demands and an enduring democratic political culture, new constitutions have been promulgated and a complex transition program put into motion in the hopes that some institutional means could be found to overcome trends toward societal inertia. To this end, modifications in the federal system have been developed along with the incorporation of a variety of nonmajoritarian policies.

On the eve of the new Third Republic, it is instructive to examine the past performance of these "consociational" policy instruments and gauge what lessons they hold for the success of the latest try at democracy. The Nigerian case is also important for Africa as a whole, as it represents the potential that nonmajoritarian, democratic elements of governance hold as both a unifying force and a means to preserve societal diversity. Before this can be accomplished, it will be necessary to consider the dynamic nature of consociational practices in light of governance.

GOVERNANCE AND CONSOCIATIONAL
DEMOCRACY IN AFRICA

In Africa, where democracy is "widely approved but everywhere in doubt," open public participation in politics has tended to be characterized by divisive struggles among ethnic groups over power and resources (Sklar 1986:115). Resulting conflicts have led to a general paralysis of productive political activity, a demobilization of participatory institutions, and the seemingly ineluctable turn toward authoritarian mechanisms of rule. In keeping with the governance approach, it is apparent that these conditions generate the need for the creation of legitimate, accountable institutions that promote a less conflictual order, with positive outcomes and benefits attainable for all parties through active participation.

Consociationalism encompasses a variety of democratic policy mechanisms that temper zero-sum, majoritarian practices with cooperative agreements arranged between representatives of rival segmental groups. Through the use of noncompetitive mechanisms, power sharing, and consensual decisionmaking, the integrity of existing segmental groups is preserved, while primacy is placed on the maintenance of national unity. Although federalism represents perhaps the most familiar policy mechanism of this type, no rigid formula need be applied to achieve like results in consociational democracies. Rather, a pragmatic, overarching spirit of tolerance finds expression in both formal means, such as constitutional rules and legislative acts directed at policy issues, and unofficial compromises adopted in the midst of policy implementation (Daalder 1971; Lijphart 1985a; Elazar 1985).

Critical to these arrangements is the degree of mutual understanding that can be engendered among politicians through the formation of a cooperative, grand coalition.[1] Such conventions as proportionality principles, segmental autonomy, and mutual vetoes become necessary policy instruments in order to provide guarantees that a balance of interests is assured, while special consideration is given for disadvantaged groups and minorities (Lijphart 1977:100). Yet the prospective success of these kinds of arrangements is heavily dependent on internal political exchanges that funnel the circulation of political resources down to the grassroots of society. This occurs at two levels of social interaction: horizontal relations founded in negotiations held among political leaders; and vertical relations between leaders and their communities—relations that have been called "high" and "deep" politics in the context of Africa (Lonsdale 1986:136). These exchanges have been shown to rely on the existence of vast associational networks cemented together by interconnected personal loyalties and a variety of communal ties (Lemarchand 1972). For the most part, these patron-client networks endure because of the absence of other societal institutions that offer adequate legal guarantees of physical security, status, and wealth (Sandbrook 1972:109).

It is in this structural relationship that political interaction reflects the exercise of legitimate power, positive reciprocity, and accountability so critical to the success of governance (see Hyden, Chapter 1). The legitimacy of these arrangements rests on the extent to which elite representatives, as community patrons, can obtain a significant slice of the "national cake" without engendering too much enmity from competing elites and their communities (Barrows 1976; Joseph 1987). This can be a delicate and somewhat tenuous arrangement. Without some normative consensus over the politician's role of representing community interests, the secretive nature of elite negotiations would be surrounded with acrimony and distrust (Dunn 1986:162). Where there is a shortage in awareness and close personal contact between political patrons and their respective communities, a wide range of abuses are possible, even to the point of deteriorating into repressive activities (Steiner 1981).

Most democracies in Africa never developed accommodative practices precisely because political parties became coercive instruments in the hands of bureaucrats soon after independence. As one faction or another took over complete control and systematically eliminated all opposition elements, patrons lost touch with their clients and turned to a reliance on brute force (Lemarchand 1988:151). In other parts of the world this pattern has contributed to the progressive abandonment of nonmajoritarian democracy, oftentimes spurred by blatant violations of agreements by one or more parties, declining pecuniary resources, uncontrollable outbreaks of civil disorder that invite military intervention, civil war, or interference from foreign powers that alter the balance of power among segmental groups (Lijphart 1985b).

A number of distinctive consociational policy instruments have emerged in the course of two democratic experiments in Nigeria. It is to these arrangements, their dynamic character, and the potential that these practices hold for African governance, that we turn now.

INTOLERANCE AND ETHNICITY IN THE FIRST REPUBLIC

Ethnic consciousness in its modern context arose in Nigeria during the colonial period as British authorities brought together some 250 variously defined linguistic groups under one administrative banner. Many ethnic identities were discovered only after enterprising ethnic leaders seized the initiative in rallying people with heretofore unrealized cultural backgrounds in the promotion of their political aspirations. It was at this time that "a myth of unbridgeable differences was propagated which the population internalized" (Nnoli 1978:136). A catalyst for solidifying ethnic differentiation was created with the liberalization of representative institutions in the early 1950s, enjoining community leaders to appeal to community traditions and ties in gathering support for aspiring political parties. This process was accelerated as the Nigerian federal government became the center of competition over highly prized amenities.

The federal structure of First Republic endowed the country with a substantial degree of regional autonomy at the time of independence in 1960. National politics therefore centered on interethnic relations between the three largest groups (the Hausa-Fulani, Igbo, and Yoruba), each of which enjoyed hegemony in a separate regional unit despite the existence of substantial numbers of other ethnic minorities. National authorities at the federal level possessed few constitutional powers and owed most of their loyalties to one or another regional governor (Adamolekun & Ayo 1989:158). This autonomy was backed up by substantial revenue-generating sources in each of the regions, amounting to almost 50 percent of fiscal outlays. With complete control over marketing boards, extensive regional bureaucracies, and law enforcement, "the large regions recklessly threatened the federal center in order to extract political capital" (Elaigwu 1988:179).

Differences among the three regions were exacerbated by a historical legacy left by colonial administrative policy. The two regions of the South were imbued with a fairly well-educated populace and many favorable opportunities for diversified economic development. The impoverished North, on the other hand, was saddled with all of the trappings of economic underdevelopment typical of other Islamic cultures of the interior savannas of West Africa—fragile agricultural and pastoral economies, weakly developed infrastructure, and virtually no Western educational endowment. Through a policy of indirect rule that favored the existence of indigenous political rulers, British colonial authorities further perpetuated these divergent forms of social organization (Melson & Wolpe 1971).

Accommodational Failure and Ethnic Domination

The first demands for consociational political arrangements arose at this time as Northern politicians sought to allay inequalities through preferential job placement policies in the federal bureaucracy and the military officer corps. Compensatory quotas were also implemented in federally funded secondary schools. With a larger population than either region in the South, it was a foregone conclusion that Northern politicians would hold sway in national negotiations over these issues. However, determined opposition from key Southern leaders meant that the only way that such plans could be accomplished was to unite the three regions under a coalitional program. A number of influential Northern politicians began to believe that this was possible only through the consolidation of the entire federation under one political force dominated by their Northern-based Nigerian People's Congress (NPC) (Bamishaiye 1976; Diamond 1988).

The intensity of such efforts brought about the emergence of a powerful coalition between the parties of the Northern and Eastern Regions. The arrangement was resisted in the Western Region, where loyalties were divided between Obafemi Awolowo's Action Group (AG) and Nnamdi Azikiwe's National Congress of Nigerian Citizens (NCNC). Interested in creating a party that aspired to truly national proportions, Awolowo vehemently resisted such efforts at autonomous accommodation. The emergence of any form of grand coalition, such as had existed under colonial auspices in the years 1951–1954, was therefore inhibited from the very beginning. As adversarial relations ensued in the federal parliament, the AG in the West suffered successive legislative defeats, capped by the humiliating loss of a third of its territory with the creation of a new Mid-Western Region in 1962. Further tension arose with the announcement of the 1963 census results. Population figures released by the federal government showed a strong numerical advantage of 54 percent in favor of the Northern Region, with the rest apportioned equally between the two Southern Regions. Allegations of cheating and falsification of federal records abounded, and the census results were vociferously challenged in both the Southern press and the federal courts.

These pressures were compounded in 1963 when the AG was torn apart by personality conflicts. Conditions worsened as a splinter group aligned with the Northern coalition emerged in the form of the Nigerian National Democratic Party (NNDP). In the following year electoral violence and a general breakdown in civil order in the Western Region brought about the unprecedented suspension of the Western Region legislature and the jailing of the outspoken minority opposition leader Awolowo. To add further insult to the AG, local governments in the West were suspended by the federally appointed caretaker government of NNDP leader Samuel Akintola, who put in their place select "management committees" that utilized control over local tax collection, licensing, and police forces to consolidate political hegemony in the West (Post & Vickers 1973:233). To a lesser degree, such abuses were also followed in other regions of the country where each party had determined to establish local dominance. This was most evident in areas in the North where local communities resisted the domination of the NPC, as among the Tiv ethnic minority and the *talakawa*-supported[2] Northern Elements Progressive Union in Kano Division (Tseayo 1980). Ethnic minorities in the Eastern Region who resisted Igbo domination through the NCNC party were similarly maltreated.

National elections in the following year led to an intensification of intolerance exhibited in the widespread incidence of electoral abuses and intermittent outbreaks of communal violence. In the end, it was a result of these factors, combined with the brazen character of political corruption, that justified the armed forces' putting an end to democracy at the beginning of 1966 (O'Connell 1970).

Assessing Accommodational Failure in the First Republic

Given the nature of competitive, majoritarian politics in the First Republic, negotiated compromises fell apart quickly in the harsh struggle over scarce resources and unchecked power. Attempts by the Northern-dominated federal government to impose programs that were designed to rectify past inequities were greeted with suspicion and animosity. To this end, public policies founded on principles of proportionality were interpreted as an unacceptable loss of power by many Southern politicians. Such fears were encouraged in an environment in which the stakes of political office were equivalent to survival: "the dominant concern of the vast majority of participants in politics at all levels during the early 1960's, was the receipt of the largest possible share of benefits in the shortest period of time" (Post & Vickers 1973:47). The uncontrolled scramble for resources exacerbated by a zero-sum, winner-take-all electoral system only exacerbated hostility among politicians. The general disregard for the rule of law eventually resulted in a general breakdown in reciprocal relations among hard-pressed patrons and their constituent communities.

Much of the blame for the failure of democratic institutions in the First Republic must also be attributed to a weakly fabricated federal structure. The three regional units comprising the federal system were unbalanced economically and demographically, leading to long-simmering feelings of acrimony and distrust among elites. The limit of only three regions compounded this sentiment because the three dominant parties attempted to represent a host of ethnic conglomerations—many of which carried strongly held ethnic resentments against the dominant regional majority group.

Although the federal structure allowed for significant autonomy in the conduct of local affairs, it failed to shield these units from the machinations of rival political forces. The propensity for rival parties to exploit cleavages in other regions thus polarized the character of political interactions. In this way, fitful attempts at attaining ethnic autonomy by the many smaller segmental groups were greeted by the major political parties with acts of Machiavellian intrigue or the use of local police and hirelings for brutal repression. In the absence of any viable mutual veto in the Senate, regional politicians were at the mercy of the collective efforts of other regions. This was most clearly evident in the deplorable manner in which the Western Region was manhandled by a federal government dominated by the other two regions. The acceptance of the 1963 census by the federal government would also have been impossible if such a veto were in operation. There could be little productive reciprocity among both politicians and client communities in the charged atmosphere of brazen abuse of law and widespread civil strife. Through a succession of increasingly violent crises, centrifugal pressures took on a momentum that never allowed a spirit of national reconciliation to surface.

ETHNIC ACCOMMODATION AND CENTRIFUGAL FEDERALISM IN THE SECOND REPUBLIC

Thirteen years of military rule between the First and Second Republics led to many changes in the federal structure of Nigeria. Most significant was the increasing subordination of the state governments to federal control. Overturning the provisions of the 1963 Constitution, the federal military government completely restructured the federal system, adding to its exclusive control such important areas as education, university administration, petroleum production, and the coordination and direction of development plans (Ukwu 1980; Oyovbaire 1984:234). All of this was made possible by the progressive concentration of financial power in the federal government that had resulted from an enormous windfall in petroleum-generated wealth. Over the period from 1969 to 1979, federal outlays rose almost twenty times from 548.2 million naira (N) to N18.5 billion. The extent to which the federal government assumed superiority over fiscal policy in relation to the state governments is illustrated by the fact that federal spending rose from 60 percent of all outlays in 1968/69 to approximately 87 percent by 1980/81.[3]

It was during this period that many key elements of accommodation were first introduced. These included a true quota system for all federal recruitment, representation of the states in national governmental bodies, and proportional allocation of federal resources (Jinadu 1985). Greater autonomy among the diverse array of ethnic groups was also provided in 1976 through a redesigned federal structure that now numbered a total of nineteen states. This arrangement allowed for independent representation of formerly neglected groups through nine states that were composed of ethnic minorities. A reorganization and expansion of local government in the same year was designed to further extend representation to the many smaller ethnic units in the country within each state.

With the trauma of explosive interethnic conflict and a three-year civil war still fresh in the minds of military leaders, major departures from the old design were incorporated into the Second Republic Constitution as well. The Westminster parliamentary model was abandoned in favor of a more centralized federal arrangement, modeled after that of the United States, that included a strong presidential chief executive balanced by a powerful bicameral legislature. Yet the new constitution incorporated several significant modifications on majoritarian democracy that included "elaborate arrangements for sharing power, adjusting conflicting interests and permitting autonomous participation" (Elaigwu & Olorunsola 1983:299).

Elite Compromise or Conspiracy?

One means of moderating the intensity of divisive political conflict is the formation of a grand coalition from among principal parties. Unproductive quarreling is avoided through negotiated compromises made possible through a broadly based coalition government. The most important characteristic of such arrangements is not any particular institutional apparatus, but rather "the participation by the leaders of all significant segments in governing a plural society" (Lijphart 1977:31).

No explicit rules for the formation of a grand party coalition were written into the Second Republic Constitution. However, specific provisions were put into place that favored the creation of a governing body that was widely representative of all the states in the federation. The president was mandated to appoint at least one minister from each of the nineteen states in the process of selecting members for the cabinet. In conforming to this provision, President Shehu Shagari chose all of his cabinet from his own supporters in the National Party of Nigeria (NPN) and the Nigerian People's Party (NPP). Although this did not constitute a grand coalition embracing all parties, it did represent an "ethnic" grand coalition because "it included persons selected from among the political class of the various ethnic groups aggregatively represented in the nineteen states of the federation" (Jinadu 1985:90).

In the first twenty months of the Second Republic, competition between several of the parties was tempered by working alliances that had been forged on the basis of this coalition. In part, this was necessitated by the absence of a true majority in the bicameral legislature. A formal accord with Azikiwe's NPP gave his Igbo party a share of key offices and promises of favoritism in the allocation of federal projects in exchange for cooperation. Overtures were also made to bring in Aminu Kano and the moderate wing of his People's Redemption Party (PRP), as well as Waziri Ibrahim's Great Nigerian People's Party (GNPP) in late 1979, with little success. Although Shagari's coalition was aided by a number of key opposition senators who gave the NPN pivotal support in the interests of preserving national unity, determined opposition from the Yoruba-supported Unity Party of Nigeria and the two smaller parties prevented any true consensual arrangement from emerging (Diamond 1983:48; Jinadu 1985:89). This strident opposition eventually came under the informal auspices of an alliance of nine "progressive governors," all of whom claimed solidarity on the basis of mutual hostility against Shagari.

While the ruling coalition between the NPP and NPN broke down over alleged abuses of power by the Shagari administration, it is notable that other attempts were made at interparty accommodation. Power-sharing agreements were eventually forged between the NPN and dissident factions of the GNPP and the PRP in the midst of preparations for the 1983 elections. Further efforts in coalition building were, however, dashed with the alignment of Awolowo's UPN, Azikiwe's NPP, Waziri's GNPP, and the a faction of the PRP led by Michael Imoudu into a newly formed Progressive Parties Alliance (PPA) in the middle of 1982. Yet this group was not brought together with the intention of accommodating national interests in an alternative grand coalition of sorts. Awolowo, Azikiwe, and Waziri remained bitter rivals while at the same time sharing mutual aspirations for the presidency. In fact, among all the parties, only a small faction of the beleaguered PRP actually advocated the formation of a new grand coalition. Rather, the PPA came together only as an alliance of convenience with the express purpose of unseating Shagari and the NPN.[4] In the period leading up to elections held in 1983, any further possibility for cooperation among the parties was nullified in an environment wherein "political intolerance and inflexibility [had] become perhaps the dominant feature of the interaction between the parties" (Diamond 1983:63). Negotiations among party leaders and the Shagari government were geared toward achieving zero-sum victories, so that such sensitive issues as the allocation of federal revenue and the location of development projects, new universities, hospitals, and other amenities became a tool for manipulating compliance with the ruling NPN (Ayeni & Olowu 1988:212).

The complex nature of the federal structure also made it difficult to form a grand coalition among the five parties. The Muslim North was dominated by the NPN but had shown strong support for the PRP in both Kano and Kaduna states. The GNPP controlled many seats in Borno, Gongola, and Sokoto states. The central "Middle Belt" ethnic minority states were unevenly represented by all five parties, while the pattern of representation in the South was hardly clearer. Although the UPN showed significant strength in all four Yoruba states, and the NPP dominated the two Igbo states, other southern ethnic groups were represented by a jumble of parties that included the NPN, UPN, and NPP in significant numbers. The tendency of "outsider" parties to make attempts at winning over dissident ethnic groups and factions within rival parties further complicated the picture. In this endeavor, the NPN was most successful, winning over anti-Awolowo sentiment in Ogbomosho and several other prominent Yoruba communities, as well as exploiting strong resentment against the Igbo in Rivers and Cross River states in the East. Where the lines of party representation were drawn imperfectly, consistent representation of segmental interests through a disciplined party system was complicated and difficult to manage.

The ubiquitous existence of an elite "political class," comprising a mixed group of bureaucrats, politicians, and varying elements of the bourgeoisie, has been identified in a number of studies of Nigeria (Dudley 1973; Sklar 1979; Diamond 1988). It has been contended that this group, aided by its access to immense wealth generated by the oil boom, has acted cohesively to further its collective interests. In many ways, party alliances during the Second Republic "crossed ethnicity, region, and religion as impressively as any political coalition in modern history" (Diamond 1982:655). By all accounts, this group had the potential for building a cohesive grand coalition of the five parties.

Yet during periods of open political competition it took very little provocation for these people to revert to all-too-familiar practices of electoral misconduct and violence. Few cared for the formalities of law when extremely high stakes were on the line in the possession of elected offices (Joseph 1987:37). In addition, most politicians involved at the highest levels had previously served in some capacity in the First Republic. Having been exposed to all the fructuous rewards that office holding could bring, few demonstrated any interest in abandoning adversarial tactics. For all intents and purposes, they exhibited little evidence of having learned from the traumatic lessons of the past, nor did they show any sense of mutual tolerance and reciprocity—sentiments that are critical for the success of consociational bargaining.[5]

Proportionality in Resource Allocation

The use of a neutral and impartial standard of allocating national resources to all segments of the population stands as a vital element of consociational democracy. Through the equitable division of civil service appointments and government subsidies, a spirit of mutual accommodation can be engendered, thus paving the way for more-difficult and politically sensitive negotiations (Lijphart 1977:38–39). More than any other issue, this nonmajoritarian practice was made explicit in the Second Republic Constitution. The 1978 Constitution is worth quoting at length on this point: "the composition of the Government of the Federation or any of its agencies and the conduct of its affairs shall be carried in such a manner as to reflect the federal character of Nigeria . . . ensuring that there shall be no predominance of persons from a few ethnic or other sectional groups" (Nigeria 1978:14, 3–4). These guidelines were constitutionally mandated for all appointments in the federal public services and armed forces, the allocation of public revenue and capital projects, and the composition of such important federal executive bodies as the Council of States, the Federal Electoral Commission, the National Economic Council, and the National Population Council.

The pressure to fulfil this constitutional mandate began immediately following Shagari's electoral victory. Debates in the federal legislature alleged that the distribution of top-level management positions in government ministries and public corporations had been biased in favor of the Yoruba. Shagari therefore dismissed many key Yoruba civil servants in federal government agencies in his first year of office. Although this action placated partisan pressures, it only embittered the Yoruba and solidified their resolve to oust Shagari and his allies from power (Gboyega 1984).

The implementation of proportionality principles was surrounded by controversy from the very beginning. This resulted from the fact that no specific ethnic allocation formula was spelled out in the constitution, nor was any settled in subsequent negotiations. Rather, allocation was to be apportioned solely on the basis of the nineteen states—a system that was flawed from the start because none of Nigeria's states possesses a perfect demarcation between ethnic groups and boundaries. Several states have mixed populations of Muslim and Christian adherents, despite common membership in one ethnolinguistic group. Other states have a predominant ethnic group that has been polarized among many subethnic groups and clans, while still others contain no ethnic groups with any clear majority in numbers (Osaghae 1988:15). More importantly, there was no clarification drawn between minority or majority ethnic groups, or North-South cleavages—both important in rectifying inequalities of the past (Jinadu 1985:93).

Controversy paralyzed subsequent proceedings of the national legislature, which was charged with monitoring the selection of federal appointments and ensuring compliance in resource allocation. This was particularly true in the distribution of federal revenue to the nineteen states. With such enormous resources at stake, the allocation formula represented the most significant source of patronage. The president stood to benefit the most from a formula that favored the federal government, since resources under his own direction could be used to favor states with an NPN majority. Opposition parties sought a greater share of federal resources for their supporters dispersed in nine states and therefore sought to secure more fiscal allocation to the state treasuries. In addition, legislators from the states with larger populations resisted allowing the federal largesse to be doled out equally, while petroleum-producing states in the East engaged in a bitter struggle over receiving a larger share of benefits (Adamolekun & Ayo 1989:170).

Proportionality and Electoral Representation

Proportionality provisions extended to the realm of electoral politics also led to rising tensions and acrimony. The Constitution specified that each presidential aspirant must garner not less than one-quarter of the votes cast in two-thirds of all states to qualify for a runoff or absolute victory. This measure was to ensure that agreements arranged by the president would contain nationwide legitimacy by bringing about the emergence of a truly national figure acceptable to most geographic sections of the country. Despite an enormous amount of controversy over the exact interpretation of this electoral formula, the Supreme Court and departing officials from the Obasanjo administration determined that Shagari had attained these percentages in the necessary thirteen states in 1979.

Elements of proportionality were also reflected in the organization of political parties, which were required to reflect the federal character by establishing a viable political presence in each state of the federation. This included both the physical presence of party offices and the presentation of candidates for seats in the national races. Other requirements stipulated that national officers of each party should reflect Nigeria's ethnic diversity by originating from no less than two-thirds of the nineteen states, and that neither emblems nor public pronouncements could contain ethnic or religious connotation. Enforcement of these stringent qualifications was provided through the Federal Electoral Commission (FEDECO), which was to act as an impartial arbiter. Ironically, there were no restrictions on specifying a federal origin for party finances, thus allowing the bulk of funds to originate from ethnic blocs and a few wealthy elites.

While all parties earnestly sought to reflect these provisions, the well-financed NPN was the most successful in attaining a truly federal representation (Omoruyi 1990; Diamond 1983). It dominated in the largely rural Hausa-Fulani areas of the North, among ethnic minorities throughout Nigeria, and even made minor inroads in Yoruba and Igbo states. Much of this success was attributable to the manner in which NPN leaders skilfully employed a zoning system. Key offices were subjected to a rotating formula based upon four predesignated ethnic zones, so that the dominance of any particular group would be obviated. The other major parties attempted to dole out key positions to members of the major ethnic groups as well, but the course of elections in 1979 made it palpably obvious that most support came from their respective ethnic bases. Although the well-financed UPN and NPP managed to place viable candidates for election in virtually every electoral district in the country, the GNPP and PRP organizations were virtually nonexistent outside of their enclaves in the North. This becomes demonstrably clear when 1979 election results are grouped by region as in Table 5.1.

Collaboration among diverse ethnic elements in virtually all the parties became strained over the issues of state creation, the appropriate division of resources, and alliance strategies. This led to intrafactional conflicts that erupted into a large number of expulsions, crossovers, and disciplining measures by the end of 1981. Both the PRP and GNPP were torn apart over whether or not to cooperate with the federal government through an accord with the NPN. The PRP eventually split into two factions that positioned national party leader Aminu Kano against the two PRP governors, Abubakar Rimi and Balarabe Musa. Eventually, both factions ran candidates in the 1983 elections, each claiming the exclusive right to wear the mantle of the party. When a majority of the GNPP national executive committee led by Shettima Mustapha voted to expel their charismatic party chairman and presidential candidate, Waziri Ibrahim, he promptly responded by personally expelling the entire committee for "subversive activities." The dispute finally ended in 1982 when anti-Waziri factions opted to abandon the party altogether and join either the NPP or UPN.

Similar troubles rocked the masterfully crafted ethnic conglomeration in the NPN. President Shagari attempted to placate spiraling centrifugal tendencies by enlarging his executive cabinet to an unwieldy number of forty-five ministries, each of which were filled with politically favored appointees. The executive boards of the multitudinous parastatals were similarly overstaffed at great expense in order to accommodate these growing pressures. Suspicions continued to arise over the religious background of cabinet members and other high appointees—as no provision for this identity was incorporated into the state-based zoning formula. Many contended that a bias in favor of Muslims was evident, as they were given control over such highly sought-after positions as Defense, Trade and Industries, and Internal Affairs (Ayoade 1986:86; Forrest 1985:8). This sentiment was fueled by allegations from the opposition press that the NPN was dominated by a powerful cabal of Northern politicians dubbed the Kaduna Mafia. Undercurrents of hostility also surfaced over Shagari's renomination to presidential candidacy in 1983, as it was alleged that this action "raised the specter of northern domination; the bane of the politics of the First Republic" (Okpu 1984:119).

Table 5.1 Seats Won in the Federal House of Representatives
and Senate by Region, 1979 Elections

	NPN	UPN	NPP	GNPP	PRP
Far North					
House	75	1	3	25	50
Senate	14	0	0	4	7
Middle Belt					
House	45	12	15	8	0
Senate	15	4	4	2	0
Southeast					
House	37	2	58	4	0
Senate	6	0	12	2	0
Southwest					
House	10	96	2	0	0
Senate	0	25	0	0	0
Total House	167	111	78	37	50
Total Senate	35	29	16	8	7

Source: The figures are derived from Adamu and Ogunsanwo 1983.
Note: The following states are grouped under regional headings: Far North comprises
Sokoto, Kaduna, Kano, Bauchi, and Borno; Middle Belt, Kwara, Niger, Plateau, Benue,
and Gongola; Southeast, Anambra, Imo, Rivers, and Cross River; and Southwest, Lagos,
Ogun, Oyo, Ondo, and Bendel.

The NPN was eventually accused of influence peddling and abuse of
office in subsequent attempts to adhere to federal character requirements for
elections. Allegations of partisan manipulation of electoral rules began in
1983 when the Nigeria Advance Party (NAP) was approved for participation
in the 1983 elections, despite a previous disqualification by the FEDECO in
1978 on grounds of poor national representation. Since the party appealed to
anti-Awolowo sentiments among the Yoruba, it was widely believed that the
NAP had been approved in order to draw critical votes away from the UPN in
the West. Later accusations centered on the manner in which FEDECO
officials and federally appointed judicial panels struck down appeals by
aggrieved opposition governors who had lost their incumbency despite
enormous margins of victory in 1979. The partisan manipulation of
registered voter lists was also raised after the FEDECO administrative
secretary, Stephen Ajibade, was found to have revised the 1979 list in his
home district from 48,216 names to 214,500 for the 1983 election.
These activities increased exponentially in the 1983 elections as

operatives from all the parties resorted to avoidance mechanisms in order to meet imposed standards (Falola & Ihonvbere 1985:216). In Borno state, for example, underage children were allowed to register and vote, while in Plateau and Niger states fake ballot boxes that were prestuffed with thumb-printed ballots were switched with genuine boxes on the way to counting stations. In many other states police and polling officials were openly bribed by party officials, while thugs were hired to keep people away from polling booths (Babalakin 1986). All in all, these practices undermined any credibility the elections might have had in the eyes of the people, so that the "landslide victory" that had returned Shagari and the NPN to power was greeted with remorse in many sections of the country. Acts of mass carnage and destruction of property reported in at least eight states in the course of the campaign and its aftermath gave credence to Awolowo's statement that "it is the first time that elections have been won in such a massive manner and nobody rejoices."[6]

Centrifugal Pressures for Autonomy

Most consociational democracies have involved agreements allocating a significant degree of autonomy over local affairs to constituent segmental groups. These guarantees, which are an enshrined principle in any federation, are intended to ensure that participation by minority parties will be maintained (Lijphart 1977:41). This spirit is reflected throughout the Second Republic Constitution, where independent legislatures and administrative machinery were allotted to each of the nineteen states. The states were also given complete control over operating budgets, education, agriculture, housing, health, local governments, and chieftaincy affairs, and direction over local infrastructural development. Concurrent powers were quite substantial as well, including revenue collection, parastatal management, education, and electrical power generation.

Yet these impressive guarantees of segmental autonomy were to prove inadequate in the face of the maelstrom of pluralistic pressures. The all-consuming imperative of patronage among constituent communities meant that substantial outlays were made by state governments to expand education, build infrastructural projects, and provide such desirable amenities as health clinics, electricity, and pipe-borne water. Yet few states could provide the revenue necessary for these expansive plans, as most governors and state legislatures had suspended existing collection of local taxes in the interests of gaining popularity over rival patrons (Ihinmodu 1982). The result was that by 1983 over 90 percent of all state and local government revenue was coming exclusively from federal sources. This situation was to persist as long as the federal treasury was abundantly supplied with revenue from petroleum (Ayeni & Olowu 1988:215).

Increasingly irresponsible expenditures at all levels of the federal system eventually led to a situation in which accounts were thrown into a deficit situation. From a healthy budget surplus of N2.5 billion in 1979, the balance of accounts had fallen to a N3 billion shortfall by 1982. Profligate mismanagement of foreign loans meant that external debts had risen to an alarming N62 billion by 1983 from an earlier N8.5 billion in 1979. All nineteen states of the federation had also fallen into debt that ranged over N300 million in five states and totaled N4.428 billion altogether by March 1983.[7]

Under these circumstances, state governors elected from opposing parties had difficulty bargaining with the Shagari government for a larger share of federal revenue. At the same time the Shagari government sought to overstep opposition politicians at the state level through direct funding of public welfare projects of all types. The governors of opposition states responded in turn by delaying or withholding cooperation at all levels in order to discredit federal officials (Ayo 1988). Among the most celebrated incidents of this nature occurred in Oyo state, where UPN governor Bala Ige ordered the demolition of two public housing projects begun under federal direction because his office had not given officials authorization to use appropriated land. In a like manner, a federal road construction plan was halted in progress by NPP governor Jim Nwobodo in Anambra state on the pretense that the project was improperly utilizing funds that were supposed to go to the state government. And in Bendel state the federal government was taken to court by UPN governor Ambrose Alli on the charge that services and development projects being undertaken by federal authorities represented an encroachment on state powers guaranteed under the constitution (Nwabueze 1985:75–77). Other incidents included the seizure of federal property and attempts at providing alternative public services that paralleled existing federal facilities (Elaigwu 1988:180).

Resistance from opposition states became increasingly combative against the Shagari administration over the latter years of the Second Republic. Tensions initially mounted over concern with abuse levied against Balarabe Musa, the outspoken PRP governor of Kaduna state. After the 1979 election the NPN-controlled Kaduna state assembly conspired against Musa by refusing to approve appointments of state commissioners, voting down a succession of legislative proposals, and eventually passing a much-publicized motion of impeachment on trumped-up charges of abuse of office. The opposition governors were outraged and accused Shagari of complicity in these tactics. Suspicions also arose over the hostile attitudes of federal police toward non-NPN governments, who were accused of harassment and deliberate neglect of duty in serving opposition governors. In response, two opposition governors from Oyo and Anambra states set up paramilitary "road safety" police forces under their direct supervision.

But no issue raised the ire of opposition governors more than the placement of presidential liaison officers in each state capital. Intended to provide direct supervision over federal agencies and programs in each state, their presence was seen as an unwarranted interference, and most were never officially recognized by state governments. The air of mutual suspicion created by these federal appointees was only worsened when many "PLOs" were encouraged by the Shagari administration to oppose state governors as NPN candidates in the 1983 elections (Nwabueze 1985:82).

Conflicting imperatives in the federal system also appeared in the ongoing issue over state creation. In the interests of diffusing pressures for greater segmental autonomy, the constitution allowed for the addition of new states into the federation should certain stringent criteria be met. While no interest lobby was successful in pushing through a new state proposal during the four years of civilian rule, an inordinate amount of time and energy was devoted to this issue in the legislature. By one account, legislation was pending in various official circles for the creation of fifteen new states in 1983, while other proposals were even being tendered for the conversion of all 450 federal electoral districts into separate states (Diamond 1982:659). The universal appeal of this issue is borne out by the fact that platforms of all five parties contained promises for the creation of new states in both elections (Forrest 1985:7).

Spiraling pressures in the federal system also emerged in relations between local government councils and state officials. The constitution allowed state legislatures to create new local government constituencies, supervise council elections, and dissolve councils established by the military in 1976. The zeal with which this exercise was pursued is illustrated by the fact that between 1979 and 1983 state governments raised the total number of local government areas in the federation from 301 to an estimated 850 (Gboyega 1985). Many governors hoped to garner electoral support through patronage allocated through these newly created administrative units. In exchange for their votes, loyal constituencies stood to benefit enormously through the construction of new infrastructural developments and employment opportunities that came with the establishment of newly created council areas. This exercise was also given momentum by the strict terms of the constitution, which specified that incumbent governors should receive no less than one-quarter of the votes cast in two-thirds of all local government areas.

These unchecked expressions of autonomy eventually led to the virtual elimination of local government as a third tier of the federal structure. Although federal funds provided the bulk of revenue for local government, the constitution specified that this money was to be dispersed through the auspices of state governments. In reality, few funds actually trickled down to local governments, as these resources were diverted into the pockets of powerful state-level politicians and their supporters. This trend was augmented by the increasing number of local government councils that were dissolved, and subsequent usurpation of responsibilities by state officials or delegated state parastatal agencies (Adamolekun & Ayo 1989:173). The proliferation of new local governments in all of the states also created insurmountable problems, as no additional funds were provided by federal authorities under the terms of the revenue-sharing formula. Intercommunal conflicts also exploded over this period as competition over resources ensued between local governments controlled by a party differing from that which dominated the state legislature or governorship (Smith & Owojaiye 1981; Nwankwo 1984).

Assessing Accommodational Failure in the Second Republic

In many ways, the introduction of several nonmajoritarian mechanisms in the Second Republic Constitution could have enhanced governance by accommodating segmental pressures. Yet there is no evidence that any kind of commitment to dampen overly parochial concerns ever materialized. The fractious alliance that emerged under Shagari's party banner at the close of 1979 never embodied more than superficial elements of consociational representation. Without any willingness to cooperate among party elites, no consensus could be arranged over an appropriate formula for the proportional division of federal resources. An arrangement based solely on states proved to be glaringly inadequate for Nigeria's diverse ethnic landscape, thereby robbing the political arena of a potentially vital building block for other agreements. As a result, negotiations were surrounded by accusations of betrayal and mistrust, as is evidenced by the bitter splits that occurred in several parties over just this issue.

Insofar as a shared consensus did exist, few productive measures were taken to strengthen trust among ethnic representatives left out of initial negotiations. Rather, outright favoritism shown to NPN supporters and their states, and flagrant disregard of the interests and autonomy of opposition states only perpetuated animosities initiated with the 1979 election controversy. Although coalition-building efforts continued up until the 1983 elections, there never emerged any real commitment to lay down majoritarian politics for cooperative endeavors.

Lingering power imbalances between the states and federal government also contributed to the air of mutual suspicions and animosity by exacerbating fears of ethnic domination. Multifarious jurisdictional battles over appointments to key patronage positions and constant calls for the creation of new states only added weight to an already overburdened legislative agenda. This situation was of course worsened by the conspicuous absence of any form of mutual veto, which could have provided some relief from the charged atmosphere of mutual hostility. An active and impartial federal judiciary also would have lessened these pressures.

The absence of tolerance among Nigeria's national leaders has been attributed to the machinations of a rather amorphous elite political class that went out of control while pursuing class-based strategies of hegemonic control over the state (Diamond 1983, Falola & Ihonvbere 1985; Marenin

1988). Indeed, there is little doubt that much of the acrimony among elites is attributable to intemperate personality conflicts and quarrels dating back to the First Republic. Even more important, however, was a general breakdown in reciprocal relations among elite representatives and their constituent communities. The deleterious combination of global recession, a precipitous decline in oil revenue, and accompanying problems with financial solvency meant that fewer resources were available to sustain massive spending outlays (Joseph 1987:28; Jinadu 1985:98; Bach 1989). As the flow of funds were cut short amid rising inflation and unemployment, productive bargaining at all levels of the federal structure became increasingly difficult to sustain. The large number of uncompleted government projects, squandering of resources, and mounting evidence of corruption in office stretched the limits of reciprocity at all levels of government (Okuridibo 1987).

In the context of Nigerian politics, the popular legitimacy of politicians largely rests upon their ability to fulfil expectations of rewards for their community through preferential access to the national treasury.[8] Experience has shown that this is accomplished either through legal transfers in the form of community patronage projects, or through personal funds doled out through private channels. In the course of the Second Republic, it is evident that as long as community demands were being satisfied "corruption" of this type was largely tolerated. However, the decline in resources by the middle of 1981 meant that promises of patronage went unfulfilled while economic conditions deteriorated. As a result, popular attention shifted to the personalized side of political corruption.[9] Having benefited enormously as gatekeepers of the public treasury, politicians now became the target of increasingly severe reprobation from the press and public at large. Critical elements of trust and accountability were eroded, giving rise to popular resentment against all politicians (Falola & Ihonvbere 1985:108). As politicians lost their ability to satisfy the demands of their communities, their accountability was threatened unless they resorted to violating the law. It is notable that accusations of ethnic favoritism resurfaced at this time as well (Bach 1989:26). Pressures to maintain expectations of reciprocity and an unwillingness to face the consequences of relinquishing power by any of the parties eventually brought out the kind of desperate electoral stratagems that were reminiscent of the First Republic.

GOVERNANCE AND POLITICAL ACCOMMODATION IN THE THIRD REPUBLIC

Nigeria is now in process of ushering in another era of democratic rule under the auspices of a new, Third Republic Constitution. Unfortunately, the new design does not embody the innovative audacity of its predecessor. Once again, a presidential system has been resurrected, supported by a bicameral legislature and an expansive federal bureaucracy. The Third Republic preserves what has been called "the constitutional hegemony of the federal government" by equipping this tier with an equally substantial number of exclusive powers (Ayoade & Suberu 1990:154). Wide discretion has also been given to the federal government to legislate on matters considered incidental or supplementary to this list, as well as to promote "fundamental objectives and directive principles" of enumerated policy.[10] In the past, similar language was used to justify direct federal intervention in areas of authority presumed to be residual matters under the direct sway of the states.

More importantly, it is unlikely that the retention of a heavily centralized federal system will demonstrate any greater capacity to contain the complex admixture of centrifugal ethnicity and patronage politics so characteristic of Nigeria. The most significant change, restricting the number of political parties to two federally funded conglomerations, cannot possibly promote the formation of a grand coalition or other consensual power-sharing agreements. There is little room provided for autonomous representation of the many groups that make up Nigeria's diverse ethnic landscape within the structure of only two broadly representative parties. This was clearly demonstrated by ongoing dissensions within the NPN agglomeration during the Second Republic, which was the only party to veritably aspire to this status. The new constitution also reproduces the mystifying language of the federal character proportionality rule almost to the letter. As in the past, attempts to interpret and apply this principle to Nigeria's complex federal structure will engender feelings of alienation among slighted groups, raise fears of ethnic domination, and furnish a strong inducement for the costly and impractical addition of more states.

It is also unlikely that attempts to enhance the integrity of the third tier of local government through direct federal supervision of elections, redistricting, and transfers of funds will provide intended guarantees of segmental autonomy. The imbalance created by the loss of a substantial sphere of independent authority will only add more fears of domination from whatever ethnic coalition manages to capture the federal center. To this end, it is unfortunate that a stronger and more independent judiciary has not been created. This body, which has been so abused by past federal governments, could offer a potential counterweight to the overwhelming concentration of power at the federal center, while at the same time easing fears of dominance held by state governors.

The enshrinement of Nigeria as a "welfare state" in the constitution and the substantial outlays this will entail also suggest that the tradition of statism will remain, despite a substantial privatization program. The deplorable condition of the economy, exacerbated by a rise in unemployment, crippling inflation, and an absence of much-needed investment in declining industries will mean that few opportunities for advancement remain outside of the petroleum-funded state sector. Given the retention of a winner-take-all, majoritarian electoral system, there is little reason to doubt that the intensity of competition over the spoils of office will be of a magnitude equal to that of earlier periods. With a chronic shortage in available capital, the delicate bonds of reciprocity will be strained to dangerous proportions, portending difficult centrifugal pressures on the federal system similar to the last years of the Second Republic.

The Nigerian case suggests the limitations that constitutional mechanisms embody if they fail to be grounded in the dynamic character of society (Harbeson 1986). Halfhearted attempts at incorporating elements of consociationalism in the midst of a US–style plural democracy in the Second Republic achieved little in the context of deeply engrained patronage politics and ethnic social identification. At the same time, the distance that Nigeria traveled between the First and Second Republics reveals that a generous infusion of capital and creative determination can bring about a substantial restructuring of the constitutional mechanisms of rule. The undisguised idealism of Olusegun Obasanjo's military administration of 1978 has not been replicated in the sober constitutional design of Ibrahim Babangida's administration. Although the record is yet to be written, the creative potential of politics in Nigeria may have to wait until another democratic constitution is fabricated some time in the future.

CONSOCIATIONAL POLITICS AND AFRICAN GOVERNANCE

Lijphart's (1985:130) assertion that consociational democracy reflects "a rational and purposive response to the facts of pluralism and interdependence" reminds us of the compelling potential that such practices offer for the creative use of politics. This approach has much to offer in overcoming societal inertia because it does not necessitate any changes in the existing ethnic fabric of African societies.[11]

It is worthwhile to consider the viability of incorporating consociational practices in the framework of democratic governance in Africa for three reasons. First, the glaring absence of a tolerant political culture in most African states does not bode well for the immediate adoption of competitive forms of pluralist democracy. The negative attitudes that many hold toward governmental authority have resulted from decades of arbitrary rule as well as outright neglect. As a result, most identification and trust in Africa remains tied to local forms of informal social organization (Chazan 1982). With this in mind, consociational practices offer a means to incorporate existing patterns of political participation into larger segmental parties, without making demands for integration.

Second, a large number of states in Africa are imbued with demographic characteristics that favor the creation of consociational arrangements. Few states are dominated numerically by a majority ethnic group, and many enjoy a rough equivalence in size among major segmental groups (Rothchild & Foley 1988:260). While no state possesses complete socioeconomic equality among segments, fairly small populations mean that a rough balance of power is conceivable given the right combination of committed leaders and resources. Where ethnic groups have suffered decades of neglect or mistreatment, they are assured of representation in the center while still retaining a measure of autonomy "to retain their identity and alleviate any feelings of hopelessness and political suffocation" (Nicol 1986:171). The renewed interest in human rights in Africa is also supportive of the creation of mechanisms that would honor the integrity of segmental autonomy and minority representation.

Third, the fact that many states have utilized power-sharing mechanisms in the past as a means to diffuse segmental pressures is suggestive of an incipient tradition of elite accommodation. The use of proportionality principles in revenue allocation and quotas in employment, for example, has been identified in such diverse countries as Benin, Malawi, Kenya, Tanzania, Zambia, and Ghana. Notable attempts to incorporate divergent societal representatives into a nondemocratic grand coalition of sorts have also been manifest at various times in Kenya, Côte d'Ivoire, and Zambia (Berg-Schlosser 1985; Rothchild 1986). Although such variants of "hegemonial exchange" have no doubt brought some stability, they have failed to make any provision for the legitimate participation of the majority through truly accountable democratic institutions. To this end, all have been found lacking in providing guarantees for segmental autonomy and minority vetoes, as is evidenced by the dearth of viable federal systems throughout the continent (Ayoade 1978). Yet the current level of tolerance for the emergence of multiparty systems and "reassertion of civil society" (Kunz 1989) in states across the continent indicates that an environment for democratic segmental representation is being created.

With these positive factors in mind, it is possible to develop an appreciation for the significant obstacles that remain. Most fundamentally, the absence of abundant material resources poses a serious limitation to the implementation of consociational agreements. The potential for productive negotiation and comity in the past was clouded by long-standing jealousies and antagonisms originating from egregious social and economic inequalities that represented a holdover from colonial era policies. Because priorities rarely centered on the promotion of national integration, few attempts were made at spreading out the benefits of economic development in an even manner (van den Berghe 1971; Young 1985). Imbalances created by objective demographic factors such as population and geographical dispersion were therefore compounded by differences in religion, education, and access to economic opportunities. Substantial pecuniary investments necessitated by consociational mechanisms were largely outside the capabilities of most states at independence. At present, the scale of outlays in most countries cannot be large and must be managed carefully through attention to proportionality principles.

Even more critical is whether traumatic memories of short-lived experiences with plural democracy in the past will engender a shared sentiment of mutual tolerance and accommodation among segmental elites and their constituent communities. The absence of nonmajoritarian mechanisms in many of the early democratic experiments in Africa was most directly attributable to a fitfully short period of state formation combined with numerous distortions created by the colonial presence. Fears of nationalist agitation led colonial authorities in most states to discourage the meeting of segmental elites in any common national fora (e.g., legislative councils, political parties) until a very late and hurried point in the decolonization process. As a result, a tradition of political accommodation among the leaders of segmental groups was never permitted to develop.

In many states years of struggle over resources and single-minded strategies of domination have created antagonisms that pose severe threats to stability if unleashed in an environment of competitive, majoritarian democracy. Without a vital commitment to moderating the scale of conflict through consensual mechanisms, there is much reason to believe that governance will continue, as Sklar (1986:122) so dismally predicted, to founder "in a rising tide of tears and social despair."

NOTES

1. Objective demographic conditions considered to be broadly favorable to the formation of consociations are the absence of any majority segmental group; rough equivalence in size among segmental groups; small number of segmental groups; socioeconomic equality among segments; geographical concentration of segmental groups; and small population size. More-subjective conditions are a past tradition of accommodation and the existence of an overarching loyalty to the territorial integrity of the national state—a sentiment that has been found to be developed especially through the existence of external political threats (see Lijphart 1977, 1985b).

2. The Hausa word *talakawa* is used to refer to commoners but also has connotations of economic degradation.

3. These figures are taken from Nigeria 1980a, b.

4. As one inside account reveals, "the relationship between the two old politicians [Zik and Awo], was an exercise in mutual deceit" (Omoruyi 1990:210).

5. Past research has indicated that the allegiance to the "idea of democracy" is mixed at best among the Nigerian elite (Beckett & O'Connell 1977).

6. Quoted from "Awolowo Interviewed," *West Africa*, November 21, 1983, p. 2674.

7. See Central Bank of Nigeria, Economic and Financial Review for 1979–1985.

8. In Nigerian politics corruption tends to be regarded as intolerable only when it becomes personalized, and community demands are ignored (see Peil 1976:49; Williams 1987:45–46; Joseph 1987:67).

9. The manner in which this occurred is described in several excellent accounts of the 1983 elections at the local level, see Apter 1987; Olurode 1987; Miles 1988.

10. See Nigeria 1989: ch. 2, sect. 14–22.

11. This form of governance has already entered the discourse of political reform in South Africa from a number of angles (see, e.g., Rotberg & Barrat 1980; Boulle 1984; Lijphart 1985b).

6

Liberalization, Governance, and Political Space in Ghana

Naomi Chazan

The 1980s were a period of kaleidoscopic change in African history. As the beginning of the decade was marked by a debilitating cycle of economic and political crisis and its midpoint by a series of policy readjustments, political liberalization became the prevailing theme at its close. The upheavals of recent years rekindled the interest of both observers and practitioners in basic issues of political authority and political change, while simultaneously evoking a growing dissatisfaction with prevailing approaches to understanding these phenomena. In this context, a wide variety of new analytical tools has been generated, and a great deal of theoretical and conceptual experimentation has taken place.

The recent experience of Ghana furnishes an excellent opportunity to scrutinize some of the components of current debates and to assess their utility. The rise of the populist regime of Jerry Rawlings under the Provisional National Defence Council (PNDC) banner on December 31, 1981, accelerated the political disorder, social tensions, and economic immiseration that already wracked the country. As one astute observer commented, "in any examination of tropical Africa in 1982 . . . it would be absurd not to recognize the collapse of the Ghanaian state" (Hodder-Williams 1984:233). Two years later Ghana was one of the first African countries to accept the conditionalities of the International Monetary Fund (IMF) and to adopt its structural adjustment program. At the end of the decade the PNDC, by then the longest-lasting military government in Ghanaian history, had completed a complex series of district assembly elections as the first stage in a self-proclaimed process of designing a viable mode of civilian rule. Clearly, substantial changes have occurred in Ghana in recent years. What is the nature of this reordering? How has this process taken place and why? What do these alterations mean for understanding patterns of power restructuring and directions of political change? And what are the implications of the Ghanaian case for comprehending similar processes elsewhere?

These questions focus attention on the problem of governance, the core issue of African politics at the beginning of the fourth decade of independence

(Hyden 1988). Governance is defined along the lines suggested by Hyden (1989:2) as the capacity to establish and sustain workable relations between individuals and institutional actors in order to promote collective goals.[1] Implicit in the notion of governance is the assumption that neither the character nor the locus of effective authority in society is preordained (Lofchie 1989). Politics is conceived of in broad terms to encompass both the formal realm of official institutions and practice and the hidden realm of informal power relations. Such an approach provides insights into patterns of reciprocity, co-optation, coercion, and repression associated with the state, as well as modes of societal construction, resistance, and withdrawal (Le Vine 1989:4). The examination of the interaction between these spheres is necessary in order to grasp the real structures of authority in particular contexts (Lomnitz & Lomnitz Adler 1989; Chazan 1987:29).

Governance, consequently, is concerned with uncovering viable regime forms as well as degrees of stateness—the capacity to entrench the authority of the central state and to regularize its relations with society (Marenin 1987:61; Callaghy 1984:32). Stateness is not akin to statism. The former accentuates the authority of the state, the latter its hegemony. Stateness presumes the existence of a modicum of reciprocity and trust, whereas statism emphasizes centralization and domination.[2] Recent Africanist scholarship has pointed to the deleterious effects of the relationship between statism and political enfeeblement. As Richard Sklar (1983:13) put it, "statism, the most general form of coercion, is the graveyard of socialism as well as democracy." In contrast, stateness, it is generally conceded, is essential to governance, because it links the authority of official institutions to the legitimacy and consent of civil society.

In statist frameworks, as Hyden remarks in Chapter 1, the transformation of the relationship between official organs and societal associations requires the legitimation of power and the injection of norms of accountability. In other words, it focuses on the separation of social, economic, and political authority through the delineation and preservation of political spaces. The concept of political space possesses organizational, material, mobilizational, and normative dimensions. At its foundation it involves the emergence of a separate consciousness and sense of purpose derived from the elaboration of a new normative lexicon rooted in basic values of trust and reciprocity.[3] Political spaces are created, occupied, and protected through the molding of autonomous structures based on shared concepts of authority and binding norms that guide the political conduct of members and may pose a challenge to reigning power schemes (Bayart 1986:118–120). They may also be penetrated, contested, or abandoned if they do not maintain a participative mass, a volume of exchanges, and a density of political goods. Although political spaces may multiply, they are limited because, as real or potential structures of action, they are also defined in terms of the political resources, people, and relationships involved.[4]

In the contemporary African environment the establishment of autonomous political spaces is a prerequisite for the emergence of civil society, which itself is a condition for the assertion of stateness and the entrenchment of workable patterns of governance. The formulation of viable rules of the political game at the heart of the concept of regime cannot proceed without the construction and maintenance of these distinctive components of the political terrain.

How do political spaces emerge in authoritarian settings and how are they subsequently preserved? Our purpose here is to explore the changes that have occurred on the Ghanaian political scene through an examination of the creation, the contestation, and the protection of political spaces in the country. The types of constraints limiting institutional, social and individual actors at specific junctures will be identified, the range of choice delimited, and the substance and consequences of specific decisions assessed (Horowitz 1988). On this basis, it will be possible to draw some conclusions about the nature, direction, and process of power transformations in Ghana specifically and to offer some comments on the dynamics of political change in other parts of Africa.

The pattern of political reordering in Ghana in the 1980s followed a particular, disjunctive sequence.[5] By the time of the installation of the government of the Third Republic under Hilla Limann in 1979 a rupture had already occurred between failing state agencies (which had consciously divested themselves of responsibility for the welfare of the bulk of the citizenry) and large segments of the Ghanaian population (Ninsin 1987). The populist phase of the PNDC (1982–1983) not only accentuated the confrontation between state and society but also exacerbated the degree of social fragmentation. The second stage of PNDC rule (1983–1987) witnessed the beginning of the assertion of autonomous spheres of political action both in the official and societal realms. The third PNDC period (since 1987) has coincided with (not always successful) attempts at the reintegration of these overlapping spaces. In Ghana, therefore, a break with the constraints imposed by the postcolonial hegemonic configuration first led to a severe power implosion that then enabled the development of autonomous political spaces and the subsequent effort to revise the rules of the political game in line with more-interactive principles. Changes in circumstances, concerns, and priorities therefore had an important bearing on the nature and outcome of political transformation in the country.

The process of political restructuring was the result of a series of piecemeal, at times seemingly contradictory, adjustments. Individuals, groups, and government leaders constantly altered their course of action in light of specific events and conditions in other sectors. The absence of a grand design contributed to the vacillations that characterized this period in Ghanaian history; it also permitted the development of a measure of responsiveness heretofore absent on the Ghanaian political scene.

The outcome and meaning of these initiatives is still unclear. Superficially, the changes that Ghana is undergoing resemble former attempts at the retrenchment of ruling coalitions (this time through the civilianization of the military) and the reassertion of hegemonic forms of domination. At the same time rural-urban terms of trade have been reversed, new elites independent of the state have emerged, and the political logic of former periods may no longer obtain. The fluid relationship between political actors is still being clarified.

The explanation for this dynamic rests in the conjuncture of a complex set of factors. Ethnic, cultural, demographic, economic, and historical variables, as well as external forces, play a role. So do the composition, interests, and concerns of key social groups. The Ghanaian experience, however, underlines the importance of immediate political conditions in delineating the range of political choice. Particular political events precipitated changes that altered the balance of power in the country and directly affected the selection of specific political measures.[6]

The main contention of this exploration is that in Ghana, the conditional employment of the exit option by many individuals as a form of boycott of official policies has worked to reinforce the importance of political voice (Hirschman 1970:33, 167) because the emergence of disconnected political spaces hastened the search for an overarching concept of the general interest.[7] The convergence of long-term processes of socioeconomic transformation and short-term responses to existing realities has made the state a more integral part of politics in Ghana. At the same time Ghanaians, through their various activities, are joining to put the state in its place (Chazan 1987:3). A spatial, interactive model of governance may yet replace the hegemonic schemes of the immediate postcolonial generation.

THE DEMISE OF HEGEMONIC STRUCTURES

Embryonic political spaces existed in Ghana since the imposition of colonial rule in the country.[8] The British system of indirect government nurtured a fragmented form of social control that relied on the status and power of local patrons (Migdal 1988:141). The anticolonial struggle challenged the legitimacy of the colonial state and its rooting in indigenous law without creating substitute bases of legitimacy or altering the patronage foundation of the power apparatus (Crook 1987). Successive Ghanaian governments attempted to fortify state institutions and to establish central authority. The quest for state supremacy,[9] pursued by different means, resulted in the creation of an organization of domination controlled by elites who derived their power from their proximity to the state and competed for authority with other groups in society.[10] The competition between state institutions and other social forces was expedited in Ghana by frequent regime changes and by a regressive pattern of central power deflation.

Statist orientations began to develop in Ghana immediately after independence. In order to consolidate his position and deflect criticism, Kwame Nkrumah curtailed opposition, reinforced his Convention People's Party (CPP), and used the administrative apparatus as a means of compensating regime loyalists. A dualistic, political and administrative, model of decisionmaking emerged that enhanced the position of state functionaries while undermining the rational norms of bureaucratic organization (Amonoo 1981). The rapid and costly expansion of the state apparatus, coupled with inefficiency and mismanagement, led to a deterioration in Ghana's standing in the international donor community and to growing economic malaise. Key ethnic and professional groups voiced their discontent through the rejection of Nkrumah's brand of African socialism and, increasingly, through noncooperation with government authorities. The combination of hegemonic rule on the one hand and social resistance on the other hand was established during this period.

The policies of successive governments reinforced and exacerbated this pattern. The National Liberation Council (NLC), which ousted Nkrumah in 1966, oversaw the return to civilian rule in 1969. The leadership of the Second Republic was composed of professional and rural Akan elites who had constituted the main opposition to the CPP's ruling coalition composed of youthful urban residents and minority ethnic groups. The Progress Party of Prime Minister K. A. Busia, although committed to democratic norms (Busia 1967), nevertheless possessed an elitist aura and was embedded in one ethnic faction of Ghanaian society. It proved incapable of either significantly ameliorating economic conditions or reducing growing regional and social disparities.

On January 13, 1972, the army intervened once again. The second period of military overrule under the leadership of I. K. Acheampong (1972–1978) was associated with the systematic abuse of the state for personal gain, the further deterioration of the economy, external neglect, the alienation of large portions of the population, the relinquishment by the state of responsibility for social welfare, and increasing state fragility (Oquaye 1980; Chazan 1983).

Ghana was pummeled by a series of political upheavals in the late 1970s. In the summer of 1978 Acheampong's Supreme Military Council (SMC) was ousted by Fred Akuffo, who, at the head of SMC II, surrendered to the demand to restore civilian government. On June 4, 1979, several weeks prior to the scheduled elections, a radical group of young soldiers headed by Flight Lieutenant Rawlings ousted the Akuffo government in a particularly violent coup (Okeke 1982; Awonoor 1984). The Armed Forces Revolutionary Council (AFRC) conducted a punitive campaign against the bureaucratic and military establishment and called for greater probity in public life. The turbulence wrought by the first Rawlings intervention interrupted, but did not halt, the installation of an elected civilian government dominated by a northern coalition headed by Limann.

The leaders of the Third Republic, however, were handicapped not only by an economic morass of monumental proportions, governmental institutions in disrepair, and a public suspicious of all government, but also by the ongoing presence of Rawlings, who continued to monitor their every move from the political sidelines. The civilian regime attempted to reinstate elite responsibility and adherence to the rule of law, but the patronage systems it revived served only to highlight social inequities, increase competition in leadership circles, and magnify the gap between state and society.

On December 31, 1981, Jerry Rawlings carried out his threat to intervene once again in the political arena if the Third Republic did not meet his expectations. By the time of the second Rawlings takeover Ghana was enveloped in a multifaceted crisis of governance. State agencies, misused by a series of weak and capricious leaders, by overbloated bureaucratic structures, by avaricious and contentious elites, and by a variety of parochial interests, had lost much of their capacity to formulate and execute policy. Many individuals and social groups had effectively abandoned the formal arena and renounced its extractive and instrumental norms. The economy, too, was on the verge of collapse: production rates were substantially below 1970 averages; agricultural output was stagnant; alarming shortages were recorded in basic commodities; the debt burden had increased; and foreign investment had ground to a standstill (Rothchild & Gyimah-Boadi 1986). The confrontation between a detached (albeit hardly autonomous), exploitative, and porous official apparatus and a fractured and withdrawn society had peaked.

This situation imposed severe constraints on all political actors and drastically limited their range of choice. Both military and civilian leaders had been discredited. Political instability was endemic, and the severity of the crisis could not be exaggerated. These conditions evoked divergent reactions from the new rulers and from heterogeneous social groups.

The PNDC came to power on a wave of popular protest that rejected the totality of previous regime directions and favored the pursuit of radical alternatives. The "Rawlings Revolution" was, in the eyes of its designer, first and foremost a political undertaking (Ray 1986:17–25). Confirmed in his belief that "Ghana may not be that rich but she is the political light of Africa" (Rawlings n.d.:2), Rawlings defined the PNDC's goal as the rearrangement of the foundations of Ghanaian politics through the transformation of the relationship between rulers and ruled, between the haves and the have-nots, between state and society. The creation of a new social order and a just political system was seen as an end in itself (Jeffries 1982).

The Ghanaian brand of populism introduced by the PNDC at its inception advocated moral reform through the eradication of the oppressive institutions and practices associated with elite privilege and popular exclusion from public affairs. People's power, in the eyes of the ideologues of the first phase of the Rawlings era, translated into mass involvement in overseeing the affairs of the economy and the society. Direct democracy and social justice were viewed as mutually reinforcing (Pellow & Chazan 1986:78–79). While rejecting liberal models of democratic government as neocolonialist and unsuited to Ghanaian conditions, Rawlings underlined the principles of reciprocity, accountability, and national independence. The promise of a "new" democracy and the allied concern with implementing direct mass engagement in public affairs were not, however, accompanied by a coherent exposition of goals and objectives (Ninsin & Drah 1987). The PNDC's initial populism advocated rebellion and reform, and highlighted a concern with the values and conduct of Ghanaians, but did not contain a constructive blueprint for their realization (Kilson 1987:50–51).

In early 1981 Rawlings set out to implement his moral crusade without establishing any firm priorities or precise deadlines. This task was eased somewhat by the fact that the PNDC was beholden neither to the military nor to the dominant civilian establishment in the country (the coup that brought it to power was an act of rebellion against both senior officers and ruling elites). By striking out against all former political leaders, the December 31 takeover challenged the entire structure of power distribution in the country since independence. At least at the outset, the PNDC was more bound to its own vision than to the interests of any organized sector of the Ghanaian population. Moreover, the campaign it conducted against elite groups during its first year in office further weakened the power of state-linked social strata (Yeebo 1985). The PNDC could thus rely on the support of the previously dispossessed without having to compromise its populist program to placate any particular pressure group.

To augment participation, the PNDC (which from its inception included civilians) established an entire network of popular institutions including people's and workers' defense committees (PDCs and WDCs), public tribunals, investigative bodies, mobilization squads, and monitoring bodies (National Defence Committee n.d.). The PNDC also strengthened a series of supportive movements, including the New Democratic Movement, the June Fourth Movement, and the Kwame Nkrumah Revolutionary Guards. A new form of institutional dualism emerged as popular institutions were designed to coexist with rather than displace established ministries, corporations, and government agencies, which, unlike the situation during the Nkrumah period, were expected to operate in accordance with bureaucratic norms (Bing 1984; Ghana 1982).

The PNDC used new organizations to carry out a campaign against what it considered to be the enemies of the revolution. These included former government officials as well as traders, professionals, and entrepreneurs. The techniques employed in this connection were particularly repressive: killings, incarcerations, public beatings, and summary trials were commonplace (Gyimah-Boadi & Rothchild 1982). Popular organs were also mobilized to implement portions of the PNDC's initial economic policy, which included campaigns to evacuate cocoa from the countryside, monitor the enforcement of price controls, and enforce sanitation regulations in the urban areas (Ahiakpor 1985). The net effect of these efforts was to wreak havoc in what was already a chaotic situation. Social relations inevitably deteriorated. Professionals, religious leaders, university lecturers, lawyers, market women, senior civil servants, army officers, and ex-politicians were either persecuted or ridiculed. Those skilled personnel who escaped the officially sanctioned witch-hunt emigrated in droves. By the beginning of 1983 Ghana was depleted of most of its educated class (Rado 1986:563). Moreover, the radical rhetoric of PNDC ideologues repelled potential donors and further weakened Ghana's bargaining posture in the international arena. Conditions in the country were nothing short of disastrous. Food was often unavailable, infant mortality rose, per capita income declined, social services broke down, the road system become impassable, and daily life became simply miserable (UNICEF n.d.). By destroying the social backbone of the state apparatus and emasculating administrative structures, the original PNDC may have succeeded in eradicating some of the sources of official abuse; it also undermined the autonomy of public institutions and eliminated social mediations. As a result, official power became embedded in a very narrow—radical-military-urban—segment of the Ghanaian social order.

The reactions of most people to the revolutionary zeal of the first phase of PNDC rule was to withdraw as much as possible from the reach of government. The aim of this disengagement was twofold: to establish a barrier between individuals and unpredictable regime agents; and to ensure a modicum of survival in conditions of immense adversity. Unlike previous informal activities, societal adaptations to the constraints of the early 1980s in Ghana were not merely a continuation of past patterns or a response to the withdrawal of official services (Herbst 1990), they were also concrete attempts to fulfil basic needs in the face of enormous exigencies.

The widespread employment of survival strategies at this juncture was thus directly related to scarcity, to the absence of basic commodities, to impeded access, to the futility of the quest for influence on formal institutions (Lomnitz 1988:6–9). Its proliferation was accelerated by the stringent level of controls imposed by the PNDC in its attempt to regulate the flow of goods. Four major coping techniques were honed to deal with the situation (Azarya & Chazan 1987). The first involved suffering and finding ways of managing, of accommodating to reduced circumstances. Arbitrary laws were ignored and others flouted. Silent means were used to resist perceived exploitation (Crisp 1984:5–6). A second mechanism revolved around the burgeoning informal sector. The elaborate (and explicitly illegal) parallel market became the most important funnel for the distribution of goods and a significant setting for petty manufacturing and small-scale agricultural production. Heavily organized, the informal sector developed norms of interchange that were carefully enforced by popularly backed arbiters (Robertson 1983; Clark 1988). A third survival strategy consisted of self-encapsulation, primarily in the rural areas, which included a shift from export to food cropping and self-provisioning on a broad scale (Posnansky 1984). And finally, some individuals turned to emigration as a mode of survival, with some 2 million people exiting the country at the turn of the decade (Brydon 1985).

These activities were conducted by a variety of social groups, some of which dated back to the precolonial and colonial periods; others were relatively new constructs. These consisted of primary associations (households, villages, kinship groups, and local development societies); occupational groups (traders, teachers, farmers); youth and women's organizations; and religious communities. And while some associations had a clear ethnic foundation, most groups highlighted functional concerns, partially because of the centrality of survival issues and partially because broad ethnic identities could not furnish organized answers to concrete problems. Evolving social networks did, however, provide alternative frameworks for local communal identification, placing a premium on friendship and personal ties. They also served as vehicles for the expression of alienation from the existing political order and as breeding grounds for the construction of alternative value systems (Agyeman-Duah 1987:620). On a small and disparate scale, new rules of social interaction were enunciated.

The outcome of the refinement of coping mechanisms was to expand the scope of the political sphere outside the official realm and to assert its importance in the daily lives of Ghanaians. These activities (which included the fortification of communal adjudication systems, the establishment of neighborhood patrol groups to ensure safety, and the development of enforcement devices in the markets) served to further constrict the penetrative capacities of state institutions and to create de facto pockets of rebellion against official repression (Le Vine 1989:4–9). Survival strategies, however, remained a necessity, a mode of fending that carried the kernel—although hardly the organizational and material attributes or scope—conducive to the emergence of autonomous political spaces.

The decisions and actions of official leaders and social groups in Ghana in the first period of PNDC rule diverged. Formal policies served to solidify the rupture between enfeebled state organs and most social groups, whereas survival strategies magnified the fragmentation of civil society. The shrinkage of the formal political arena and the social enclosure that ensued created a power vacuum at the center and set in motion a process of power dispersion. The demise of hegemonic structures was not, however, accompanied by the concomitant assertion of independent political spaces. Indeed, the key characteristic of this period in Ghanaian history was the lack of autonomy of political structures and their collapse into socially embedded parochial networks.[11]

In Ghana, however, the dismemberment of the official realm contained the potential for a more significant reorientation (Robotham 1988:25). The new rulers of Ghana differed qualitatively from their predecessors; their insulation from previous elites enhanced, at least temporarily, their own cohesion and room for maneuvering. Moreover, despite the failing economy, the centrality of the political project was continuously underlined. While this emphasis prompted the formation of vying factions in the short term, it also focused attention on issues of political authority and legitimacy in the long run.[12] The ability to rearrange priorities and to explore the latent possibilities ingrained in these openings was the challenge facing social and institutional actors eighteen months after Rawlings's second coming.

THE CREATION OF POLITICAL SPACES

The calamitous conditions engulfing Ghana in 1983 were compounded by the onset of a serious drought and by the January expulsion of over a million Ghanaian citizens from Nigeria. The feasibility of the escape option was consequently circumscribed, redirecting attention to the design of strategies on the domestic front. In addition, the PNDC's position was assailed by a series of coup attempts, rendering its leaders not only vulnerable but also particularly sensitive to public currents. Clearly a substantive reevaluation was in order.

The problems facing the PNDC were manifold: it had to revive failing public institutions, restore a semblance of control over the economy, and restructure the basis of its relationship with disenchanted social groups (Chazan 1988a:14). Its success depended not only on its ability to augment its resources and to reinstate a degree of autonomy but also on its capacity to inject specific contents into its radical worldview. The process of moving from protest to reconstruction required the delineation of priorities and the formulation of specific guidelines for their realization. The tone was set in a statement by Rawlings in which the prior emphasis on direct action was buttressed by a stress on hard work. "Fellow citizens, production and efficiency must be our watchwords. Populist nonsense must give way to popular sense" (Rawlings 1983:10). Participation was thus equated with responsibility as well as accountability.

The essence of the PNDC's decisions in 1983 (which paved the way for the second phase of its rule) was to separate economic from political concerns and to concentrate first on the amelioration of economic conditions. The new economic policy revolved around the PNDC's decision to accept the conditionalities imposed by the IMF and the World Bank and to adopt an economic recovery program (ERP) based on market principles (Jonah 1987). The ERP consisted of a stabilization regimen—including a massive devaluation, budgetary streamlining, the removal of subsidies, and increased prices to producers (Ghana 1983a, b)—and a structural adjustment program (which entailed the divestment of unprofitable state corporations and the streamlining of the civil service). On the political level a National Commission for Democracy (NCD), headed by Justice D. F. Annan, was established and charged with the task of designing a "true" (as distinct from "new") democracy, based on Ghanaian "tradition, history and culture" (Ghana n.d.b:10). With the creation of the NCD the political agenda shifted from action to thought, whereas economic activities gathered momentum.

The setting of these regime priorities was undoubtedly triggered by the severity of the crisis, expedited by the extent of the shredding of the fabric of political life in the country (Callaghy 1990), and facilitated by the separation of the regime from powerful social groups, by the weakness of its opponents (Rothchild & Gyimah-Boadi 1989:243), and by Rawlings's ability to distance himself from the radical components of the initial PNDC. It is doubtful, however, that this reorientation constituted a complete turnabout in regime outlooks. The decision to stress certain concerns at the expense of others is best understood as a reasonable strategic response to prevailing conditions and pressures from below (Robotham 1988:14). If anything, Rawlings's reformulated emphases highlighted the conceptual ambiguity inherent in the PNDC's early populist proclamations and the need to move beyond generalizations to the specification of concrete goals. In this process, the experimental, piecemeal nature of regime strategies was accentuated.

The move away from direct democracy necessitated an institutional restructuring. By late 1983 all the original members of the PNDC except Rawlings had been replaced. The new PNDC consisted of the heads of the major structures of government. With the addition of the coordinating secretary, (Prime Minister) P. V. Obeng, to the PNDC in July 1985, a measure of harmony was achieved between the political and administrative wings of the executive (EIU 1987:5). In conjunction, the network of popular organizations was revamped. The National Defence Committee was dismantled, and the PDCs and WDCs reorganized as Committees for the Defence of the Revolution (CDRs). Members of all classes were invited to participate in their activities (Committee for the Defence of the Revolution 1986). The purpose of the National Mobilisation Programme, originally set up to assist in the absorption of Ghanaians expelled from Nigeria, was changed, and its local auxiliaries (titled Mobilsquads) were directed to assist in community development efforts (Mikell 1989). At the same time some parastatals were closed and others were drastically reorganized. More significantly, the centrality of the bureaucracy and the courts was reaffirmed, and a campaign was launched to attract skilled Ghanaians residing abroad back to the country.

The outcome of this restructuring was to rationalize, at least to some extent, the organization of the regime. First, the distinction between civilian and military leaders was blurred.[13] Second, administrative and political elites were merged, thus linking, "through multiple office-holding, the major institutions of government" (Crook 1989:213). Third, political institutions were separated more clearly from administrative organs, and the balance between the two rectified. Fourth, key bureaucrats were protected from political pressure and their position stabilized (this was especially true of the economic team headed by Finance Secretary Kwesi Botchwey). And fifth, a premium was placed on technocratic skills and on adherence to the bureaucratic norms of efficiency and discipline (Dunn 1986). A degree of order was imposed on the state apparatus at the same time as it was placed more firmly under PNDC control.

The most visible regime activities during PNDC II were directed toward economic rehabilitation. The government scrupulously adhered to its economic plan and in return received significant capital injections from abroad. By 1985 economic indicators showed some improvement. The gross domestic product had increased by 13 percent, inflation was reduced to 20 percent, exports had risen by 76 percent, the transportation system was being repaired, and government expenditures were down. More to the point, goods were available in the market, food was plentiful, and even though income disparities grew, the PNDC had begun to turn around the economy (World Bank 1986; Ewusi 1986).

Achievements in the political arena were far more ambiguous. While populist rhetoric persisted, the defense committees lacked clear guidelines and failed to become rallying points for popular participation (Agyeman-Duah 1987:641). Plans for the decentralization of administrative authority and decisionmaking responsibilities did not proceed beyond the dissemination of written documents (Ghana n.d.a.). And the NCD devoted more attention to redrawing electoral districts than to elaborating a new model of civilian rule. In fact, when asked when Ghanaians could expect to elect a government, Justice Annan stated that "the time-frame will be determined by the speed with which Ghanaians come to realize the meaning of democracy" (*West Africa*, October 27, 1986:2255, as quoted in Agyeman-Duah 1987:622).

PNDC moves, economic accomplishments notwithstanding, continued to be greeted with large doses of skepticism. The main beneficiaries of the new economic measures were the rural dwellers. A reversal of the urban-rural terms of trade favored the population in the countryside at the expense of the residents of the main cities (Callaghy 1990), and the pattern of rural exodus that had prevailed since the colonial period was halted (Ghana 1984). But middle-class urban groups, still smarting from the indignities suffered after the 1981 takeover and resentful of the influx of expatriates in the form of IMF and World Bank consultants, did not hasten to cooperate with the government. They were joined by the trade unions and the students, who in a series of strikes began to express their explicit opposition to regime policies. The National Union of Ghanaian Students (NUGS), as in the past, became the mouthpiece of regime opponents, demanding full democratization and cautioning against the reappearance of instances of official abuse. The Ghana Trade Union Congress (TUC) made demands for wage adjustments, which were picked up even more forcefully by individual unions. Perhaps most significantly, the radical groups that had formerly constituted the backbone of the PNDC withdrew their support, accusing Rawlings of betraying the revolution. As the restructured PNDC coalesced, the ideological argument between left and right was revived with intensity.[14]

The disorder that marked PNDC I was replaced under PNDC II by a calmer, if hardly more equitable, political climate. At the same time signs of official corruption and malpractice reappeared. A "culture of silence" had set in, one that left the people aloof from government, and the vision of popular democracy more remote than in the past. Thus, structural adjustment at this juncture was not accompanied by any significant movement toward political reform.

The meaning of these changes cannot be overestimated. Regardless of appearances, the shifts that took place under PNDC II were neither a retreat from radical positions nor a return to hegemonic patterns. Rather, they reflected a subtle molding of a distinctive political space at the state level. The normative objectives of the government had been fleshed out. The reorganization of official agencies promoted a heretofore absent structural independence while simultaneously reducing the size of the state apparatus. The role of the state in Ghanaian society was redefined as privatization, subsidy withdrawals, and cost recovery programs narrowed the spheres of official intervention (Jonah 1989:51). The resource base of the state was augmented, not insignificantly, by the injection of foreign capital. And the mobilizational scope of the state was, at least potentially, broadened with the apparent shift from urban to rural support bases (Gyimah-Boadi 1989).[15] By 1987 the Ghanaian state was far more autonomous and far less intrusive than it had been in the past.

Developments at the state level between 1983 and 1987 had important repercussions for social relations. In Ghana, as elsewhere, precisely because formal government structures were initially enfeebled, and when reorganized their penetrative capacities were curtailed, more room was available for the elaboration of associational life (Bratton 1989a). The network of occupational, service, local community, and religious organizations expanded substantially during this period (Jonah 1989:34). At the same time, the wariness of central government that existed before was perpetuated. The social developments that took place in the first half of the 1980s stressed norms of reciprocity, leadership responsibility, and accountability, while acknowledging the need for watchfulness based on a not inconsiderable measure of suspicion and cynicism (Callaghy 1987). Both self-awareness and silence were nurtured in these settings.

Interactions during this period concentrated heavily on the rapidly expanding informal sector. Economic activities in this sphere included the development of microindustries and small manufacturing cooperatives, the expansion of local markets, shifts in patterns of agricultural production, and the creation of new distribution networks (Daddieh 1987). By the mid-1980s it was estimated that the informal sector accounted for fully 85 percent of employment in the country (Jonah 1989:15). Concurrently, certain social services were taken over by voluntary organizations, including sanitation, housing, and major aspects of health and education. A different breed of elites emerged as a result. These entrepreneurs were not, like many of their predecessors, either associated with the state or dependent on its resources. New avenues of accumulation and class formation developed, leading to the emergence of a group of "nouveau riche" Ghanaians who flourished at the expense of salaried employees (Jonah 1989:15–19).[16] Despite the social inequalities that emerged in the informal sector, in many respects, as Richard Sklar (1987) has indicated, the enlargement of local economic activities was, by virtue of the cooperative decisionmaking involved, in itself a political act of democratic assertion.

The variety evident in the informal sector pointed to an important restructuring of social life. While specific groups carved out their own spheres of independent action and began to amass their own resources, they also encouraged the development of wider communication networks based on lateral transactions. Thus, to establish an effective distribution system, it became necessary to spell out relations between producers, food contractors, transporters, traders, and potential clients (Clark 1984). The development of new forms of pluralism thus led to a greater degree of societal interlocking. Patterns of social interaction coalesced separately from the state but, while neither ignoring its presence nor rejecting its significance, disputed the centrality of its authority (Chazan & Rothchild 1989).

In the social (as in the official) realm distinct political spaces surfaced in Ghana during the course of the 1980s. The entrenchment of social organizations, coupled with the growth of autonomous accumulation channels and the concomitant crystallization of member identification with group objectives, resulted in the shaping of separate economic, social, and political niches bound by explicit rules and culturally prescribed values (trading networks and revivalist cults provide but two, divergent examples). The ideologies that developed in these settings did not coincide with official tenets. They were not, however, necessarily in open confrontation.[17] As straddling became the norm, the emergence of discrete political spaces reasserted the state in innovative ways. The expansion of the informal bolstered the formal. To be sure, the fortification of social organizations and the prevalence of cultural diversity did serve notice that politics did not coincide with state structures and that official monopolies would no longer be entertained. At the same time, however, the boundaries of the state were recognized and internalized. The employment of modified exit options thus came together with the enhancement of new forms of engagement in the state orbit.

A process of political redistribution took place in Ghana in the mid-1980s. Government structures and social groups established their own independent organizational and material networks and consciously endowed them with meaning. The operational range of the state and of other social associations differed qualitatively from the hegemonic patterns of early independence and from the constrained possibilities that existed when political structures became embedded in social segments at the beginning of the decade.[18]

The result of these processes was twofold. First, since the possibility of exploring options beyond the borders of Ghana diminished, its geographic framework was recognized as the arena of political action. Both social groups—from professional associations to farmers' cooperatives—and formal institutions coalesced on a countrywide basis. Somewhat counterintuitively, the freedom from the state in Ghana reaffirmed the freedom to determine its character (cf. Hyden 1989:7). Second, and simultaneously, the recreation of a measure of stateness was not accompanied by the development of binding norms of governance. The political spaces that emerged at this juncture, albeit not always openly antagonistic, were in fact too separate. No adequate means were designed to regularize political relations, and no integrating formula was articulated. Growing disparities within and between the various spheres and the lack of elite cohesion in each of these settings highlighted the absence of mediations. The emergence of fortified political fragments did not, at this stage, promote greater interaction. If in the first years of PNDC rule political structures became too embedded, at the end of the second PNDC phase these distinct structures had become overly autonomous.

THE PROTECTION OF POLITICAL SPACES

The dilemmas facing Ghanaians in 1987 were different than those they had confronted five years earlier. Economic liberalization, far from increasing popular involvement in government, actually exacerbated social cleavages and delayed political reform. Income inequalities fueled a new wave of discontent, and the PNDC found it increasingly difficult to explain that without its economic initiatives the situation would be substantially worse (Callaghy 1990). The growing autonomy of the state had not been translated into a greater capacity to manage social relations. The problem of legitimacy loomed large as the decade drew to a close.

In 1987 the PNDC, increasingly preoccupied with the negative ramifications of the social inequities that had surfaced during the implementation of the structural adjustment program and by growing disaffection in urban quarters, decided once again to reassess its path. A third phase of political reordering ensued, one in which the government attempted to gain control of political spaces by correlating its populist notion of people's power with participation in formal institutions.

The adjustment of priorities at this juncture involved the reinstatement of political concerns on a par with economic ones and the establishment of a more direct linkage between political and social issues. This adaptation was articulated in two major instruments promulgated on July 1, 1987. The first, the National Programme for Economic Development (Ghana 1987b) established targets for economic growth in the post-ERP era. Besides detailing production goals, the new plan underlined the importance of promoting the human face of structural adjustment. It suggested that "sustained work at both economic and political levels will be required" (Ghana 1987b:21).

The second document dealt specifically with the PNDC's political program. Faced with the need to capitalize on rural support without giving urban opposition an effective outlet for mobilization (Callaghy 1990), the government decided to begin the process of political reform by conducting local elections. The limitations of the period of "true" democracy were identified, and a new phase of "real" democracy, involving a shift from theorizing about politics to legislating new political institutions, was launched. The declared purpose of the District Assembly elections was to "democratize state power and advance participatory democracy and collective decision-making at the grassroots" (Ghana 1987a:1). The district assemblies were presented as "the bodies exercising state power as the people's local government" and "an important step in the PNDC's programme of evolving national political authority through democratic processes" (Ghana 1987a:1–2). The procedures set forth in what has come to be known as the Blue Book delineated means for ongoing participation at the district level and included specific provisions for monitoring, recalling, and periodically rejuvenating local leadership (Ayee 1988).

The 1987 reorientation constituted another example of the piecemeal nature of Ghanaian policymaking during the Rawlings tenure. Once again, the regime exhibited a sensitivity to the implications of unfolding conditions for its own standing, and engaged in a substantive reconsideration to maintain its position. At this turning point legitimacy needs demanded a more concerted effort at civilianization (Austin 1985:101). The flexibility inherent in the PNDC approach did possess a degree of constancy. Its bottom-up approach, expressed through a purported commitment to meeting the needs of ordinary Ghanaians (and thereby, not coincidentally, ensuring its own durability), continued to dictate vacillations in regime strategy.

Preparations for the local elections, which included a prolonged voter registration exercise and the delimitation of electoral districts, took over eighteen months. During this period some of the adverse effects of structural adjustment became more apparent (the growing debt burden, gross income discrepancies, rising prices). At the same time the government enjoyed some respite as external investments increased and credit lines were extended. The political atmosphere, however, did not improve. The PNDC continued to employ repressive measures, violate human rights, and curtail freedom of speech and assembly. The election exercise was hardly conducted in a democratic climate.

In December 1988 the first series of elections was held in the Ashanti, Western, Eastern, and Central regions (designated as Zone I of three electoral zones). The last round of balloting was completed on February 28, 1989. The final results indicated a record number of candidates standing for office (12,842) and, for Ghana, an extraordinarily high turnout of 58.9 percent (T-Vieta, 1989:510–511).[19] Not insignificantly, participation rates were substantially higher in the remote Upper East and Upper West regions (62 and 67 percent respectively) than in the Greater Accra region (44.3 percent), Kumasi (45 percent), or Legon (11 percent). Many urban associations rejected the government's program, claiming that its objective, far from being an initial building block toward true democracy in Ghana, was in fact a sophisticated technique to restore state hegemony. These groups, whose appeal gathered momentum in 1990, called for a comprehensive transition to full constitutional government (Mensah 1989). Thus, the district assembly elections, while verifying the rural support base of the PNDC, accentuated the extent of urban disaffection and highlighted the regime's inability to penetrate into the political spaces carved out by informal structures in the cities.

The local elections may have contributed to stabilizing PNDC rule. They did not, however, supply an adequate response either to the regime's need to attract backing in the urban areas or, more vitally, to the problems of state legitimacy and regime authority that induced the transition to PNDC III. The challenge of "how to respond further to the democratic desires of politically alert citizens" (Agyeman-Duah 1987:642) remained unanswered. Rawlings was clearly aware of the problem. On the tenth anniversary of the June 4 intervention, he asked Ghanaians to make accountability an "irrevocable, nonnegotiable policy of Ghana" (Ephson 1989:952). But Rawlings's willingness to subject his regime to the type of scrutiny he imposed on his predecessors could not prevent a rising demand for a more formal political liberalization. At the end of the decade the dominant mood in the country was one of impatience with populist and local substitutes for real and meaningful democratization (Robotham 1988:33). People are "waiting for populist spectacles to be replaced with the structures and substance of democracy" (Bentsi-Enchill 1989:953). The publication in early 1991 of the NCD's proposals for a return to civilian rule did little to reduce these demands (National Commission for Democracy 1991).

The third phase of PNDC rule has been marked, to date, by an unfulfilled regime quest to gain control of political spaces by forming institutionalized channels of participation. Such a task cannot be accomplished through rituals that merely prop up regime dominance and recall the statist tendencies of yesteryear. It entails both the coordination of the heterogeneous network of diverse authority locations through the establishment of regular mechanisms of interaction between existing political spaces and the formulation of mutually acceptable rules of the political game. Autonomous political groups (from students and trade unions to traders and political associations), by openly demonstrating their resistance in speech and action to what they view as statist designs, have suggested that the affirmation of stateness could further governance only if the definition of political liberalization is equated with power deconcentration and if the formalization of reciprocal arrangements is pursued more systematically. Whether the PNDC can meet this challenge is still unclear; what is not debatable is that integrative bodies cannot be established in Ghana without recognition of political spaces and accommodation to their structures (Sklar 1987).

DEMOCRATIZATION AND GOVERNANCE: SOME IMPLICATIONS

Ghanaian politics underwent a process of transformation in the course of the 1980s. Shifts in regime policies were but a superficial display of a more fundamental process of power restructuring. From a condition of severe power deflation and pervasive political enfeeblement, some political spaces were constructed simultaneously on the official and social levels (Chazan 1988b). Current debates over the substance and form of political liberalization are reflective of efforts to design an overarching scheme for effective interchange.

Political reordering in Ghana took place through a process of power disaggregation and subsequent reconstruction. State decay paved the way for the creation of autonomous social niches and for the rehabilitation of state agencies. The formation of political spaces involved the development of organizational independence, resource control, membership commitment, and a separate consciousness derived from an awareness of shared experiences and common interests. These attributes were consolidated through a series of periodic adjustments in response to immediate economic and political circumstances. The cumulative effect of these decisions was to imply that political life in Ghana was moving in more-coherent directions, in part because other alternatives had been foreclosed.

The nature of the emergent political design was more spatial than vertical. The dispersion of power locations and the creation of political niches with a significant human mass, a density of goods, and a growing volume of activity, required a new kind of political architecture, one that respected political spaces and sought innovative ways to bring them together. Such a formula has not yet surfaced in contemporary Ghana; what is nevertheless apparent is that the organization of political structures in the country today differs from that which prevailed at the beginning of the decade.

The Ghanaian experience has an important bearing on current debates about the capabilities of African states. The most significant feature distinguishing the Ghanaian state in the 1980s from the state in the preceding twenty years is its enhanced ability to implement its policies. This capacity is partially a result of the particular pattern of reorganization of decisionmaking structures that took place in the country. In Ghana, far from protecting the bureaucracy from political pressures, the tendency has been, at least on a declaratory level, to subject official agencies to ongoing political scrutiny. This process was made possible by the reduction of competition in ruling circles through the achievement of a modicum of leadership cohesion. In Ghana this coalescence was a consequence of the discreditation of postcolonial ruling groups; in other countries the same objective may be achieved through centralization (Allen, 1986).

Some lessons may also be drawn from the dynamics of state empowerment in Ghana. During the course of the 1980s Ghanaian officials used foreign capital to tie the state more integrally to the agricultural base of the domestic economy. The dependence of the state on urban interests diminished, allowing political leaders a latitude not enjoyed by their predecessors. Economic liberalization, however, as Hyden suggests in Chapter 1, while sharpening political sensitivities, did not provide guarantees for orderly political change. Indeed, the case of Ghana verifies Hyden's assertion that economic improvement is an insufficient precondition for the assertion of legitimate authority. Political decisions, based on a revised political logic, rather than solely economic ones, clearly played a role (Bratton 1989b:570).

The Ghanaian experience raises important questions about issues of governance that lie at the center of these processes. In Ghana fortification of official capabilities came together with the molding of autonomous spaces. At first, state centrism in Ghana encouraged state weakness precisely because it fueled a grassroots determination to avoid the domain of formal politics. The deleterious cycle of hegemonic repression and societal resistance was attenuated only with the creation of more-autonomous spheres of social action (cf. Fatton 1988:3). The subsequent emergence of new entrepreneurial elites set in motion innovative patterns of social stratification and highlighted class cleavages (Konings 1986). In the Ghanaian example, therefore, efficient governance appears to be a function of the reduction of state dominance and the growth of vibrant spaces that constitute a crucial sign of political engagement.

Finally, the incomplete nature of political reordering in Ghana highlights the centrality of political ideas in the restructuring of political relationships. The absence of a clear conceptualization of the general interest and its authority corollaries prevented the formulation of an alternative set of rules governing political transactions. More to the point, it exacerbated the debate between differing symbolic systems and impeded the coalescence of a common consciousness (Migdal 1988:80). Informal norms of political conduct could not act as a substitute for a lucid delineation of shared values. In this context, therefore, future political developments remain unpredictable, since the rules underlying governance have yet to be explicated.

Political transformation in Ghana has thus involved changes on the societal as well as on the state level. Analyses rooted in only one of these perspectives furnish decidedly partial explanations of political dynamics in the country. By combining insights derived from these two approaches, it is possible to illuminate political processes, better uncover political trends in specific countries, and pinpoint some of the spatial requirements necessary for the development of viable patterns of governance.

The Ghanaian pattern of political reconfiguration relates profound processes of reordering to the creation and attempted consolidation of political spaces. While the Ghanaian model confirms the integral connection between improved governance and the consolidation and preservation of autonomous political networks, similar developments in other statist frameworks in Africa and elsewhere have not necessarily followed the same course or yielded similar results. The understanding of the pace and outcome of contemporary political liberalization experiments may, however, benefit from the insights gleaned from the Ghanaian experience and from the tools honed to grasp its complexities. The diverse forms of stateness and the multiple rules of governance being negotiated in many parts of the world today may better be grasped through a systematic comparative study of the circumstances, mechanisms, and meaning of the emergence of political spaces and their relevance for the coalescence of vibrant civil societies.

NOTES

Multiple thanks are due to Michael Bratton, Goran Hyden, and Victor Le Vine, who commented on an earlier draft, and to the Harry S Truman Research Institute for the Advancement of Peace at the Hebrew University of Jerusalem, for the support and facilities that made the preparation of this chapter possible.

1. Also see Hyden, Chapter 1: governance is defined as "the conscious management of regime structures with a view to enhancing the legitimacy of the public realm."

2. This analysis relies on Fatton (1988:3–7), although the conclusions drawn from these distinctions differ.

3. The normative aspects of political space are implicit in some recent writings (Bayart 1989:280–315; Hyden 1989:2) but have not yet been sufficiently explicated.

4. I am indebted to Victor Le Vine for helping to pinpoint the structural connotations of the concept of political spaces and for suggesting some of the terminology employed here.

5. The pattern of the development of political spaces in Ghana, which

involved a process of severe power deflation at the state level, is not necessarily the only sequence possible. In especially strong states political spaces emerge within the context of, and in opposition to, existing power structures. The emergence of political spaces in situations of national liberation struggles is just one example.

6. This point is made and elaborated in Chazan 1989:326. Some portions of this chapter draw heavily on this piece.

7. The relationship between the definition of a general interest and the prospects for liberalization is elaborated in Heper 1986:4–15.

8. The importance of the contextual historical facets of contemporary state development in Africa are highlighted in Bayart 1989.

9. Forrest (1988) uses the term *state hardness* to describe this process, which usually resulted in various forms of statism, although not necessarily in greater degrees of stateness or improved governance.

10. For the process of the creation of the modal African state see Callaghy 1984. The relationship between state and class formation is discussed in Diamond 1987.

11. This is the position adopted by Price (1984), although his reasoning differs from that presented here.

12. On the distinction between factions (discrete social aggregates) and factionalism (the process by which they are mobilized), see Lemarchand 1987:149–151.

13. This was a major deviation from the alternating military/party system that had existed in the country since independence (see Pinkney 1988).

14. See the recent debates between Kwame Ninsin (1987, 1988) and James Ahiakpor (1988), and the ideological divisions apparent in Ninsin and Drah 1987.

15. The rural support for the PNDC was verified in the 1988–1989 District Assembly elections. Participation rates were higher in the rural areas than in the urban areas, while turnout rates in the large cities were particularly low (the Northern, Upper West, and Upper East regions averaged well over 60 percent participation rates, whereas voting in Accra was only 44.3 percent).

16. For an excellent comparative case study see MacGaffey 1987.

17. Bayart's (1986, 1989) suggestion that the African state stands in opposition to civil society has increasingly been challenged, most recently by Bratton (1989a) and Chazan (1990).

18. For a detailed examination of the range of activities of voluntary organizations and their interaction with governments, see Michael Bratton's masterful analysis (1989b).

19. For a comparison of participation rates see Chazan 1986.

7

Grassroots Legitimation of Military Governance in Burkina Faso and Niger: The Core Contradictions

Pearl T. Robinson

The major problem in the sphere of political analysis is to know not so much how a regime defines itself as what objective function this self-proclaimed definition has in the political game which the regime is playing.—Paulin Hountondji, *African Philosophy* (p. 93)

No serious consideration of liberalizing trends in present-day Africa can credibly ignore the phenomenon of participatory institutions established by military regimes. Nigeria's former president, General Olusegun Obasanjo (1987:13–14), implied as much in a speech before the Council on Foreign Relations in New York when he insisted that "not all military regimes are unrepresentative and more tyrannical . . . than the civilian governments they replaced." Of course, the general's views are at least in part conditioned by his own professional commitments, and by his unique perspective as the person who shepherded Nigeria's transition from military rule to multiparty government under the Second Republic. But a benevolent rendering of the soldier-state is vulnerable to a multitude of challenges.[1] Wole Soyinka (1972:183), for one, has denounced the moral legacy of military rule, which, in his judgment, creates "a vacuum in the ethical base" of politics, a vacuum that all too often is filled by the military ethic of coercion. These divergent assessments of the legacy of military rule are rooted in two fundamentally different notions about what sustains legitimacy. For Obasanjo, the efficiency of the state apparatus and of the economic system are essential; for Soyinka, what matters most is whether the political order can be validated as just and right. Their positions converge in the mutual recognition that the legitimacy of military rule is problematic.

Typically, soldiers who seize power rationalize their intervention by denouncing the abuses of a corrupt and inept civilian (or military) government, and by proclaiming their intent to correct those abuses. The logic of this form of intervention dictates a period of rehabilitation, followed by an orderly return to civilian rule. As Eboe Hutchful (1986:803) reminds us, the legitimacy of "corrective" military regimes is predicated on their self-proclaimed impermanence. Yet the reality is that most of Africa's soldier-politicians have been reluctant to return to the barracks—opting instead for longevity in office as the risks of losing power decrease over time (Bienen & van de Walle 1989:19–23).[2] But the determination to hold on to power undermines a corrective regime's internal structure of justification—thus rekindling the problem of legitimation. In many such cases, the ethos of grassroots participation emerges as an alternative legitimizing rationale.

Today we see a widening trend of African military regimes fostering institutional arrangements that allow for direct participation of the populace in local-level decisionmaking. How are we to understand these developments? Do they amount to something other than the long-standing practice of soldiers devising structures that provide a modicum of civilian support?[3] Are these proliferating grassroots councils indicative of a drift toward political liberalization, or are they merely schemes to cover an iron fist with a velvet glove? Although the surge of local-level councils sponsored by military rulers is clearly not the product of a single ideological orientation, scholars have generally focused on politics in Marxist states that emphasize revolutionary ideology and class struggle (Allen et al. 1989; Bienen 1985; Hutchful 1986; Keller 1988; Rothchild & Gyimah-Boadi 1989). As a result, not much is known about participatory structures established by military governments to promote corporatist-style patterns of representation and the harmonization of class differences.

THE TWO CASE STUDIES: BACKGROUND

This analysis is an attempt to bridge that gap by identifying, in a preliminary way, some of the common elements of participatory governance in two contrasting experiences of military rule in the West African Sahel. Our case studies of Burkina Faso and Niger highlight the class-based politics of Captain Thomas Sankara's Révolution Démocratique et Populaire and the corporatist framework of General Seyni Kountché's Société de Développement during the fluid period of civil-military relations, when these leaders initiated regime changes and encouraged experimentation with new forms of grassroots participation. Following Fernando Cardoso (1979:38), regime is used here to refer to both "the formal rules that link the main political institutions" and "the political nature of the ties between citizens and rulers."[4]

Employing a framework that stresses the dynamics of rhetoric and response, I will examine the official discourse on participatory politics under the two regimes and describe the range of behavioral responses to the delineation of new political space. For our purposes the comparable time frames are 1983–1987 in Burkina Faso and 1979–1984 in Niger. These intervals define windows of opportunity when military rulers encouraged a surge of new entrants to join the political fray.

Characteristics common to both countries during these periods included an asymmetrical dualism in the leadership structure and an emphasis on legitimation strategies that engineered popular involvement in public affairs while promoting redistributive or distributive economic policies. Official support for participatory governance was channeled into structures created by the state, sometimes to the peril of institutions rooted in civil society. And in both cases the participatory surge short-circuited after the demands of a debt crisis and aid donor conditionality converged with the consolidation of a more monolithic leadership structure.

It is important to note that, long before the period we shall be examining, Burkina Faso (known as Upper Volta prior to 1984) and Niger began developing two quite distinctive cultures of politics. Despite the shared legacy of French colonial rule, the populations in these neighboring countries have differed markedly in their receptivity to hegemonic patterns of social and political practice. The contrasts are evident in the degree of Islamic penetration (between 25 and 50 percent in Burkina Faso, over 90 percent in Niger),[5] the structure of both the party system and the trade union movement (pluralistic in Burkina Faso, corporatist in Niger until 1990), and even in the praxis of the coup d'état (between 1960 and 1989 six coups in Upper Volta/Burkina Faso, one in Niger). The only successful coup attempt in Niger during the thirty-year period from independence to 1990 was instigated by a small group of army officers acting clandestinely. But when Sankara assumed power in Upper Volta's fifth coup, he reiterated a pattern begun seventeen years earlier by a group of civilians who stormed the National Assembly, denounced the economic priorities and corrupt practices of the government, and demanded that the army take command (Skinner 1989:208–209).

Beyond comparing and contrasting the specifics of the Burkina Faso and Niger experiences, my more general argument is that increasing numbers of African military regimes can be expected to promote the establishment of localized, participatory structures as a response to the rise of legitimation problems. Jürgen Habermas's (Habermas 1979:178–205) discussion of legitimation problems in the modern state provides an explanation of the political dynamics that are at play.

In the real world of politics, governance is inseparable from regime legitimation. Legitimacy is a psychological relationship between governors and governed. It is a belief on the part of the governed that those in positions of political authority have a right to exercise that authority. Defining legitimacy as *a political order's worthiness to be recognized*, Habermas (Habermas 1979:178) problematizes the legitimacy of a political order as "a contestable validity claim." He thus frames a dynamic analytical approach that addresses the gap between legitimacy—which is a shared belief of the governors and the governed—and legitimation problems—defined operationally as a process of contestation in which one side denies while the other asserts legitimacy. To bridge this gap, regimes resort to legitimations—devices that establish "how and why existing (or recommended) institutions are fit to employ political power" (Habermas 1979:183). The process is variable but ongoing. Although constitutionalism and an official opposition may serve to institutionalize the legitimation process and render it less cataclysmic, legitimation problems occur under all types of regimes. They are at the core of governance. We turn first to the problems of legitimation in Burkina Faso.

BURKINA FASO

Revolutionary Charisma

Our starting point is a brief review of Captain Thomas Sankara's political legacy. The thirty-four-year-old Sankara seized power on August 4, 1983, at the nadir of an extraordinarily chaotic period in Upper Volta's political history that began with the overthrow of President Sangoulé Lamizana in November 1980. After fourteen years in office Lieutenant General Lamizana, the former army chief of staff who in 1966 heeded the demands of the crowd to evict the civilian government, was ousted by Colonel Saye Zerbo. A rapid succession of events followed in the aftermath of that coup. Zerbo was toppled by a group of junior officers and privates in November 1982. Three weeks later Major Jean-Baptist Ouedrago emerged as head of state presiding over a newly formed Conseil de Salut du Peuple (CSP). Four factions reportedly vied for influence within the CSP.[6] Sankara, who headed the progressives, served as prime minister from January 11, 1983, until his arrest on May 17. He was freed in June after Captain Blaise Compaoré, commander of the paratroop unit stationed near the Ghana border at Pô, staged a revolt and threatened to march on Ouagadougou. Finally, on the evening of August 4, Compaoré led a military column into the capital, overthrew President Ouedrago, and named Sankara chairman of a newly created Conseil National pour la Révolution (CNR).

Assuming power in his country's fifth coup d'état and heading a coalition government that bore the seeds of factionalism, Sankara faced severe legitimation problems from the outset of his presidency. Corrective measures ranked high on his political agenda, but the record of failed military rule precluded any simplistic assertion of corrective legitimacy for the new regime. Although the CNR initially relied almost entirely on the charismatic appeal of its young leader for legitimation, Sankara never moved to institutionalize his charisma (Skinner 1988). Instead, he insisted on locating legitimacy in the realm of "the people." Legitimation was thus a prime motivation for regime changes that sought to associate the structure of formal, authoritative power with popular participation in governance (Collier 1982:8). New participatory institutions at the grassroots level were designed, at least in part, to respond to issues arising from the regime's contestable validity claim.

Within a short period of time Compaoré emerged as the number-two personality in the government. His relationship with Sankara was so close that the writer Mongo Beti, recounting an intimate dinner hosted by the head of state during the 1985 PanAfrican Film Festival in Ouagadougou, described Campaoré as "the President's shadow."[7] Although the nature of this ill-fated friendship remains a matter for speculation, its political import lies in the fact that it served as the underpinning of the dualistic leadership structure that came to characterize the regime. Within the CNR, Sankara and Compaoré worked in tandem but embodied contradictory tendencies: Sankara's grandfather was the Fulani slave of a Mossi prince; Compaoré the son of a Mossi chief. Sankara was charismatic, Compaoré enigmatic. Sankara readily admitted to being a revolutionary ideologue, Compaoré was reportedly "wary of clichés and meaningless formulae" (Onwordi 1988:2028). When remarks by President Sankara intimated a readiness to put to death two union leaders who had been arrested on treason charges, Compaoré, in his role as minister of justice, questioned their detention and firmly opposed their execution. For a while the give-and-take personified in this relationship functioned as a practical impediment to the consolidation of one-man rule. But the failure to institutionalize viable conflict-regulating mechanisms within the inner circle eventually took its toll. As the contradictions became identified with contending factions, they erupted into fratricidal battles that ultimately led the regime to self-destruct.

The threats to regime survival, however, were external as well as internal. In fact, Burkina Faso's relations with international capital markets proved a major fault line of instability. Expressing the desire to end neocolonial practices and capitalist exploitation endured under previous governments, the CNR sought to reject political and institutional relations that might jeopardize its economic priorities. Shortly after coming to power the new leadership nationalized all land and mineral rights. In the face of a rapidly rising debt burden inherited from the past, it opted for a self-reliant, people-oriented economic policy, and repudiated austerity proposals put forward by the International Monetary Fund (IMF) (*Africa Research Bulletin*, Econ. Ser., October 15–November 14, 1984:7478). Initiatives such as these eventually closed the door on an IMF standby loan, and Sankara's 1987 decision to suspend payment on the debt resulted in a cutoff of Western aid flows as well as financing from the international development banks. Making a political virtue out of an economic Dunkirk, the CNR and its supporters extolled grassroots participation and political mobilization as morally preferable substitutes for foreign capital.

In contrast to the typical practice of Africa's corrective military regimes during the 1960s and 1970s, Burkina Faso's young coup makers did not impose a blanket ban on political parties or hold themselves aloof from politics. Political to the core, they changed the name of their country, moved quickly to transform domestic and international policies, and projected a revolutionary populist program driven by the rhetoric of class struggle. Eager to encourage broad participation in the political process, the regime initially accommodated itself to Upper Volta/Burkina Faso's pluralistic political culture of multiparty politics and militant trade unionism.[8] In fact, during Sankara's entire term in office, no less than five Marxist parties remained active either as members of the government or as vocal opponents of state policies.

In this highly charged environment where the political order was openly contested, redistributive policies and new norms for political conduct became essential elements in the process of legitimation. Accordingly, problems of privilege, poverty, family development,[9] and government corruption rose to the top of the political agenda. The regime's ethical stance extended beyond issues of government corruption and included the recognition that public policy choices have normative political implications. A statement by Joséphine Guissou Ouedrago, minister of family development and national solidarity under Sankara, underscored the importance of grassroots participation to the success of this endeavor:

> It is not for nothing that the name of the country has been changed to Burkina Faso, which means the country of dignity, the country whose inhabitants express integrity. You cannot respect yourself and at the same time extend your hand for alms and believe that everything must come from abroad. . . . We want people to understand that they do have resources, not only economic and physical resources, but the resources of their mind—creative ideas—the resources of their physical strength, so many resources to make the most of. If we continue in this direction, there is no reason we shouldn't win. In any case, there is no alternative [Pradervand 1989:167].

As the CNR moved to implement redistributive policies, it took aim at the privileges enjoyed by the bureaucratic bourgeoisie and sought to redeploy state power in support of peasant farmers, herders, and the urban poor. Government employees, who accounted for less than 0.3 percent of the population and consumed more than 60 percent of the national budget (Skinner 1988:444), proved highly vulnerable targets for the regime's populist politics. Salaries of mid- to upper-level careerists in both the army and the civil service were slashed, while rural producers saw their taxes cancelled, and bottom-tier government workers received wage hikes. Mandated early retirements and large-scale layoffs were then instituted to further cut the wage bill and offset the tax relief extended to small farmers and herders ("Burkina Faso," *Africa Contemporary Record* 18 [1985–1986]:B10–B15). As part of its ongoing campaign to reshape public norms and values, the CNR established a number of national solidarity funds (e.g., for railway construction, employment training programs, victims of natural disasters, and the handicapped) and required mandatory contributions by all salaried workers (*West Africa* 3604 [1986]:2018–2019).

Changes in the structure of institutional power were yet another facet of the legitimation process. Administrative functions were decentralized, and judicial responsibilities reassigned. In a bid to end "feudalism," the CNR removed traditional chiefs from official involvement in local administration and installed a system based on elected Comités pour la Défense de la Révolution (CDRs) in the villages, urban neighborhoods, and in the workplace. These new committees were authorized to intervene in local political and economic matters and to initiate self-help development projects at the grassroots level. The CNR also set up Tribunaux Populaires Révolutionnaires (TPRs) to try officials accused of political corruption and economic crimes such as embezzlement.

The new-style participation, with its revolutionary committees and peoples' courts, was channeled through institutions created by the state and directly responsible to the CNR. As each locally elected CDR pressed to impose its hegemony in a given arena, changes in the structure of participation and the concomitant shift in economic priorities sparked struggles for control of political space. The antagonists included defiant trade unionists, contingents of university and *lycée* students, and political parties representing extreme left as well as conservative tendencies. Additionally, many of the CDRs fell captive to local political conflicts and became battlegrounds for settling old scores involving chieftainships or family feuds (Skinner 1988:449; see also Sankara 1987:162–180).

But the unions proved to be the Achilles' heel of the regime. Since 1964 the syndicalist movement has functioned as an unofficial political opposition in Upper Volta/Burkina Faso. The pattern is ingrained, and it did not end with the August 4 revolution (Kabeya 1987). Although the coalition of forces that backed Sankara when he came to power included three militantly left-wing parties[10] and their affiliated unions, the CNR's redistributive policies jeopardized the economic interests of many union members, who are largely public sector workers. Over time, virtually all of the key trade unions withdrew their support and began to denounce the political order as antidemocratic.

Burkina's trade union movement had weathered a single-party system and remained politically autonomous and highly pluralistic through four military governments, but the CNR changed the rules of the political game. Oriented toward the peasantry and the poor, the radical young leaders did not consider the support of organized labor a sine qua non for their political survival or the legitimacy of their regime. In fact, the denunciation of "neocolonial" unions as enemies of the people took on a cardinal importance in their overall strategy of legitimation (Bamouni 1986:18–19, 135–137). Union leaders were jailed on charges ranging from embezzlement to plotting with foreign agents. The firing of over one thousand teachers who staged a two-day strike and the imposition of new restrictions on union activities were coupled with a head-on assault against union hegemony by the CDRs vested to represent workers in the workplace. When eleven unions published a joint statement that accused the CNR of threatening democracy and curbing the freedom of organized labor, Sankara met with three unions still supportive of the regime and barred his harshest critics from joining the talks ("Burkina Faso," *Africa Contemporary Record* 17 [1984–1985]:B435–B436). Finally the May 1987 arrest on treason charges of Soumane Touré, secretary-general of the militant Confedération Syndicale Burkinabè, and Salif Kaboré, a fellow union leader, attracted the attention of Amnesty International when the two men were threatened with execution. Although Compaoré's intervention ended this particular crisis, the practice of waging class struggle against the labor aristocracy proceeded unabated and continued to serve the objective function of legitimation.

Meanwhile the CNR was beset by internal factionalism fuelled by the Marxist parties represented in the government.[11] Sankara long prevailed by playing one faction off against the other, but the destabilizing consequences of this ploy shifted the balance from legitimacy to coercion as the basis of public authority. In June 1987 Sankara floated the idea of dissolving all political groupings—possibly as a prelude to creating a unitary party (Otayek 1987). There was no immediate follow-up, but the matter resurfaced when Sankara, Compaoré, Major Jean-Baptiste Lingani, and Captain Henri Zongo reportedly debated the advisability of restructuring the party system during a fateful meeting on October 8, 1987. We may never know how the issues were framed or who advocated what, but it is clear that the debate was heated and that Compaoré and Sankara were on different sides.[12] In a preemptive move by his comrades in arms, the president was arrested and executed on the eve of the CNR meeting he was to chair on October 15. With his death, an innovative attempt at governance that captured the political imagination of progressive idealists across Africa and around the world came to an abrupt end. Under Sankara's successor, Captain Blaise Compaoré, only the rhetoric of revolution survived.

The Rhetoric of Revolutionary Populist Participation

The public pronouncements made by the slain president during his tenure in office configured a new discourse on participation that became one of the defining features of his regime. Drawing excerpts from Sankara's speeches, it is possible to reconstruct the ideal of participatory governance that the Révolution Démocratique et Populaire was trying to project. Because the rhetoric of mobilization is susceptible to a wide range of interpretations (if indeed it reaches a receptive audience), the messages transmitted may not necessarily be the messages received. But this very ambiguity encouraged people to subvert the conventional norms of political behavior. Through statements such as the ones that follow, Sankara provided cues aimed at promoting and reorienting popular involvement in politics.

An operational definition of "the people." Disaggregating the population as a whole into class strata, Sankara defined the people as those segments of society in which the regime based its support. Although it was a matter of considerable pride among politically progressive Burkinabès that the new ideology identified women as a critical category, the gap between official rhetoric and the reality of women's status often left much to be desired:

> The people, in the current revolution, are composed of:
> 1. The . . . working class, which is young and few in number, but which has proved through continuous struggle against the employers that it is a genuinely revolutionary class. . . .
> 2. The petty bourgeoisie, which . . . is very unstable and which often vacillates between the cause of the popular masses and that of imperialism. . . . It is composed of the most diverse elements, including small traders, petty-bourgeois intellectuals (government employees, students, private sector employees, and so on), and artisans.
> 3. The . . . peasantry, which is composed [primarily] of small peasants who . . . are attached to their small plots of land. . . .
> 4. The lumpenproletariat, a layer of declassed elements who, since they are without work, are inclined to hire themselves out to reactionary and counterrevolutionary forces to carry out the latter's dirty work [Sankara 1987:39–40].
> There is something crucial missing: woman. She has been excluded from this joyful [revolutionary] procession. . . . And yet the authenticity and the future of our revolution depend on women [Sankara 1987:201–202].

The enemies of the people. Given the importance of the class struggle to the legitimation process, it was necessary to define the enemy. Sankara also took pains to situate the conflict with the unions in the context of the class struggle:

> Who are the enemies of the people? They are that group of bourgeois who enrich themselves dishonestly through fraud and bribery, through the corruption of state officials. . . .
> Who are the enemies of the people? They are the men in politics who travel through the countryside exclusively at election time. . . .
> The enemies of the people are also beyond our borders. Their base is among unpatriotic people here in our midst at every level of our society—civilian and military men, men and women, old and young, in town and country alike. These enemies from abroad—neocolonialism, imperialism—are among us [Sankara 1987:11–12].

Concerning the regime's incessant battles with organized labor, Sankara declared: "Is this a conflict with the workers, the working class, or with the leadership? It's a conflict with the leadership, not with the workers. . . . These same workers are in both the CDR's and the unions. It's only the leaderships that are not at all pleased. And that's natural. It's because of their petty-bourgeois outlook" (Sankara 1987:105).

The goals. The CNR sought to mobilize popular participation behind an omnibus program of agrarian, administrative, educational, and economic change. The revolution was said to have a dual character—democratic and popular, and the articulation of gender equality took on special significance:

> [The revolution's] primary tasks are to liquidate imperialist domination and exploitation and cleanse the countryside of all social, economic, and cultural obstacles that keep it in a backward state. From this flows its democratic character.
> Its popular character arises from the full participation of the . . . masses in the revolution. . . . [A] new machinery is being constructed that will guarantee the democratic exercise of power by the people and for the people.
> Organized into CDR's, the people acquire not only the right to review the problems of their development, but also to participate in making decisions and carrying them out. . . .
> The final goal of this great undertaking is to build a free and prosperous society in which women will be equal to men in all domains [Sankara 1987:30, 40–43, 49].

Restrictions on political freedoms. In a speech made during his stint as prime minister in the government of President Ouedrago, Sankara took a hard line against dissent: "[I]n no way do we wish to put an end to freedom. But we say that the freedom to criticize brings with it the freedom to protest. And freedom for honest men should not mean freedom for the dishonest. We will strip the liberties of those who use the freedoms created by the CSP to attack the [government] and, in that way, to attack the Voltaic people" [Sankara 1987:15–16].

As president, Sankara was prepared to deny the political rights of disaffected elites while at the same time making allowances for a more gradual transformation of peasant attitudes. Debate among those judged committed to the regime was encouraged:

> While the revolution equals repression of the exploiters and our enemies, it can only signify persuasion for the masses—persuasion to take on a conscious and determined commitment to the struggle.
> Unity among revolutionaries is undoubtedly a stage we will have to go through in advancing the organization of the vanguard. . . . We should, however, guard against a barren, monolithic, paralyzing, and sterile kind of unity. . . . We need thoughts and activities that are rich with a thousand nuances, all put forward courageously and sincerely in the framework of accepting differences and respecting the need for criticism and self-criticism, and all directed toward a single, bright goal, which can be none other than the happiness of our people [Sankara 1987:238].

Through his rhetoric, Sankara helped to create a political environment in which power was decentered, the old order could be openly challenged, and ordinary people might dare to take political risks.

Responses of the Populace to the Regime's Participatory Rhetoric

The nuances and ambiguities embedded in Sankara's rhetorical pronouncements on revolutionary populist participation allowed for broad interpretive latitude by people in the various strata.[13] While a systematic assessment of the range of responses to the new participatory rhetoric is beyond the scope of this analysis, the point remains that in the absence of such an assessment, we cannot hope for anything more than an impressionistic understanding of what revolutionary mobilization implied—either in personal terms or with respect to regime legitimation— for the broad spectrum of Burkinabè citizenry. Without making any claim to be representative, it is nevertheless possible to focus on available accounts, based on testimony and observation, to probe the ways in which people, variously situated, responded to the new politics of participation.

Sankara acted as a lightning rod, drawing supporters and critics alike to assert or deny the validity of the new regime, but many Burkinabè were ambivalent about the import of these changes for their own lives. *Afrique Asie's* brief sketch of one young Ouagadougou resident's attitude toward the campaign against feudalism is a case in point. Commenting favorably about the government's get-tough policy with the emperor of the Mossi, Mogho Naba Ousmane Congo, the young man remained noncommittal regarding his own behavior:

Many people respect the Mogho Naba, but I believe that Sankara was right to oblige him to pay his electric bills. After all, if it is not he who pays, then it would be the people who must pay for him, and they do not believe that this is good. We young people cannot live like our parents. Even in the countryside, people do not agree to give their sisters as presents to the Mogho as they did in the past. . . . I will not behave like my father, but I do not yet know how I will behave. I shall wait to see what the future holds for me [quoted in Skinner 1988:450].

But for Halidou Sawadogo, a Mossi peasant leader in the village of Séguénega, there was no such equivocation. From his vantage, the revolution was a fulfillment of the expectations of independence. It brought a government that was more responsive to rural people and committed to eradicating the corruption and exploitation of past regimes. Queried by a Swiss journalist about the changes under Sankara, Sawadogo explained: "The Independence granted us in 1960 changed almost nothing. . . .

After Independence, it was anarchy. Tax money was squandered—it just disappeared. If the farmer did not pay his taxes, he went off to prison. . . . Farmers did not reap the benefits of Independence until 4 August 1983, the day President Thomas Sankara came to power in Burkina Faso. It's only now that we feel we are independent" (Pradervand 1989: 57).

It is not surprising that the young urbanite and the peasant leader differed in the relative intensity of their support for the regime. But even among people similarly situated, the level of enthusiasm for participatory mobilization varied. For a glimpse at how this drama was played out in four Mossi villages circa 1986, we have the scenarios presented by Robert Maclure (1988) in his study of rural animation programs in Burkina Faso. Maclure worked in a rural province between March 1981 and August 1983 as the field director of a rural development project sponsored by a nongovernmental organization, and he returned to the same locale for dissertation research from September 1985 through January 1987. He is thus able to provide before-and-after observations of how the local residents responded to changes wrought by the revolution.

Regarding day-to-day life in the villages, Maclure noted that "the intrusion of the State has been particularly dramatic" since 1983. The village CDRs, which were the "acknowledged conduits of government policy," assumed official authority (previously held by village chiefs and elders) over local administration and minor litigation as they proceeded to translate the policy of bottom-up development into concrete community actions. Among other tasks, the CDRs formulated and oversaw the implementation of village development plans, mobilized village work parties for government construction projects, and recruited young men for paramilitary training. The representatives on these councils, reportedly not democratically elected and drawn largely from the ruling lineages, were charged with explaining a wide range of government policies to their fellow villagers—including the abolition of rural levies, the mandatory possession of identity cards by all adult citizens, the obligatory establishment of first aid posts in all communities, and the abolition of forced marriage. Maclure notes that the authority of the local CDRs was reinforced by a squad of gendarmes and provincial police stationed in the region, and by a nearby military encampment (Macclure 1988:80).

The broad scope of these interventions could not fail to have an impact on the lives of the peasantry, but their consequences were far from uniform. For some villagers, the advent of the CNR brought an exhilarating sense of empowerment; others perceived the new order as a set of burdensome obligations. Thus Maclure (1988:115–116) found that while the majority of rural people in the province perceived the significance of regime change, most remained aloof from the governmental process.

NIGER

Neotraditional Corporatism

Turning next to Niger, we find several striking parallels with the Burkinabè experience. Although the young Captain Sankara and the aging General Kountché were worlds apart in their respective political philosophies and leadership styles, both pursued legitimation strategies that extolled the virtues of popular participation in governance. To be sure, politics under Sankara and Kountché had little in common: the former espoused mobilization around issues of class conflict and antiimperialist struggle; the latter promoted a corporatist vision of society based on class harmony and the interdependent functions of an organic whole. Yet both headed regimes that established local-level councils with oversight responsibilities for development initiatives and directed significant new resources to the countryside.

Kountché seized power in a 1974 coup d'état and remained in office until his death in November 1987. His predecessor, President Diori Hamani, had consolidated a one-party state under the Parti Progressiste Nigérien (PPN) shortly after independence, but the clientelistic PPN never gained broad-based popular support. With an economy based on groundnut exports, Niger ranked among the world's poorest countries when a devastating five-year drought beginning in 1968 exacerbated the endemic problems of scarcity, maldistribution, and political corruption. By 1971 several disgruntled government functionaries were openly challenging the legitimacy of one-party rule and calling for competitive elections to seats in the National Assembly (Baulin 1986:89–99).

Once in power the new rulers proceeded to instal a neotraditionalist military regime. Officers from the armed forces were named to head government ministries, all seven administrative *préfectures*, strategically sensitive *sous-préfectures*, as well as the state bureaucracy charged with food aid and famine relief. The Conseil Militaire Suprême (CMS) revived the moribund Association of Traditional Chiefs from the colonial past, launched the moderately reformist Islamic Association of Niger, and fashioned a national youth movement called the Samariya, modeled after a Hausa age-grade association. The organizational utility of state-sponsored neotraditionalism was explicitly enunciated by President Kountché, who declared that the Islamic Association's mission was to promote the ideological application of organized Islam at all levels of national life (Triaud 1982:37), while the Samariya served as "the cornerstone of any attempt in mobilizing the masses" (Kountché 1979).

Condemning the civilian regime for its misplaced priorities, Kountché (1974) identified famine relief and drought control as his government's most urgent priorities. Fortuitously, the military takeover coincided with a return of the rains, an unprecedented influx of development aid, and new wealth from the exploitation of Niger's uranium reserves. World market conditions for uranium benefitted from the oil price shocks induced by the Organization of Petroleum Exporting Countries as uranium prices increased sixfold between 1973 and 1979. With this confluence of events Niger's overall gross domestic product, adjusted for inflation, increased at an annual average rate of 7.6 percent between 1976 and 1980, peaking at 13 percent in 1979, while uranium's contribution to export earnings grew from 19 percent in 1971 to nearly 88 percent in 1979 (Toh 1984:1–2). In fiscal year 1978/79 the uranium sector contributed 21 percent of central government revenues and financed about 80 percent of the state's investment outlays (Toh 1984:Table A.13).

The upshot of these developments was Kountché's announcement on the first anniversary of military rule that the time had come for the state to "assume its responsibilities" and create a *société de développement*. He spearheaded an ambitious government program to build roads; drill village wells; construct rural clinics and urban housing; increase the availability of electricity; and expand training opportunities for teachers, health personnel, and agricultural cadres. State-sponsored irrigation schemes became the key component of the Ministry of Rural Development's strategy to reduce chronic food deficits and expand the commercial production of rice and cotton. Additionally, regional productivity projects were established in each préfecture to promote surplus production of millet and sorghum. Although water projects and productivity packages proved to be more-effective devices for distributing patronage in the rural areas than for transforming the rural economy, the regime vaunted these highly visible initiatives as tangible evidence of its "corrective" legitimacy.

But toward the end of 1979 a precipitous fall in the price and demand for uranium, below-average rainfall, and rapidly rising public debt resulted in economic contraction and a conjunctural crisis. During 1979–1981 the budget deficit soared from CFA fr 14.2 billion to CFA fr 64 billion. Although uranium still accounted for 76.4 percent of export earnings in 1982, its contribution to central government revenues for that year dropped to 8.4 percent (Toh 1984:3, Tables A.11, A.13). These dislocations proved politically troublesome because they pulled the economic plug that was sustaining Niger's newfound prosperity and exposed the regime's contestable validity claim.

In October 1979, at the crest of rising expectations, Kountché appointed Lt. Col. Adamou Moumouni Djermakoye president of a national commission to consider an institutional framework for a société de développement. Djermakoye, who at the time was the number-two personality in the regime, propelled the venture with a series of speeches that highlighted the importance of participatory development. Meanwhile the Five Year Development Plan (1979–1983), which boosted allocations for mass-level health care, educational reform, local-language literacy, and the promotion of popular participation in development actions, was put on hold.

Initially, the notion of a société de développement was tied to the expectation of continued economic growth, but by the time the commission issued its report in June 1981, the earlier concept of a social welfare–maximizing development society had been stood on its head. With the state's resource base shrinking, the société de développement emerged as the institutional backstop for a new strategy of governance devised to implement a politically precarious shift in national economic policy. That shift consisted of initiatives and reforms prompted by bilateral and multilateral aid donors: renewed attention to export markets for livestock and animal products, cuts in social spending, privatization of parastatals, reduction of agricultural subsidies, a downsizing of development schemes, and revival of commercial groundnut production. Faced with a legitimation crisis, Kountché was anxious to build a popular consensus in support of his rule. As the regime focused its rhetoric more pointedly on the salutary effects of grassroots participation in socioeconomic development, the institutions of the société de développement became the embodiment of that consensus.

The société de développement was built from the bottom up, but its component parts were neither locally initiated nor autonomous from the state. In fact, field staff from the Ministry of Rural Development's rural animation service were assigned the task of creating a network of local conseils de développement (CDs) sufficient in scope and number to incorporate the entire Nigerien populace into grassroots assemblies. The state determined the list of constituent associations: farmers' and herders' cooperatives; the Samariya; the Nigerien women's association; the chiefs; the Islamic Association; the consolidated trade union; the merchants' and truckers' guilds; retired soldiers; and griots (praisesingers). Competitive election to the councils was ruled out as unnecessarily costly and divisive. Instead, each association was instructed to select its representatives by consensus. A national assembly drawn from the membership of local councils was convened in August 1983, and in January 1984 President Kountché named a new commission to consider a charter for the société de développement.

The société de développement was structured into five tiers of CDs—village, local, subregional, regional, and a national assembly called the Conseil National de Développement (CND). Each tier corresponds to a rung in the administrative hierarchy, and at each level the local administrative authority was to sit as president of the corresponding CD. Thus village chiefs and canton chiefs were the designated leaders of village and local CDs, the sous-préfets headed the subregional CDs, and Niger's military préfets functioned as presidents of all seven regional CDs. The CMS appointed a civilian administrator to preside as president of the CND. By design, the CND was a consultative body that lacked legislative authority (Dagra 1985).

Apparently structure does matter. Data from my 1983–1984 field work reveal that virtually all the CDs ratified government proposals to increase existing tax rates and fees, tap new sources for local taxation, enhance tax collection efforts, and involve the chiefs in the recovery of agricultural credit arrears.[14] CDs in the pastoral zone ratified a variety of initiatives aimed at bringing nomadic herders under tighter governmental controls. These measures ran the gamut from urging pastoralists to destock their cattle and adopt range management practices, to insisting that they enroll their children in school and cease carrying firearms. At the same time administrative officials used the CDs as a forum to press the point that the days of big government spending were over. Councilors were repeatedly instructed to inform their constituents that the state could no longer be counted on to carry the costs of building classrooms, drilling wells, and providing free medical care.

Although the new participation was corporatist by design, between 1979 and 1984 the rules of the political game were at times fluid. To borrow a Hausa phrase, this interval marks what can be called the *shan iska* period of military rule—a time when sporadic political openings made it possible to "breathe fresh air." By the end of shan iska, Niger's military government had abandoned the posture of a transitional corrective regime and moved to institutionalize itself with a corporatist grid of participation and control. What is of interest to us here, however, is how manifestations of a pluralist political ethos occasionally broke through this highly centralized command structure.

The Rhetoric of Participatory Development

Examining the dialectical relationship between the military regime's evolving rhetoric of participation and the varying responses of elements within the populace, we move toward a more dynamic conceptualization of participatory politics in Niger. During the period in question there were two dominant voices articulating the ideal of participatory governance that was to be implemented through the structures of the société de développement.

President Kountché, who never relinquished his role as the ultimate lawgiver, always stressed evolutionary change and the slow, deliberative nature of the process required to build a national consensus through the institutions of the société de développement. His conception of grassroots participation was paternalistic and characterized by an unwillingness to regard the mass population as a mature citizenry ready to engage in full-fledged political life. Djermakoye, on the other hand, used rhetoric that suggested confidence in the people's capacity for self-governance. In his role as president of the national commission for the société de développement, he toured the country for three years, making speeches about the importance of the project to Niger's development. The language embedded in some of these texts extended interpretive latitude to listeners within the attentive public who were ready to respond to any credible indication of a liberalizing trend. It is important to note, however, that both Kountché and Djermakoye hail from the aristocracy and were united in their conviction that traditional elites had to be central to any process of participatory reform.

Until Djermakoye's demotion to a post as préfet in October 1983, the coexistence of two official narratives enriched the vocabulary of political possibility. The following excerpts indicate how the introduction of rhetorical ambiguity opened up new political space by seeming to give official support to a move toward popular participation in governance.

An operational definition of "the people." For Kountché, the CND reflected the complementarity of social relationships among Nigeriens, and he took pains to define the army as an emanation of the people. By contrast, Djermakoye suggested that the peasantry was a subordinated majority that was at risk of being manipulated by the army:

President Kountché:

> What a beautiful example . . . to see seated, side-by-side, the farmer and the herder, the producer and the consumer, the seller and the buyer. What a beautiful example to see in a single institution, united all together, the employer and the employee, the chief and the subordinate, the administrative official and the citizens under his charge. . . .
>
> What a beautiful example to hear, [speaking] in unison, the national army in the midst of its . . . people. This is proof that in a country like ours, the army is . . . an integral part of national life, and should no longer be either set apart or marginalized [Commission National 1983:99–100].

Lieutenant-Colonel Djermakoye:

> [The Nigerien people] consists primarily of farming and herding peasants—a preponderant majority—more than 90 percent—to whom we the minority continue to dictate the laws.
>
> To want to build a new Nigerien nation without taking this situation into account would be adventurous demagoguery. The Supreme Military Council is not ready to let itself slide down that slippery slope, even though our positive accomplishments over the last five years in the areas of food security, improved conditions for workers, [and] rehabilitation of the economy might tempt us in that direction [Commission Nationale 1983:19].

The structure and character of the new participation. Considerable thought was given to the modalities for organizing and channeling participation. Kountché clearly wanted the state to remain firmly in control of the process and had a one-sided view of politics. Djermakoye spoke of reciprocity and encouraged the citizenry to assume greater responsibility for the affairs of the nation:

President Kountché:

> Schematically, I would compare the société de développment to a pyramid, in which the popular will expresses itself from the bottom up and can organize itself for [development] management at each level. The base of the pyramid will cover the entire territory of the country, organized into development cells. The scaffolding will be left up to imagination and adaptation. What will be essential is the assurance of effective participation for all the sons and daughters of the nation in the decisions that concern them [Commission Nationale 1983:9–10].

Lieutenant-Colonel Djermakoye:

> The société de développement will be a structure for dialog—the kind of dialog that the Supreme Military Council has always been willing to engage in—where information circulates from the base to the summit, and from the summit to the base. Thus all Nigeriens, whatever their place in society, will feel themselves concerned with the future of the country [Commission Nationale 1983:15].

> We want to engage the Nigerien people on the path of . . . dialog, concertation, and collective reflection in order to find within ourselves, in our own genius, the indispensable elements for national construction [Commission Nationale 1983:19].

The limits of acceptable participation. During the first five years of military rule avoiding the scourge of party politics took precedence over any notion of participatory governance. Even during the shan iska period Kountché remained cool to the prospect of partisan mobilization, but Djermakoye spoke of the need to extend the parameters of political involvement.

President Kountché, speaking to the representatives in the CND:

> In this role . . . you must put aside all demagoguery, all sectarianism or partisanship. . . . Only the interests of the nation should [guide] your actions. You must therefore transcend personal sentiments so that your council does not become a closed arena of internal quarrels [Commission Nationale 1983:102–103].

Lieutenant-Colonel Djermakoye:

> The concept of the société de développement responds to the expectations of our people, who see in it the best instrument to permit the . . . full flowering of their legitimate aspirations and to begin an apprenticeship and the actual practice of democracy [Commission Nationale 1983:34].

> [To] ward off the prospect that participation may slacken and become only a slogan, certain conditions must be met: creation of a veritable cult of participation; administrative reform adapted to this new

approach to development; utilization of national languages by our administrative cadres . . . ; and full use of the immense possibilities that our mass media offer for a wide-ranging program of animation, education, and information for our population.

. . . The path of participation, of dialog, of tolerance is the only answer to the historical challenge of building the Nigerien Nation [Commission Nationale 1983:96].

Djermakoye's prescription for the conditions needed to breathe life into the new rhetoric could very well have served as a blueprint for events that were to follow. Indeed, the shan iska period was in large part a phenomenon tied to the mass media and dependent on political communications conducted in the public realm. The decision to promote the use of indigenous languages in fora sponsored by the CND augmented the possibilities for interactive exchange.

Responses to the New Participatory Rhetoric

It should come as no surprise that grassroots responses to these bifurcated messages ranged from alienation to engagement. On the one hand, a 1985 study of popular participation in Western Niger found that 34.3 percent of the five hundred respondents surveyed were unaware of the existence of their own village CDs. In this same sample, 46.8 percent did not know why the CDs had been created, while 79.2 percent reported having no knowledge about the operations of their local councils (Sidikou & Charlick 1985). On the other hand, the depth of involvement in several high-visibility, ad hoc events conducted under the auspices of the CND stands in sharp contrast to the apparent shallowness of the formalized processes in most local CDs. One explanation for this discrepancy is that the CDs, as creatures of the state, were tightly controlled by the Interior Ministry—a bureaucracy with a penchant for acting behind closed doors. Typically, agendas for the CDs were preset and passed down through the administrative hierarchy, while grievances and interests articulated during the meetings were frequently not referred up the line.

Nevertheless, some of the civilian personnel involved in laying the groundwork for the société de développement sought alternative means to carve out new political space. With the aid of radio and rural television,[15] French-speaking elites as well as indigenous-language audiences were drawn into the forum of political debate. The commission charged with drafting a charter for the société de développement organized a series of lectures under the patronage of the CND and invited prominent intellectuals such as Cheikh Anta Diop, Samir Amin, René Dumont, and the Nigerien historian André Salifou to spell out their views on issues of critical importance to Niger's development. Public lectures by distinguished scholars with strongly held ideological positions were rare in Niger at the time, and these events drew large, enthusiastic audiences. Salifou's lecture on the political history of

Niger was simulcast with an interactive telephone hookup so that people could call and engage in on-air debate. In response to one question, Salifou expressed reservations about the notion, enshrined in the société de développement, that consensus must be the basis of a viable political community. He countered with the argument that political life "requires the courage to discuss issues, to disagree, and to make decisions on the basis of majority rule. Consensus avoids clear positions and delays the resolution of problems."[16]

The president of the CND, Oumarou Mamane, brought rural audiences into this process with meet-the-people tours. His visit to the predominantly Fulani rural town of Torodi was memorable as an occasion when herders publicly raised issues of government corruption, ethnic participation, and resource distribution. This open-air meeting, conducted in three languages (Hausa, Djerma, and Fufulde) with concurrent translation as necessary, was staged both to publicize the société de développement and to encourage pastoralists to cull their herds. Musicians, dancers, and a crowd numbering in the hundreds were present when the CND president began to explain the government's concern that a bad rainy season had resulted in insufficient pasture to support the herds. He went on to relay the government's decision that the best way it could help the herders was to advise them to sell their cattle.

To an audience consisting largely of Fulani pastoralists, such advice rang hollow. Moreover, it skirted the issues that most herders consider to be the real sources of difficulties in their lives. Mamane invited the audience to respond to his remarks, but initially no one stepped forward. Only after the CND president offered his personal guarantee of protection to anyone willing to speak was the silence broken by a man who asked to be pardoned for what he was about to say because "talakawa [common folk] aren't supposed to say bad things to important people."[17] This herder detailed his experiences with customs agents who routinely extorted payments every time he took his cattle to and from pastures across the border into Burkina Faso. As he talked, fear diminished, and long lines formed at each of the battery-powered microphones installed to facilitate dialog. For more than two hours, Torodi was transformed into a people's forum where rural residents recited a litany of grievances suffered at the hands of state officials.

Denunciation of corruption, complaints of excessive fines levied against the owners of animals that wander into farmers' fields, criticism of the government for not drilling wells to facilitate watering animals in zones where mixed agriculture is practiced:[18] the talk drifted toward charges of an antipastoralist bias in government policies and programs. The ethnic overlay was made explicit by a Fulani chief from the Dogon Doutchi region who complained that no Fulanis had been chosen to sit on local or regional CDs in his district. In addition, he protested the secrecy that surrounded the selection of local-level councilors—a process to which he as a chief had remained oblivious until after the fact.

The Torodi encounter was filmed in its entirety and broadcast nationally on television and radio. Hausa- and Djerma-speaking co-anchors described the town as a multiethnic community where "herders and farmers live together in peace." They characterized the meeting as an demonstration of what could be expected in the new société de développement being launched by the government. Viewers and listeners were presented with images of people who spoke freely while state officials listened, appeared responsive, and promised to investigate irregularities. Although antigovernment criticism was wide-ranging, the Fulani chief's ethnic claims were notably the only remarks singled out as problematic. Editorializing, one of the anchormen explained that the chief had misunderstood the nature of the sociéte de développement. He then instructed the media audience that the institutions of the société de développement make no provisions for ethnic representation. Only national identity and national interests could have legitimate standing.

The contrast between the tightly controlled realm of the CDs and the openness of the media-linked arenas described above is striking. In the former, interest articulation was closely monitored and dictated by the state; in the latter, it was self-directed and spontaneous. But the CDs were institutionalized, while the media fora were scaled back after 1984. The return to civilian rule under a one-party state in January 1990 seemed to put prospects for political pluralism on hold for an indefinite future. Within a year, however, political protests involving students, mine workers, unions, and urban residents forced the government to legalize multipartyism and announce plans for a new constitution. By the winter of 1991 Niger had eighteen political parties. In the wake of such cataclysmic political changes, the experience of shan iska will likely serve as a referent for future political actions.[19]

POLITICAL PRAXIS AND THE LIMITS OF LEGITIMATION

Our examination of experiences in Burkina Faso and Niger has revealed the ways in which two ideologically disparate military regimes turned to grassroots participation as a medium for legitimation. Both regimes accorded the people an important symbolic role in their legitimation strategies. Yet at a more fundamental level, what these two systems have in common is an attempt to project legitimacy through the façade of quasi-democratic institutions, while at the same time trying to overcontrol politics. As we have seen, the ensuing contradictions enabled at least a few individuals to openly challenge the validity of the regime. Ironically, in both cases the objective function of grassroots participation was subversive of the rulers' intent.

At this juncture it is difficult to make broad generalizations about the limits of popular participation in Africa's soldier-states. Much more work needs to be done on the comparative politics of grassroots councils and their functioning in military regimes. Following the model used here, such studies might examine the dialectical relationship between leaders' rhetoric and popular responses, as well as the interplay between formal structures and officially sanctioned informal arenas of participation. Both have an immediate bearing on how far governance issues will be taken seriously.

As these two case studies have illustrated, the African state's fragile political sphere is besieged by external and internal economic constraints. Thus grassroots councils per se provide no assurance of effective or responsive governance—either under civilian or military rule. As we have seen, such councils can be manipulated by national political elites or become the vehicles for ratifying unpopular policies dictated by the IMF or bilateral aid donors. Moreover, the convergence of autocratic outcomes in revolutionary populist Burkina Faso and neotraditional corporatist Niger implies that the very fact of military rule begets a crisis of legitimation. Once a military regime crosses the Rubicon of corrective legitimacy in search of a more permanent rationale for its authority, the relative balance between coercion and legitimacy inevitably reverts to coercion. The scope for governance is concomitantly reduced.

NOTES

This chapter was drafted while the author was a visiting member of the Institute for Advanced Study, with support from the National Endowment for the Humanities and the Ford Foundation. Elliott Skinner, Donald Rothchild, Naomi Chazan, and Crawford Young are acknowledged for their comments on earlier versions.

1. For a quantitative assessment that analyzes the balance sheets of thirty African military and civilian regimes over a twenty-five-year period and concludes that the civilian regimes outperformed their military counterparts in all the areas of comparison, see Liebenow 1985.

2. Bienen and van de Walle found that African leaders face a high risk of losing power in the first years of their rule, after which the risk decreases sharply. The relationship holds for both military and civilian rulers.

3. It is commonplace for soldiers to govern with the assistance of the civilian bureaucracy and technocrats. Many military regimes also establish local-level councils. For an analysis of how Uganda's General Idi Amin used councils of elders and the ways in which Sudan's General Ga'afar Numeiri structured civilian participation, see Kasfir 1976b.

4. Collier (1982) applies Cardoso's approach to the African experience.

5. Islam reached both territories in the eleventh century, but by 1960 when more than 90 percent of Nigeriens had embraced the faith, Muslims formed an estimated 20 to 25 percent of Upper Volta's population. The Mossi, who are Burkina Faso's largest ethnic group, have been described as "the principle island of resistance to Islam" in precolonial Sudan (see Skinner 1958).

6. Bamouni (1986:70–71) reports that the CSP consisted of two

conservative factions, a nationalist faction headed by President Ouedrago, and a progressive faction.

7. Mongo Beti makes this point in his preface to Bamouni 1986 (p. 7).

8. For example, in the elections following the return to civilian rule in 1978, seven political parties participated, and four candidates ran for president. Before Sankara came to power, trade unions numbered over thirty, and strikes were endemic.

9. The notion of "family development" emphasizes the necessity of associating social development with economic development. A transformative model for addressing the status of women, it served to put issues such as polygamy, bride price, female circumcision, sex education, abortion, family planning, and prostitution on the public agenda as legitimate policy concerns. Along with the promotion of income-generating activities for women and the establishment of child care facilities on a mass level, this approach resulted in a radical—albeit ill-fated—proposal to establish a social wage for housewives.

10. The Ligue Patriotique pour le Développement (LIPAD), the Union des Luttes Communistes (ULC), and the Parti Communiste Révolutionnaire Burkinabè (PCRB) all had ministerial posts in the first CNR government.

11. By 1987 there were four groups in the coalition government: the Union des Luttes Communistes-Reconstruite (ULC-R), the Union des Communistes Burkinabè (UCB), the Groupe Communiste Burkinabè (GCB), and the Organisation des Militaires Révolutionnaires (OMR).

12. Skinner (1988:453) cites the claim that Sankara opposed the creation of a monolithic party. Otayek (1987), among others, suggests that Sankara's insistence on the need for a unitary party led to his demise.

13. A sketch of the revolution's ideological basis, as well as its political and economic organization, is provided by Guy Martin (1987).

14. This account is based on my analysis of reports filed on local, subregional, and regional CD meetings held in Gaya, Dogon Doutchi, Magaria, Tchin Tabaraden, Abalak, and Maradi; participant observation at regional CD meetings in Zinder and Dosso; newspaper accounts of CND meetings; and personal interviews (for a detailed analysis of the system, see Robinson, forthcoming).

15. Radio Niger broadcasts daily in six national languages. Locally produced public affairs programming is a staple of Nigerien television. TV sets are generally accessible in public places—including rural areas, where community centers are equipped with electric power generators, or merchants and chiefs may make their sets available for public viewing.

16. André Salifou, Débat-Télé, "Histoire Politique du Niger," December 1983 (author's translation). Within a year Salifou was removed from his post as dean of the Faculty of Education at the University of Niamey. Observers have attributed his dismissal to remarks made during this broadcast.

17. This account is reconstructed from a 1984 Radio Niger tape recording of the "Débat de Torodi."

18. In the arid pastoral zone to the north, the government drilled a network of boreholes that eventually led to a serious problem of overgrazing around these water points. For the Torodi herders, however, the perception of inequitable resource allocations was paramount.

19. Albert Hirschman (1984:42–44) refers to this phenomenon as the Principle of Conservation and Mutation of Social Energy.

8

The Rise and Fall of a
Governance Realm in Kenya

Joel D. Barkan

Goran Hyden argues that the governance realm of a political system is that area bounded by two variable conditions that determine the relationship between the rulers and the ruled: (1) the *actor dimension*, or the personal expectations individuals have for each other's behavior; and (2) the *structural dimension*—the institutionalized procedures, or rules of the game—operative in a particular polity.

Not all political systems have established or maintained a governance realm. Those which have are systems wherein the basis of interaction between the rulers and the ruled is that of legitimate authority or reciprocity, and where the procedures that structure these relationships maintain accountability, trust, or both, between the actors involved. Political systems with a governance realm are thus systems wherein there is a measure of bargaining, compromise, and tolerance among competing interests, and between those who exercise political authority and those who are subject to it.

The existence of a governance realm is dependent on a regime's adherence to a predictable and legitimate set of procedures that regulate the exercise of political authority and the competition between claimants for state resources. Procedures that are frequently changed are never institutionalized. Procedures that do not provide for a significant measure of bargaining and reciprocity between the rulers and the ruled, and between competing claimants, will not be regarded as legitimate.

It is no coincidence that the diminution of the governance realm across Africa has accompanied the spread of personal rule (Jackson & Rosberg 1982). Where the exercise of political authority is monopolized by a head of state who rules by decree and where such rule is marked, as it typically is, by abrupt changes in the rules of the game, the establishment or maintenance of a governance realm is impossible. Although Hyden's concept of a governance realm is applicable to all political systems, it is addressed primarily to African polities because of the breakdown of governance across the continent. In this context, the case of Kenya is particularly instructive, because it is perhaps the only African state to establish a robust governance realm and then dismantle it.

I will chronicle and explain the rise and fall of a governance realm in Kenya from the late 1950s through 1990 by considering five questions: (1) what were the normative and institutional elements of Kenyan political life that constituted a governance realm from the mid-1960s to the early 1980s? (2) what conditions gave rise to the establishment of a governance realm? (3) to what extent were these conditions unique to Kenya and explain what is often termed "the Kenyan exception"—Kenya's record of greater political stability and economic performance compared to other African countries? (4) why was the governance realm in Kenya dismantled after becoming a distinctive feature of Kenyan political life? and (5) what does this dismantlement suggest about the prospects for establishing or reestablishing a governance realm in Kenya and other African countries?

ESTABLISHING A GOVERNANCE REALM: THE KENYATTA ERA

A robust and resilient governance realm was established in Kenya during the 1960s and maintained until approximately 1983. It resulted from a combination of three factors: (1) the peculiarities of Kenya's transition to independence from 1958 to 1963; (2) the shrewd and skillful leadership of Kenya's first president, Jomo Kenyatta; and (3) the tradition of self-help among the Kenyan population. These factors resulted in the establishment of a no-party state that provided a clearly defined arena for a limited but significant measure of political competition—a semicompetitive system in which patron-client networks linked the state and civil society together (Barkan & Okumu 1978) and provided for a measure of accountability by the rulers to the ruled. Most important, the Kenyan state during this period was predictable. Clear norms and procedures were evolved for regulating the relationship between state and society—norms that were accepted by both the rulers and the ruled, and that remained constant over time.

Kenya's Transition to Independence

In contrast to most African colonies, Kenya was the home of a white settler community,[1] which retarded and complicated the country's transition to self-rule. Although Britain and France began the transition in most colonies by the mid-1950s (Fieldhouse 1986), the future of Kenya remained in doubt as the settlers resisted the rise of African nationalism while the nationalists mounted an armed insurrection in 1952 known as the Mau Mau Rebellion. Although the colonial government contained the rebellion within two years, it declared a state of emergency that lasted until 1960. Under the emergency, Kenyatta and other nationalist leaders were jailed. Their political party, the Kenya African Union, and all other nationwide political organizations were banned. The British government, however, committed itself to Kenya's eventual independence.[2]

As was their practice in other colonies, the British sought to transfer political power to an indigenous elite in Kenya by phasing in a parliamentary system of government. The procedure followed was to hold a series of elections to transform the Legislative Council (LEGCO) from an appointed and advisory body into an elected legislature responsible for making government policy. Through these elections, the proportion of LEGCO members elected on the basis of universal suffrage rose until it exceeded 90 percent. At this point, a provisional government would be formed by the leader of the majority party or majority coalition of parties. Independence would follow within a few months.

To commence this scenario in Kenya, the first elections for African representation in the LEGCO were held for eight of thirty-two seats in 1957. A second round for six additional seats was held in 1958, but the continuation of the emergency required that candidates in these elections form campaign organizations only at the district level. These district organizations were typically clientelist organizations created by individual candidates to mobilize support among the members of their ethnic group.[3] Thus, when nationwide political parties were legalized again at the end of the emergency in 1960, the leaders of the new parties were faced with an array of district organizations that they had to accommodate. The result, hastened by the intention of the British to hold a third round of elections for thirty-three seats in 1961, was the rapid formation of two nationwide coalitions of district organizations—the Kenya African National Union (KANU) and the Kenya African Democratic Union (KADU).

As the professed heir to the Kenya African Union (KAU), KANU was the coalition of those organizations that had emerged in the districts that had provided KAU with the core of its support before the emergency. These areas included the districts of Central Province and the eastern part of Rift Valley Province, populated mainly by the Kikuyu people, and the districts of Eastern Province, populated by the Embu, Meru, and Kamba peoples. District-level organizations in Nyanza Province, the home of the Luo and Gusii peoples in western Kenya, also joined the KANU coalition.

As the party of the Kikuyus, Luos, Kambas, and Gusiis, KANU drew most of its support from four of Kenya's five largest ethnic groups.[4] As the party of the Kikuyu, Embu, and Meru, KANU was also the coalition of those groups which were among the most prosperous and politically mobilized as a result of their proximity to Nairobi and the spread of cash-crop agriculture into their areas of residence. In essence, KANU became the coalition of "the bigs," "the mobilized," and "the haves," and drew the core of its support from groups that constituted 60 percent of Kenya's population.

By contrast, KADU was the coalition of "the smalls," "the unmobilized," and the "have-nots" in that it was composed of district organizations located in relatively undeveloped areas inhabited by smaller ethnic groups who had not participated in KAU. These included the Abaluhya people in Western Province, who are 14 percent of Kenya's population but who are relatively poor; the Kalenjin peoples, who reside in the western side of Rift Valley Province; the Mijikenda peoples of Coast Province and most of Kenya's seminomadic peoples scattered across the arid and semiarid expanses of northern and northeastern Kenya, and the southern Rift Valley. Although geographically vast, the population base of KADU was barely a third of Kenya's population.

KANU demonstrated its numerical advantage in the elections of February 1961 by winning nineteen of the thirty-three seats, with 67 percent of the vote. A major campaign issue for KANU was the release of Jomo Kenyatta, who had remained in jail since 1952. In response to KANU's overwhelming victory, the colonial government freed Kenyatta in August after which he assumed the presidency of KANU and reinforced the party's claim to being the successor to KAU.

A fourth election, held in May 1963 under a new Constitution negotiated by KANU and KADU, paved the way for Kenya's independence. The Constitution provided for a bicameral legislature with a lower house (the House of Representatives) of 129 members of which 117 were to be elected from single-member districts. The results paralleled those of 1961. KANU won seventy seats, with 54 percent of the vote, while KADU won thirty-two, with 26 percent. The remainder was divided between minor parties and independent candidates. As the majority party, KANU formed the first elected African government, with Jomo Kenyatta as prime minister, in June. Independence followed on December 12.

The elections of 1961 and 1963 extended the proliferation of clientelist organizations across Kenya as branches of KANU and KADU were established in each new constituency to elect local notables who stood for election under one party's banner or the other's. With few exceptions, each constituency was populated by people of the same ethnic group who extended overwhelming support to candidates affiliated with one party.

From a distance, Kenya appeared to be a two-party state. In reality, the two coalitions functioned as a no-party system. With independence, those elected began to scramble for state resources to pay off clients in their home areas. The issues separating individual members of KANU and KADU were thus mainly distributive rather than programmatic in nature. KANU sought to consolidate the dominant position of the bigs, the mobilized, and the haves, while KADU sought to defend the smalls and the have-nots against such domination.

The only significant programmatic difference between the two parties reflected this concern. Whereas KANU sought to achieve Kenya's independence under a constitution that provided for a strong centralized government, KADU sought a federal arrangement known as Majimbo to protect the members of its minority coalition. Under pressure from the British, KANU agreed to Majimbo to expedite the elections of 1963 and the final transition to independence. However, once in power Kenyatta's government dragged its feet on implementing federalism, particularly the establishment of eight regional legislatures with the authority to enact their own budgets. By the middle of 1964 Kenyatta and KANU had effectively shut KADU out of the political process and hence any meaningful access to state resources.

As members of a minority coalition in what had in essence become a unitary state, KADU parliamentarians had no option but to fold their party into KANU. By the end of 1964 Kenya became a de facto one-party state as members of KADU joined KANU "in the interests of national unity." A new Constitution was passed that scrapped Majimbo and provided for a presidential form of government with Kenyatta as its head. KANU had become Kenya's sole political party, but it remained a loose coalition of local and regional clientelist organizations that were monoethnic in character.

The Kenyatta Factor

As the patriarch of Kenyan nationalism, Jomo Kenyatta played a role in the development of his country's political system that is instructive for those concerned with the establishment of a governance realm. Soon after becoming the president of KANU in 1961, Kenyatta realized that the formation of a single and centralized nationalist party would be very difficult because of the existence of many district organizations. The proliferation of such organizations had entrenched the power of many local notables to the point that they could not be controlled by Kenyatta and other leaders of KANU. Unable to amalgamate these personal organizations into a single party, Kenyatta determined that his best strategy was to rise above the fray and tolerate the activities of local bosses so long as they did not challenge his authority as the head of KANU and later as the head of state. Rather than suppressing leaders who sought to maintain and fortify their local power bases, Kenyatta assisted and manipulated their efforts by selectively dispensing or withholding patronage needed for this task.

The collapse of KADU and the wooing of its deputy leader, Daniel arap Moi, into the KANU fold is a case in point. Rather than suppress KADU during the period immediately before and after independence, Kenyatta starved the party into extinction while incorporating its most important pieces into his regime. By elevating Moi to the vice-presidency of KANU, and later to the vice-presidency of Kenya, Kenyatta strengthened KANU by co-opting Moi's organization intact (Throup 1987). Kenyatta's strategy of allowing local and regional leaders to maintain political followings of their own, provided they supported his regime, set the norms of governance for the rest of his tenure as Kenya's president.

Between 1965 and 1969 Kenyatta was faced with the emergence of a new opposition party, the Kenya People's Union (KPU), formed by dissident members of the House of Representatives and Senate. Concerned that Kenyatta and KANU had forsaken the objectives of independence, particularly a more equitable distribution of Kenya's limited farmland, the leaders of the KPU professed to offer a socialist alternative. Given the direct and ideological nature of this challenge, the government systematically harassed the party and its leaders. A special election was called in 1966 to force the nineteen representatives and ten senators who had defected from KANU to renew their electoral mandate. Twenty of the twenty-nine dissidents lost their seats in what became known as the little General Election, and in 1969 the KPU was banned.

At the same time as he suppressed competition between parties, Kenyatta began to institutionalize a significant measure of competition within KANU. Beginning with the parliamentary elections of 1969, and continuing through the elections of 1974 and 1979, almost any adult member of KANU who supported the party's election manifesto could become a candidate for parliament. Parliamentary elections were open contests that usually attracted multiple candidates, but contests limited to those who refrained from challenging the regime. Parliamentary constituencies were also made smaller and more socially homogeneous prior to the 1969 elections by the merger of the House of Representatives and Senate into a unicameral National Assembly of 158 elected members and twelve appointed members.

The net effect of these changes was to turn parliamentary elections into a series of local referenda on the ability of individual incumbents to secure state resources for their home areas (Barkan 1976). Campaign rhetoric focused on distributive issues rather than programmatic alternatives. Notwithstanding these limitations, Kenyatta's commitment to the regular holding of elections that were both open and fair strengthened his regime and contributed to the establishment of a governance realm. Because elections were truly competitive, incumbents were held accountable for their activities and forced to be attentive to the concerns of their constituents. Those elected thus wielded legitimate albeit limited authority, and in turn legitimized the regime. The electoral mechanism also pruned away officials whose records at constituency service were poor and whose continuation in office would have detracted from Kenyatta's leadership.

Kenyatta's rules for distributing patronage also encouraged incumbent parliamentarians to be attentive to their constituents. During the late 1960s Kenyatta increased the number of government ministries and hence the number of cabinet ministers to approximately twenty. The number of assistant ministers rose to over forty. These positions were coveted because of their prestige, perks of office, and especially the access they provided to state resources. With more than one-third of the National Assembly receiving ministerial appointments, Kenyatta developed a powerful tool for maintaining support from prominent politicians and ensuring that they remained popular in their home areas.

Initial appointments of cabinet ministers invariably went to veteran politicians including several (e.g., Daniel arap Moi, Jeremiah Nyagah, Masinde Muliro) elected before 1963. Members of the National Assembly elected in 1963 and after were appointed assistant ministers. Relative newcomers were left on the back bench. The criteria for appointment became clearer following the elections of 1969 when 26 percent of the ministers and 37 percent of the assistant ministers lost their seats. Members of parliament (MPs) who had been reelected two or more times could expect cabinet appointments, while those who had been reelected once were most likely to be named assistant ministers. These criteria were maintained in subsequent appointments following the elections of 1974, 1979, and 1983, but have eroded since the election of 1988.

Notwithstanding these "rules" of appointment, the percentage of ministers and assistant ministers who lost their seats in successive elections remained roughly the same as in 1969. For example, in 1983, 19 percent of incumbent ministers and 41 percent of incumbent assistant ministers who sought reelection were defeated. The advantage of holding a ministerial position and incumbency to win reelection was also clear. While roughly four-fifths of cabinet ministers could anticipate reelection, the proportion for backbenchers was about half. Challengers, on the other hand, faced formidable odds. Between 1969 and 1983 only 11–20 percent of all challengers won election.[5]

Two additional aspects of Kenyatta's patronage system deserve mention. The first is that once given a ministerial position one's tenure in office was usually secure until the next election. Kenyatta reshuffled his cabinet infrequently, and when he did virtually all incumbents retained their rank if not their portfolios. The second is that ministers, assistant ministers, and even some backbenchers who were regarded as particularly valuable to the regime were also appointed to the statutory boards of government marketing agencies for agricultural commodities, regulatory agencies, and state-owned corporations (parastatals). As with ministerial appointments, appointments to statutory boards carried an array of perks and access to resources that could be funneled back to one's constituency or traded for same. In sum, the basis of Kenyatta's system of patronage was not mere loyalty to the regime, but loyalty coupled with a demonstrated ability to represent a public constituency and renew one's electoral mandate.

Kenyatta also contributed to the establishment of a governance realm by maintaining a high degree of professionalism and autonomy in the civil service and judiciary. Although he appointed all members of the Public Service Commission, which in turn made all senior appointments in the civil service, members of the commission could not be removed for reasons other than infirmity or misconduct without referring the matter to a special judicial tribunal. Professional competence, as demonstrated by a record of high performance, was the principal criterion for appointment. In marked contrast to the membership of the statutory boards, all members and former members of the National Assembly were excluded from serving on the Public Service Commission.

This is not to suggest that the political significance of many senior appointments in the civil service was ignored. By positioning himself above day-to-day politics at the constituency level, Kenyatta relied heavily on the civil service, particularly the Provincial Administration, to project the authority of the central government across rural Kenya. Provincial commissioners (PCs) were given considerable autonomy over the administration of their areas but reported directly to the Office of the President.[6] PCs were rarely transferred, and their tenure in the same province often lasted from five to ten years. The result is that PCs often became powerful lords in the realms they administered. District commissioners also held their positions for a minimum of two to three years, sometimes more. The result was the presence in rural Kenya of a strong and competent administration that enjoyed the confidence of the president—the "steel frame" of the Kenyan state.

Kenyatta's commitment to maintaining a professional civil service can also be explained by the ethnoregional base of his regime and his position as the leader of a regime representing the the bigs, the mobilized, and the haves. The core of Kenyatta's support came from members of his own Kikuyu tribe. As residents of one of the most developed regions in Kenya, and because of their greater access to educational facilities before independence, Kikuyu held a significantly larger proportion of the positions in the civil service than their proportion of the population. Kikuyu historically entered the civil service before the members of other groups, and in greater numbers because of their superior educational qualifications. Thus, Kenyatta's commitment to maintaining a professional civil service was also a commitment to maintaining Kikuyu dominance and responding to the expectations of his core constituency.

Kenyatta also maintained a professionally run and independent judiciary. Appointments to the judiciary were made by the Judicial Services Commission, which was appointed by the president and chaired by the Chief Justice of the High Court, who was also appointed by the president. Judges on the High Court, however, had life tenure and could not be removed for reasons other than illness unless an independent tribunal concurred there were grounds for dismissal.

Complementing Kenyatta's commitment to a professionally run state was his tolerance of a relatively free press and the emergence of autonomous associational life. The norms for both were the same as for electoral politics; as long as the press and private associations did not challenge Kenyatta's authority directly, it was permissible to offer muted criticism of government policy. The press regularly provided a forum for the public debate of issues on which Kenyatta's government had not taken a final position. Debate within the National Assembly was given extensive coverage, as were disputes between regional leaders, local politics, and the activities of private associations. Perhaps most significant for the creation of a governance realm, private associations and interest groups were free to organize their respective constituencies, articulate their concerns, and lobby the government.

Within these norms of permissibility, a wide range of associational life made its presence felt in Kenyan society. These included professional associations and economic interest groups such as the Law Society of Kenya, the Chamber of Commerce, the Kenya Manufacturers Association, the Kenya Farmers Association, and the Central Organisation of Trades Unions (COTU); church organizations of various denominations; Kenyan-based nongovernmental organizations such as the National Christian Council of Kenya and Maendeleo Ya Wanawake (Women's Development Association); powerful ethnic welfare associations including the Gikuyu Embu Meru Association (GEMA) and the Luo Union; and community self-help development organizations known as Harambee. Whereas professional and economic associations served mainly urban constituencies, a distinctive feature of other associations was the extent to which they established linkages between the Kenyan state and rural society. The importance of the intermediary roles played by these organizations cannot be overstated. On the one hand, these organizations broadened the social base of the Kenyatta regime. On the other, they served as counterweights to the state and fostered a process of bargaining and mutual accommodation between the regime and civil society.

Although Kenyatta's regime was an authoritarian one, especially during its latter years, and while he ruthlessly repressed any direct challenge,[7] it was not a system marked by the excesses of personal rule found elsewhere in Africa and later in Kenya itself. Kenyatta never sought to monopolize all sources of authority. Although invariably referred to as *Mzee*, the Swahili term of respect for a wise elder, a cult of personality was never developed around the president. Subordinate officials such as prominent cabinet ministers were not reduced to political eunuchs but featured as pillars of the regime. While Kenyatta's Kenya was not democratic, it was nonetheless a relatively open and resilient system with multiple secondary centers of power and a measure of real competition—and hence accountability—at the local and regional levels. Kenyatta's regime was also a predictable system, a necessary condition for the creation and maintenance of a governance realm.

Self-Help and Rural Civil Society

The third significant factor that contributed to the establishment of a governance realm during the 1960s and 1970s was the proliferation and autonomy of local self-help development organizations known as *Harambee*.

Although the developmental significance of Harambee organizations has been discussed extensively in the literature (Winans & Haugerud 1977; Mbithi & Rasmusson 1977; Thomas 1985), their political significance has been regarded as something of a sideshow—a defensive activity by the peasantry to carve out a measure of political space vis-à-vis central political authority (Holmquist 1980). It was, and may again become, much more (Barkan & Holmquist 1989).

Because most Kenyans, like most Africans, are small farmers, the existence or nonexistence of a governance realm ultimately turns on the nature of peasant-state relations. Where there are relationships of reciprocity and bargaining between state authorities and the peasantry, there will be governance. Where there are no such relationships, there will not. The existence of these relationships, however, depends in turn on the emergence of associational life across the countryside; that is to say, civil society among the peasantry. In rural Kenya the most significant component of civil society apart from the church is Harambee.

By the mid-1980s there were between fifteen thousand and twenty thousand Harambee self-help organizations in Kenya. The specific number is difficult to determine, but there are several hundred groups in most districts.[8] Almost 90 percent of all members of rural communities join Harambee organizations, and more than half are members of four or more groups. The principal activity of these organizations is to provide basic social welfare services and infrastructure to participants. The construction and staffing of primary and secondary schools, health clinics, cattle dips, local water systems, and feeder roads and bridges account for most self-help activities. Only a handful of groups produce goods for the market.

Members of local communities organize themselves to provide social welfare services and infrastructure on a self-help basis because few individuals can obtain these services on their own. On the other hand, members rarely join to produce goods for the market because almost all production of agricultural commodities is done on a household basis. Although Harambee projects are exercises in collective action, they are not highly prone to free riding because they are usually the only source of services for which there is widespread public demand.

Self-help first emerged among the Kikuyu in the late 1930s and 1940s to establish educational facilities not provided by the colonial state and to assert African independence. The establishment of the Kenya Independent Schools was both politically and developmentally significant and laid the basis of what later became a nationwide movement of grassroots organizations. Self-help was also practiced among the Luo who formed the Luo Thrift Association and the Kavirondo Tax Payers Association in the 1940s. Following independence, Kenyatta and his government repeatedly urged all rural Kenyans to engage in self-help efforts similar to the efforts that had established the independent schools. Such efforts were called Harambee after the official motto on Kenya's coat of arms. The term soon became part of Kenyan political rhetoric, as Kenyatta ended most of his speeches with several exhortations of "Harambee!"[9]

Kenyatta first urged the formation of self-help groups to reduce the volume of demands on his government for rural services. As in other African countries, popular expectations for rural services rose sharply at independence but were far more than the state could provide. The encouragement of Harambee was also consistent with Kenyatta's strategy for dealing with local and regional political leaders. By urging rural residents to engage in self-help and to seek assistance from their elected leaders on the one hand, and by allowing leaders to build a political base through such assistance on the other, Kenyatta forced most politicians to pay more attention to the needs of their constituents than to matters of central government policy. The combination of the regular holding of elections and Harambee cemented the link between development and politics at the local level while leaving Kenyatta free to make policy at the center. This combination also made Harambee the principal arena of local politics insofar as incumbent leaders and would-be leaders could not ignore the demands of self-help groups. Harambee became the nexus where civil society in rural Kenya met the state, and thus a critical institution of the governance realm.

In this regard, Harambee established clear norms of social interaction between state and society as well as within local communities. In addition to the expectation that elected officials would advance their political careers by assisting self-help, civil servants at the district and national levels developed criteria for providing state assistance to different types of projects. For example, by the late 1970s and early 1980s it was clear to most rural residents that if they constructed a secondary school building according to blueprints provided by the Ministry of Education, and established an effective organization for administering the school, collected school fees and recruited an initial complement of teaching staff, the ministry would eventually provide certified teachers and take over the school. Assistance to rural health clinics by the Ministry of Health evolved in the same manner. The creation of the Rural Development Fund supported by the Nordic countries and the Dutch provided a modest yet significant pool of funds that was dispensed by the district administration to match local initiative. The establishment of the microprojects program by the European Economic Community, as well as assistance provided self-help groups by foreign nongovernmental organizations (NGOs) including CARE, reinforced the evolving relationship between local communities and the state.

Harambee also reinforced and reflected norms of reciprocity and accountability within local communities, and more broadly between the center and periphery of Kenyan society. Notwithstanding the extent to which elected leaders and district officials responded to self-help, all projects were (and remain) substantially self-financed during their infancy. More than 85 percent of all projects never receive state assistance of any kind. This is because most projects are primary schools and child care centers serving small catchment areas, while projects that receive state support are large efforts such as secondary schools or health centers that serve several adjacent communities. State assistance flows to large projects partially because they are more-complex efforts that require both financial and technical assistance to succeed, but also because elected leaders are more likely to lobby on behalf of large projects.[10]

The financing of Harambee thus falls mainly on the members of the local community. During the Kenyatta era funds for Harambee were raised in cash, labor, or kind, and evolved into an informal community income tax. All members of the community, no matter how poor, were expected to contribute and were often subject to intense pressure to do so. Those who were relatively rich, however, were expected to pay substantially more than those who were poor—and did (Barkan & Holmquist 1989). This pattern of contributions suggests that Harambee has fostered a measure of reciprocity between those who are dominant in rural communities and those who are not.

Self-help has also fostered a relationship of reciprocity between the residents of rural communities and those who have migrated from these communities to urban areas—especially civil servants and professionals. As with the rural rich, members of the urban salariat are expected to make regular contributions to self-help in their home communities to maintain respect and hence full "citizenship." Although it is impossible to estimate the amounts of these transfers, they are considerable. Urban workers regularly collect contributions from each other to support self-help back home. The expectation that residents of the center have obligations to those on the periphery thus parallels and reinforces the expectation that the state must be responsive to rural interests. By giving rise to such expectations, Harambee has helped establish the norms that maintain a governance realm.

DISMANTLING A GOVERNANCE REALM: THE MOI ERA

When Jomo Kenyatta died in office in August 1978 he was succeeded by the vice-president, Daniel arap Moi, as specified by Kenya's Constitution. A Kalenjin and former leader of KADU, Moi became the head of a regime that had suffered toward the end of Kenyatta's life from the declining health of its leader and rising corruption. Moi was also soon faced with an array of pressures on the Kenyan economy that were beyond his immediate control. The end of the world coffee boom in 1979, the dramatic rise in the price of imported oil in 1980/81, the world recession of 1981/82, and the continuation of a 3.9 percent annual rate of population growth combined to slow fifteen years of economic advance. Severe droughts in 1979–1980 and again in 1984, which necessitated large importations of food, further complicated the economy. Per capita income in the rural areas declined. By the early 1980s Kenya had also exhausted most first-stage options for establishing import substitution industries, with the result that the number of new jobs in Kenya's cities could not keep pace with rising numbers of migrants from the rural areas.

Despite these pressures, and partly in response to them, Moi embraced a populist approach to governing based on what he termed his *Nyayo*[11] philosophy of "peace, unity, and love." Although boosting Moi's popularity in the short run, Nyayo raised public expectations beyond what his government could deliver. Most important, Nyayo was a harbinger of personal rule and the diminution of the governance realm.

The Nyayo Variation of Personal Rule

Moi began his presidency in 1978 with a highly publicized crackdown on corrupt associates of the old regime, and on ethnic welfare unions, particularly GEMA.[12] Both moves were an effort to undermine members of the Kikuyu establishment and serve notice to the Kikuyu community as a whole that the new regime was not beholden to it in the manner of the old. Moi next decreed that the government would provide all schoolchildren with free milk and implement a policy of universal primary education. In 1983 the president announced that Kenya would restructure its educational system to provide eight years of primary education, four years of secondary school, and four years of university training instead of three.

Although welcomed at the time of their announcement, Moi's decrees were indicative of an approach to governance that soon became the modus operandi of his presidency. Four characteristics mark this approach. First, the president would suddenly announce new directions in policy without extensive deliberation with his advisors or the heads of departments charged with their implementation. The civil service, on the other hand, was expected to implement the new directives without question, even if implementation was impossible or would cause serious disruptions and incur heavy costs. The decisions to provide free milk and restructure the educational system are two examples. The government was forced to go slow on the first, while the second has put severe strains on the system.[13]

Second, government resources were to be reallocated to meet the basic needs of Kenya's have-nots, primarily those residing in regions that were once the cores of the old KADU coalition of which Moi had been a leader. By stating that the government would provide expanded welfare opportunities to the *wananchi* (Swahili for "common people"), Moi sought to redirect resources away from the ethnoregional base of the original KANU and the Kenyatta regime. Notwithstanding its populist overtones, Nyayo was never intended to mitigate class inequities, but to reduce inequities between ethnoregional constituencies. Kikuyu, including the poor, soon learned that Nyayo was not for them.

Third, new policy decisions were to be articulated as the personal decisions of the president rather than as policies of his government. The distinction was not immediately apparent to observers of what had been a strong presidential system but emphasized the extent to which political authority was to be monopolized by Moi alone.

Fourth, public debate of new policy initiatives was discouraged and ultimately forbidden. Only praise was acceptable. To question, even to help the government fulfil a stated objective, incurred the president's displeasure. By 1982 the semifree press that had operated throughout Kenyatta's tenure came under intense pressure and began to practice self-censorship.[14] Meaningful debate in the National Assembly also dwindled, especially after the elections of 1983. MPs who questioned the wisdom of a particular policy or who sought to modify government policy were soon branded as disloyal, and in some cases expelled from the legislature and ultimately KANU. Regime policy and procedure became less predictable as Moi expressed increased distrust of those who did not follow the Nyayo line. With uncertainty came both fear of the president and sycophancy to ward off his suspicion.

Institutional Changes

In 1982 Moi began a series of institutional changes that entrenched Nyayo. The first was a constitutional amendment to make Kenya a de jure one-party state. Although Kenya had been a de facto one-party system since the demise of the KPU in 1969, the president felt it necessary to formally ban opposition parties to consolidate his rule. Moi's perspective of the role of KANU and opposition parties differed from his predecessor's. Whereas Kenyatta had viewed KANU as a coalition of local and regional clientelist organizations that embraced a diversity of interests, Moi came to view the party as a mechanism to control leaders with independent followings.[15]

The evolution of KANU. The amendment to formally make Kenya a one-party state, and the events that gave rise to it, signaled the transformation of KANU in the late 1980s. The amendment was rushed through the National Assembly in response to the intention of Oginga Odinga, the former head of the defunct KPU, to form a new opposition party. Odinga had been readmitted to KANU and politically rehabilitated by Moi when he was expelled again in 1979 for criticizing Kenyatta posthumously. If such troublesome critics as Odinga were to be expelled from KANU to put them in political limbo, they could not be permitted to form new parties once outside.

The amendment to make Kenya a one-party state was passed in May 1982 and provoked much public discussion, which resulted in a crackdown on the press and an attempted coup by the Kenya Air Force in August. The regime in turn became more manipulative and repressive as Moi sought to undermine the influence of prominent cabinet ministers and others who had developed independent bases of power. In marked contrast to Kenyatta, Moi did not view prominent elected leaders as people who maintained popular support for his regime, but rather as rivals who threatened it.

The first to fall in 1983 was Charles Njonjo, the former attorney general and then minister of constitutional affairs who had engineered Moi's constitutional succession to the presidency. Following a script that was to be repeated to dump other leaders, Moi's office first leaked rumors that an unnamed cabinet minister had engaged in "traitorous" behavior by discussing state secrets with a foreign power. Discussion of the rumors soon surfaced in the press and subsequently in the National Assembly where the name of the "disloyal" individual was revealed. Ministers of lesser status and backbenchers seeking to curry presidential favor then jumped on the bandwagon to vilify the "disloyal" member and demand his expulsion from the Assembly and KANU. In Njonjo's case, the leader targeted to fall was also tried for sedition and pardoned by the president before leaving public life. Several other popular ministers, most notably G. G. Kariuki, the minister of state in the Office of the President, were also implicated in the "Njonjo affair" and drummed out of the National Assembly and KANU.[16]

Moi also made use of the party to undermine cabinet ministers about whom he had doubts. Once party branches at the district and constituency level were revitalized by the election of new officers in 1985, these organizations became autonomous bodies that were not always part of the clientelist networks maintained by elected officials of long standing. Where an MP or a cabinet minister did not succeed in electing one of his supporters to a party position, the branch organization could become a source of opposition from below. Where backbenchers or assistant ministers controlled party branches in their constituencies, instead of the cabinet minister from the region, there was also a potential for challenging the authority of the regional boss. This tension between established leaders of cabinet rank and lesser leaders who held positions in the party increased in September 1988 when a new round of elections was held by the party to elect branch officers. Several established Kikuyu leaders were severely challenged and in some cases defeated in elections that many felt were rigged on orders from Moi. The political decline of Kenya's former vice-president, Mwai Kibaki, can be interpreted in these terms. Kenneth Matiba also faced such pressures and was ultimately forced out of the cabinet and expelled from KANU in December. A prominent Kikuyu leader and businessman, Matiba was detained in July 1990 along with Charles Rubia, the former mayor of Nairobi. Having been expelled from KANU, both men had publicly called for the end of the one-party state.

During the Kenyatta era challenges to ministers and assistant ministers from below were rare except at election time. Today they are regularly encouraged by Moi to weaken the authority of leaders of national stature. This is particularly true in Central Province where local party officials perpetually snipe at MPs and especially ministers. Rather than use the emergent party apparatus to mobilize regime support at the grass roots, Moi has used the branch organizations to promote endless rounds of factional infighting to break up clientelist networks that were once used to advance ethnoregional interests. The practice of expelling prominent leaders from KANU, a practice that increased markedly in the late 1980s, has been pursued with the same objective.[17]

Changes in electoral procedure. Moi's penchant for undermining prominent regional leaders instead of standing on their shoulders in the manner of Kenyatta also explains his intervention in the electoral process. As discussed above, almost anyone wishing to stand for office during the Kenyatta era could do so; elections were conducted honestly and turnout was high. The nature of the system began to change in 1983. Although electoral procedures remained the same, the president became actively interested in the outcomes of roughly three dozen contests. In some constituencies candidates were prevented from running by being persuaded to withdraw or declared ineligible by KANU. In others the president publicly endorsed the candidates he favored. Only rarely were the results falsified, and many of those elected were not favored by Moi.

To achieve greater control over the electoral process, the president announced several controversial changes of election procedure in 1986. Most controversial was the introduction of a queuing system of public voting where the casting of secret ballots was replaced by voters lining up in a field behind the agents of candidates holding pictures of each contestant. Although queuing was only to be used at the first stage of elections for the National Assembly to determine the three finalists for whom secret ballots would then be cast, the fear and intimidation that accompanied the procedure reduced turnout to a historic low. In the 1988 elections, Kenya's seventh since independence, only 23 percent of those eligible voted despite highly publicized efforts by KANU to register a record number of voters. The number of formal complaints of fraud filed with the election commission after the election was also the highest in Kenya's history.

A second controversial procedure, specifying that candidates receiving 70 percent of the vote at queuing time would be declared elected, contributed further to the widespread view that many of the elections had been rigged. The appointment of Josephat Karanja to be Kenya's vice-president after the election caused particular outrage. Karanja received 92 percent of the vote in the first round of the election but drew only 4,196, or 8 percent, of the 51,155 registered voters in his constituency. Thirty new parliamentary constituencies were also created prior to the elections. While the new constituencies and redistricting provided for a more accurate representation of Kenya's population, the increase from 158 to 188 constituencies narrowed the power bases of some established politicians.

The changes in electoral procedure, coupled with the president's use of local KANU organizations to undermine established leaders have restructured the relationship between the state and society and in the process reduced the governance realm. Under Kenyatta, the criteria for candidates' winning elections were clear, and the electoral process determined who held high office other than the president and who did not; today people are not sure. The net result of the changes is that neither the party nor elections generate support for the regime.

Perhaps in recognition of this weakness, Moi appointed a special Review Committee of KANU in July 1990 to hold public hearings on the future of the party and the electoral system. More likely, the president was responding to increased pressure from inside and outside the country that Kenya democratize its political system. Internally, Moi has been faced by a rising chorus of critics who include leaders of professional and private voluntary associations, prominent clergy, and human rights activists who refuse to be cowed by detentions, harassment, and other means—including torture—that the regime employs to subdue its opponents (Amnesty International 1987). Externally, the regime has come under pressure from major donor countries and international aid agencies, particularly the United States and the World Bank.

A major subject of the debate on democratization is the question of whether Kenya should become a multiparty system to reestablish a measure of political competition. Moi has resisted the idea of opposition parties vociferously, arguing that more parties would lead to ethnic conflict and that the calls for change are made by foreigners meddling in Kenya's internal affairs, or their local agents. Notwithstanding Moi's position, testimony submitted to the KANU Review Committee included numerous statements by Kenyan lawyers, journalists, and clergy that it was time to legalize opposition groups and modify election procedure. Criticism was also expressed about the increasing practice of expelling party members with whom the president disagreed. At a meeting of party leaders held in December 1990 to discuss the report of the Review Committee, Moi announced that while he still rejected a multiparty system, the most objectionable aspects of the electoral system, queuing and the 70 percent rule, would be scrapped. Expulsions from KANU, which dropped sharply in 1990, would also be stopped. At a subsequent meeting of party leaders, held in June 1991, the president announced a return to an open system of elections whereby "anyone" will be able to stand for election to the National Assembly.

Administrative and judicial reform. Just as Moi has sought to restructure the party and electoral system to undermine the authority of prominent elected officials, so too has he tried to undercut the authority of senior members of the civil service, especially the Provincial Administration. As discussed above, district commissioners (DCs) and provincial commissioners were important pillars of Kenyatta's regime and held their positions for many years. Moi began altering the system soon after he became president. By 1980 all but one of the eight PCs he inherited from Kenyatta, including all four Kikuyu, were retired from the civil service, while the exception, Simeon Nyachae, was brought to Nairobi as a permanent secretary (and later chief secretary) in the Office of the President.[18] In a parallel move, roughly half of the DCs were transferred out of the Provincial Administration to other departments. Kikuyu administrators were affected disproportionately by these transfers, while a disproportionate number of Kalenjin officers were promoted to become DCs or assistant DCs. Tenure of both PCs and DCs under Moi appears to be shorter than during the Kenyatta era, but most hold their positions for at least two years.

In 1982 Moi announced a major restructuring of the Provincial Administration, known as District Focus for Rural Development (Kenya Office of the President 1987). As stated later by the president, District Focus would achieve three objectives: (1) "the people will be directly involved in the identification, design, implementation and management of projects and programmes" for rural development; (2) "the decision-making structure will centre around the districts themselves [and] minimize the delays that often characterized centralized decision-making systems"; (3) "most fundamentally, the allocation of resources will be shared more equitably, by being directed to areas of most need" (Moi 1985).

District Focus embodies several of the most salient features of Nyayo in that its rhetoric is populist and egalitarian while its substance has enabled Moi to exert greater control over political and associational life in the countryside. The centerpiece of District Focus is a series of administrative procedures for planning rural development at the district level, and for writing the annual budget and forward budget for each district in the district rather than in Nairobi. These procedures have provided rural residents with new opportunities to participate in the formal process of decisionmaking but have not empowered the rural poor because the district administrative team orchestrates the planning and budgetary process (Barkan & Chege 1989).

The result is that District Focus has greatly constrained the autonomy of Harambee organizations and the involvement of elected officials in self-help by requiring that all projects seeking government assistance be reviewed by the District Development Committee and subordinate committees at the location and sublocation levels. Although the establishment of these committees has provided Harambee organizations greater access to the administrators who control the Rural Development Fund and other monies to assist self-help, the net effect has been a reduction in the extent to which Harambee organizations can extract state aid.[19] Elected officials, particularly leaders of long standing who had built their political careers by assisting Harambee, have also been major losers. Although its stated purpose was to increase public involvement in the decisionmaking process, District Focus has reduced much of the free wheeling and bargaining that previously characterized the relationship between the state and organized interests across rural Kenya.[20]

By shifting the locus of decisionmaking for rural development from the headquarters of government ministries in Nairobi to the district administration, District Focus has also bypassed the PCs and representatives of central ministries at the provincial level. The new procedures have thus permanently blocked the reemergence of the provincial administrative fiefdoms that characterized the Kenyatta era.

In August 1988 Moi sought to further extend his control over the civil service by instructing the National Assembly to amend the Constitution regarding the tenure of members on the Public Service Commission. Whereas before the amendment the president appointed all members of the commission but could not dismiss them without referring the matter to an independent tribunal of legal experts, Moi now acquired the power of dismissal. The amendment also gave the president the authority to dismiss judges and members of the Judicial Services Commission, while the police were given wider powers of detention. Individuals suspected of capital offenses can now be held for up to fourteen days without charge. These moves were widely viewed as having compromised the independence and professionalism of both the civil service and the judiciary, and as undermining human rights.

Associational Life and Human Rights

Consistent with his Nyayo approach of establishing direct control over all arenas of authority, Moi has also reduced the autonomy of private voluntary associations. As noted in the first section of this chapter, Kenyatta gave free rein to five types of voluntary associations that flourished during his presidency and broadened the social base of his regime. While pushing their own agendas, these organizations helped establish a system of informal rules and procedures through which state and civil society accommodated each other.

Under Moi, these rules have been suspended or modified, with the result that the relationship between state and civil society has been greatly strained. As noted above, Moi began his presidency by banning ethnic welfare associations. These organizations had often maintained close relationships with regional political leaders and reinforced the clientelist structures that were the foundation of the Kenyatta regime. Because these organizations tended to be vehicles of the bigs, the mobilized, and the haves, their banning was intended to reduce the power of those ethnoregional interests that were never part of the old KADU-Moi coalition. Indeed, in the years immediately prior to his ascension to the presidency, members of GEMA had figured prominently in an attempt to prevent Moi from succeeding to the presidency by changing the Kenyan Constitution. However, by banning ethnic associations, the president removed a significant network from the web of associations that cemented state and society together.

Moi's transformation of Harambee has had a similar effect. Although Harambee had evolved into a social movement that became the principal arena of electoral politics, it is important to remember that most self-help groups were autonomous organizations with little or no contact with the state. These organizations, moreover, were most numerous in regions of high population density and regions that were relatively more developed than others; in other words, in the regions of the bigs, the mobilized, and the haves. As such, Harambee posed a dual threat. They were the base of the clientelist networks of the politicians Moi sought most to destroy. And they were an autonomous movement of the ethnoregional interests he wished most to contain.

Beginning early in his presidency and continuing throughout the 1980s, Moi has sought to delink the Harambee from electoral politics and capture the movement from above. Moi's tampering with electoral procedure and the transformation of KANU together with the implementation of District Focus have largely accomplished the former. To capture the movement, Moi has played a highly visible role raising funds for local self-help groups as well as for several large projects that he favors. Whereas Kenyatta's approach to Harambee was mainly one of exhorting local communities and political leaders "to do more," he rarely became involved in raising funds for particular projects.[21] Most self-help organizations, particularly small ones, were left to generate their own revenue, while large groups would attract assistance from local or regional leaders. By contrast, Moi has made frequent tours of the countryside to attend large fund-raisers planned by the Office of the President with the district administration. At these gatherings the presidential entourage typically rolls into a selected district to raise funds for many small projects at one time; for example, all Harambee primary schools in the district. The event is preceded by several weeks of collections in the area by government chiefs directed by the district administration. These collections, which are tantamount to a mandatory tax, are then presented to the president at the fund-raiser. The president himself makes his own contribution, as do members of his entourage, which includes cabinet ministers, senior civil servants, and other notables currently in his favor.[22] The funds collected are subsequently divided among all projects, with the result that the entire exercise generating revenue is out of the hands of those who run self-help. Funds collected for large projects favored by the president, such as the Kabarak Secondary School in the president's home region and the Moi Airforce Academy in Nairobi, are simply monies extracted from rural dwellers. Because funds are rarely collected for large projects within the district visited by the president, the process does little to bolster the prestige of the local member of the National Assembly. In short, small Harambee organizations lose their autonony, while large ones and their patrons have been largely cut out of the process.

Space does not permit as detailed an analysis of the regime's treatment of other forms of associational life, but the pattern is similar. Organizations that used to function independently have been steadily brought under presidential control in the name of assisting the wananchi and distributing resources more equitably across ethnoregional interests. In 1989 COTU and Kenya's largest women's organization, Maendeleo ya Wanawake, were forced to affiliate with KANU. Although neither of these organizations ever challenged the president, the fact that most of their leaders and members are from the bigs, the mobilized, and the haves made them too large to function on an independent basis. Professional and "public interest" organizations have also come under fire. The Law Society of Kenya has had a long history of speaking out in support of an independent judiciary, and in recent years several of its officers and prominent members have protested the decline of human rights and changes in electoral procedure, and praised a multiparty system. Some of these individuals, most notably Paul Muite, Gibson Kamau Kuria, and Gitobu Imanyara, the editor of the *Nairobi Law Monthly*, have been periodically detained in an effort to silence their criticism of the regime. In the process, their plight and that of others in detention has been widely reported by the international press and drawn world attention to the seamy side of Nyayo.

Other major associations, particularly those dominated by Kikuyu, have likewise been subjected to presidential pressure. In 1983 the powerful Kenya Farmers Association was forced to reorganize as the Kenya Grain Growers Cooperative Union in an effort to reduce the influence of rich Kikuyu landowners. During the second part of the decade the government sought to discredit the Kenya Tea Development Authority, a parastatal organization that operates mainly in Central Province, by authorizing the establishment of so-called Nyayo Tea Zones under separate administration in western Kenya. The National Council of Churches of Kenya (formerly the National Christian Council of Kenya) as well as prominent clergy have also come under attack as each has called for a liberalization of the electoral and party system. So too have apolitical groups such as the Greenbelt Movement, an organization dedicated to environmental preservation that had the temerity to question a plan by KANU and the management of the *Kenya Times* to construct a sixty-floor office building in the middle of Uhuru Park in downtown Nairobi. Where leaders of organizations have voiced direct criticism of regime policy, the individuals expressing such views have been vilified as disloyal and branded as subversives and traitors by sycophantic supporters of the president in the National Assembly and other fora. Such leaders have been subjected to harassment by the police, including unannounced searches of their personal residences. Others have been detained.

The Kenya government has also moved to regulate and control the more than 140 NGOs operating in the country. Many of these NGOs are based and funded from outside Kenya (e.g., CARE, Technoserve), while others are national NGOs established by Kenyans. Because these organizations constitute independent sources of authority, and their operations are dispersed across rural Kenya, the government has viewed them with increasing suspicion. Indeed, by their very nature numerous NGOs seek explicitly to empower the rural and urban poor, and thus create a potential source of opposition to the regime. To regulate NGOs, the National Assembly passed the Non-Governmental Organizations Coordination Act in November 1990, which requires that all NGOs register with the government to continue their operations. NGOs that remain unregistered are deemed under the act as having committed an offense. A key provision of the act is the establishment of a Coordination Board to set guidelines (including a code of conduct) for the operations of NGOs, and monitor their activities. The board, whose chair is appointed by the president, may refuse to register any organization whose activities are "not in the national interest." The board may also cancel or refuse to renew certificates of registration. In brief, the act gives the government unlimited power to constrain NGOs with which it does not agree (Kenya 1990).

CONCLUSION

Although never a pluralist democracy in the Western sense, Kenya established a governance realm during the Kenyatta era that linked state and society together in a manner that legitimized the exercise of political authority. Clear norms were established in respect to the nature of political competition, the roles of elected officials, civil servants, and judges, and the parameters for associational life. A wide range of procedures were adopted that gave operational and institutionalized meaning to these norms and made the system predictable. Kenyans did not enjoy the rights of citizens in a democratic polity, but they could expect that the state would be held accountable for its performance. The state could be influenced; it could be bargained with. Above all, the state was not an arbitrary entity from which the average citizen sought refuge.

In the thirteen years since the death of his predecessor, Daniel arap Moi has consistently sought to fragment and capture all independent bases of authority to reduce his dependence on institutions controlled by ethnoregional interests that were never part of his political coalition. In the process he has established a form of personal rule that seeks to exert authority directly vis-à-vis the Kenyan population, thus bypassing established institutions and power brokers. Because, with few exceptions (e.g., District Focus), Moi has not sought to replace established institutions with new ones, existing institutions have been undermined, especially the informal procedures that had previously established a predictable relationship between state and society. In the process, the governance realm in Kenya has collapsed.

The principal lessons of the rise and fall of a governance realm in Kenya are two and consistent with conventional wisdom. First, the existence and maintenance of a governance realm is, by its very nature, dependent on a measure of tolerance on the part of the rulers for the ruled. Where rulers cannot accept a plurality of autonomous institutions, there can be no governance realm. Put simply, it makes a difference who governs at the top; individuals count notwithstanding the myriad of domestic and external pressures that bear upon their regimes.

Second, institutions count. While it is necessary to have a tolerant ruler to maintain a governance realm, such a ruler is not sufficient. As discussed by Hyden, the actor dimension must be complemented by an appropriate structural or institutional dimension if a governance realm is to emerge and be sustained. Clear procedures must be implemented that guarantee a measure of trust and accountability between the rulers and the ruled, and that do so over time. Put differently, the polity cannot merely be tolerant, it must be predictable. As noted in the discussion of Kenyatta's Kenya, the institutions that provide for a governance realm need not be democratic in the Western concept of the term. Such institutions as Kenya's electoral system during the 1970s are examples of adherence to a predictable set of procedures, in the context of an authoritarian regime, that provide for a governance realm. The informal procedures regarding the Kenyan press and associational life are others.

Can Kenya recreate the governance realm that existed in the country until the early 1980s? Can the type of governance realm that once existed in Kenya be replicated elsewhere in Africa? Turning to the first question, the answer must be a qualified "yes." While many of the practices employed by Kenyatta during his presidency could be resurrected by Moi, the impact of these practices may no longer be the same. By rescinding the queuing practice and announcing that anyone can run for Parliament, Moi has, in essence, stated his intention to at least formally restore the electoral procedures of the previous era. However, unless these moves are accompanied by a return to an earlier version of Harambee, a hands-off policy toward associational life (including NGOs), a free press, an independent judiciary and improved record on human rights, and a willingness to accept and even nurture a stable group of prominent albeit subordinate leaders, the reform will yield little. Indeed, such changes in the electoral system alone could result in a zero-sum political game in which ethnoregional interests compete more aggressively for an ever smaller resource pie. Put differently, the very condition Moi fears most—that he will be overwhelmed by demands his regime cannot satisfy— could be the outcome. On the other hand, the same outcome could also result from a blanket return to previous practice. Having repressed and fragmented many of Kenya's political institutions, any lifting of the lid from the organizations and individuals that have borne the brunt of Nyayo may result in excessive, uncoordinated, and destructive opposition to the regime or its successor for opposition's sake. A situation similar to that now unfolding in the Soviet Union could emerge in Kenya. Moi, in short, like Gorbachev, may be faced with Hobson's choice: to do nothing will result in a further erosion of the legitimacy of his regime; to go back or partially back to the status quo ante is no guarantee of success.

Can the Kenyan experience of the 1970s be replicated elsewhere in Africa? Again, the answer is a qualified "yes." As in Kenya, there is no logical reason why steps cannot be taken to undertake meaningful reform elsewhere. The recent experience in Benin and with elected local government in Nigeria suggest that new procedures and rules can be implemented to create or recreate the structural dimension required for a governance realm. Here, again, there are also risks. Unless the nascent institutions established to make the state more accountable respond adequately to the level of public demands unleashed by reform, the reform will be short-lived. The existence of a governance realm is an essential feature of any legitimate regime, but a governance realm is also a fragile set of relationships that can be easily undermined if the principal actors are not tolerant and respectful of each other's existence. Like a good marriage, governance requires hard work and self-restraint by all partners if it is to endure.

NOTES

1. At its height in the mid-1950s Kenya's white settler community numbered approximately sixty thousand or 1 percent of the colony's population—much smaller than its counterparts in Southern Rhodesia (Zimbabwe), Angola, Mozambique, and South Africa.

2. The process of decolonization in Kenya, and the policies pursued by the British to buy off settler resistance to African rule, cannot be discussed here. For details see Gordon 1986; Leys 1975; and Wasserman 1976.

3. District organizations usually mobilized members of only one ethnic group because the boundaries of most districts were drawn to conform to the natural boundaries between ethnic groups. The same pattern continues today, three decades after independence.

4. Although ethnic statistics have not been kept since the 1969 census, Kikuyus account for approximately 21 percent of Kenya's population, Luos 14 percent, Kambas 11 percent, and Gusiis 7 percent. Embus and Merus account respectively for 5 and 2 percent (Kenya 1970:69).

5. Although only 21 percent of all challengers won in the 1988 parliamentary elections, the figures should be treated with caution due to widespread rigging of the final results.

6. Until the early to mid-1970s, when advancing age forced him to shorten his working day, Kenyatta maintained close, at times daily, personal contact with his PCs.

7. The assassinations of Tom Mboya and J. M. Kariuki, and the suppression of Oginga Odinga and the KPU are examples of how far the regime would go to subdue any direct challenge or perceived challenge.

8. A register of Harambee organizations is kept by the community development officer at the district headquarters of the rural administration. Between 375 and 500 self-help organizations are listed on the registers of most

districts, but the number varies considerably with the population density and overall level of development in the area. There is also substantial double counting and undercounting. Our estimate, which may be somewhat high, is based on the existence of forty administrative districts.

9. Pronounced "hah-ram-bay," the term was originally a Swahili word meaning "Let us pull together."

10. There is some evidence that suggests that political leaders avoid small projects. Because small projects serve small catchment areas, politicians are often wary of taking up their cause lest they be criticized for being responsive to only one part of their constituency.

11. Nyayo is the Swahili word for "footsteps." Moi initially used Nyayo to stress that his regime would follow "in the footsteps of Kenyatta," but by mid-1979 the new president made it clear that the footsteps to be followed were his own.

12. All ethnic unions were ordered to wind up their affairs and disband by June 30, 1979.

13. Yet another example was Moi's sudden announcement in May 1988 that Kenya's three universities would change their standards for admissions and accept an incoming class of more than nine thousand applicants, more than three times the number for which places existed. Most outside observers agree that the quality of higher education has been severely compromised by this jump in enrollments.

14. The editor of Kenya's oldest English-language daily, the *East African Standard*, was sacked after he questioned the move toward a one-party state. KANU then established its own paper, *The Kenyan Times*, to propagate Moi's views and make clear the politically correct line. Despite continuing pressure and threats, the press has remained relatively free, and at times even lively.

15. Under Kenyatta, KANU was a moribund organization that emerged only at election time to certify those standing for office. No national party conferences of delegates from branch organizations were held from 1966 until after Kenyatta's death in 1978. Although a conference was held in 1978 to elect a new slate of national officers, branch organizations continued to languish until 1985 when new officers were elected for the first time in nineteen years.

16. Variations of this theme were employed later to get rid of Josephat Karanja, whom Moi appointed as Kenya's vice-president in 1988 but dumped in April 1989.

17. The number of expulsions has steadily risen. Between 1982 and 1987 four members were expelled, including Oginga Odinga and Charles Njonjo. In 1988 ten members were expelled, and in 1989 the number rose to fifteen.

18. Nyachae himself was forced to retire in December 1986 and thwarted from standing in the 1988 elections.

19. This was not by accident. Following the Ndegwa Report in 1982, which recommended that the Kenya government substantially reduce expenditures on social welfare services, especially education, the government concluded that it was essential to gain greater control over Harambee. Control was also desired to increase the proportion of self-help projects, particularly those supported by the Rural Development Fund, that were successful. See also the government's sessional paper of 1986, *Economic Management for Renewed Growth* (Kenya 1986:29–30).

20. In June 1991, the president announced that henceforth, the chairmen of the District Development Committees would be elected. If implemented, this reform might partially restore an aspect of the bargaining process that once characterized state-society relations.

21. One exception to this practice was collections for The Gatundu Hospital in Kenyatta's home location.

22. It is assumed by most observers that the president's contributions are made from funds in the Office of the President. Contributions made in the name of cabinet ministers are collected from civil servants in the ministry prior to the event. Contributions by civil servants are now deducted from salary checks—in effect a tax on white-collar workers.

9

Rwanda: Recent Debates Over Governance and Rural Development

Catharine Newbury

When Rwanda regained its independence from Belgium in 1962, expatriate experts predicted impending doom. It was assumed this small, landlocked, densely populated country was destined to remain forever a backwater of poverty—"a museum-piece of postcolonial underdevelopment," as one Rwandan specialist put it. A quarter-century later Rwanda's bustling economy and proliferating development projects presented a picture very different from the gloomy predictions of outsiders. Despite daunting challenges, by the end of the 1980s Rwanda had achieved significant improvements in transport infrastructure, innovations in rural services, and advances in training and competence of government personnel. Teachers, nurses, and other government employees received salaries that, although not generous, allowed them to live decent lives. All but one of Rwanda's ten major towns were linked to the capital by paved roads, regularly maintained. Public transport was available and affordable.[1]

Rwanda was still an overwhelmingly rural country; more than 90 percent of the population earned their living from agriculture, producing food and cash crops on smallholder farms. Nonetheless, the 1970s and early 1980s saw increased production in both food crops and coffee, Rwanda's major export. The international aid community has applauded such advances. A 1989 World Bank report singled out Rwanda as a "successful case of adaptation," where government policies had successfully encouraged growth in agricultural production: "Rwanda avoided the urban bias so common in Africa. Government remained attentive to the farming majority in determining pricing policy, exchange rate policy, fiscal priorities, and effective rural institutions" (p. 105). The report praises the Rwandan government for providing an "enabling environment" that encouraged growth in agricultural production, by allowing market forces to determine food prices and by trying to insure that coffee producers received a substantial share of the export price (World Bank 1989:105). Here then is one image of Rwanda—a success story that belies the general pattern of political malaise and economic collapse characterizing many African states in recent years.

Another view sees Rwanda in a less favorable light. Some observers have asserted that, whatever its positive reputation among external donors, the state in Rwanda is authoritarian and repressive. This view notes official corruption and the growing gap between the living standards of the wealthy and most rural dwellers. The policies of ethnic and regional favoritism that benefit the majority Hutu ethnic group and the northern regions of the country in the distribution of government resources are seen as distorted development and objects of anger to people elsewhere. Rural development programs have provided few benefits to the mass of the rural population, it is charged, and many Rwandans resent the tight control of the party and exactions by government officials at the local level (see, e.g., Cros 1989, 1990b, d; Press 1990).

Rather than two static sets of observations, these contrasting portraits reflect ongoing discussions within the country. They represent deep philosophical assumptions on how to assess development, and about what orientations are desirable for the future—centralization or democratization, individual accumulation or social distribution. Although oversimplified, these images help to shape external observations, molding how outsiders interpret the government's intention to move toward political renewal, announced in 1990. Neither image is entirely accurate, but each does portray a part of recent Rwandan political realities; so this is not simply a discussion over the facts. The debate over these images—the interactive process—is as important as the content. It conveys something that outsiders often miss: the involvement, energy, and participation of Rwandans themselves in shaping their own shared future.

The debate also reveals interesting contradictions in the structures and goals of the state itself, contradictions that result from both structural and conjunctural factors, and from both internal and external influences. Rural development policy is one domain in which such contradictions are dramatized. On many occasions the Rwandan government has reiterated its commitment to rural people and pledged its efforts to alleviate rural poverty. Government officials, the president foremost among them, are proud of their agricultural policies, praised in the World Bank report cited above. Moreover, from the government's point of view, policies to promote rural development reflect responsiveness to the rural majority.

This is why recent debates over rural development policies in Rwanda are so important. As articulated in the writings of Rwandan intellectuals, expatriate development experts, and government officials, the focus of this evolving terrain of struggle has been the plight of rural people in the country and how rural development policies are helping or harming them. Pervading the discussions is an implicit subtext: the debate over accountability. Goran Hyden (Chapter 1) defines governance as effective management of the public domain, a type of governmental behavior that fosters authority, reciprocity, trust, and accountability. The debates over rural development policies in

Rwanda reflect concern for all of these characteristics, but with a particular emphasis on accountability and reciprocity.

At issue is what rural development programs are doing and who is benefitting. These debates indicate strains in the relationships between rural producers and the state; they also provide insight on the likely impact of recent decentralization measures promising increased responsibilities to the communes, Rwanda's local administrative entities.

As part of a program for political reform and economic renewal, the Rwandan government has designated communes (with an average population of about fifty thousand people) as "nodules of development." Commune authorities are called upon to seek funding from external donors for local development projects and to generate enthusiasm among rural producers for a new government program of agricultural intensification. Do these measures simply shift the administrative load (and revenue base), or can this new orientation be viewed as enhancing governance? To what extent does the decentralization policy offer possibilities for political renewal, for participation by peasants in decisions that affect their lives, and for increased accountability of the government to its citizens?

Asking such questions broadens the field of analysis and makes it imperative to consider the context in which these changes are occurring. We will look first at the nature of the contemporary Rwandan state and the orientation of its development planning, then examine contradictions in Rwandan's development agenda that may well limit the capacity of communes to carry out the new roles assigned to them, and undermine the goals of the agricultural intensification policies. We will conclude with a survey of challenges (external and internal) confronting the state in 1990: the plummeting price of coffee on the world market; a serious famine; and the invasion of Rwanda by armed insurgents from Uganda. In microcosm, these represent Rwanda's larger structural problems: its vulnerability in the international economy; its internal tensions (many related to its population density); and the explosive potential of the country's political configurations (often historically created), both within and beyond its borders. In response to these difficulties and the wave of democratization sweeping across Africa in 1990, Rwanda's president announced a series of political reforms; these will be briefly discussed.

DECOLONIZATION AND THE POSTCOLONIAL STATE

In a bloodless coup on July 5, 1973, Major-General Juvenal Habyarimana seized power from Grégoire Kayibanda, the first president of independent Rwanda. Habyarimana claimed he was establishing a "moral revolution" to build upon the political revolution of 1959–1962 in which Kayibanda had played a key role. The 1959 revolution, led by members of the Hutu ethnic group, overthrew the highly centralized monarchy that had ruled Rwanda before and during colonial rule (under Germany before World War I, and thereafter under Belgium, as a League of Nations Mandate and United Nations Trust Territory). Although colonial power retained the monarchy, it also transformed what had been a hierarchical but flexible system into a more rigid, bureaucratic colonial state, and one that intensified ethnic divisions. Members of the Tutsi group had predominated in the influential offices before European arrival, but the resources placed in their hands under colonial rule greatly enhanced their coercive and extractive powers and narrowed the social range of the elite to several dominant lineages. Consequently, the gap widened between Tutsi officeholders and the rest of the population (mostly, but not exclusively, Hutu), as administrative qualifications changed and Tutsi were favored in access to schools, jobs, and other opportunities in the modern sector.[2]

By the 1950s colonial demands for labor, taxes, and obligatory cultivation, as well as the extractions and often brutal conduct of many chiefs, had created bitter resentments and a lively political consciousness among rural dwellers. Not all Tutsi were rich and powerful, but virtually all of the chiefs and others who did become rich and powerful during the colonial period were Tutsi. Thus cleavages that subsequently developed between Tutsi (a minority in Rwanda) and Hutu (the vast majority of the population) were not just ethnic, but social as well, reflected in distinct class status (Chrétien 1985; C. Newbury 1978, 1980, 1983, 1988; Vidal 1973, 1985).

During the 1950s Kayibanda served as editor of a Catholic newspaper, in which he and other educated Hutu called attention to the political, economic, and social inequalities in the country. These outlets gave voice to the grievances of rural Hutu (Ntezimana 1978; Bart 1982); today's debates over political power and class stratification flow in currents that are deep and powerful. Hutu leaders also began to create organizations that could defend Hutu interests. Kayibanda headed one of these, originally called the Mouvement Social Muhutu (MSM), later transformed into a formal political party, PARMEHUTU (Le Parti du Mouvement de l'Émancipation Hutu); PARMEHUTU had its principal following in the central and northern areas of the country, regions now included in the prefectures of Gitarama, Gisenyi, and Ruhengeri. Other Hutu activists formed a different party, APROSOMA (Association pour la Promotion Sociale de la Masse), with its base in the South and the West. While PARMEHUTU adopted an ethnic platform, pro-Hutu and anti-Tutsi, APROSOMA initially articulated a different ideology, seeking to represent the interests of all poor groups, Tutsi as well as Hutu. These predominantly Hutu parties competed with the two major parties organized by Tutsi: UNAR (Union Nationale Rwandaise) was a monarchist party that aimed to preserve the monarchy and crush Hutu resistance; the RADER party (Rassemblement Démocratique Rwandais), organized by younger educated Tutsi *évolués*, favored progressive reforms and a constitutional monarchy (Lemarchand 1970; Linden & Linden 1977; Murego 1975; Newbury 1988).

In November 1959 the simmering tensions in Rwanda erupted into violence near Gitarama in central Rwanda and quickly spread, first to the North and South, later to other regions as well. The Belgian administration switched its support to the Hutu groups, and in 1960 election results for burgomasters and councils for the new communes gave Hutu candidates an overwhelming victory. By the time Rwanda regained its independence from Belgium in 1962 the monarchy had been abolished and Tutsi authorities had been expelled from power; many fled the country. The new republic to emerge from the revolution was governed by a Hutu president, Kayibanda, with an elected National Assembly (Harroy 1984; Lemarchand 1970; Linden & Linden 1977; Murego 1975; Newbury 1988; Ntezimana 1978; Reyntjens 1985; Vidal 1973).

During the first eleven years of postcolonial rule APROSOMA and other groups disappeared from the political landscape as PARMEHUTU moved to monopolize political space. Kayibanda's government came to be dominated by individuals from central Rwanda, his home region. Such favoritism heightened regional tensions and helped to provoke the 1973 coup. Moreover, despite the Hutu orientation of the Kayibanda government, the representation of Tutsi, both as teachers and students in high schools and postsecondary institutions, and in the ranks of salaried workers, remained significantly higher than their percentage in the population. Resentment against Tutsi in Rwanda intensified in the early 1970s with the ethnic violence in Burundi, in which thousands of Hutu were massacred by Burundi's Tutsi-dominated government (Reyntjens 1985:502–503).

In February and March 1973 Tutsi workers and students in Rwanda became the target of a wave of anti-Tutsi sentiment. The "disorder" that began as ethnic conflict soon mushroomed into something broader. Tutsi teachers and students were expelled from schools, and employees were fired from their jobs; some suffered physical harm or lost their belongings (Reyntjens 1985:502–503). In some areas the attacks took a populist cast, and shops owned by wealthy Hutu merchants (including a few prominent politicians) were looted. Personal threats were directed at both Hutu and Tutsi. On some hills in central Rwanda, Tutsi residents were told to leave, and their homes were burned. In Musanza, near Ruhengeri in the north, Hutu whose origins were in the south and central areas of the country were forced to leave. As Reyntjens (1985:503) points out, "the movement clearly went beyond the level of ethnic struggle and became more a conflict between classes and regions, in which the north openly opposed the central and southern portions of the country."

The coup of 1973, then, was precipitated by conflict between Hutu and Tutsi but also reflected regional and class rivalries among Hutu. The army, dominated by northerners, acted to expel from power the Hutu leaders of central Rwanda.[3] These events should not be seen simply as background, but as representative of the continuing regional and ethnic tensions that the government of the Second Republic—itself born from such tensions—has had to contain. Such was the rationale Habyarimana used for his focus on organizing a strong, effective state apparatus during the first years of his rule. The process of centralizing and reinforcing the postcolonial state, begun under Kayibanda, was greatly intensified under the Second Republic. But such policies have precipitated new tensions. Strong state structures have not always benefitted rural agriculturalists; they have also been seized upon to benefit individual power holders. In recent years regional and class divisions have been increasingly apparent, and in some cases have been openly flaunted by certain individuals.

From early on, Habyarimana's government included substantial numbers of civilians; it later shifted further from a military to a predominantly civilian government. In July 1975 a new political organization was launched, the Mouvement Révolutionnaire National pour le Développement (MRND). (The MDR-PARMEHUTU, Rwanda's single party under the Kayibanda government, had been abolished after the coup.) MRND, incorporating all Rwandan citizens, had as its stated goals the fostering of unity and cooperation among ethnic groups and regions, and mobilizing the population for development. The party claimed to encourage "responsible democracy," meaning "the free expression of ideas on condition that they are seen as useful to the collectivity and are articulated publicly" (Mfizi 1983:61).

A Constitution for the Second Republic was promulgated on December 20, 1978; a week later Habyarimana (the only candidate) was elected as president by close to 99 percent of the popular vote. In December 1981 elections were held for a national legislative body, the Conseil National de Développement (CND). Presidential and legislative elections were held again in 1983 and in December 1988 (Reyntjens 1988:827; 1989; EIU 1989a:41–42).[4]

Speeches by Habyarimana and pronouncements in government documents have emphasized the government's commitment to a policy of *équilibre* (balance)—or attempts to reduce conflict and encourage harmonious relations among Hutu, Tutsi, and Twa. To promote affirmative action, the Second Republic introduced a system of quotas regulating access to postprimary education and employment, based on the percentage of each group in the population. (Officially, Hutu are about 90 percent of the population, Tutsi some 9.5 percent, and Twa less than 1 percent.)[5] Regional considerations are also supposed to be taken into account in admissions to secondary school and university, and in appointments to ministerial posts and other high offices such as prefect (Biloa 1990). Nevertheless, regional favoritism has not been eliminated from Habyarimana's government: Rwandans from outside the North consider that Hutu northerners have an inside track in obtaining government employment, scholarships to study abroad, and other opportunities. Access to education has been particularly sensitive, since the number of places in secondary schools is severely limited, and the few positions of salaried employment are usually open only to degree holders (Cros 1989).[6]

Rwanda's state structures are permeated with a strong hierarchical ethos, patterns of top-down decisionmaking, and networks of client relationships. The CND (legislature) has served as a forum of debate over some issues, but policymaking power has been heavily concentrated in the president's office and the Central Committee of the MRND.[7] There is thus ample evidence in Rwanda's political evolution of what Jean-François Bayart (1983:37) has called the "totalizing" strategy of postcolonial states in Africa—the tendency of those in power to try to control and direct from above many (or all) aspects of political and social activity. Also evident is the "search for hegemony," whereby the president and other powerful actors use offices and material rewards to build a dominant coalition of supporters (Bayart 1989: ch. 4).

The role of postcolonial African states as vehicles for class formation is well documented. The state serves as an instrument for domination and control; access to resources of the state, directly or indirectly, is important in shaping opportunities for people to become and remain wealthy or powerful.[8] In this context government agricultural policies may intensify class formation; such policies are often used to foster support for the government among groups it regards as important (Bates 1981). Rwanda is no exception: the economic policies of "planned liberalism" have indeed promoted the enrichment of a few; so have many agricultural policies, despite their proclaimed intent of promoting advancement of the rural masses.

THE STATE AND DEVELOPMENT

Rwanda's government has claimed a commitment to programs whose purpose is to dampen the differences created by ethnic polarization and colonial rule. But while preaching a concern for social justice, the party and government have not embraced an ideology of equality or anything approaching socialism. One reason for this is that the power holders and their allies in the military, commercial, and educational spheres have done very well by the system (Bézy 1990); an effective program of socialism stressing equality would threaten their own accumulation. The second reason is no less influential: Rwanda depends, to an extraordinary degree, on foreign assistance, directly through aid programs, indirectly by being able to operate in a favorable political climate. In an age of intense ideological competition, Rwanda's international patrons would not be pleased with an orientation toward socialist rhetoric or goals.

Still, it is important to recognize that the state in Rwanda has not been merely a predator, and it can point to some moderate development successes.

What accounts for these successes? Part of the explanation seems to lie in the quality of leadership. But this was changing in the 1980s. By then, leaders who had experienced colonial rule personally, and who had lived through and participated in the revolution, were approaching retirement (age fifty-five in Rwanda). They were being replaced by younger officials who had never experienced colonial rule, whose concerns were to consolidate and extend their own economic power, and whose commitment to economic justice and to the welfare of rural Rwandans seemed markedly attenuated. And as the power balance gradually shifted between generations, so the emphasis of policy goals shifted ever so subtly.

At least as important as the choices made by leaders are structural features that may be beyond the rational influence of the leaders—variables such as the prices of major commodities on the world market, the regional economic environment, the availability of foreign aid. For example, a critical feature of Rwanda's development strategy has been to solicit foreign aid, and the government has displayed considerable skill in impressing foreign donors (EIU 1989a:53, 55). Rwanda has presented itself as a small country struggling courageously against the odds, with the political stability and administrative competence to show positive results from aid. It has thus been seen as an attractive investment for aid administrators who wish to show successful aid programs. Between 1980 and 1986, for example, there was only one year in which new commitments for foreign aid (grants and concessional loans) totaled less than $200 million; in 1987 new aid commitments increased to $340 million. Allocations of such funds, considered as part of a separate "development" budget, were almost as large as the government's annual operating budget for ordinary expenses (EIU 1988:56, 1989a:55).

Thanks in part to large infusions of foreign aid, Rwanda's balance of payments has been generally favorable compared to that of other African countries. However, the emphasis on foreign-funded projects has entailed heavy costs as well. The ratio of administrative costs to implementation is high, and there are many questions as to how effective many of the aid programs have been (Godding 1984, 1989). During the 1980s the trade gap grew as expenditures for imports increased progressively while export prices fell. Not since 1979 has Rwanda achieved a current account surplus. Yet until the mid-1980s Rwanda's debt service remained moderate. Even at the end of 1987 gross debt owed constituted less than 28 percent of the gross national product, "one of the lowest ratios in sub-Saharan Africa" (EIU 1989a:57). Despite increasingly difficult economic conditions during the decade, Rwanda made it through the 1980s without a structural adjustment program and did not incur large debts to the International Monetary Fund. It is ironic, in fact, that the World Bank should wax so eloquent about the success of an economy that had not had a structural adjustment program to guide it. As one report noted dryly, it was Rwanda's good fortune that it did not contract large loans with private commercial banks in the early 1970s—the time when petrodollars were being recycled in the form of loans to Third World countries (EIU 1988:57). But from 1986 the decline in world prices of coffee and tea had serious repercussions for Rwanda's balance of payments. Whereas Rwanda's reserves in hard currency could cover 5.3 months of imports in 1986, this had declined to only two months at the end of 1989. And Rwanda's external debt rose from FRW 7.4 billion (Rwandan francs) in 1982 to FRW 50 billion in 1988 (Kaïdi 1990:42).

External factors favorable to Rwanda's economic stability in the 1970s went beyond the willingness of outside donors to provide funds, equipment, and personnel to aid in development programs. Rwanda also benefitted enormously from the economic collapse of its three largest neighbors; in recent years Kigali has become a communications, service, and supply center for large areas of eastern Zaire, southwestern Uganda, and northwestern Tanzania. But this represents a conjunctural benefit: were the neighboring economies to function at anywhere near their potential, they would not only deprive Rwanda of much of its windfall profits (especially in the commercial and transport sector) but also threaten the productive base. In a changed economic environment Rwanda could become a dependent terminus rather than an autonomous economic hub. Three examples will suffice. Rwanda benefits greatly by exporting coffee grown in Zaire but sold in Rwanda, as Zairian coffee producers (and government officials) seek to escape the corruption and exploitation of the state-run Zairian coffee-purchasing network (D. Newbury 1986). And currently Rwanda exports cement to Zaire. The Zairian cement factory on Lake Kivu is capable of producing at lower cost than that of Rwanda; if the Zairian factory were to recommence operations, this could not only deprive Rwanda of export earnings but potentially threaten Rwanda's small cement industry. Finally, many missions, development agencies, schools, and medical networks in neighboring countries kept offices in Rwanda during the 1980s; were the conditions in those countries to stabilize (or, alternatively, were conditions in Rwanda to deteriorate as they did in late 1990), the existing ties might quickly atrophy.

Politically, too, Rwanda has profited from its position as a buffer between Zaire, Uganda, and Tanzania. Because of his country's economic and political vulnerability, Habyarimana has actively cultivated friendly ties with neighboring states, attempting in particular to rebuild a modus vivendi with Burundi. However, the presence and precarious status of Rwandan refugees in surrounding countries, especially Uganda, has remained a festering problem ("Right to Choose" 1988; Guichaoua 1989:151). The tenuous nature of these ties was dramatically illustrated in October 1990 when Rwanda was invaded by exiles based in Uganda (United States Committee for Refugees 1991).

Internally, the Rwandan government has frequently reaffirmed its interest in promoting rural development to ameliorate rural living conditions.

Kayibanda, the former president, is still revered by rural Rwandans for his clear commitment to the needs of rural people—an involvement that was critical to his conception of political mobilization and leadership at the time of the revolution. To some degree (although diminishing over time), this has remained an enduring legacy for the Second Republic. Recognizing that Rwanda was and would remain primarily an agricultural country, Habyarimana's government was initially attentive to rural concerns, and government policy attempted to expand services to the rural areas. One particularly visible example was the establishment of government-run Banques Populaires (with at least one branch in each commune). In the 1970s the government also established a network of local producer cooperatives and created OPROVIA, a government agency that purchases beans and sorghum from producers at favorable prices; this was supposed to serve as an alternative outlet to compete with private traders, who tended to set up regional monopsonies or who established informal agreements to hold down prices paid to the producers.

Critics charge that such initiatives have received insufficient support from the government to function effectively (Mugesera 1986). Although the commitment to rural areas is still embedded in political rhetoric, it sometimes appears more rhetorical than material. This tendency has increased as contradictions have appeared between the government's announced commitment to improving the lives of peasant producers and the economic ideology of "planned liberalism" officially adopted in 1980. A government publication describes planned liberalism as follows: "The national economy must be planned: that is why the MRND opted for *planned liberalism*. It protects *private property* and supports *private initiative*, but gives primacy to the interest of the collectivity. It says no to unrestrained capitalism, no to socialism or extreme collectivism that stifles freedom and individual initiative. The creation of state-owned or mixed ownership enterprises is recommended, and cooperatives are encouraged" (Mfizi 1983:63; emphasis in original).

This development orientation assumes that it is possible to improve peasant living standards while at the same time encouraging rapid class development and an unrestrained private sector, whose only real sources of income are found among the peasant community. Thus it is government policy to make credit available to private entrepreneurs so as to foster growth in trade, construction of buildings, and small industries. As Jean Rumiya (1985:7) has noted, some impressive gains were associated with this approach: Kigali, the national capital, grew in size; paved roads encouraged development of an improved transport system; the number of automobiles increased; and the country was able to procure sufficient amounts of gasoline, construction materials, and food products.

However, few benefits from this growth trickled down to the rural masses, and planned liberalism led to significant changes in value assumptions. Wealth is no longer measured by the standards of the society itself, nor does the government try to promulgate a communal conception of shared wealth. Instead, with the model of the international aid experts close to hand, wealth is assessed by reference to industrialized societies. In the past a man was seen as wealthy if he farmed two hectares of land, owned a bicycle and a radio, built a solid house, and provided education for his children. But now,

> with the appearance of fortunes acquired in the corridors of the administration and through trade . . . the symbols of wealth have changed: villa, automobile, bank account, salary, etc. . . . The prototype of the wealthy man is no longer the well-off peasant, respected by his peers, or the government official who returns to his hill, but the city dweller, preferably in Kigali, whose living standard attains an international level in the areas of leisure, transport, or lodging. This paradise has a strong attraction for youth. . . . But in this type of competition, there are only a few winners [Rumiya 1985:8].

One effect of economic changes during the 1980s has been a growing gap between rich and poor as well as a more vigorous assertion of class interests by those in power. As government officials increasingly became absorbed in this class, and younger administrators failed to understand or adopt the principles of the revolution (based to some degree on opposition to accumulated wealth of some at the expense of others), the government backed away from support of programs to sustain rural incomes and rural well-being. Official corruption increased, and there were allegations of lavish spending by certain state officials (Legum 1988:B379–B380).

The widening gap between rich and poor is not a strictly urban-rural division; reports by government agencies as well as international organizations indicate significant differences among rural dwellers in size of landholding and access to farm inputs and other resources, and show that Kigali has a massive poor segment (Bézy 1990:32; Donnet 1989; Marijsse 1982). Rural inequality translates into widespread poverty for the majority. Fernand Bézy (1990:32) cites a government survey published in the mid-1980s that estimates per capita expenditures for consumption among Rwanda's peasants at less than 11,763 FRW per year (about US $157); such "pauperization of peasants has exceeded the limits of what is acceptable." There is, moreover, an important regional dimension to the inequalities. Almost 90 percent of government investments in the rural sector during 1982–1984 (excluding the development budget funded by foreign aid) went to four prefectures: Kigali (in the center); Cyangugu (in the southwest); and Ruhengeri and Gisenyi (both in the north). Gitarama Prefecture, with the largest population outside Kigali, received only 0.16 percent of government funding; Kibuye Prefecture received 0.84 percent. "Thus 20% of the population shares about 1% of the national funding" (Guichaoua 1989:173).

Unemployed youth openly blame the state for the lack of land and jobs they face; parents blame the state for the paucity of post-secondary school places available for Rwanda's children; and people of diverse backgrounds blame the state for what is seen as the failure of rural development projects to make a significant difference in living standards of Rwanda's rural poor. The external aid agencies, therefore, have been backing a state apparatus that is increasingly distant from the population. It is a scenario well known in Africa and beyond.

AGRICULTURAL INTENSIFICATION
AND COMMUNES AS NODULES FOR DEVELOPMENT

The growing gap between state and people is apparent both in political rhetoric, as policies have become more hortatory than instrumental, and in political receptivity, as the population has become more cynical about government programs that do not function or that in fact support the commercial classes or government officials rather than peasants. This attitude will affect how rural people react to new efforts by the government to combat the deepening agrarian crisis: from the mid-1980s the Rwandan government has been preaching the need for food self-sufficiency and "agricultural intensification"—improvement of yields on existing cultivated acreage. The agricultural intensification program will attempt to encourage the use of improved seeds, fertilizers (including compost), and insecticides (Mbugulize 1986:7–8), and will promote greater regional specialization in particular food crops. Meanwhile, coffee has remained the country's main export crop and major source of foreign currency; the government regularly exhorts rural producers to increase coffee production. Yet, because land is scarce, peasant producers augment coffee acreage at the expense of food production.

As part of its planning for agricultural intensification, and in an effort to achieve greater coherence in the plethora of agricultural development projects operating in the country, the Rwandan government has assigned additional responsibilities to the rural communes (local government units) and has instructed them to serve as foci for development efforts (Niyibizi 1987). Some foreign aid donors view this policy as a positive step forward; it permits nongovernmental organizations (NGOs), for example, to deal with communes directly in planning and executing development projects, hence avoiding some of the bureaucratic tangles associated with the larger macropolitical environment (DAI 1986, vol. 1:85). The policy of increased autonomy for communes also dovetails with aid strategies encouraged by the World Bank, intended to provide support for rural collectivities (Guichaoua 1989:183). In its 1989 report, *Sub-Saharan Africa: From Crisis to Sustainable Growth*, the World Bank stresses the important role that local governments ought to play in development, even though they are "weak and underfunded." While this report cites Rwanda as a model to be emulated, it is worth noting that the World Bank goal is not necessarily the well-being of rural people, but enhanced ability of the state to extract taxes and delegate authority: "The initiative shown by Rwanda's communes in mobilizing citizens for road improvements, tree plantings, and soil conservation illustrate the potential. Developing competent and responsive local governments is central to capacity-building. It implies stronger powers to raise revenue locally and a clearer delegation of authority and responsibility" (World Bank 1989:58). Within this context, policies of "decentralization" and "reviving local government" (World Bank 1989:58–59) are recommended: "Many of the problems of the town and rural communities can only be solved locally; solutions imposed by the central authorities are likely to fail. The objective should be to capitalize on the energies and resources of the local people."

Rwanda's communes have been effective in promoting reforestation and antierosion measures. Critics wonder, however, how effective the commune in Rwanda can be as a dynamic vehicle for development. If development is taken to mean improvement in the living standards of the mass of the population (a goal articulated by the government in many fora), it is hard to see how the commune as presently structured can promote this. One problem is underfunding—a bigger drawback than the World Bank report acknowledges. Provision of more fiscal autonomy to the communes is, of course, beneficial to the central government in this period of austerity. But this means that Rwanda's communes have little in the way of resources. Some support comes from the central government in the form of salaries for certain officials working for the commune, and for teachers; communes can also request loans and grants from a central government fund set up for that purpose. Otherwise, the communes must fend for themselves to procure revenues; they rely on local community labor (*umuganda*) and on raising revenues through levies on the population, livestock and market taxes, and so on. Deficits in commune finances are therefore common; in 1985, for example, 51 percent of the country's communes had to request loans to balance their budgets (DAI 1986, vol 1:71).

Another problem is the multiple demands placed on burgomasters, the officials who administer the communes. To do his job effectively, a burgomaster needs to be an entrepreneur—to cultivate links with important central government officials, to build relationships with donor agencies, and to solicit ties (in French, *jumelage*, or twinning) with, for example, towns, provinces, or schools overseas. Some communes have greater opportunity for such ties or have more resources or skills to contribute to this end; one result, already evident, is aggravated regional inequality among communes. To an important degree, therefore, the welfare of the commune is dependent on the burgomaster's luck or skill in foreign relations. Unfortunately, this is just one more task to add to an already long list of obligations; it is generally agreed that burgomasters are overworked, saddled with too many, and too diverse, responsibilities. "The burgomaster is expected to play the role of Everyman" (DAI 1986, vol. 1:71).

President Habyarimana himself has recognized that the new role of communes places additional burdens on burgomasters. In a 1988 speech he exhorted the burgomasters to practice "self-sacrifice and creativity" in adapting to their new roles. The commune, he explained, consists not just of buildings and communal officials. Rather, it is "the *symbiosis* between leaders and followers [who are] determined to be authors of their own development in a Responsible Democracy" (Habyarimana 1988:34–35). The role of a burgomaster is not just to sit in his office

> as if he is a chief [*umutware*] receiving visits from citizens [*abaturage*] who come to pay court. Rather the burgomaster should mobilize the population to engage in actions that contribute to development. . . . The burgomaster . . . must support the agriculturist-herders [*abahinzi-borozi*] in their daily efforts, so that they can defend themselves against the unrepentant parasites [*abamunyunyuza imitsi*][9] who look out only for themselves. The burgomaster is . . . the protector [*umushumba*; lit., shepherd] of [the commune's] inhabitants, the person who looks out for the interests of the agriculturist-herder who sacrifices himself each day for our benefit [Habyarimana 1988:7, 35].[10]

Critics point out that the structures within which a burgomaster works are not conducive to making him a representative of the popular masses. For example, burgomasters can hardly be regarded as autonomous of the central government; whereas in the First Republic they were elected officials, under the Second Republic burgomasters are appointed by the president and are under the direct authority of the Ministry of the Interior (DAI 1986, vol. 1:84; Guichaoua 1989:179).[11] The commune, like other Rwandan government structures, is a hierarchical structure that fosters top-down decisionmaking. Each commune is divided into administrative sectors; since 1985 the representatives from each sector who sit on the commune council have been chosen through elections by the local population (DAI 1986:71). During regular meetings at the commune, these representatives attempt to make known the concerns of their constituents. But it is clear that the burgomaster is in charge; all too often the burgomaster's role has been simply to tell the councilors what to do and instruct them to communicate this to the population. From the point of view of the population, the burgomaster represents the power of the central government, and the most evident role of the commune is to collect taxes, dues for MRND, fines, levies for schools and health installations, and so on (Guichaoua 1989:179–180).

Rwanda's government acknowledges many of these problems. In the 1988 speech cited above Habyarimana alluded to the issues of funding and autonomy for communes and delineated central government measures to address such difficulties. But he blamed the communes as partly responsible for problems of underfunding. In addition to poor planning and poor fiscal management, the president castigated "narrowness of vision" and "short-term thinking" as key constraints to growth in the commune budget and development in the communes. Short-term thinking, the president continued, is reflected in "fear of taking initiative under the pretext of waiting for instructions from above," in an "intellectual inferiority complex," and in the use of "brutality and coercion toward subordinates." The president noted problems in the use of umuganda labor; criticized the proliferation of taxes ("These contributions are necessary but they should not bankrupt the population"); and encouraged recent initiatives to establish private schools (Habyarimana 1988:35–40). He also exhorted the authorities to consult the population:

> In our country, in all our communes, the agriculturist-herders constitute the majority. But they are not the most educated. However their work must now be revolutionized. . . . We have undertaken our program for self-sufficiency in food. This program will be carried out primarily thanks to the agriculturist-herders. But how will they be able to achieve this if they do not understand the goals of this program, . . . if they are not listened to, if . . . they do not dare to defend their interests against the traders and intellectuals who are allowed to do what they want?
>
> We must have confidence in the population, they must be consulted on everything that has to do with their development. . . . The communes that have carried out these instructions are clearly developing more quickly than the others [Habyarimana 1988: 43].

Analysts familiar with commune politics and administration wonder how encouragement of participation by local producers will be implemented in the communes as currently structured. A look at the role of agricultural extension officers (*moniteurs agricoles*) who work for the commune will illustrate this point. Since colonial times these officials have enforced various rules regulating agricultural production: digging antierosion ditches on hillsides; proper planting and care of coffee trees; installation of compost piles; pruning of banana plantations. Anyone who ignores the regulations is subject to fines; thus the population views the agricultural extension officer as a type of policeman. These officials do little in the way of agricultural extension (demonstrating new seeds and techniques), although some do aid coffee growers in use of sprays for coffee trees (Guichaoua 1989:180; Bagirameshi, Bahizina & Barnaud 1986). And almost no effort is made to provide extension services to women (Ubonabenshi Ngango 1987).

As part of its agricultural intensification program, the Rwandan government plans to introduce a revamped agricultural extension service. This service will use extension workers trained in new production techniques to make regular visits to farm sites. Yet it does not appear that this system will promote participation by rural dwellers in agricultural policymaking. As one donor study observes, "T[raining] & V[isit] is a hierarchical, top-down system of working with farmers and the local population in which the extension agents look up, not down—that is, they are accountable to their superiors and not to their clients. A system such as this is perfectly suited to existing Rwandan structures and, if adopted, may contribute little to improving agricultural production" (DAI 1986, vol. 1: 85). The report suggests that the new extension system might respond to the concerns of farmers "if . . . some accountability is built in, if some decentralization is allowed, and if local empowerment is encouraged." What is needed, the authors insist, is the creation of consultative, participatory structures that involve discussions with rural people who are to be affected by projects and programs, to give them roles in both planning and implementation. The report recommends encouragement of local farmer organizations as a vehicle for such participation (DAI 1986, vol. 1: 85).[12]

André Guichaoua would concur about the need for strong organizations at the grassroots. Yet his study shows that local power structures are not conducive to the growth of strong, assertive political organizations. The existing administrative structures in communes hinder peasant organization, and thus "leave the responsible positions and strategic areas of economic and social life in the countryside (commercialization, supplies, credit, transport, etc.) to people who are partially outside the rural milieu (traders, absentee landlords, civil servants, and military personnel). [These structures] also [make] it impossible to avoid the traditional process of polarization of wealth and concentration of competence and power benefiting an 'elite' and the capital" (Guichaoua 1989:187).

DEBATES: POLICIES AND PRACTICES IN AGRARIAN CHANGE

Such reservations about the role of communes in development echo concerns being voiced by many in Rwanda as part of a lively ongoing debate over what agricultural intensification can and should mean, what obstacles block efforts to raise peasant incomes, and what should be done to promote rural development. Insights on these debates are provided in *Dialogue*, a monthly periodical based in Kigali, as well as in articles by Rwandans and expatriate development personnel published in international journals. Four of the themes evoked in these writings are of particular interest for this discussion: the vulnerable position of rural producers vis-à-vis the market and government failure to foster peasant involvement in formulating agricultural and pricing policies; the bureaucratic behavior and extractive practices of commune authorities; the shortcomings of large-scale rural development projects funded from abroad; and the government's neglect of rural women in planning for agricultural intensification.

There is general recognition of the need for increased agricultural production. Although production has increased over the years, this has resulted mainly from increased acreage being cultivated (and less left fallow). What increases in production have occurred have barely kept pace with Rwanda's rapid population growth (Mbugulize 1986:7–9). It is generally recognized as well that to be successful agricultural intensification programs will require adequate incentives for rural producers. It is precisely in this area that some observers see a glaring weakness in government policy toward the rural areas.

Despite the government's public pronouncements about improving incomes for agriculturists, most producers remain in a dependent and vulnerable position vis-à-vis the market (read traders and merchants who buy their produce). The terms of trade for rural producers declined gradually over the period 1970–1986 (Itangishaka 1988:27); since the mid-1980s the decline has been more severe. And while the price of coffee to growers has been relatively stable (120 FRW, raised to 125 FRW in 1986, and then lowered to 120 FRW in March 1990), prices of goods rural people buy (clothes, salt, blankets, kerosene, building materials, etc.) have increased, especially during the 1980s. "This deterioration in peasant income is all the more serious when seen in the context of rising expenditures in both agricultural and nonagricultural spheres: medical care; children's school fees; house construction; marriage costs for a family member; various taxes" (Itangishaka 1988:27).

The vulnerability of peasants is dramatized in the practice of *kwotsa imyaka*—selling off a portion of one's anticipated harvest of food or coffee at much less than prevailing prices, in order to obtain ready cash. The price per kilo of coffee that prevails in such transactions sometimes amounts to only 50 percent of the official price. While illegal, this practice is common (Itangishaka 1988:28–29). Its prevalence reflects the poverty and powerlessness of many people in the rural areas—and their seasonal needs for cash to pay school fees, for example, or to buy food during the period of *soudure* (belt tightening) while awaiting the next food harvest. Some local cooperatives have attempted to combat this practice by making advances of cash available to their members. And in some regions of the country the Banque Populaire has experimented with granting special loans to address such needs (Itangishaka 1988:29).

Peasants are also vulnerable in that they are at the mercy of traders who pay them a low price for their produce as a means of recovering transport costs, while charging high prices to consumers (see Bézy 1990:37–39). This is not just an issue of rural-urban prices. Several regions of Rwanda are "food deficit" areas, and at certain seasons must purchase food from other regions that have a surplus. The government has attempted to intervene to prop up prices to producers, while keeping prices to consumers relatively low. But these "measures . . . put in place to defend the income of the peasant have been not only insufficient but also ineffective" (Itangishaka 1988:30).[13]

Another critic suggests that government efforts have been ineffective because rural producers are seldom brought into discussions on these issues. As René Sibomana, head of the Boy Scouts Association in Rwanda, explained in a 1988 interview, "it is astonishing that peasant producers are never invited to attend meetings [*réunions de concertation*] on price agreements. It is almost as if traders buy peasant merchandise out of the kindness of their hearts, as some sort of philanthropy. And unfortunately, that is close to the truth, since neither TRAFIPRO nor OPROVIA can take the place of the traders to reach peasants in their own milieu" (Sibomana 1988:18). TRAFIPRO, a parastatel cooperative, and OPROVIA, a state marketing agency, purchased a limited range of crops from cooperatives and farmers at favorable prices.

These observations indicate potential pitfalls in the government's effort to encourage regional specialization in food crops. Rather than producing all the different crops needed for their own consumption, producers are to be urged to specialize in particular crops and purchase the rest of their food, using the income from the crops they market. But many farmers would prefer not to depend for their food needs on a market they know to be volatile (Little & Horowitz 1987:255; 1988:272).

A second concern focuses on top-down decisionmaking in governmental structures. The commune comes in for criticism. "Defending peasant incomes requires defending peasants both against traders and against commune administrations that, instead of supporting the peasants, burden them the more with taxes of all kinds" (Sibomana 1988:18).

Increased distance between civil servants and the population and a lack of responsiveness to popular concerns have become commonplace. An editorial in *Dialogue* in 1988 deplores this situation, noting that when a poor person goes to government offices, municipal courts, or medical clinics he is made to feel as if he should "apologize for his poverty." Most of the poor are peasants; they ought to be (but often are not) treated with respect (Ntamahungiro 1988:12–13). Concentration of power in the hands of a few undermines accountability.

> Rampant bureaucratization poses a real danger for our country. It has gotten to the point where government officials no longer feel accountable to the population. The concentration of political, economic, and social power in the hands of a few has become so marked as to threaten the entire development process. The bureaucracy stifles us, even crushes us. . . . It's hardly . . . possible for new ideas to emerge, especially coming from the younger generation. It's always the same persons who participate in all the meetings, assemblies, and conferences, and who make the same proposals. They alone make the decisions [Sibomana 1988:25].

In contrast to reservations about communes noted by expatriate observers, Sibomana hopes that the new focus on communes may serve to remedy problems of top-down decisionmaking: "the projected decentralization policy giving greater autonomy to the Communes should loosen up the situation and allow direct contact with peasants on their own terrain, enhancing their ability to defend themselves" (Sibomana 1988:25).

Most important, though, Sibomana argues, is increased organization of peasants to defend their interests. "In fact, [people in] the rural areas have always organized themselves and defended themselves because they've succeeded in making a living up to now. The problem is to go beyond this stage and [for them] to regroup themselves in organizations for producing and marketing" (Sibomana 1988:20). Such organizations, Sibomana argues, should be formed by the people themselves, not by outsiders such as national deputies or civil servants; relying on outsiders can act as "a brake on the self-determination of cooperative members," since "the interests of peasants aren't necessarily the same as those of civil servants" (Sibomana 1988:20–21).

A third area of concern about rural development policies has focused on the shortcomings of large-scale development projects funded by external aid. These projects, found in every prefecture and usually encompassing several communes, are supposed to promote improved agricultural production and better animal husbandry. Funded through external bilateral and multilateral aid agreements, the projects expend substantial sums of money each year. Critics fault the large projects for their emphasis on infrastructure (houses for personnel, warehouses for supplies, construction of commune buildings) and inadequate attention to improving rural living standards. Some critics deplore the shift from an emphasis on integrated rural development that characterized project activities in the 1970s to a more narrow emphasis on production techniques and developing improved seeds and cattle-breeding techniques in the 1980s. Others assert that the projects have done little to diffuse improved seeds and agricultural techniques to the population and have failed to develop systematic collaboration between project administrators (usually expatriates) and commune and prefectoral authorities (Godding 1984, 1987, 1989; Nkundabashaka 1987).

Despite the stated purpose of these projects to aid the rural masses, it appears that the major beneficiaries are the expatriates, who receive generous salaries and benefits, Rwandan employees of the projects, and a small minority of "progressive farmers." In a study of OVAPAM, a World Bank project in northeastern Rwanda, René Lemarchand (1982:71) found that, far from fostering redistribution, the project tended to increase existing inequalities and create new ones; it also served the political interests of powerful political actors: "a development project such as the OVAPAM is generally seen by . . . power-holders as a system of spoils designed to reinforce what power they already hold, and only secondarily if ever as a means of reducing rural poverty."

Inadequate protection for rural producers from exploitation by traders, bureaucratic behavior of commune officials, and large-scale development projects that favor bureaucratic over programmatic goals are thus among the problems noted by critics of Rwanda's rural development efforts.

A fourth concern focuses on the role of women in development. Rwanda's government prides itself on attention to women's concerns and claims a commitment to improving women's economic and social status. However, Rwandan women continue to experience discrimination in many spheres. Landrada Mukayiranga, one outspoken critic who heads the office of Popular Education and Family Welfare in Rwanda's Health and Social Affairs Ministry, has called upon the government to reduce gender discrimination by guaranteeing women equality of legal rights, by insuring the right of inheritance for women, by incorporating women into decisionmaking bodies at all levels, and by providing equality of educational opportunity for girls at the secondary school and university levels (Mukayiranga 1986).

Other critics argue that government attention to women and development issues has scarcely moved beyond rhetoric; too often "integrating women into development" is interpreted as providing women instruction in knitting and sewing, cooking nutritious meals, and planting vegetable gardens. Rwandan women, like women elsewhere in Africa, play important roles in producing both food crops and cash crops (Nimbona 1988:64–65). A United Nations Development Programme (UNDP) study found, for example, that more than 80 percent of the labor associated with the care and harvesting of coffee trees in Rwanda is performed by women (UNDP 1980). Yet government rural development policy gives little attention to the productive roles of women.

Odette Ubonabenshi Ngango, an agricultural economist, wants this to change. Noting that some 22 percent of Rwanda's rural households are headed by women, and these households are among the poorest in the country, she deplores the inadequate attention to women's needs on the part of the government and NGOs. To bring about improved agricultural yields, she notes, will require the active participation of rural women. Efforts to introduce changes in the rural areas by government and NGOs must therefore take into account women's productive roles. Formulation of projects should include consultations with rural women, to find out what types of changes they desire and are willing to support (Ubonabenshi Ngango 1987).[14]

The enthusiastic responses of rural women to a pilot program sponsored by the IWACU Center in Kigali provides support for a new approach. IWACU provided modest loans and technical support to self-help cooperative organizations among rural women. Initial results from twelve sponsored projects were positive; women successfully organized themselves into local groups that undertook projects such as installation of gristmills and encouragement of income-earning activities for women (Nimbona 1988).

CRISIS AND RENEWAL: PROSPECTS FOR THE FUTURE

In July 1989 the International Coffee Agreement on quotas for coffee sales was abandoned. The world price of coffee then plunged to about half of its level earlier in the year, with serious implications for countries such as Rwanda (coffee provides almost 80 percent of Rwanda's export revenues). The effects of this precipitous decline rippled through the local economy, bringing another round of austerity measures and forcing the government to reduce the price paid to coffee producers. A serious famine in the center, South, and West during 1989–1990 further weakened Rwanda's deteriorating economic situation and generated intense criticism of the government for its dilatory response to the crisis.[15] In early 1990 the government began negotiating a stabilization program and a package of structural adjustment policies with the World Bank and the International Monetary Fund; in November 1990 the Rwandan currency was devalued by 40 percent. As could be expected, prices of many commodities (such as rice, sugar, gasoline) quickly inflated—by as much as 35 percent or more (Munyarugerero 1990c).

Observers of the coffee economy in Rwanda have constantly stressed the importance of coffee for the operation of local markets. So the reduction in the coffee price and the inflation accompanying devaluation will hurt not only producers (by undercutting their buying power) but also the traders/merchants who buy coffee from producers and sell consumer goods to them. Commune finances will also likely suffer, as well as the morale of common citizens and government officials alike.

The Rwandan government has claimed that its agricultural intensification and food self-sufficiency programs respond to the concerns and desires of the rural majority. It has further insisted that increased food production is compatible with continued emphasis on cash-crop production (mainly of coffee and tea) (Robins & Ndoreyaho 1988). The crisis conditions of the early 1990s will put these government assumptions to a severe test. Even before the crash in coffee prices some peasants preferred to neglect coffee trees and put their energies into planting food for sale—knowing that they would get a better return on their land and labor.

Yet regulations prohibiting the uprooting of coffee trees and mandating proper care of the trees have been on the books for years (Bart 1980). Will the government refrain from using coercion to promote coffee production, should price incentives evaporate? Or will the government be tempted to enforce regulations on care of coffee trees more stringently?[16] Increased coercion would do little to inspire enthusiasm among rural dwellers for government plans and programs, and could seriously undermine government credibility.[17]

Severe economic crisis within Rwanda contributed to the precipitation of a political crisis; 1990 saw many of the trends noted earlier in this chapter coming to a head. Amid the horrors of famine and the rigors of economic austerity measures, rampant *affairisme*, official corruption, and the lavish life-style of certain officials and merchants appeared all the more reprehensible. In mid-1989 the Catholic newspaper *Kinyamateka* began openly to publicize facts about the famine, official corruption, and land accumulation by high officials—subjects that were being ignored in the official media. From January 1990 other Rwandan intellectuals joined in public criticism of the government. Emboldened by events in Eastern

Europe, and influenced perhaps by the proliferation of protests in Zaire and elsewhere in Africa, they founded several new local newspapers that publicized economic and social conditions in the country as well as official corruption. The Rwandan security service clamped down and brought legal action against several journalists.[18]

Pressures for political reform continued to build during the second half of 1990. In May, Rwanda's Catholic bishops published a letter to Christians calling for social justice, respect for human rights, freedom of the press, and an end to nepotism, favoritism, and bribes. The letter condemned corruption in the courts, inequities in umuganda (unpaid community labor), land accumulation by the wealthy at the expense of the poor, "diverse forms of theft," and the "desire to get rich quickly without any effort" (Les Evêques du Rwanda 1990).[19]

Toward the end of May a clash between university students and gendarmes in the southern town of Butare resulted in the death of one student and injuries to five; students at both the Butare campus and the Ruhengeri campus in the North then went on strike. Here was one more indication of the volatile social climate engendered by the famine, by bitterness over regional favoritism, and by the restiveness of youth aware of openings to democracy occurring elsewhere (Cros 1990c).

Although initially Habyarimana had been reluctant to embrace multiparty democracy (Cros 1990a), he began to seize the initiative and propose political reform. Responding to multiple internal pressures and concerned about international opinion, he announced on July 5, 1990 (the seventeenth anniversary of his regime), a series of constitutional changes to be introduced over a two-year period. These would entail a move away from single-party rule and a reduction of the power concentrated in the president's office; Habyarimana would remain head of state and government but would relinquish his roles as head of the MRND, the Central Committee of the MRND, the CND, and the Judicial Council. A national charter would be drafted, specifying procedures for the transition to multiparty politics. In addition, several unpopular programs would be revamped, including animation (singing, dancing, slogans, games during which employees demonstrate loyalty to the state)—to be reduced from once a week to once a month—and umuganda. The president promised to allow more freedom for the press and to allocate government jobs on the basis of merit and ability. He instructed the next MRND Congress, scheduled for December 1990, to discuss these constitutional changes (Cros 1990d).

On September 21 Habyarimana appointed a Commission of National Synthesis and instructed its thirty members to draft the National Charter (Munyarugerero 1990a, b). Only a little over a week later, on October 1, 1990, a well-armed force of Rwandan exiles based in Uganda invaded the country. Calling itself the army of the Rwandese Patriotic Front (RPF, an exile organization), this group claimed that its goal was to establish a democratic government in Rwanda that would allow the return of all Rwandan refugees (Press 1990).[20]

As 1990 drew to a close, it appeared that Rwanda's army had won the October War, successfully repulsing the invaders. Nevertheless, the RPF forces seemed capable of continuing a guerrilla offensive through incursions against areas in the North near the Ugandan border (United States Committee on Refugees 1991). Habyarimana energetically pursued diplomatic initiatives, consulting with his counterparts in Zaire, Burundi, Tanzania, and Uganda. He asked them (and European allies) to support his efforts to arrange a cease fire and negotiations with the RPF, and to organize a regional conference to address the problem of refugees. In a major reversal of his previous stance, he agreed that Rwandan exiles who wished to return to Rwanda would be allowed to do so ("Uganda/Rwanda: Picking Up the Pieces" 1990).

Following the October War Habyarimana also accelerated the process of internal political reform. Responding to criticism from the RPF and other exile groups, he announced that ethnic labels (Hutu, Tutsi, Twa) would no longer be recorded on identity cards. In effect this meant abandoning the quota system (Munyarugerero 1990a, b; "Uganda/Rwanda: Picking Up the Pieces" 1990). The timetable for the move toward multiparty rule was speeded up, and a draft version of the National Political Charter was completed in December 1990. Following several months of public discussion, this charter was to be revised and then voted on in a national referendum before June 15, 1991. Once approved, the charter would pave the way for changing the Constitution to allow multiparty competition (Munyarugerero 1990a).

CONCLUSION

At the beginning of this chapter we looked at two contrasting images of Rwanda—one portraying a well-organized state successfully developing its economy and people against formidable odds; the other showing an authoritarian, repressive apparatus governed by corrupt officials and riven by regional and ethnic inequities. The analysis of debates over agricultural policy then showed how Rwandan government attempts to construct the first image (that of a successfully developing society responsive to the rural majority) have fallen short, in part because of the growing predominance of features characteristic of the second image.

These images are relevant also to current discussions over democratization in Rwanda. In the latter part of 1990 a heated debate was shaping up among Rwandan intellectuals as to what form the transition toward political renewal should take. In publications such as *Kangura*, *Le Démocratie*, *La Relève*, *Dialogue*, and *Kinyamateka*, writers discussed the failings of Rwanda's one-party state and called for multiparty democracy as well as greater citizen participation, more public accountability, responsible leaders who adhere to the rule of law, and increased opportunities for citizens to form organizations. Desires for progress toward governance were evident. Most attention focused on the process of change itself; by the end of 1990 few analysts had specified what difference a multiparty democracy would make in terms of substantive policies, and how a limited, democratic government would deal with the challenges of rural development noted above.

Implicit in discussions over democratization in Rwanda is the assumption that combating the rigid authoritarian state (the second image) would foster its opposite (the first image). A corollary assumption, seldom articulated explicitly, is that the process of political renewal as it is presently being pursued will redound to the benefit of Rwanda's rural majority. Yet there is no guarantee that such will in fact be the outcome. We have explored problems of lack of responsiveness in the elaboration and execution of rural development policies and commune administration. To what extent will the moves toward political renewal change this? While those calling for multiple parties, competitive elections, limited government, and a lifting of restrictions on the press agree on the need for an end to authoritarian rule, there are divergent views as to how economic development should be encouraged and what kind of society the new government will foster.[21] The rigors of the structural adjustment program and economic austerity associated with the low coffee price are likely to exacerbate tensions. Similarly, in the wake of the famine the government hopes for substantial foreign aid to advance its agricultural intensification program. As currently structured, this program is unlikely to foster greater government responsiveness or enhance the government's credibility among the rural masses.

As Rwanda's politicians shift from immersion in the formal aspects of democratization and governance and begin to consider substantive policy issues, it will be important for them to keep in mind the contradictions embedded in current development efforts. For while it is understandable that debates over agricultural policy have been pushed to the sidelines in the context of the multiple crises facing Rwanda in 1990, the problems with rural development have not disappeared. Participants in the ongoing efforts to achieve political renewal in Rwanda can benefit from thinking about governance as conceptualized in this book. They also should consider the guidelines of the 1990 Arusha conference on how to foster participatory democracy and development.[22] Only if such concerns are confronted will it be possible to forge governmental structures that are truly responsive to the rural majority.

NOTES

This revised version of a paper presented at the Annual Meeting of the African Studies Association in Atlanta (November 2–5, 1989) has benefited from the comments of John Harbeson, David Newbury, and Pearl Robinson. The data derive from documentary and published sources, but my interpretations have been shaped by observations during field work in Rwanda in 1970–1971, a short visit in 1988 funded by a travel grant from the University of North Carolina, and a six months' stay in 1989. The chapter was written during residence as a visiting member at the Institute for Advanced Study in Princeton, with funding from the National Endowment for the Humanities and the Rockefeller Foundation Resident Fellowship in the Humanities Program. I wish to thank these individuals and institutions, while absolving them of responsibility for the views expressed here.

1. Positive gains had been made in Physical Quality of Life Indicators as well. Life expectancy was estimated at forty-nine years in 1987, and between 1965 and 1987 the infant mortality rate declined from 141 per thousand to 124 per thousand. In 1965 the proportion of Rwandans of primary school age attending school was 53 percent; by 1986 this had increased to 67 percent (World Bank 1989:221, 272, 274). Adult illiteracy rates remained high, especially among women, but by the end of the 1980s the government had launched an ambitious adult literacy program assisted by the United Nations Children's Fund (UNICEF).

2. The political dimension of this process is considered at greater length in Newbury 1988.

3. On the coup, its causes and its aftermath, see Decraene 1974; Reyntjens 1985 (esp. 501–508), 1986.

4. Administratively the country is divided into eleven prefectures, each headed by a prefect appointed by the president; prefectures are divided into communes. MRND committees at the prefectoral level must approve candidates for the legislature, and normally two candidates are listed for each seat. Thus, while there has been no choice of presidential candidates in presidential elections, some choice is permitted in election of national deputies. There has been significant turnover: in the 1988 elections nonincumbents won twenty-six of the seventy seats in the CND. Two Tutsi were elected, the only Tutsi allowed to run; no Twa were elected; and eleven seats in the legislature were held by women (EIU 1989a:42; Ntamahungiro 1989:8, 10). There were no women prefects or burgomasters, but several women held positions as assistant prefects.

5. In 1956 Hutu made up about 83 percent of the population, Tutsi 16 percent, and Twa about 1 percent (Maquet & d'Hertefelt 1959:86). Many Tutsi were killed in the "events" of 1959–1964, while thousands of others fled the country. Some Tutsi who remained in Rwanda managed to have the label recorded on their identity card changed to Hutu. Currently many contemporary sources describe the ethnic composition of Rwanda as about 85 percent Hutu, 14 percent Tutsi, and 1 percent Twa.

6. On Rwanda's educational system see Hoben 1989.

7. In 1990 members of the Central Committee (appointed directly by the president) numbered twenty-six; included among them were a university professor, several ministers, three women, and two prefects (Biloa 1990:36–37).

8. See, e.g., Cooper 1981; Callaghy 1987; Joseph 1987; Kasfir 1983, 1987; Newbury 1984; Sklar 1979; Schatzberg 1980, 1988; Thomas 1984; Young and Turner 1985.

9. "Parasite" scarcely captures the graphic image conveyed in Kinyarwanda: "those who suck away all the force [of their victims], turning them into skeletons."

10. This speech, delivered in Kinyarwanda, was published in the Kinyarwanda original and an official French translation (Habyarimana 1988). My rendering is based on both the Kinyarwanda and French versions.

11. Usually burgomasters are selected to administer their natal commune, but prefects, who are also appointed by the president, hold office only outside their home region.

12. Jean-Pierre Godding (1987:98) suggests that to encourage participation by peasants in agricultural change the government should abolish moniteurs agricoles. This would save money and would force commune authorities and planners to rely upon and listen to the producers themselves, who are often more knowledgeable about local conditions than are the *monagri*.

13. For a critique of agricultural pricing policy see Mugesera 1986.

14. Research by Joachim Voss in Ruhengeri provides strong support for Ubonabenshi's argument. In a study of how to introduce improved varieties of beans, he found that selecting seeds, sowing, and storage were tasks performed by women. Therefore, any attempt to diffuse new seeds would require "a dialogue with the women, since they will play the determining role in the choice of seed types" (Voss 1987:46).

15. Food shortages during the first half of 1989 later escalated into widespread famine caused by irregular rains during the short rainy season of September–December. In December 1989 the government called for outside aid, yet even then there were delays in communicating with international organizations prepared to help. Official reports say at least three hundred people died of hunger; the numbers would be larger if one includes those weakened by hunger who died of disease. Hundreds of people, especially men, left their home regions in search of food. The famine affected prefectures in the Center, South (such as Butare), and West (Gikongoro was especially hard-hit, but Cyangugu was spared), and several communes in the East.

16. Little and Horowitz (1988:272) believe that in such circumstances the state would resort to coercion "to assure coffee's place as Rwanda's preeminent source of foreign exchange."

17. As the EIU commented in 1989, "given the close relationship between leaders' fortunes and those of their countries' economies, the collapse of the ICA is likely to be the indirect cause of the fall of several heads of state in the next year or two: Juvenal Habyarimana may not be the most vulnerable, but he will have cause for concern" (EIU 1989b:6–7).

18. Among those charged with slandering public officials and undermining popular confidence in the government were the director of *Kinyamateka*, Abbé André Sibomana (a Catholic priest), and three of his journalists. They were charged with having tried to discredit the government by writing that political authorities were embezzling money, seizing land, and ignoring the law, and that journalists and others in Rwanda were afraid to speak out about problems confronting the country (Cros 1990e; "Procès au redacteurs du journal *Kinyamateka*" 1990). Although several journalists from other papers were convicted and punished, Abbé Sibomana and the three *Kinyamateka* journalists were acquitted in September 1990.

19. The bishops directed particular attention to the plight of the poor:

> How can one remain silent when one sees how the little people tighten their belts, in order to find money for the poll tax and other contributions required at every turn, while this money goes into the pockets of certain [people] who pillage the common fund. . . . How can one remain silent when one sees that the sums of money intended for development projects for the people are not being used for this purpose in their entirety; rather the bulk is diverted [to benefit] . . . the persons in charge of these projects? [Les Evêques du Rwanda 1990:14–15].

20. Many of the Rwandan exiles who participated in the invasion were

officers and regulars in Uganda's National Resistance Army (NRA). Insecurity about their future in the NRA (there were indications that people of Rwandan descent might be demobilized) and insecurity among civilian Rwandan exiles faced with regular episodes of harassment helped to precipitate the invasion (United States Committee for Refugees 1991). Despite RPF claims to represent the interests of both Hutu and Tutsi, within Rwanda this organization is viewed as being dominated by Tutsi, with strong monarchist associations ("Uganda/ Rwanda: Picking Up the Pieces" 1990).

21. Compare, for example, the views of two of the Rwandan intellectuals who contributed to the special issue of *Dialogue*, on "Démocratie et Multipartisme au Rwanda." Emmanuel Ntezimana, a university professor, calls for a government that will promote equity and provide basic human needs to the popular masses (Ntezimana 1990). Jean-Damascène Ntakirutimana, administrative director of Générale de l'Informatique et des Etudes (GENIE), hopes a future multiparty government will allow energetic entrepreneurs to accumulate land and develop it as a means to increase agricultural production (Ntakirutimana 1990).

22. See *African Charter* 1990; Gran 1990; Howard 1986: ch. 4; Paul 1990.

10

Local Organizations, Participation, and the State in Urban Tanzania

Aili Mari Tripp

Voluntary organizations in Third World countries have sometimes been described as societal forces that undermine state strength by pressing excessive demands and whittling away at state resources through parochial networks (e.g., Migdal 1988). The experience of urban Tanzania during the crisis years of the 1980s suggests that such a characterization, while applicable in certain contexts, also has its limitations. In fact, during this period people in Tanzania were forced to withdraw their reliance on the state for resources and to depend more on their own efforts through the activities of voluntary organizations and other survival strategies. Where organizations placed demands on the state, it was frequently to lift unduly limiting government restrictions or to make government policies more responsive to private economic and other initiatives.

In the 1980s in Tanzania, local voluntary organizations became increasingly important in providing alternatives to the state's limited resources and succeeded in diverting demands that might otherwise have overwhelmed the state. They helped avert an even more serious legitimacy crisis than the country's leaders already faced. These organizations emerged where the state's ability to guarantee security, adequate incomes, and various social and public services declined. Sometimes they provided avenues for meaningful participation where organizations affiliated with the ruling party, Chama cha Mapinduzi (CCM),[1] left little room for creativity and autonomy. The accountability required in the operation of many voluntary associations frequently served as a challenge to the absence of such accountability in many party and government institutions. Finally, pressure from some of these groups began to result in positive changes in the state's agenda, opening up new political spaces and bringing some policies more in line with various societal imperatives.

Thus, in the 1980s the Tanzanian state began to retreat from its heavy interventionism that had undermined voluntary associations in the 1960s and 1970s. It allowed for the growth and revitalization of this sector, sometimes openly, but often simply by its inability to do anything to curtail its activities. The experience in Tanzania was not unlike that of other African nations in this regard (Bratton 1989b:569). Somewhat ironically, the new vulnerability of the state allowed for the strengthening of civil society and the potential for a new set of relationships between the nongovernmental organizations and the state.

The shifting emphasis away from statist approaches and the greater prominence of societal initiatives reveal a deeper dynamic at work in which the rules of governance have begun to be renegotiated. In analyzing these political processes, Hyden's use of the notion of governance (see Chapter 1) allows us to take the spotlight off the government and other formal legal institutions of the state where necessary in order to give greater play to a broader array of forces. This is especially important in the Tanzanian context, where formal legal institutions reflect only a fraction of real popular participation. Popular participation in new voluntary associations, as I will show, is slowly bringing about changes in the rules of the game, changes that are being gradually reflected in various policy measures.

Not all, however, would see the strengthening of societal participation in this way as a positive development. For example, Migdal argues that many Third World states are ineffective because social control is fragmented in a number of relatively autonomous social organizations that act as power centers operating along their own rules. He lumps small families, neighborhood groups, clans, clubs, communities, and even large foreign-owned companies into this category of social organizations. The state is only one organization, albeit an important one, among many groups. There does not exist one set of rules guiding social behavior. Rather, there are a number of competing sets of rules, of which the state advocates one set (Migdal 1988:29–31). For the state to be strengthened, Migdal says that societies must be weakened (generally through war, revolution, or mass migration) so that a new distribution of social control can emerge with the state at its center.

Samuel Huntington (1968:4) posited another kind of critique of participation in the late 1960s, suggesting that rapid social mobilization had outpaced the development of political institutions, especially parties, causing a decline in the political order and undermining the authority, effectiveness, and legitimacy of the government. Huntington's argument on departicipation emerged as a critique of the earlier view that participation was integral to political development (Chazan 1982:171). In the African context, Kasfir (1974:18) echoed this view, suggesting that departicipation is conducive to political modernization and that high rates of participation may lead to more-polarized factions and civil war.

Migdal (1988:138) argues that the state in many Third World countries "has become a kind of great benefactor without the control or power one might think should stem from such beneficence." In a similar vein, Marenin (1987:65) referred to the African state, commenting: "Everything is asked of the state, much is expected and the state is perceived as the most powerful, first and final guarantor of general welfare, economic development and individual advancement." In the earlier Tanzanian context, Hyden (1980:31–32) suggested that peasants and patrons made demands on the state for more schools, dispensaries, water, and roads but were unwilling to cooperate when it came to official policy demands on them. He wrote: "What had been a state with limited access was now turned open to a flood of popular demands. As most politicians had ridden to power in support of these demands, they had great difficulty in resisting them. . . . The economy of affection tended to swamp the public realm, limiting the scope for decisions aimed at defending the foundation on which its existence rested" (Hyden 1983:19).

In Tanzania one still found in the 1980s ample evidence for local organizations placing demands on the state. However, more common was the frequent absence of demands on the state and the reliance on group or individual self-help solutions to meet various societal needs. Perhaps the demands would have been there if the state were in a position to make good on its promises. But during the 1980s the state's increasing inability to provide a modicum of social and public services, to ensure livable incomes for the employed, and to offer viable police protection made it necessary for local organizations to fill some of these voids. In fact, the resiliency of society and its ability to reproduce itself with considerable autonomy from the state was one of the reasons the entire fabric of society did not fall apart during years of unprecedented hardship, to the amazement even of many Tanzanians. This was true even for urban dwellers who were more dependent on the state for jobs, social services, and security than their rural counterparts. As real wages fell by 83 percent between 1974 and 1988, urban dwellers began to pursue a variety of survival strategies, including reliance on farming, emigration back to the countryside, and increased involvement in small income-generating projects such as making pastries, carpentry, and the manufacture of clothing to supplement formal wages (Tripp 1990:56).

Before discussing the new forms of participation in Tanzania, I offer a historical survey of voluntary associations in Tanzania, explaining how they became increasingly constrained in the postindependence era. I then take two kinds of local community organization, rotating savings associations and local defense teams, to explore the growth of new organizations in response to the crisis. I draw extensively from material gathered in field research in Dar es Salaam, Tanzania, between 1987 and 1988. The study was concentrated on two parts of the city, Manzese and Buguruni, populated primarily by workers and self-employed entrepreneurs.[2]

VOLUNTARY ASSOCIATIONS DURING COLONIAL RULE

Tanzania has a rich history of voluntary associations, mutual aid societies, and various kinds of self-help organizations and networks. As in other parts of Africa, voluntary associations and social networks formed the basis of social, economic, and political activity, rather than the individual (as in electoral politics) or the broader social constellation; for example, class, ethnicity. People joined voluntary associations to further their economic and political interests, to enhance their personal status, or simply to cope with a changing social environment (Chazan 1982:185; Chazan et al. 1988:72–73).

Christian and Islamic influences were among the most important social movements at the turn of the century. Increased participation in new religious organizations reflected, in part, the desire to find new ways to cope with the uncertainties of colonial rule. Islam experienced its fastest growth in Tanzania between 1916 and 1924, when the numbers of Muslims jumped from 3 percent of the population to 25 percent. This was an unsettling period, following the British conquest of German East Africa, when the British were trying to establish control. It also coincided with an influenza epidemic and famine. The Islamic brotherhoods, especially the Qadiriyya, were the most instrumental in spreading Islam during this period (Nimtz 1980:14, 57–62).

Christianity also spread dramatically from 1914 to 1944, largely as a result of the efforts of Catholic and Protestant missionaries from France, Germany, England, Switzerland, and other European countries. The French Roman Catholic Holy Ghost Fathers started the country's first mission in Bagamoyo in 1868. In Dar es Salaam, the Lutheran Berlin Mission Society began its work in 1887, soon followed by the German Benedictines and Swiss Capuchin Fathers. Various denominations and missions worked in different parts of the country, careful not to infringe on the areas chosen by other missions. By 1938, 10 percent of Tanzania had converted to Christianity, and by 1957 one-quarter of the population considered themselves Christian, with the Roman Catholics claiming the largest number of converts. The missions were responsible for most of the country's health care and education until the 1970s (Iliffe 1979:543; Swantz 1965).

In addition to these religious movements, urban voluntary associations grew during the colonial period to serve a number of different purposes. Some of the first organizations emerged to provide new migrants with social services, which in the rural areas had been previously taken care of by their relatives (Wallerstein 1964:320). In Dar es Salaam, these organizations took the form of ethnically based groups, the earliest of which was formed in 1912. By 1954 fifty-one ethnic associations were registered in Dar es Salaam. Most were burial societies, while others provided loans, informed members of job vacancies, arranged dances, and ran football teams. Some organizations were even concerned with broader issues such as rural improvement and urban welfare. Other associations brought together individuals from particular regions.[3] The traders in Dar es Salaam had the best organized occupational group, the African Commercial Association, which aimed to resist Asian competition and petty restrictions of the Township Authority.

The associations varied with respect to level of organization, cohesion of leadership, division of labor, members' ages, regularity of meeting times, registration, and dues (Iliffe 1979:389–390). People were drawn to these associations because they had a clear identification with their members, knowing that they could count on them for company and mutual support to dissipate the isolation of city life.

The Wazaramo Union was perhaps the largest ethnic organization, which by 1955 claimed thirty-five hundred of the sixty-five hundred members of registered ethnic unions. As the original inhabitants of the Dar es Salaam area, their prime concern was the advancement of their rural areas. The union lobbied the colonial authorities to withdraw their support of certain discredited local leaders and to replace them with leaders chosen by the Zaramo. The union also owned trucks to transport passengers and agricultural produce between town and country (Iliffe 1979:391).

The *beni* dance societies, popular up until the 1930s, emerged as the first nonethnic local organizations. Although primarily a forum for competition through dance, procession, and theatrical expression of combat, the societies had a strong mutual aid component to them. While African civil servants were barred from joining the beni societies, the colonial authorities never actually prohibited them. Nevertheless, the authorities perceived their multiethnic character, anticolonial songs, and satiric use of colonial military attire as a threat (Ranger 1975:15, 63–65, 92). The beni societies were eventually replaced by Western type *dansi* clubs that came to Dar es Salaam from Mombasa via Tanga. By 1954 most of the fifty-eight dance societies seeking registration in Dar es Salaam were *lelemama* women's exorcism groups (Iliffe 1979:391–392).

Soccer was introduced by the English missionaries and popularized in the 1920s. By the 1950s Dar es Salaam had thirty-eight registered soccer clubs, based on workplace or ethnicity. In addition there were clubs referred to as "schools" where members engaged in small-time *kamali* gambling or played *bao* (a game played on a board carved with rows of holes), snakes and ladders, dominoes, or cards (Leslie 1963:101). Most of these recreational forms remain popular to this day.

As in other parts of Africa, the voluntary associations were often the precursors of the nationalist movement, providing fora for advancing anticolonial ideas (Wallerstein 1964:331). The most important political organization in Tanzania up until the 1950s was the African Association (Chama cha Umoja wa Watu wa Afrika). Formed in Dar es Salaam in 1929, it brought together clerks, teachers, and civil servants to promote African unity, irrespective of ethnic, religious, and regional background. It branched out to other parts of the country in the 1930s. In 1953 Julius Nyerere became the president of the association, which a year later evolved into the Tanganyika African Nationalist Union (TANU), the political party that was to lead the fight for independence (Iliffe 1979:406–412). TANU grew quickly during the preindependence period, from fifteen thousand members in 1954 to over 200,000 members by 1957 (Coulson 1982:115–116). During this period, the cooperative movement played a key role in the nationalist movement in the rural areas. It mushroomed from 188 cooperatives in 1952 to 474 in 1957, representing 305,000 members. By 1959 the number of cooperative societies had jumped to 617 (Coulson 1982:115–116).

In the cities the labor movement was vital to the success of TANU's drive for independence.[4] Since domestic workers formed the largest occupational group in Dar es Salaam, it was not surprising that the first registered African trade union was the Cooks, Washermen and House Servants Association, started in 1939. Other unions were soon to follow, including the African Teachers Association, established in 1944, and the Railway African Association, which by the end of 1945 was the most powerful workers' organization in the territory (Iliffe 1979:396–397). In 1947 dockworkers organized the Dockworkers and Stevedores Union.

The Tanganyika Federation of Labour (TLF) emerged as the leading organizer of workers in 1955, launching a union drive that is said to be unequaled in Africa's history. By 1961, 42 percent of Tanzania's workers were unionized, compared with 12 percent in Uganda and 8 percent in Kenya in the same period. The union movement had grown from one registered union with 381 members in 1951 to a powerful movement of thirty-five registered unions in 1961, representing 203,000 members (Iliffe 1979:539). Although the colonial government had forbidden cooperation between the TFL and TANU, they jointly mobilized successful boycotts during the 1957 bus strike and the 1958 strike of brewery workers (Coulson 1982:106–107, 116–117). TFL's cooperation with TANU proved to be decisive for the independence movement.

Thus urban voluntary associations in the colonial era grew in response to a variety of different societal needs. The earliest associations took over such functions as burials that would have otherwise been carried out by kin in the rural setting. They helped new migrants assimilate into urban life by providing recreational outlets as well as companionship and mutual support. Other organizations, such as the dance societies, Muslim brotherhoods, the trade unions as well as the more explicitly political African Association and TANU, grew as a response and, in part, as a challenge to colonial domination.

VOLUNTARY ASSOCIATIONS AFTER INDEPENDENCE

Voluntary associations continued to proliferate in the postindependence years but for different reasons than during colonial rule. Independence had necessarily obliterated the anticolonial component of various organizations. Groups catering to the specific needs of migrants were not as vital as they had been in the earlier periods of migration. Associations organized on the basis of ethnicity were banned, regardless of whether they were supportive of TANU's goals. It was felt that such groups could raise "tribalistic" demands, thereby threatening national unity. Many of the tribal unions that had allied themselves with TANU and played an instrumental role in opposing the colonial administration were no longer tolerated after independence. The Native Authority system was abolished, and in 1962 and 1963 chiefs, subchiefs, and headmen were removed as officials and replaced by directly elected councilors in local governments. This process of destroying former ethnic bases of power was reinforced with the villagization process of the early 1970s, during which the size of the political-administrative units that had once been chiefdoms or parishes were broken up into smaller entities (Moore 1988:166). Similarly, even though Christian and Muslim religious organizations had been an integral part of the independence movement, after independence TANU warned religious organizations to stay out of politics (Bienen 1970:66–69).

Religious organizations, however, persisted as some of the most vital institutions in Dar es Salaam throughout the 1980s and into the 1990s. Muslims, who predominated in the city, not only attended their local mosques but often belonged to a number of related organizations, including the *tariqas* or brotherhoods. While the Qadiriyya was the most influential brotherhood in the early part of the century, indications were that the Ahmadiyya brotherhood was gaining ground in the 1980s because of its strong missionary component. Other organizations included the Muslim Welfare Society and the only government-recognized Muslim organization, the Baraza Kuu ya Waislamu wa Tanzania (BAKWATA), otherwise known as the National Muslim Council of Tanzania. Among Christians, the Roman Catholics remained the largest denomination in Dar es Salaam, followed by the Lutherans, Anglicans, Seventh Day Adventists, and a host of other, smaller churches, including the Mennonites, Baptists, and Assemblies of God.

Other popular organizational forms included professional associations, such as the Tanzanian Medical Association, and business associations, such as the Tanganyika Association of Chambers of Commerce, Dar es Salaam Chamber of Commerce, and Dar es Salaam Merchants Chamber. Welfare and health associations ranged from such religious affiliates as the Tanzania Christian Refugee Service and the Muslim Welfare Society to the Tanganyika Leprosy Association and the Society for the Blind. Women's associations included the Media Women's Association and national organizations such as the Young Women's Christian Association, while youth organizations ranged from the Scouts to such religious affiliates as the Lutheran Chama cha Vijana and the Catholic Youth Club.

While most of the organizations mentioned so far were relatively visible, the majority of groups, as in the colonial period, remained community based, informally organized, and usually not registered. In local communities one found, for example, a wide variety of types of associations, ranging from market, manufacturing, and other such cooperatives to various forms of mutual aid societies, parents' organizations, and rotating savings associations; in addition to cultural associations such as dance groups, *tarab* music clubs that played and sang Arabic songs, football clubs, and exorcism groups. In the rest of this chapter I will focus on such community-based voluntary associations in the urban setting.

RESTRICTING FORMAL AVENUES FOR PARTICIPATION

As in other parts of Africa the role of informal community organizations increased as avenues for participation in broader-based formal associations were cut off (Chazan 1982:170). The government and party expanded their monopoly control of social relations by gradually centralizing party activities, by abolishing local governments in 1972, and by absorbing, eliminating, or curtailing key independent organizations, creating new ones and preventing others from being formed.

These developments paralleled the party's gradual expansion of its powers. At the time of independence in 1961 the Parliament was supreme. By 1965 Tanzania was declared constitutionally a one-party state; in 1975 the Constitution was amended to give the party supremacy and subordinate the National Assembly (Parliament) to its leadership. This was reinforced by the party's 1977 Constitution, which stated that "all activity of the organs of the state of the United Republic shall be conducted under the auspices of the party." The National Assembly was subordinated to the National Executive Committee of the party, where all major policy decisions were made (Mlimuka & Kabudi 1985:64; Pratt 1979:221). The dominance of the party over the government was further consolidated by Nyerere's simultaneously holding the positions of president and party chairman for twenty-three years.

The crowding out of interest group activity was part of a trend of party and government expansion that saw these institutions increasingly encroach into new political, economic, and social spaces. The party's 1967 Arusha Declaration was a major turning point in this regard, after which major financial, commercial, and manufacturing companies were nationalized. In the postindependence years the state expanded its presence by increasing social services, the numbers of parastatals, and the size of the bureaucracy. By 1976 government controlled 65 percent of the country's wage employment and 70 percent of the wage bill (ILO 1982:267).

Unlike most African states, however, Tanzania had adopted from the outset an approach that saw the political participation of people as vital to the success of the nation's development plans. As Nyerere (1973:333) wrote, "indeed, as far as we are concerned, the people's freedom to determine their own priorities, to organize themselves and their own advance in welfare, is an important part of our objective . . . because only through this participation will people develop."

The party was to serve as the main vehicle for political participation. Participation was not intended to take the form of local autonomous organization or grassroots initiatives outside of the party sphere.

The party was to be a mass party, and, indeed, numerically it was large. By 1987 the party had a membership of 2,469,840 members or 11 percent of the population. This indicates a steady increase in membership, which was (for TANU) about 6 percent of the population at the time of independence in 1961 and 9 percent of the population in 1977 at the time of the formation of CCM (Bienen 1970:57; [Dar es Salaam] *Daily News*, April 24, 1987). However, the size should not be interpreted as a key indicator of the effectiveness of the party or the level of support for party leadership, which appears to have declined since independence.

The party was hierarchically structured so that at the ground level every ten or so houses had a party cell representative through whom directives from the upper echelons could be channeled. By 1987 there were 269,102 cells and 10,515 party branches throughout the country (*Daily News*, October 24, 1987). The cell structure, especially in the early years of its formation, provided effective avenues for participation at the local level. Early studies of the cells showed them to be involved in local dispute settlement, organizing development projects, carrying out various welfare activities, and even assuming police and judicial functions at times (Miller 1970:551; Samoff 1973:69). Little input, however, filtered up from the local echelons to higher authorities, although this was one of the aims of creating the cells. As Moore (1988:166–167) observed in the northern Kilimanjaro District,

> the party provides the only legitimate forum for consolidated political activity at any higher level. Formally, it consists of a great web of representative organizations linking every citizen to the state in a great chain of representation, but to date it has been easily controlled from the top. Policy is made at the top and ratification sought from below to give the proper democratic patina. . . . Since the 1970s, the national administrative decentralization of 1972 notwithstanding, power and decision making have increasingly been concentrated at the top of the party and nation.

The increasing curtailment of independent initiative within the party led political scientists to conclude that real citizen participation in formal institutions was limited (Moore 1988:167; Samoff 1979:45, 56). Local practices, forms of organization, and ways of thinking were rarely taken into account or used as a basis for policy development.

The lack of input at the local level prompted one party branch leader, a textile worker, to remark in an interview I conducted with him: "Party leaders treat people like small children and tell you, 'Don't cry, I'll give you sweets.' In the past the party was secure, and the life of the people was considered. People even came to cell meetings at that time. Today they come only if we press hard for them to come. At that time it was something to be a party leader. Now if you come around they don't want to be troubled by you." Another party cell leader I spoke with explained why the party's top-down approach had not worked: "You can't force people to go along one narrow road. People have their own *akili* [minds, intelligence]. They aren't going to go along with force."

In the early 1970s the party bureaucracy was strengthened from the regional down to the ward levels, leaving salaried party bureaucrats with more power than elected officials of comparable rank. At the same time the government eliminated potential channels for participation when it launched a decentralization program and abolished local governments in 1972, replacing them with regional and district representatives who reported directly to the prime minister's office.

Local government in Tanzania had been patterned along the lines of the British local government system, which had responsibility for managing the schools, dispensaries, refuse disposal, and all key public services. The Dar es Salaam Municipality was established in 1945 as the first local government. At independence in 1961 it became an urban council. With the 1965 establishment of the one-party state, local governments came under greater control of the party but remained under the central government ministry in charge of local governments (Kulaba 1989:217–219).

The 1972 decentralization program, in effect, made local governments accountable not to the people, but to central government, which controlled funds and personnel. Theoretically, decentralization could have meant more opportunities for genuine participation, better comprehension of local conditions, faster implementation of policies, and better coordination between government departments. Decentralization was described in the press as a move toward greater democratization to encourage local participation in decisionmaking and planning. But even though decentralization shifted senior officials to regional and district offices, it did not result in the devolution of decisionmaking power to the people. For this reason decentralization has been widely regarded as part of the trend toward further strengthening the presence of central government in the locality (Coulson 1982:254; Kleemeier 1984; Mlimuka & Kabudi 1985).

In addition to the expansion of party and government control, the party found even more direct ways to restrict local participation. Like the colonial authorities who feared that voluntary associations would serve as "unconscious nurseries of democratic life," the new leaders saw the unbridled expansion of voluntary associations as a threat to the dominance of their states (Liebenow 1986:234; Wallerstein 1964:333). Tanzania was no exception as the party set out to co-opt or eliminate existing organizations and form new ones under its aegis.

Throughout the early 1970s local political and economic organizations were systematically undermined. In the urban areas the trade union movement was significantly curtailed, while in the rural areas the cooperatives were replaced by crop authorities in 1976, bringing them more under direct state control. Like local governments, they had been relatively accountable to the local communities prior to their removal (Kleemeier 1984:187). Genuine local grassroots initiatives in the countryside were also crushed in this period. The Ruvuma Development Association was a case in point. It succeeded in organizing communal production and providing social services to its members. Its autonomy and emphasis on democracy and self-reliance were perceived as a threat by regional authorities, who disbanded the association in 1969. As Samoff (1974:69) wrote, "In Tanzania, party policy frowns on the formation of interest groups in general, and economic interest groups in particular. . . . It is assumed that the political functions performed by interest groups in other polities—especially interest aggregation, articulation and communication—are performed by TANU and its auxiliaries and that interest groups, which could be used to form competing centers of power, are both unnecessary and dangerous."

By the early 1980s the ruling party had five affiliate organizations under its wing: the Union of Tanzanian Women; the Youth Organization; the Union of Tanzanian Workers; the Union of Cooperative Societies; and the Tanzanian Parents Association.

The suppression of independent organizations was problematic for both the authorities and society. As Liebenow pointed out, it represented a loss of creativity and different perspectives regarding alternative courses of development. Given the party's limited resources and revenues, it could ill afford to assume the services and functions of such organizations even if it wanted to. As a consequence, the party had to bear burden of failure in times of crisis, contributing to its demise in legitimacy (Liebenow 1986:234). Similarly, Hyden argued in the early 1980s that the strategy that circumscribed the activities of local institutions merely to terms set by the state ultimately "outlived itself." He argued that nongovernmental organizations (NGOs) had the critical task of establishing new forms of linkages with the government, replacing the predominance of regulatory linkages between the state and NGOs (Hyden 1983:128–130).

TRUST AND ACCOUNTABILITY AT THE GRASSROOTS

As avenues for formal participation were cut off, people relied more on their own organizations for meaningful social interaction, especially the less visible community-based organizations. People felt they had more autonomy and control in their own organizations, which usually gave them the freedom to express differing interests. One Young Women's Christian Association (YWCA) leader, for example, explained her preference for working in an independent association over the party-run organizations she belonged to: "we work in the YWCA and our [income-generating] projects because we can use our creativity and do what we want" (Marja-Liisa Swantz, May 23, 1989). The level of organization; the accountability and integrity required of leaders; the financial contributions and the enthusiastic participation in many of these voluntary associations—community-based and national ones alike—contrast sharply with the general level of participation in the party-affiliated organizations. The comparison between informal and officially sanctioned women's organizations provides a case in point.

One of the most popular organizations among urban women are rotating savings societies called *upato*, formed to pool and save money. The proliferation of these organizations in recent years reflects the fact that women are significantly more involved in income-generating projects and have more cash at their disposal. Half of all self-employed women I interviewed in my survey of Manzese and Buguruni reported participating in such societies (Tripp 1989a).

The small upato societies were organized in offices, in marketplaces, and in neighborhoods, where people participated with others of diverse ethnic groups and religious backgrounds. While I found a slight preponderance of participants from coastal ethnic groups (Zaramo, Matumbi, Ndengereko, Zigua, and Kwere) relative to the general ethnic breakdown of women in the survey, women of all of Dar es Salaam's many ethnic groups participated in these societies (I found in my survey alone forty-seven different ethnic groups).

The number of members in these societies ranged from five to fifty-seven. Women pooled on the average between 20 and 30 percent of their monthly income from their small businesses. The majority put money into the kitty every five days, thus making contributions six times a month. Each woman had her designated turn to draw from the pooled money. Women liked to make frequent deposits because if money sat around the house too long, it was likely to be spent. One-fifth of those who participated in these upato societies were involved in second savings societies as well.

One of the ways the upato organizations ensured accountability was by hiring a "secretary-treasurer" or *kijumbe* (literally translated as go-between or special secret messenger) to collect the pooled money and redistribute it. She herself, however, could not belong to the society and could be dismissed if she failed to carry out her obligations to the group. In some of the larger societies participants provided the name of the next of kin, who was responsible for making her installment should she fail to contribute. This person could also claim the kitty were she to die before it was her turn to claim it.

In the past, women participated in such societies, but rather than pooling money, they pooled *khangas* (cloths) and food. One woman, also a cell leader, said that she had been in such a society since 1972 when clothes and shoes were put into the kitty. At that time she belonged to a group of twenty women friends who started pooling money *kutunzana*, which is an endearing way of saying in order to care for or to look out for one another. Now they had adopted what she called a "new style" of upato involving money, where friends of friends were allowed to join.

Women said they saved to clothe their children and to pay for their education; that is, school fees, uniforms, and school supplies. Women also used their upato savings to expand their business or to get their project going again if it collapsed. Others saved to build houses. Women also saved for themselves, although this was after they felt they had taken care of their family's needs. One spinach seller I interviewed at a market said that she and her friends spent their extra money on clothing and getting their hair fixed. She explained, that "these days women want to buy khangas [colorful wrap-around cloths] from Mombasa and China. Women want *rasta* [hairpieces woven into the hair to make longer braids] and wigs. It costs to have these and have your hair relaxed or curled."

The one characteristic of these savings societies that was stressed time and again by women was the fact that they necessitated trust in order to function. As one woman who put 300 Tanzanian shillings (Tsh) into the kitty two times a month said, "Because we trust ourselves we can save on our own." She was a seamstress who also made and sold fried *maandazi* buns. Another woman, who along with eighteen other women put Tsh 100 in a kitty every three days, made a similar point: "upato is like putting money in the bank, but you need trust."

Like the upato societies, the activities of the YWCA in Buguruni and Manzese also testify to the viability of independent women's organizations. In both these areas of Dar es Salaam the YWCA has been successful for over two decades in the projects it initiated. In Buguruni the YWCA ran a women's hostel, while in Manzese it ran a women's group, a gardening project, and a nursery school of eighty children, operated by two teachers.

In contrast, the role of the local party-affiliated Women's Union (UWT) in Buguruni and Manzese tells a much different story. As in many urban areas, the UWT initiated cooperatives in the form of stores, bars, and farming projects. Little, however, had come of its efforts. In one Manzese party branch as many as ninety-two women had been organized in 1982 to participate in income-generating projects, including a store that sold flour, charcoal, and pastries. Almost predictably the women reported that the cooperative fell apart, and by 1987 the store sat empty—I witnessed only one solitary cat sleeping on its shelves. Accusations of mismanagement and theft of money were the reasons it fell apart, I was told.

When I talked to the national UWT leaders about the problems in organizing cooperatives and women's groups, they offered the standard answers, blaming the women themselves for their ignorance of how to run small businesses, their lack of management skills, their inability to keep records, and the untrustworthiness of local leaders. The irony is that in women's own organizations, such as the upato savings societies, it is precisely trust that keeps them functioning.

The problem of accountability goes deeper than this. A year after independence the women's section of TANU was transformed into the UWT, making it the first party affiliate. UWT committees were formed at national, regional, divisional, and branch levels with an elected chair and party-appointed secretary at each level. The UWT was subordinate to the party at each of these levels. Its program dealt with issues relating to child care, maternal health, nutrition, day care centers, and income-generating projects. Kaniki described the organization in the late 1950s as unquestionably "one of the most effective instruments of the party" (Kaniki 1974:14, cited in Geiger 1982, 59). Since that time, however, the UWT's effectiveness as an organization repeatedly came into question (Geiger 1982:52; Rogers 1983:27). Because it did not have a popular mass base, the UWT was largely dependent on the party for funding, which according to the union's leaders meant that they had to go without adequate personnel, transport, and other resources. Its party-derived organizational mold rarely allowed the UWT to incorporate or utilize existing forms of association among women as starting points for their own mobilization efforts. Instead they attempted to impose preconceived notions of how women should organize themselves, usually in the form of cooperatives, rather than drawing from the strength of such existing organizational forms as savings associations, ritual cult groups, dance societies, age and neighborhood groups, and other mutual aid organizations. As Swantz (1985:160) observed, "this meant also that women's own needs for meeting together were not considered when the activity list of the new association was planned, and that the capabilities of women leaders in the preceding social organization were not consciously incorporated. These are fundamental reasons for the difficulties the UWT has encountered in trying to bring the ordinary women into the local branches as active members, or even to arouse their interest."

Thus, it is not difficult to see why women tended to prefer involvement in their own organizations over involvement in party-mobilizing efforts. Where party channels limited local input, independent groups encouraged such initiatives. Moreover, the kind of accountability and organizational efficiency so often demanded of the leaders in voluntary associations provided alternate standards against which to measure the operation of party and government organs.

MEETING SOCIETAL NEEDS

Apart from a preference for local forms of organization, people established voluntary associations to meet societal needs that the government could no longer respond to effectively. "You scratch your back where your arm reaches," exclaimed one local beer maker while explaining to me how in hard times you do what you have to in order to survive. His motto of self-reliance is a familiar theme in Tanzania. Tanzania is a country whose leaders espoused self-reliance as a key tenet of its socialist ideology. Self-reliance was the watchword used by the party and government with little consistency in a variety of ways, including the willingness to exist without foreign aid; nonalignment with the great world powers; the pursuit of a strategy of internally based growth; the Africanization of the labor force; rural development (in contrast to urban development or industrialization); and minimization of dependence on central government through decentralized decisionmaking (Coulson 1982:299). It is, however, this last interpretation that gained the greatest currency in people's minds when the government's top-down forms of rule came into conflict with their survival strategies, which most considered their way of pursuing self-reliance. Ironically, during the recent crisis years people had to become more self-reliant than ever before, not because of the party's self-reliance policy, but often in spite of it (Swantz 1988). Some of the most self-reliant endeavors people initiated met with state opposition, even when these measures posed no obvious threat to the stability of the nation or its leaders.

Where the state's attempts to exert monopolistic control over society and the economy exceeded state capacity to regulate social relations and allocate resources effectively, people's own organizational structures often emerged to fulfil a variety of societal needs. The state's growing inability to guarantee adequate police protection, ensure that wages bore some relation to the cost of living, and provide basic social and public services led people to form their own organizations to cope with some of the difficulties they faced. Chazan (1982:177) argues that the growth of such informal groups in Africa has been an indication of the breakdown of state operations. Informal strategies can represent a form of "disengagement" from the state that Azarya (1988:7–8) describes as "the tendency to withdraw from the state and keep at a distance from its channels as a hedge against its instability and dwindling resource base."

Local security has been one such area in Tanzania where people's inability to rely on the state apparatus led to the formation of independent security teams, even in the urban areas. Local party leaders at the cell level in Manzese and Buguruni favored using their own security systems, believing the police could not be trusted because they were so frequently bribed by criminals. One local party leader in Manzese echoed the sentiments of many other cell leaders when he commented that "there are many gangsters in this area. Everyone knows who they are. You know everyone in your neighborhood and what they do. But people are afraid to report criminals. If they report them to the police, the police arrest the gangsters, who pay them a bribe of Tsh20,000 each and ask who reported them. Then they go and attack the person who reported them. If you are going to report someone, you had better be prepared to move." Another cell leader in Buguruni, also a shopkeeper, said that "we know who are criminals, but if we report them today they will put them in jail for two days and then they will be out and our lives will be threatened. That is why we are silent." The cell leaders feared the collusion between the police and gangsters not only because it rendered the police virtually useless, but because they believed the police to be the criminals' chief source of arms (rifles and pistols), since there are no private legal sources of such weapons in the country. One cell leader said: "We ask for weapons but we can't get them. It is strange, because robbers get them. Where do they get them? It is most likely that they use bribes."

Realizing the police would be of little help, many local leaders began around 1987 to organize their own local security teams, involving local citizens who would patrol their own areas at night at approximately ten-day intervals. These defense teams carried *fimbo* (sticks), *rungu* (sticks with knobs), *shoka* (axes), and *panga* (machetes) as weapons. The defense teams in Dar es Salaam were patterned along the lines of other such organizations that had sprung up throughout the country in the 1980s for similar reasons: the lack of confidence in the state's ability to provide adequate security, and the collusion between police and criminals. In Dar es Salaam they are called *jeshi la jadi* (traditional defense organizations) or *sungusungu*, which literally means large black biting ants. In the Shinyanga and Mwanza Region, where these organizations have been most prominent, they are also called *wasalama* or *busalama*, derived from the Nyamwezi word *busungu* or poison (Abrahams 1987:182).[5] In Singida and Iringa they are called *siafu* or red fierce biting ants (*Daily News*, September 27, 1986).

Nyamwezi villagers have explicitly linked sungusungu to earlier customary obligations to respond to an alarm call from a neighbor. In fact, although sungusungu is a new phenomenon, it is modeled along the lines of traditional dance societies, cultivating teams, spirit exorcism associations, hunting groups, threshing teams, and other such forms of neighborhood organizations. These other forms were distinct from support provided by kinship relations and by the historical chieftainships and the postcolonial local governments. Although they frequently borrowed the nomenclature of chieftainship, Abrahams points out that, in fact, the Nyamwezi sungusungu teams are much closer in resemblance to the 1950s neighborhood threshing groups and their "millet chiefs," which were, in fact, opposed to chieftainship. Instead the sungusungu "chiefs" are often diviners and medicinal experts who prepare medicines to protect members of the organization. In addition to the chief and second in command, there are officers who are appointed to bring people together for assemblies, and a secretary who keeps records or proceedings and issues membership receipts (Abrahams 1987:183–185, 192–193, 195).

The government's response to sungusungu teams has been uneven throughout the country. In the northwest, for example, regional and district leaders frequently saw the teams as a challenge to their own authority and at times tried to suppress their activities (Abrahams 1987:186; *Daily News*, March 3, 1987, p. 1) After years of parliamentary debate about the legalization of sungusungu and intermittent calls by national leaders to recognize the defense teams, in 1990 Minister of Home Affairs Augustine Mrema directed the districts of Dar es Salaam to formalize them (*Daily News*, November 22, 1990). At the same time he threatened to take stern measures against members of the Police Force who tried to frustrate the move because, as he explained, "people know that members of the police are too few for the big task." He also charged his ministry to work on statutory regulations that would empower cells and wards to form councils to legally deal with criminals. Within two months of organizing the patrols the number of murders in the city dropped dramatically from seventy-one to five, and armed robbery cases dropped from forty-eight to six (*Daily News*, January 11, 1991).

NEW FORMS OF LOCAL PARTICIPATION

As we have already seen in the case of the rotating savings associations and the local defense teams, new organizations have emerged for a variety of reasons. Some, like the rotating savings associations, independent cooperatives, even a recently formed Association of Businesswomen, reflect the entry of new sectors of the population into small-scale entrepreneurial activities, partially as a response to the decline in real wages of employees in the formal sector.

Other organizations, such as the local defense teams, sprung up to provide services and other resources the state could no longer provide. New ethnic and region-based welfare organizations were formed around 1987 in Dar es Salaam to raise funds for flood relief, orphanages, AIDS victims, health and educational facilities in their home regions and to serve as burial societies. These organizations include a Wahaya association, Wanyakyusa Residents of Dar es Salaam, Mtwara-Lindi Residents of Dar es Salaam, and two Wachagga associations representing Rombo and Moshi Vijijini. The associations resemble the ethnic welfare and burial societies that emerged in Dar es Salaam in the first part of the century to help new migrants cope with the transition from rural to urban life. In discussing the emergence of new ethnic and region-based welfare associations in Tanzania, it is important to note that other new associations have been organized along lines that cut across these cleavages, even at the community level; for example, rotating savings associations. This was as true in the early 1990s as it was during the colonial period when trade unions, professional associations, dance societies, sports clubs, cooperative unions, and most importantly the independence movement drew from broad and diverse membership bases. A careful study of the composition of urban organizations shows both strong horizontal and vertical links of association. In this sense many local groups play a positive role in creating national affinities that go beyond parochial interests, suggesting possibilities for the strengthening of civil society as the state becomes more attuned to the needs of the nongovernmental sector.

Other organizations formed to meet new needs the state was unable to respond to. Even though the government had taken over the development of child care centers, the new pressures on women to become self-employed had increased the demand for day care centers, forcing parents to create new organizations to build and operate centers of their own.

As people mobilized themselves to meet new needs or to meet needs the state could no longer fulfil, some organizations did make demands on the state. But rather than demanding greater resources from the government, they called on the government to lift its numerous and often tedious restrictions in order to make it easier for people to cope with the economic difficulties they were facing. The kinds of demands people made on the government had to do, for example, with easing licensing restrictions on the poor, ending militia harassment of vendors, and abolishing party restrictions on its members with two incomes. Organizations representing the business sector pressed for an environment more conducive to the private sector, demanding, for example, an investment code that would streamline investment registration procedures and laws. Organizations such as the Metal Engineering Industries Development Association tried to get the state to play a role that would facilitate and protect the development of local private capital. Thus, the focus of popular demands was not so much a question of extracting goods from the state, but rather on getting the state to extricate itself from society and strengthening its role as a facilitator of independent initiatives.

STATE RESPONSES

Chazan (1989:169, 175) has shown how voluntary associations in Africa were able to influence specific policy decisions, affect the composition of political leadership, and in some cases even induce fundamental revolutionary change in the political system, including shifts from military to civilian rule by electoral means and shifts from one-party to multiparty politics. Chazan and Rothchild (1989:34) argue that in Ghana, voluntary organizations are part of the political dynamics that "ensured that governmental capacities and performance would mirror at least some social interests; simultaneously they have provided a real check on government excesses. Thus, social concerns and political possibilities are integrally linked through the composition of coalitions and the direction of their activities from the bottom up."

In Tanzania these same kinds of readjustments were visible, however slow and imperfect. Voluntary associations provided pressure points that formally and informally, openly and through noncompliance, helped force the state to change or reconsider many of its rules. While it would be premature to conclude that major democratizing currents were emerging or that Tanzanian politics was adopting a pluralistic face, nevertheless there were small signs of new political openings. In some instances the state eased its restrictions tacitly, by turning a blind eye to various activities that it could not openly condone without relinquishing certain key ideological principles.

In Tanzania in the middle of 1990 the party launched a restricted public debate over whether a multiparty state should be permitted and for the first time allowed the state-controlled media to discuss the limitations of press freedom in the country. Independent publications and newspapers were openly sold on the streets of Dar es Salaam. These measures were coupled with a growing recognition of the importance of independent voluntary organizations for national development. In April 1991 the party Central Committee decided that its mass organizations (i.e., the national trade union, the cooperative union, and the national women's, youth, and parent's organizations) could draw their own constitutions, develop their own programs, and elect their own leaders, which in effect would make them independent of the party.

Pressure from voluntary organizations was reflected in such lively parliamentary debates as the discussions over the funding of independent self-help projects, the legalization and protection of sungusungu, and the privatization of medicine. The Medical Association of Tanzania, for example, fought and in 1990 won the right for physicians to legally treat private patients after putting in a day's work at the government-run hospitals, which paid them little more than the minimum wage.

The legalization of various associations was in part a realization that these associations could no longer be suppressed and that they inadvertently took pressure off the government and party to provide various services and resources. But legalizing them was also a way of making it easier to monitor their activities. This was probably the case with the new government endorsement of the Tanzania Traditional Healers Association, which was reestablished in 1990, having been dissolved ten years earlier. In a meeting with the minister of health, Philemon Sarungi, the healers complained about how they had been "neglected and undermined" by the government (*Daily News*, February 25, 1991). Already in Mbeya the new relationship between the government and the healers' association had resulted in the healers agreeing to cooperate with the government health care system in a campaign to prevent AIDS.

In other instances the authorities simply ignored organizations such as the ethnic and region-based welfare associations that previously had been prohibited on the grounds that they would threaten national unity. Part of this tolerance may have come from the government's incapacity to suppress them. But part of it also came from a growing realization that these associations were not inherently divisive and that their contribution to social welfare at this time outweighed other considerations.

Although these were important signals of a new openness in Tanzanian politics, these observations should be tempered by a recognition of the limitations on freedom that persisted even as new freedoms appeared. For example, only those organizations that had party approval could conduct political debates around multiparty democracy, while the president appointed a commission to coordinate the debate for one year (*Daily News*, April 19, 1991). Shortly after appointing the commission, the administrator-general revoked the registration of the promultiparty Tanzania Legal Section Trust (TANLET) because it had proposed a national seminar on multiparty democracy in April 1991. The administrator-general wrote to TANLET: "from now on you are precluded from participating, organizing, sponsoring, facilitating directly or indirectly in any political activities or providing political platform to any person or organ" (*Daily News*, March 27, 1991).

Thus, the newness, fragility, and uncertainty of the consequences of such political openings could easily lead to quick reversals of policies that promote greater openness in the political process. Many powerful forces still have strong interests in preventing changes that would further erode their economic and political base.

CONCLUSION

In spite of these continuing limitations on popular participation, some important changes are occurring as voluntary associations take advantage of new political spaces created by the decline of state capacity. These developments in Tanzania, with parallels in other parts of Africa, may indicate the beginnings of some long overdue adjustments in state-society relations that would make the state more responsive to societal needs and preferences. Thus the problem of instability comes not from the existence of local institutions per se, but rather from the way in which such organizations are inserted into the larger polity and the way in which the state deals with them.

This is especially important when it comes to analyzing the role of associations based on ethnicity, religion, or kinship. When pitted against one another such affiliations have all too often fueled debilitating conflicts that have undermined the functioning of the state apparatus. But it is necessary also to point to the sustenance such ties have provided people in times of crisis. As in most countries, such affinities are not intrinsically divisive in Africa, nor do they automatically erode the state from within.

In summary, I have tried to show how Tanzania's government and ruling party absorbed, co-opted, eliminated, and curtailed the activities of key independent organizations, including trade unions and agricultural cooperatives, in the years following independence. Nevertheless, voluntary associations and networks, especially informal ones, continued to play a central role in the country's political, economic, and social life. In the 1980s they increased in significance as Tanzania plunged deeper into economic crisis. People formed new organizations and revitalized such old ones as rotating savings associations, local defense teams, and mutual aid organizations to cope with the growing economic and other uncertainties of life.

The official recognition of various informal associations, such as the local defense teams and the local healers' association, represented the opening up of new political spaces and the reconstruction of state-society relations in such a way that the state was forced to act more in accordance with various societal imperatives. It was possible in the 1980s to begin identifying some new productive reciprocities between the rulers and the ruled, thus enhancing the possibilities for governance, as described by Goran Hyden (Chapter 1).

Instead of increasing pressures on the state and making demands on the state for resources it could not deliver, local voluntary organizations provided people with avenues through which to find their own solutions to everyday problems of guaranteeing food, income, physical security, and other social and public services. These strategies, often pursued by thwarting state regulations, which at first glance might appear to have undermined state authority, might actually have served to enhance state legitimacy. They took the heat off the government to live up to past guarantees and allowed people genuine and autonomous avenues to seek their own solutions. Moreover, some of these strategies forced the government and ruling party to make open as well as quiet retreats from past heavy-handed interventions in politics and economics, thereby enhancing the state's legitimacy. In all these ways, the existence of these private strategies decreased demands placed on the state.

The concern of Huntington and others that political development requires departicipation does not hold up to the recent experience of Tanzania and many other African countries. The question is of particular importance, as boundaries of state and societal control are being reevaluated and reinterpreted not only in Africa, but worldwide. The retreat of the state, the opening up new spaces for local participation, and the strengthening of civil society offer new possibilities for a renegotiation of bases for state-society relations and for the construction of more-productive relationships between the public and private sectors.

NOTES

1. The ruling party was called the Tanganyika African National Union (TANU) prior to 1977, when it merged with the Afro Shirazi Party to form Chama cha Mapinduzi.

2. Together with a research assistant, I conducted a cluster survey of 284 residents, approximately three hundred informal interviews with self-employed entrepreneurs, a snowball survey of fifty-one middle- and upper-income residents engaged in sideline businesses, and around three hundred interviews with local party leaders at the lowest level of ten-house cells. We carried out all these

interviews in Swahili. In addition, we interviewed party and government leaders from the cabinet and Central Committee levels down to the regional, district, and branch levels.

In Manzese and Buguruni we talked with local religious leaders, teachers, and other important community figures as well as leaders and members of local organizations, both formal and informal. These included women involved in the Union of Tanzanian Women projects, members of the party's youth organization (VIJANA), Muslim imams (prayer leaders), and Ahmadiyya brotherhood leaders, Catholic and Lutheran ministers and lay people, organizers of local defense teams, people running manufacturing and market cooperatives, members of dance societies, educators at a City Council–sponsored Nutrition Center, women involved in *upato* rotating savings societies, managers of football clubs, and many others. We also spoke with national leaders of the Women's Union and its small projects branch (SUWATA), the Young Women's Christian Association, the Family Planning Association (UMATI), the Tanganyika Association of Chambers of Commerce, the Dar es Salaam Chamber of Commerce, the Association of Tanzanian Employers, and the Tanganyika Tea Growers Association, among others.

3. One of the earliest ethnically based organizations was the Pogoro Union formed in 1912, followed by the Chagga Association and Mbisa group of Northern Rhodesia, formed in 1919. By 1921 the Nyamwezi, Sukuma, Ngoni, Pare, and Sudanese had formed their own associations. The Ukami Union, founded in 1938, brought together members of the Kwere, Luguru, Kutu, Zigua, Doe, Vidunda, and Sagara and Kami ethnic groups. In the early 1950s the Nyakyusa and Fipa also formed associations. Regionally based organizations included the Nyiramba Association, the Mbaha Union, the Marui Association, the Buganda and Bukoba Natives Association Dar es Salaam, and the Nyasaland and Northern Rhodesia Association (Leslie 1963:40–56; Iliffe 1979:390).

4. The first trade unions were formed by Asians in the 1930s, including the Union of Shop Assistants of Tanganyika and the Asiatic Labour Union of Sikh carpenters (Iliffe 1979:346).

5. In the Kahama area the defense teams were initially called Chama cha Busalama. Chama can mean club, association, or party. Regional authorities forced them to drop this appellation because of its latter connotation, reflecting some of the apprehension these organizations have caused the authorities (Abrahams 1987:185).

11

Initiatives From Below: Zaire's Other Path to Social and Economic Restructuring

Janet MacGaffey

Zaire's long-standing economic crisis and the poverty of the majority of the population, despite the country's enormous natural wealth, are notorious. Wages are so low compared to prices that virtually no one is paid a living wage. The country is plagued by transport and communication difficulties, a corrupt and ineffective administration, industry working far below capacity, scarcities of all kinds, and a huge foreign debt. In this system, in which political interest governs the operation of the economy, little optimism seems possible. Yet investigation reveals people confronting the seemingly insuperable problems of survival in such conditions by taking matters into their own hands and organizing an unofficial economy and other parallel social institutions to offset the failure of official ones. Through this unofficial system, people are challenging an oppressive state and restructuring society without recourse to violent revolution. I will give details of this process and consider its implications for governance in the sense that is discussed throughout this book.

Second economies exist in most countries of the world, and the extensive literature on them has focused primarily on their economic implications. In contrast, my study of the second economy of Zaire (MacGaffey 1987: ch. 5; MacGaffey et al. 1991: introduction) has stressed that it is essentially a political phenomenon and that it has been a factor in the process of class formation since independence. Other recent studies have emphasized the political aspect of second economies in countries as far apart economically as well as geographically as Peru and Hungary. Hernando de Soto, in his book *The Other Path* (1989), describes the informal economy of Peru, existing largely outside the law, as an alternative, peaceful form of revolution, a contrast to the violence of the Shining Path guerrilla movement.[1] Ivan Szelenyi sees private producers among peasants and workers as forming a new class of "socialist entrepreneurs" in the socialist economy of Hungary. They have not overthrown the bureacratic class but have forced concessions from bureaucrats in a "silent revolution from below" (Szelenyi et al. 1988:4–5).

A perception of second economies as spontaneous, popular efforts to transform society has implications for the issue of governance. In Chapter 1, Goran Hyden expanded this concept beyond the task of running a government or making critical choices; he looks at power as an exchange and not just a zero-sum game. In this sense governance is characterized by reciprocal behavior and legitimate relations of power between governors and governed, thus differing from rule, which does not presuppose legitimation in these relations. Hyden sees governance as the core of politics. It presupposes trust coupled with accountability and allows us to look at initiatives aimed at structural change that emanate from both state and society, from the top and the bottom of the system. I will describe here initiatives coming from the bottom to see how effective is the restructuring they bring about at the level of concrete everyday reality, and to specify the extent to which they must be matched by initiatives from above.

In Hyden's terms, the challenge to existing structures by political actors must emanate from the top as well as from the bottom for a fully successful transformation. It is clear, however, that the potential also exists for change from the top to follow and build upon changes initiated from below, a consideration that seems particularly timely given the current move in Zaire in the direction of a multiparty system, and the recent events in Eastern Europe. There is also the possibility for successful gains for subordinated classes in improving their conditions of life even if changes from the top do not occur. As Szelenyi (Szelenyi et al. 1988:9) observes, "power is not a zero sum game—workers can make important and lasting gains, even if capitalists or bureaucrats lose little or nothing."

Is it justifiable to use the term *revolution* for these nonviolent initiatives from below and the restructuring they bring about? Revolution usually implies the overthrow of government by organized violence, a new class taking control of state and society, and a shift in the power base, but as Hyden suggests, change is possible without apocalyptic intervention. We will see what changes in society Zaire's burgeoning second economy has brought about. Do these changes constitute a hidden revolution? What light do recent political developments shed on this question? What gains have the subordinated classes made?

We will begin by looking at how revolution from below has taken place in Hungary and Peru. De Soto (1989:xiv) describes the informal economy of Peru as "the people's spontaneous and creative response to the state's incapacity to satisfy the basic needs of the impoverished masses." People operate in this economy not "to live in anarchy, but so that they can build a different system which respects a minimum of essential rights" (p. 55); through informal activities they are able to confront the mercantilist state rather than succumb to it. This state is one in which the economy is governed by politics, not by markets, and where entry to the market is restricted not free. To survive in Peru's cities, migrants have had to make a living outside the law in informal trade, to construct and live in informal housing, and to set up an informal transportation system. In these ways they challenge a legal system that does not "honor the expectations, choices, and preferences of those whom it does not admit within its framework" (p. 12), but enacts laws that favor special interest groups and discriminate against the interests of the majority. People thus effectively resist a state that has never expressed their will or catered to their needs and have restructured society to meet these needs.

Peru's other path for transforming society from below is paralleled in the activities of Hungary's subordinate class of peasants and workers, which is producing a revolution within state socialism in a process of "socialist embourgeoisement." The emergent, marketlike second economy existing outside the state economy is empowering unskilled or semiskilled peasant-workers through part-time family agricultural production (Szelenyi et al. 1988:8). Peasant workers supplement their wages with private production, ranging from garden produce to livestock raising and small-animal production, to hothouse agriculture in plastic tunnels. These activities are relatively autonomous from the state and are so extensive that they account for 34 percent of the gross farm product. Six out of ten Hungarian families engage in food production; in 1982, 90 percent of the rural and 30 percent of the urban population grew agricultural products (p. 31). Szelenyi believes that many peasant-workers have managed to transform the disadvantages of their semiproletarian position into an advantage. He stresses not the omnipotence of the dominant class but the power of peasants and workers and the limits of bureaucratic domination (p. 4).

In both Hungary and Peru people struggle to cope with the inadequacies of the official system to meet their needs. Through initiatives coming from below, they have challenged existing structures, modifying them or creating new ones; in the process they are transforming society. We will now look at similar initiatives in Zaire and at the transformations they have brought about, and then assess to what extent they have restructured or revolutionized society. What are the implications of this process for the issue of governance?

INITIATIVES FROM BELOW IN ZAIRE

A brief account of the Zairian polity and economy under President Mobutu Sese Seko is necessary to give the context for the expansion of Zaire's second economy. The strategy for the reconstruction of the state after Mobutu came to power in 1965 was to develop a public sector strong enough to serve the economic interests of the new state-based class. This strategy failed as the administrative capacity of the state became increasingly ineffective in the years after independence. This decline was a result partially of the colonial legacy of a low level of education and lack of experience of Zairians in management and government, partially of the seemingly unbounded greed of a powerful few of the new governing class, and partially of economic problems that have deprived the state of resources.[2]

Some of these economic problems have their roots in colonial policy, which neglected food production and developed an economy to export primary raw materials for the benefit of industry in the metropole. Others result from the efforts of the new dominant class to use state position to acquire control of the economy, culminating in Zairianization of foreign-owned businesses in 1973 and, after its failure, in retrocession in 1976, in which businesses were returned to their former foreign owners but with Zairian partners. This indigenization drastically disrupted industry, commerce, and agriculture, and caused an abrupt decline in state revenues. Other causal factors of the deepening economic crisis into which Zaire has spiraled since the late 1970s are the decline in copper prices on the world market, the increase of world petroleum prices, and a huge national debt arising from unwise and costly investment during the economic boom of the early 1970s.

The economic crisis and accompanying high inflation have resulted in a decline in real wages. In 1990 in Kinshasa, they represented 6 percent of their value on the eve of independence in 1960. In 1983 public service salaries were nominally seven times higher than in 1975, but in real terms they represented less than one-fifth of the 1975 level. Relative to 1969, prices were forty-six times higher in 1979, and 113 times higher in 1986 (Houyoux et al. 1986:10). The estimated average monthly food budget for a family of six in 1984 was Z3,037 (zaires), while the base monthly salary for a medium-level civil servant was Z750. But only about 1 million of the estimated 4 million labor force is employed at all. Urban dwellers must thus find outside the formal wage and salary system not only means for survival, but also essential supplementary income, as well as the means for any improvement in their life-style.

The decline in the effectiveness of state administration following independence, the impossibly low wages at all levels, and the rampant scarcities in consumer and other goods caused a rapid expansion in second-economy activities as people struggled to survive and make a better life for themselves. The participation of state officials in these activities accelerated the decline in administrative efficiency, further expanding the second economy and making the state less effective in enforcing its control of economy and society. Concomitantly, the state became more predatory because of the ever-increasing extortions from the population by its personnel.

That sector of a country's total economy that we call the second economy is variously referred to in the literature as the informal, underground, parallel, hidden, shadow, endogenous, irregular, or black economy. Second economy is preferable to "underground" or "hidden," because many of its activities are carried out quite openly; to "parallel" because unofficial activities intersect with official ones in many complex ways; and to "informal" because this term has come to refer to the small-scale enterprises of the urban poor, ignoring the large-scale illicit activities of the wealthy and powerful, which are of much greater significance for the national accounts and the functioning of society.

The second economy is made up of economic activities that are not only unmeasured and unrecorded but are also, in varying degrees, illegal. This illegality makes these activities essentially political phenomena: since illegality is defined by the state, it can be defined in ways that serve the interests of the politically powerful; the boundary between legal and illegal shifts over time and is susceptible to pressures that are political. In Zaire, the second economy consists of production of goods and services that is made illegal because it is concealed to avoid taxes or other charges; production of illegal goods and services; concealed income in kind, including barter; and other income opportunities that are illegal or in some way deprive the state of revenue.[3]

People avoid legal sanctions by payoffs to tax collectors, licensing authorities, and customs officials. Poachers and illegal miners give a cut to local chiefs for protection. Local authorities are bribed to turn a blind eye to the large markets on frontiers, existing purely for barter, which is illegal. Widespread evasion and disregard for the law undermines the legitimacy of the state and public morality, and also contributes to the declining administrative efficacy of the state.

We will look in turn at three of the major categories of activities in Zaire's second economy, and at the proliferation of private social services as public ones become defunct. They constitute a restructuring from below of an economy and society that fail to meet people's needs.

Transportation

Despite the fact that Zaire spends close to a quarter of the foreign exchange earned by exports to improve its transportation system, the deficiencies of this system constitute one of the most serious economic constraints. Parastatal rail and river boat services have been in steady decline since independence: they are slow; reliability and security are poor; and unit costs are high compared to other countries (twice those in Zambia or Kenya, for example). Whereas in 1984 these parastatals carried two-thirds of the country's freight, by 1988 private road transport moved about 80 percent of it. But trucks and spare parts are in short supply; the supply of fuel is irregular or inadequate; many roads are in appalling condition and, in rural areas, have often deteriorated so as to be unusable.[4] The parastatal Office des Routes, even though it now benefits from a road tax on fuel, still does not have the resources to maintain secondary regional roads. It has little knowledge of rural roads, and its funds are insufficient and sporadic. Salaries and working conditions for its personnel are poor: a director earns three to four times less than his counterpart in a private business company. Private initiative struggles to cope with this situation: local entrepreneurs pay for and organize the maintenance of some roads, so also do religious groups and some of the big companies.

In Kinshasa, the official passenger transport services are quite insufficient, and many small transport enterprises have grown up to fill the gap. A 1985 study of "informal" transport in the city found that this system operating outside the law provided nearly half the city's transportation: the parastatal bus company (SOTRAZ) carries about 30,000 passengers; informal transport (*kimalu-malu*, covered pickups with ten to twenty places; *fula-fula*, covered trucks with fifty to one hundred places; and taxibuses with twenty-five to thirty places) carries about 27,500. Although in theory all transport is fully integrated into one sector, in fact because taxes are numerous and high, many transporters evade them; they constitute an unofficial transport sector. Controls are ineffective, and the gendarmes and transport authority officials seek to extort tolls rather than make drivers respect the regulations. The unofficial system is complementary to the official one. It charges lower prices and has a greater flexibility in routes, and thus caters to a clientele that cannot afford to use the official system or that lives far from the main routes (Baerhrel et al. 1985). An informal sector driver, when his vehicle is in good condition, can make Z20,000 a month, fifteen times the wages paid to a driver by SOTRAZ.

The deficiencies of the official transportation system are thus compensated for to some degree by an unofficial system, existing outside the official one and evading state control. In Kinshasa, unofficial transport makes up for the inadequacies of the parastatal system and provides a better living for some of those who work for it.

Housing

A striking feature of the urban landscape of Kinshasa is the vast amount of half-finished construction, particularly in the "zones of extension" outside the planned areas of the city. Two-thirds of Zaire's expenditures on construction occur in the informal sector, and the consumption of cement shows that the sector is in fact comparable in size to the formal construction sector. Formal sector firms suffer from financial constraints because the government and public agencies pay their debts late and irregularly. A study made in 1985 showed that the state has largely resigned its role in urban development; taxes are not paid, laws are not applied, legal claims are overridden by those who can mobilize armed force, and confusion reigns. In response to burdensome taxation, excessive regulation, lack of access to credit, and other problems, popular initiatives have taken over and displaced state control: unplanned growth accounts for 70 percent of the residential urban area and accommodates two-thirds of the population (Delis & Girard 1985). Little capital investment is required for construction firms in the informal sector;

all that is needed to start building houses or making concrete blocks is a used concrete mixer. The relevant technology is fairly simple.

Since 1973 and the passage of the Loi Bakajika, all land has belonged to the state, which grants occupation rights and revokes them if plots are not developed and put to use. This is one reason for the amount of unfinished construction. Another is that costs have escalated: official procedures for establishing legal right to land use are tortuous and offer many opportunities for corruption and commissions for intermediaries (Delis & Girard 1985); the prices of cement and roofing continually spiral upward.[5] Houses are constructed a little at a time as people find the means to purchase and gradually accumulate the necessary materials; they then engage the services of masons, carpenters, and so forth. Meantime they may live in rudimentary housing constructed of adobe or other impermanent materials. By these means they overcome the constraints and burdens the official system imposes, with its overregulation and extortion.

Entrepreneurship: Production of Goods and Services

A multitude of entrepreneurs operate small and medium-sized enterprises in the "informal sector" in Kinshasa: they manufacture furniture, metalwork, arts and crafts, and vehicle chassis; engage in construction and market gardening; repair vehicles, tires, bicycles, shoes, radios, and watches; run restaurants, bakeries, manioc mills, and bars; make clothes, dress hair, and prepare cooked foods for street hawkers (Pain 1984:117–123). A survey by the International Labour Organisation in the mid-1980s reported twelve thousand artisanal and commercial enterprises, most of them very small (Ekwa 1986:393).

These enterprises operate on the margins of the law with regard to licensing and to taxation that is perceived as excessively heavy. Many are unlicensed. They provide more employment and income opportunities for the urban masses than does the official sector. They produce goods and services and sell them at prices the general population can afford, and also provide training through apprenticeship and opportunities on the job for the acquisition of skills and experience. Entrepreneurs often work at jobs in the formal sector as well, or have more than one informal sector enterprise. Most of these enterprises are very small, employing only three to four people. They are fiercely competitive and their survival is often precarious; many of them do not stay in business for long. They provide no benefits or job security. Hours are long and conditions of work poor, yet wages may be higher than in the official sector. Marc Pain (1984:131) reports that the level of life of traders and artisans is superior to that of wage workers.[6] In the absence of access to bank credit, venture capital mostly comes from personal savings or from contributions by family members.

These enterprises reflect the tremendous surge in individual effort and initiative in the struggle for survival, and a response to the oppressive constraints of the state in the situation of high unemployment and grossly inadequate wages.

Entrepreneurship: Smuggling and Unlicensed Trade

Popular initiatives are restructuring the deficiencies of the official marketing system: unlicensed traders and smugglers organize a distribution system that supplies urban and rural markets with food, manufactured goods, and other commodities.

Smuggling. Lack of foreign exchange means that shortages of consumer goods, vehicles, spare parts, fuel, construction materials, pharmaceuticals, and imported foodstuffs are widespread and chronic, but second-economy traders contribute to solving this problem. In the official banking system hard currency is virtually unobtainable, so traders smuggle primary export commodities in order to acquire the currency to import, or directly barter for, the goods they want.

Large-scale smuggling of Zaire's primary export commodities began in the early years of independence and has expanded rapidly since the beginning of the current economic crisis. The principal commodities involved are diamonds, gold, coffee, cobalt, and ivory. The scale of these activities is an indication of the large numbers of people involved and of the significance of smuggling for reconstructing the failing national economy.

Diamond smuggling developed rapidly in the early 1960s; by 1979 the amount of diamonds smuggled was equivalent to 68 percent of official production (5.5 million carats smuggled; official production, 8.06 million carats [Bézy, Peemans & Wautelet 1981:172]). The reforms of 1983, however, were very successful in changing this situation. Legalizing artisanal diamond mining and the creation of official, licensed counters to purchase diamonds decreased smuggling: official exports tripled in four years, increasing from 7,161 carats in 1982 to 23,233 in 1986; revenues increased 13 percent 1985/86 (Zaire. Département de l'Économie 1987:65). As a result of these reforms, the state earned foreign exchange as well as taxes and fees. Some problems remain, however. Gem diamonds continue to be smuggled, since their price is very sensitive to changes on the world market. Artisanal miners illegally mine the MIBA concession of five thousand square kilometers. around the plant where the best diamonds are to be found, and some clandestine counters are set up in this area, violating the 1983 agreement. In 1987 there were indications that smuggling was increasing again (Zaire. Département de l'Économie 1987:65–66, 201). Mbuji Mayi, the principal diamond-mining center, is plentifully supplied with consumer goods imported with proceeds of the illegal diamond trade, and wealth accumulated in this trade has given rise to a new bourgeoisie in the town (Biaya 1985).

Gold is extensively smuggled, despite the setting up of purchase counters and legalization of artisanal gold mining. After the reforms, smuggling initially decreased and official production increased. It soon decreased again, however: although exports jumped from twenty-one hundred kilograms in 1982 to fifty-two hundred kilograms in 1983, by 1986 they were down to 1,951 kilograms (Zaire. Département de l'Économie 1987:64).[7] Gold diggers in the rich gold areas of the northeast and in Kivu accept the risks of smuggling rather than take the lower prices paid by the official counters.

Ivory and coffee are the other two most lucrative commodities for smuggling. Ivory export is permitted only through the Department of Nature Conservation, but ivory, rare skins, and meat are poached from Zaire's national parks in Shaba, Kivu, and Haut Zaire. Ivory is smuggled to Europe, East and South Africa, and, especially after conservationists blocked the European market, to Hong Kong.[8] Consumer goods are imported in exchange. Meat is smoked and traded to Zaire's cities, where the supply of meat in the official marketing system does not keep up with demand (Rukarangira & Schoepf 1991). From 30 to 60 percent of the national coffee production is smuggled out of Zaire annually (in 1978 an estimated sixty thousand tonnes).[9]

Diamond, gold, coffee, and ivory smuggling has been the source of foreign exchange for importing vehicles, spares and fuel, consumer goods, medical products, and construction materials (MacGaffey 1987: ch.6). This trade ensures a plentiful supply of goods in the local stores: four to five truckloads of consumer goods, entirely paid for in gold, are imported monthly into Butembo, Kivu, from Nairobi, for example (Vwakyanakazi 1982:282–283). Coffee, gold, ivory, tea, and other commodities are also exchanged in direct barter at village markets on the Sudanese frontier for trucks and other vehicles, spare parts, fuel, and electrical appliances (Vwakyanakazi 1991). By these means, people counteract the scarcity of foreign exchange and arrange for themselves to import the goods they need that are unobtainable by official means.

In Lubumbashi, the Kenia marketplace is almost entirely supplied with foodstuffs and manufactured goods smuggled in from Zambia. They include maize flour, sugar, cooking oil, fuel, empty sacks, and miscellaneous goods. Bales of imported used clothing, plastic shoes, and spare parts stolen from the mining companies are exported in exchange. Trucks ply the road to the frontier and to the Zambian copperbelt towns daily. False declaration, under- and overinvoicing, concealment, bribery of customs officials are all utilized in this trade. Goods are also smuggled on convoys of bicycles, using forest paths to avoid the customs posts altogether. There is also a lively trade in stolen cars imported across Zaire's southern frontiers (a full account of this trade is given in Rukarangira & Schoepf 1991).

In these activities, people are not only restructuring a failing economy, some of them accumulate sufficient capital to found or expand businesses and productive enterprise that may develop the local economy. Since the 1970s, gold and coffee smuggling to East Africa has been a means to accumulate wealth for venture and working capital for African wholesale, retail, and productive enterprises in Kivu (MacGaffey 1987: ch. 6).

Unlicensed trade. In Zaire's rural hinterland producers confront a marketing system that is unpredictable and disorganized to an extreme degree. In some rural areas the distribution system broke down when the big foreign companies responsible for marketing were indigenized in Zairianization; many of them soon thereafter folded up entirely. The official marketing structure is almost defunct in many areas: produce rots in the fields or by the roadside waiting for trucks that never come.[10] In the absence of official traders, unlicensed ones have filled the gap.

In Lower Zaire, in Luozi zone, these traders, known as *lutteurs*, travel the main truck routes regularly. They take with them empty boxes and sacks for the produce they will buy, as well as products they will sell or barter: foods such as flour, salt, tea, sugar, fish, and jam; necessities such as hoes, knives, machetes, pharmaceuticals, soap, cement, and cloth; and luxuries such as cigarets and beer. They may stay two or three weeks in the countryside, collecting produce that they eventually take back to Kinshasa's markets on a truck (Makwala 1991). In the East a similar situation is reported in the rice trade of Haut Zaire. High rates of unemployment have driven people into this trade; many of them are unemployed teachers (Russell 1989:7–8, 11).

Petty commerce is the commonest means by which people supplement inadequate wages or survive in the cities if unemployed. In urban areas women's trade has become the mainstay of the majority of households (Houyoux et al. 1986). These women often operate without licenses and pay no taxes. Women sell from their houses to their neighbors, or in the markets. Poor women scrape a meager living, desperately trying to support their children when their husbands are insufficiently paid or unemployed. Women with high enough social position to have the necessary contacts and capital carry on a profitable import trade in wax-print cloth and clothing, jewelry, and shoes from Europe and West Africa to Kinshasa (Makwala 1991; Schoepf & Walu 1991; MacGaffey 1987). Their activities increase the supply of consumer goods available to those who have money.

Medical Care and Education

In addition to economic ills, social services are almost defunct in Zaire; here, too, popular initiative brings about social restructuring in an attempt to compensate for the failure of the official system.

The decline in public health services and in public education has been so bad that in many respects it can be said that these services no longer exist. In 1986 health and education each got less than 3 percent of government spending, while 23 percent went to the military and over 50 percent to political institutions (*Africa News*, June 12, 1989); in 1989 less than 8 percent of the national budget was spent on health and education combined (*Wall Street Journal*, April 9, 1990). The elite send their children to be educated in Europe and travel there themselves for medical care. For the rest of the population, those who are sick usually find that doctors, nurses, and other medical personnel must be paid a personal fee before they will deliver care; hospitals will not admit even emergency cases without advance payment; health centers lack medicines and equipment of the most rudimentary sort.

In the face of this breakdown of official health institutions, a private, popularly organized system is emerging. In Butembo, a city of 100,000 in Kivu, Zaire's easternmost region, for example, the one hospital, two small medical centers, and thirty small dispensaries that make up the available health services are all private. They provide basic medical care for the population and find their own means, legal or illegal, of importing medicines. No research has been done on the quality of care and qualifications of their personnel, but they provide some health service when it would otherwise be absent. In the rural areas of the zones of Lubero and Beni likewise, 80 percent of health services are provided by private organizations (Vwakyanakazi 1991).

Schoolteachers and administrators must often wait for months for their grossly inadequate pay, with the result that students must bribe administrators for admittance to schools and universities, and pay off teachers with money or sexual favors to pass exams. University libraries are empty of their books and journals; many buildings are derelict, and dormitories closed; laboratory facilities are lacking, and students learn from lecture notes. Schools lack books, teaching supplies, and furnishings, even blackboard chalk. In response to this situation, private schools at all levels have proliferated in towns and cities.[11] In Butembo, North Kivu, a small private university has opened. Private education is widely perceived by parents as the only solution to the drastic deterioration of the system.

All these relatively recent options add to expenses that most people find hard to meet anyway; nevertheless, they make health care and adequate education, otherwise almost nonexistent, available for those who can find the money.

ORGANIZATION, PERSONAL TIES, AND CLIENTSHIP

We will now examine the basis for organization in these alternative systems. Their activities are primarily organized on the basis of personal ties. Eric Wolf (1966:17) has argued that ties of clientage prove especially functional "in situations where the formal institutional structure of society is weak and unable to deliver a sufficiently steady supply of goods and services, especially to the terminal levels of the social order." Clientage relations, kinship and ethnic bonds, friendship, and other relations involving exchange of reciprocal favors are crucial for obtaining goods and for operating in the second economy. These personal relations constitute social assets for the poor because they create earning opportunities (Jagannathan 1987:29). They are the counterpart of the much more privileged opportunities that managerial and official position bring to the powerful for participation in the second economy.

Traders, petty producers, truckers, and retailers have elaborated ties of clientage into networks, extending sometimes over enormous distances, to organize unofficial systems of distribution and marketing that, in large measure, provide the food supply for cities and towns. Such clientship networks among traders and producers are reported in the maize trade in North Shaba and in the rice trade in Haut Zaire (Rukarangira & Schoepf 1991; Russell 1989). In Bas Zaire, producers are regular clients of lutteurs from whom they receive money in advance for their manioc, palm oil, or other produce. The lutteurs in turn become clients of truckers, from whom they get reduced rates for transporting their goods. In Kinshasa, these traders finance the market retailers by allowing them credit on the basis of personal ties (Makwala 1991). Women in trade get help in obtaining supplies through relatives living overseas or working in the local wholesalers. Kin and ethnic ties, friendship and other connections are the basis for reduced rates for transportation and favored treatment at the customs (Schoepf & Walu 1991).

Second-economy activities operate in a more regular and predictable manner than is generally the case in the official economy. Illegal trade is not haphazard and unorganized: it operates according to a system of rules known and subscribed to by all participants. Examples include standardized equivalences observed for barter transactions, set rates for bribes at unofficial border controls, arrangements set up for terms of clientage, and the reciprocal obligations of other personal ties. Reliability in this system is ensured by the trust and confidence that come from relying on personal relationships of kinship, ethnicity, and clientship.

We see here the reciprocal behavior and trust coupled with accountability that are an essential feature of governance. These personal relationships are reciprocal as specified by Hyden: "each contributes to the welfare of others with an expectation that others will do likewise"; they depend on trust, fairness, and mutual respect, on an underlying normative consensus.

BENEFITS AND COSTS

The alternatives presented by the second economy to some extent restructure and transform a society that would otherwise barely function. These transformations can be looked on as the benefits of this reconstruction.

However, they also have a negative side. We will first examine the nature of the benefits, then the very considerable costs that come with them.

The second economy provides means of survival, and of accumulating wealth, where neither is possible in the official wage and salary system. The rich and powerful have superior access to resources and consolidate their social position by participating in the second economy, but they have no institutionalized means to monopolize its activities, many of which are accessible to the general population. Ordinary people manage to survive, and in some cases live quite well or get rich, by working outside the official system. They trade without licenses, smuggle, grow crops for illegal trade, produce goods and services in the informal sector or find jobs in it (some of which pay more than equivalent work in the official economy). In these ways they overcome inadequate incomes and legal constraints, and manage to confront a predatory state.

As the official distribution system deteriorates, an unofficial system compensates. Unlicensed traders operate in defiance of state laws and keep up the supply of food to the urban areas and of manufactured goods to the rural areas. Goods that are in short supply are imported through smuggling and other unrecorded transborder trade, ensuring that they are plentiful in at least some regions of the country. Capital accumulated in unrecorded trade may be invested in productive enterprise that expands the local economy and also its tax base.

But, as De Soto points out for Peru, informality involves tremendous costs. Enterprises operating on the margins of the law must bear the expense of the bribes by which they evade controls. And they suffer not only from their illegality but also from the absence of a legal system that promotes economic efficiency (De Soto 1989:158). In Kinshasa, the difficulties artisans have in obtaining credit, supplies, raw materials, and tools not only constrain the operation of their enterprises but are also extremely time-consuming. Inadequate tools mean that product quality suffers. Furthermore, production for the most part has to be to order because working capital and stocks are so small. Similar problems impede the unofficial transport sector. In Kinshasa, the very limited access of transport operators to bank credit is a major reason for not replacing vehicles. The deplorable state of many of them, the scarcity of spare parts, and the difficulty of maintenance reduce to one-third the potential operation of this sector.

The second economy can compensate in some ways for the deficiencies of the official economy but cannot make up for the absence of centralized planning. The allocation of resources is arbitrary and not evenly or necessarily rationally managed. A glaring example is the way that Zaire's game parks, one of its valuable national resources, are being destroyed by poachers supplying ivory to smugglers and meat to feed the urban population. Another is that though some regions benefit from smuggled imports and are well supplied with manufactured goods, others are grossly deprived. In areas where private individuals manage to organize road maintenance, transportation improves; in other areas the situation remains desperate. Shortage of foreign exchange from smuggling and embezzlement means that industry is operating far below capacity for lack of essential imported materials.

Other costs that come with the second economy are labor shortages, disruption of social life, and dangerous working conditions. With the legalization of artisanal mining, Zaire has experienced a gold and diamond rush reminiscent of the American West. Men and boys abandon urban and rural wage labor and professional occupations in favor of more-lucrative mining and smuggling activities; teachers and pupils alike desert schools;[12] and unmarried or divorced women go in large numbers to the mining camps to make money by selling food or sexual and domestic services (Tshibanza & Tshimanga 1985:345). In the mining camps living and working conditions and health care are appalling. Private and public disregard for safety measures brings injury and death both in the mines and on the overloaded trucks and buses that ply rural and urban roads.

The second economy certainly does not bring equity. Access to the necessary resources for participation is extremely uneven and intensely competitive. The rich and powerful, and those who have jobs, have greater opportunities than do the unemployed, the urban poor, and rural producers. Any kind of employment brings the possibility of rendering services, creating obligations, and receiving other services in return; some jobs bring access to scarce resources or to their allocation. These rent-seeking opportunities constitute an advantage unavailable to those without jobs. The higher the position of an individual in the system, the greater the opportunity (see MacGaffey 1987:135–137). This greater access to the second economy is one of the primary benefits of state office. Although this economy does seem to be more open than the official one, and to offer more opportunities for social mobility, the gap between rich and poor continues to widen. The personal ties among the poor and powerless that are the counterpart of the rent-seeking opportunities of office for the powerful can offset inequity to only a small degree.

Despite such continuing problems, initiatives from below in Zaire's second economy have, nevertheless, begun to transform a society suffering under the depredations of the state. In second-economy activities people can make a living, market sufficient foodstuffs to supply the towns, obtain some of the goods and services they need, build houses, and get themselves to work. What is the evidence that these changes brought about by a burgeoning second economy are changing the social structure and the balance of power?

As we have seen, economic benefits are in fact offset by considerable costs. The situation seems to correspond to De Soto's (1989:152) conclusion for Peru: "lawbreaking is not, on balance, desirable, and . . . the apparent chaos, waste of resources, invasions, and everyday courage are the informals'

desperate and enterprising attempts to build an alternative system to the one
that has denied them its protection."

In Zaire, to solve these problems, to further the governance that could
bring about a real consensus between rulers and ruled, initiatives must also
come from the top. Changes in state policy to decrease onerous taxes,
provide legal guarantees to promote economic efficiency, liberalize
transborder trade, organize centralized supply sources and adequate
transportation, and make financing available would build on changes brought
about from below: trade, trade routes, production for this trade, and
organizing networks are already operating; the enterprises we have described
already serve the towns and cities. Some such policy changes responding to
the pressure of second-economy realities have occurred, largely because of
the insistence of outside agencies. In 1983, under pressure from the
International Monetary Fund and the World Bank, Zaire liberalized producer
prices, legalized artisanal gold and diamond mining, and floated the currency.
The first reform was not successfully implemented, but the legal sale of gold
and diamonds mined by individuals caused official export of diamonds to
triple in four years, and an initial increase in official gold exports. The
parallel money market was successfully eliminated until 1985 by this
monetary reform.

However, given the nature of Zaire's dominant class and a state that
operates to serve the interests of this class and especially those of the
political clique surrounding the president, one cannot be optimistic about the
likelihood of serious and sustained initiatives from above. The prospects for
development of the kind of governance discussed here do not seem very
bright.

Nevertheless, it does appear that there has been a shift in the distribution
of power. No longer are the subordinated classes dependent on jobs and the
opportunities for rents that they may provide; other sources of income have
developed as ways have been found to evade a predatory regulatory system.
Much economic enterprise has burgeoned in the second economy. Through
popular initiatives people have succeeded in defeating the state in some areas
of its oppression. This defeat is evident in the widespread inability of the
state to implement legislation and taxation. It cannot clamp down on all the
transport, construction, trading, and manufacturing enterprises that have
sprung up. It has opted out and simply ignores much of what goes on. But
the economy cannot function without these activities; they have come to
constitute an economic base for the subordinated classes that did not exist in
the early years of the Mobutu regime. It is this change, precarious and
tentative as it is, that represents a power shift in society. Although not a
revolution in the sense of a new class taking control of state and society, this
power shift represents a revolution of the sort referred to as silent and hidden
by Szelenyi and De Soto. Recent concrete political actions have propelled
this hidden revolution into a more overt form.

RECENT POLITICAL DEVELOPMENTS[13]

In early 1990 President Mobutu announced that Zaire was to change from a one-party state to a multiparty democracy. This sudden conversion to democracy was widely regarded as a means to persuade the big donor organizations to relax their supervision of presidential spending of state money. Early in 1990 the IMF and the World Bank suspended more than $100 million in quick-disbursing balance of payment funds, and the US Congress called for cuts in the $60 million a year Zaire received in foreign aid from the United States. Mobutu was angered by World Bank conditions for its loans, stipulating quarterly audits of the treasury accounts and of GECAMINES, the copper-mining company. Reportedly in 1990 the Zairian government failed to account for $400 million in export earnings.

But there are other significant contributory factors to Mobutu's change of policy. A few months prior to his announcement of multiparty democracy, Mobutu traveled around Zaire soliciting comments on his regime from individuals and groups. The flood of adverse comments, especially on the Popular Movement of the Revolution, the single party, reportedly unnerved him, as did events in Eastern Europe at this time, especially the overthrow of Nicolae Ceauşescu in Romania. In mid-April pamphlets circulated in Kinshasa, calling for three days of mass demonstrations against the president. Other concrete political pressures were applied during this period and in the months that followed. The Catholic church, long the most effective opponent of the regime, during the bishop's conference in March 1990, issued a report criticizing government corruption and the one-party state, calling for fundamental political reforms and a new constitution, freedom of speech, an end to the flight of capital overseas, and access to medical care and quality education for all citizens. Teachers went on a go-slow strike in May, demanding decent salaries and access to credit; simultaneously doctors went on strike in Kinshasa. In July civil servants began a nationwide strike to demand payment of their promised salary increases and refused to resume work, despite a government order. The same month university students demonstrated in Kinshasa, demanding the firing of the presidents of their colleges and the departure of the government.

Earlier in the year, on May 11, an appalling event at the University of Lubumbashi aroused public opinion nationwide. In reprisal for the execution by students of three government informers, the university was closed off, with the complicity of several local officials, and as many as 150 students may have been massacred by the security forces. Public protest erupted with student demonstrations in several cities, strikes by workers in Lubumbashi, and the closing of shops, public and private firms, state departments, and markets in the city. Eventually eleven of the officials involved were arrested by order of the National Assembly, including the governor of the region;

Zairians are finally having some success in making government officials accountable for their actions.

In response to internal and external political pressure, Mobutu raised government pay 55 percent and, in his speech of April 24, authorized three political parties and announced his own withdrawal from direct control of the executive (except for defense, foreign affairs, and security).

The proposed change to multiparty democracy has not been unopposed, however. On April 29 a demonstration by supporters of the popular opposition leader, Tshisekedi, who had been released from house arrest on April 24, was violently suppressed, reportedly with several deaths. Tshisekedi himself was later attacked in his house. Old-guard politicians reacted to the threat to their interests and prevented the rapid implementation of multiparty politics. Their influence is indicated in the dominance of old faces over new in the transitional government appointed by Mobutu. In a speech on May 3 he announced the phases of transition to the new political system, to culminate in elections in January 1991, and in a new constitution to be submitted to the will of the people in a referendum. Any number of parties may present themselves for election; the top three elected will become the official parties. By July forty-two parties had applied to the high court for recognition, despite the high deposit for registration, stipulated by law, of Z5 million (US$8,800). All these various initiatives reflect a readiness for political action when opportunity arises. They build on the shift in the power base in society that I have described.

CONCLUSION

This power shift that has taken place in society challenges the process whereby the dominant class has consolidated its position and attempted to close its boundaries. It has used the state to control the economy to serve its interests and has reproduced itself by recourse to educational and medical services overseas; by repressive regulations it has attempted to limit the economic development of other classes; and it has ensured the deterioration of education and health services for the general public at home. Through the second economy, however, people are able to secure some sort of living, sometimes a good one, and at least some of them can thus find the money to pay for the alternative education and medical services they have organized for themselves. The scale of their activities is best measured by investigating the second economy, but many of the activities that are part of this process of class formation are legal. Both legal and illegal are integrated into and are transforming the fabric of society.

A similar shift in the distribution of power has been discerned by Szelenyi (Szelenyi et al. 1988:8) in the state socialist economy of Hungary: "The ultimate and real source of countervailing power is self-employment, petty commodity production. Classes struggle to achieve compromises, to alter the distribution of power between the classes at the point of production and by establishing an alternative economic system."

In Zaire, this countervailing power lies in the second economy activities of the subordinated classes and the economic base that this gives them. As in the Hungarian silent revolution, Zairians have taken it upon themselves to create greater freedom of opportunity than the bureaucrats with their restrictions and constraints would ever concede. Recent political developments build from this new economic base to overt political action.

What are the implications of this situation for discussion of the issue of governance? It seems to indicate that to assess the possibilities for the development of governance in any particular society, it is necessary to investigate the historically and geographically specific parameters of class conflict. The nature and outcome of this conflict constrain the potential course of the development of governance. Analysis in terms of governance must thus follow and cannot preclude analysis in terms of class.

NOTES

I am grateful to Wyatt MacGaffey for his helpful comments and discussion of this chapter.

1. Richard Sklar (1987:712) calls the informal sector "a democratic fact—an expression of the people's will in economic organization."

2. For details see Callaghy 1984; Young and Turner 1985; and Schatzberg 1988.

3. This definition follows those proposed by Smith (1985:6–8), Mattera (1985:4–14), Blades (1982:30–33), and Gershuny and Pahl (1980:7).

4. The situation is worse in Zaire than in neighboring countries: once across the borders, roads improve.

5. The costs of cement and roofing increased tenfold between 1976 and 1982 (Pain 1984:157).

6. De Soto (1989:62) reports that in Peru informal traders earn, on average, 38 percent more than the minimum legal wage.

7. The reasons for the drop in official exports of gold are the decrease of the price on the world market, to which the counter prices are very responsive; the gap between the agreed rate to be paid by the official counters and the parallel rate offered by unlicensed buyers; the difficulty counters have in obtaining sufficient bank notes from the regional commercial banks; and insufficient counters (there are only about one-third as many as there are for diamonds). Clandestine buyers are numerous.

8. At the time of writing, the October 1989 world ban on ivory trading, agreed to by ninety countries, that came into effect January 1990 appears to have decreased the demand for ivory and forced prices down by 50 percent (*Wall Street Journal*, February 8, 1990). Poaching has reportedly declined in Kenya and Tanzania since the ban; in China and Hong Kong, ivory-carving factories have virtually closed down. Conservationists are encouraged by the poor prices African poachers are getting for ivory: at Kismayu, a transit point for ivory on the southern coast of Somalia, it was being sold with difficulty in the early summer of 1990 for only $2 to $3 a kilogram (*New York Times*, May 22, 1990). A year previously it had fetched $50 to $70 a kilogram (*Newsweek*, April 16, 1990).

9. The 1983 liberalization of export regulations decreased coffee smuggling by small producers in Kivu (Zaire. Département de l'Économie 1985:41). They now sell to official exporters rather than smuggling it across the borders by headload or on bicycles. Coffee export fraud continues, however, through over- and underinvoicing, false declaration of quality, and barter, although it is now largely perpetrated by the big official exporters and collectors (Vwakyanakazi 1991).

10. Kinshasa's population is about 3 million and is increasing at about 8.5 percent a year. Despite this increase, the hinterland of Kinshasa supplied a declining quantity of goods over a period of ten years: 50 percent fewer trucks were coming into Kinshasa from the rural areas in 1984 than in 1974. Similarly in Lubumbashi, in 1973 the number of trucks entering the city was five times greater than in 1980 (Flouriot 1986).

11. In 1974 the government nationalized the schools, 90 percent of which were previously owned and operated by the Catholic, Protestant, or Kimbanguist churches. In 1979 administration of schools was handed back to the churches, with the government paying teachers' salaries. The government pays part of the operating expenses, but not teachers' salaries, of any school that is accredited by the Ministry of Primary and Secondary Education.

12. In a study of 160 gold diggers south and east of Mbuji Mayi in 1983 and 1985, 38 percent were students or teachers (Tshibanza 1986:345).

13. Information for this section comes from *The Washington Post*, May 12, 1990; *Wall Street Journal*, April 9, 1990; *The New York Times*, April 14, 1990; *Zaire Oyé* 8 (August 1990); President Mobutu's speech of May 3, 1990, to the Legislative Council; *Africa Confidential* 31, no. 10:4–5; *Africa News*, April 30, 1990; and *Elima* (Kinshasa newspaper), July 28, 1990.

12

The Institutional Bases
of Governance in Africa

Michael Bratton & Donald Rothchild

The call for a focus on governance is timely and important, reflecting the worldwide thrust toward political and economic liberalization in the 1990s. A governance approach highlights issues of state responsiveness and accountability, and the impact of these factors on political stability and economic development. For too long social scientists dealing with Africa's development have concentrated on economic issues, overlooking the highly important political dimensions of the process. The current experimentation with structural adjustment programs requires a concern for the politics of reciprocity at the same time that these countries engineer a renewed emphasis on market-based economies (Rothchild 1991; Mbembe 1989:129). Clearly, it is time to set right the imbalance in our thinking between economics and politics and to center our attention, as Goran Hyden says in Chapter 1, on "how rules . . . affect political action and the prospect of solving given societal problems." In this sense, regime management represents a creative regard for facilitating the transition to open, legitimate, and responsive politics; the purpose of this management effort is to help Africa's states cope more effectively with their current economic and political difficulties.

The use by African state elites of arbitrary and repressive measures and their inability to apply governmental regulations throughout the national territory is a sign of state weakness or "softness." Paradoxically, the independent African state consolidates power at the political center and extracts considerable economic resources from society; yet it spends much of what it obtains on itself and lacks the capacity to spur the country's development as a whole. The weak state is confronted simultaneously with a variety of severe problems, including economic scarcity, a decaying economic and social infrastructure, the enfeeblement of the rules of the political game, the decline of regularized intercommunity relations, a deep cleavage between state and society, overdeveloped state structures, insufficient state legitimacy, and inadequate state coercive power (Rothchild & Foley 1983:314). Governance involves less in the way of administrative management (costly state-subsidized public projects and overextended and overmanned state enterprises and parastatals), and more in the way of political management; with its emphasis on developing networks of reciprocity and exchange, governance increases the possibilities of accomplishing more (building legitimate state structures and overcoming the estrangement between state and society) while spending less (Sharkansky 1979:3).

The relationship between state and society in Africa is complex, involving dynamic processes of engagement and disengagement, demands and responses. Although mutually interdependent, both state and societal elites seek to maximize their political autonomy and to assert their notions of the good society. At the same time a sense of common fate drives them to enmesh one another in constant interchanges—the state elites driven by a search for enhanced control and legitimacy, and the societal elites motivated by the need for state-controlled resources (Bratton, forthcoming). Estrangement of state and society usually proves mutually damaging, resulting in costly struggles for both sides. Yet in state-society relations, as in world politics, "cooperation varies across issues and over time" (Axelrod & Keohane 1985:226); rather than being kept apart in separate spaces (Ninsin 1990:140–141), state and society in Africa engage on certain issues while disengaging on others. Within this ongoing process of shifting ties and interactions, a governance approach has the advantage of helping to identify accommodative patterns of state-society relations that enhance political legitimacy.

THE MEANING OF GOVERNANCE

What is the meaning of governance? To date, the usefulness of the concept to theory and practice has been impaired by the lack of a precise or widely accepted definition. Webster's dictionary does not help much, indicating only that governance is a synonym for government, or "the act or process of governing, (specifically) authoritative direction and control." This interpretation refers to the actions and functions of the executive branch and asks : "how effective is government?"

The concept of governance recently entered the lexicon of comparative politics by an unusual route. It was adopted first by practitioners in international development agencies, initially with the limited connotation of effective government performance. Following political independence, African leaders turned to international donor and lending agencies for assistance in setting up government agencies and training public officials to implement public policy. At the time, in the 1960s, this type of assistance activity was called institution building rather than governance, and it began to disappear from aid portfolios as recipient countries became self-sufficient in skilled personnel. By the 1980s, however, with special reference to Africa, it was revived under the leadership of the World Bank, as an institutional "capacity-building" initiative under the rubric "governance for development" (World Bank 1989:60).

In practice, the World Bank (1989:60) defines governance quite narrowly as "the exercise of political power to manage a nation's affairs." Bank officials perceive that, in Africa, rent-seeking behavior by political elites, fueled by flows of foreign aid, has undermined governmental effectiveness. The Bank's analysis acknowledges the need for a rule of law, a free press, respect for human rights, and citizen involvement in intermediate associations. But the member governments of this multilateral body constrain it from underwriting projects in these explicitly political areas. Hence the Bank has taken a technocratic approach, aiming governance reforms at the encouragement of economic growth, rather than democratic politics. To date, its fledgling governance program concentrates on reducing the size of government, privatizing parastatal agencies, and improving the administration of aid funds (Lancaster 1990:39).

Private development agencies have elaborated a vision of governance, which directly addresses the issue of political accountability. The Ford Foundation (1990:68–69) led the way in the early 1980s with a pioneering governance program "rooted in the belief that effective government depends on the legitimacy derived from broad-based participation, fairness, and accountability." The foundation openly sought to strengthen democratic institutions, increase the participation of disadvantaged groups, and make public services more responsive to the needs of the poor. To meet these objectives in Africa, the foundation cut back assistance to governments in favor of supporting nongovernmental organizations as vehicles for civic participation and the provision of services. The key insight that distinguished Ford Foundation from World Bank governance programs was that governments do not regulate themselves; they must be checked and balanced by an active, articulate, and organized citizenry.

Thus the concept of governance gained wider meaning. It still referred to the objective capacities of governments, as reflected in technical skills and efficient management. But the concept expanded to capture a less tangible, but more essential, quality of government: the consent of the governed. When citizens regard state commands as legitimate, governmental effectiveness is more easily attained because it rests on a bedrock of voluntary compliance.

The academic literature on governance, which originates from scholars who work closely with international development or philanthropic agencies, has concentrated almost exclusively on the issue of political legitimacy. The first chapter of this book acknowledges the valuable early contribution of the African Governance Program of the Carter Center in defining governance as the study of legitimation processes and reminding us that political authority can be vested outside the formal-legal institutions of the state. Lofchie, for example, argues that the power to determine the distribution of resources in

African countries really rests with the major international lending institutions, who are able to dictate the terms of economic adjustment policies (1989:120). The point is useful that state elites are constrained in making decisions, but it does not mean that they are constrained only by external actors. In Africa, the partial abdication of sovereign authority for policymaking to the World Bank and the International Monetary Fund (IMF) has undercut rather than bolstered the political legitimacy of incumbent state elites. To explore the concept of governance fully, we must turn to the relations between the rulers and the ruled and ask whether the exercise of state authority reflects, and is condoned by, expressions of popular preference.

In this regard, Richard Joseph (1990:202) states that "the renewal of African governance will require the reinvigoration of the non-state sectors of society," based on the free association of ordinary citizens in voluntary organizations and the availability of open expression through the media, universities, and independent policy research institutes. He argues that effective governance requires institutional pluralism, communal empowerment, and meaningful popular participation. More than any other writer, Joseph (1990:202) associates governance with democracy, arguing that "the most decisive way in which [political] accountability can be achieved is through the requirement that a government's continuation in office depends on the active approval of the people as expressed in competitive elections." We would attach only the undemanding proviso that competitive elections are one among many possible mechanisms for introducing governance. In the absence of elections, or between them, state elites can take alternative measures—from public policy debates to investigations of maladministration—that can help guarantee accountability.

The main value of Goran Hyden's contributions is to move debates on governance to a level of theoretical generality. He elevates governance to an "umbrella concept to define an approach" to comparative politics, an approach that fills analytical gaps left by frameworks that have previously enjoyed prominence in the discipline (Hyden 1988:4). In particular, he hopes that a governance approach can transcend some of the forced choices that previous theoreticians have felt compelled to make: for example, between the voluntary individual actions of rational choice theory and the deterministic structure of Marxist frameworks. Using a governance approach, the analyst would be concerned with "the creative potential of politics," especially with "the ability of leaders to rise above [the existing structure of] the ordinary, to 'change the rules of the game,' and to inspire others to partake in efforts to move society forward in new and productive directions" (Hyden 1988:4, 16).

Hyden also explicitly draws our attention beyond the performance of governments to the social roots of authority. He clearly states that governance is "characterized by reciprocal behavior and legitimate relations of power between governors and governed; in this respect 'governance' differs from 'rule' which does not presuppose legitimacy" (Hyden 1988:19). Although governance is practiced by political elites, it is manifest in the conditions of the citizenry. This implies that a strong state is unlikely to emerge in the absence of a vibrant civil society. In short, governance is "the conscious management of regime structures with a view to enhancing the legitimacy of the public realm" (Hyden, Chapter 1). It concerns the institutionalization of normative values that can motivate and provide cohesion to the members of society at large. Indeed, the very development of polities is associated in Hyden's approach with an increasing range of opportunities for reciprocal relationships.

Let us summarize Hyden's claims:

1. Governance is a conceptual approach that, when fully elaborated, can frame a comparative analysis of macro-politics.
2. Governance concerns "big" questions of a "constitutional" nature that establish the rules of political conduct.
3. Governance involves creative intervention by political actors to change structures that inhibit the expression of human potential.
4. Governance is a relational concept, emphasising the nature of interactions between state and social actors, and among social actors themselves.
5. Governance refers to particular types of relationships among political actors; that is, those which are socially sanctioned rather than arbitrary.

The reader is immediately struck by the fact that the concept of governance is asked to bear the heavy weight of numerous intellectual agendas. At one and the same time governance is supposed to be an analytic framework, a description of the substance of legitimate politics, and a desirable political value. This list does not even include governance as an instrument of public affairs management or a gauge of political development. In our view, no single concept can be all things to all people. The attempt to stretch the concept of governance to perform multiple, perhaps contradictory, purposes helps to explain why its definition in the academic literature has so far been so slippery. In an effort to move the conceptual debate forward, we have selected for further discussion three aspects of Hyden's notion of governance: the normative; the analytic; and the substantive. From this commentary we seek to discern directions for future research.

Governance as Normative Value

Governance has strong normative overtones: it is the practice of good government. We welcome into contemporary discourse the revival of moral questions posed by the classical political theorists. Contemporary political scientists—in the quest to discover the political correlates of socioeconomic development—have for too long emphasized the capacity of states to penetrate and transform society and have neglected state capacity for responsiveness and accountability. Ironically, of course, these dimensions of government performance are intimately connected. Governments perform best—in the sense of achieving stated goals and doing so with the least expenditure of material and coercive resources—when they align their programs with realizable popular goals.

We also share Hyden's (1988:2) view that social scientists are participants in social processes and cannot help but hold normative preferences about policy alternatives and political outcomes. Thus the goal of theory is not only one of gaining better understanding "but also [of] making individuals aware of alternatives, of enabling individuals to realize their potential, and of highlighting the shortcomings inherent in existing situations" (Hyden 1988:31). Far from being value-free, social science is dedicated to enhancing human opportunity and solidarity.

The logic of a normative discourse, however, drives the analyst to associate good government with one particular type of regime whose applicability is assumed to be universal. Hyden (1988:41) stresses that, conceptually, governance is "preferable to democracy, which is more value-laden and tends to invoke associations with only the liberal version of it." We read Hyden to be saying that research on governance must therefore reveal and promote the variety of cultural preferences and practices that underpin political legitimation in different parts of the world. In some places the prevailing values will be pluralistic (in which the paramount value is the pursuit of individual happiness), in others corporatist (which maximizes the common good of an organic state), and in yet others more communitarian (in which the solidarity and well-being of communal groups is uppermost). And because all societies are complex structures with modernized elites superimposed on communal-minded masses, each will display a mix of universal and particular values that is to a degree distinctive. If the legitimation of the state requires congruence with prevailing social values, then we must expect to find a range of political forms that can express legitimacy.

Yet Hyden's effort to operationalize the concept of governance inevitably leads the reader to associate good government with democratic values and procedures. The indicators in Chapter 1 by which he proposes to assess such dimensions of governance as citizen influence (political participation and public accountability), government responsiveness (open policymaking, adherence to the rule of law), and normative consensus (equality and tolerance) are drawn from the canon of liberal democracy. Moreover, we tend to feel that Hyden's conception of political development (itself a highly normative idea) is insufficiently independent of his operational definition of governance. For example, both concepts rest on freedom of association, rule of law, and tolerance of opposition. If governance, development, and democracy are objectified by some of the same indicators, then one or more concepts is at least partially redundant.

Perhaps the time has come to acknowledge that the values of liberal democracy are spreading universally, especially among the growing ranks of the educated middle classes in the developing world. Prominent African intellectuals vigorously espouse the advantages of core democratic principles over the indeterminate, and possibly second-best, forms of governance based on "authentic" culture (Ake 1990:4; Anyang'Nyong'o 1987:19–20; Khapoya 1991). Political appeals to primordial values are usually made by incumbent elites who would prefer not to share power or ambitious opponents who see particularism as a path to power. And Hyden himself notes (Chapter 1), that the prospect for governance tends to be greater in a liberal democracy than in other forms of regime. It is therefore incumbent on governance theorists to specify the extent to which the norms of governance and democracy overlap and to identify the ways in which governance can promote reciprocal political relations en route to democracy.

Governance as Analytic Framework

In laying the groundwork for a theory of governance, Hyden treads a delicate path between action and structural approaches to theory. He seeks a middle ground in which individual political initiative and institutional structure mutually and positively interact.

Hyden begins with a call for the restoration of human agency to the study of processes of political and institutional development. Governance is concerned with the initiatives of political actors at all levels of the polity to create forms of association for tackling social problems. To contribute to governance, individual and collective action must to a degree be motivated by a conception of social benefit, rather than by self-interest alone. As numerous writers have noted, political behavior derives not only from selfish interest but also from moral standards and the human need for a sense of belonging (Etzioni 1988; Elster 1989; Runge 1986). The governance approach explicitly acknowledges that while political actors seek personal power and opportunities to earn wealth they also derive satisfaction from the performance of public service.

But how can such other-regarding, public-spirited aspects of political behavior be encouraged? Much depends on the structure of commands, incentives and appeals that is conveyed to political actors through public institutions. Hyden (Chapter 1) calls for the creation or reform of institutions "so as to make individual actors expend their energies in the labor of the public interest." This would involve a set of institutional arrangements by which leaders can mobilize popular energy in support of developmental action, and through which followers can keep leaders honest and accountable. In all settings, but especially in poor countries, socially responsible behavior is best supported by nonmaterial incentives such as moral exhortation and peer pressure. The real challenge is to arrange material and coercive incentives to obtain the same ends.

The governance framework does not allow us to definitively answer the question, "which comes first: action or structure?" Hyden's definition of governance as "the conscious management of regime structures" implies that he places action uppermost. But his subsequent account devotes more attention to the "structure, values, and norms" of regimes than to identifying the sorts of political actors and action that can cause regime change. Who are such actors likely to be? Presumably they include individual leaders, factions, and coalitions both within the state elite and outside of it. What sort of political resources—of ideology, skill, and organization—do they bring to bear? Those in state office probably enjoy structural advantages in access to material resources, while actors in civil society may be able to draw on greater reserves of moral or social authority. What kinds of action strategies do they pursue: confrontational or accommodative? isolated or coalitional? planned or reactive? The strategies actors pursue are partially structurally determined—for example, by the resource base—but also importantly reflect the independent choices of leaders.

The governance approach therefore renews the concern of analysts with political leadership, collective action, and the management of conflict. And the governance lens provides a fresh perspective on all these matters. It explicitly recognizes that political leadership includes a range of international and local actors beyond the state elite; that collective action can occur on the basis of shared values, rather than by coercion or selective incentive alone; and that the management of conflict can best be sustained by agreement among contending parties on procedural rules for political contestation. Governance analysis therefore begins with an assessment of the capacities of contending parties to promote or block regime-altering reforms. Its central concern is with the interactive processes of bargaining among actors in state and society over the permissible limits of politics. And it concludes by discerning whether, and on what terms, such actors strike agreements that can form the basis of stable and legitimate government.

Governance as Legitimate Politics

Hyden (Chapter 1) speaks of a "governance realm" at the core of politics that is bounded by political relationships of reciprocity and authority, trust and accountability. We interpret this as a catalog of different ways in which power is legitimated. We see the distinction between trust and accountability as analogous to Max Weber's distinction between traditional and bureaucratic modes of legitimation (Gerth & Mills 1946:295–301). This leaves reciprocity as Hyden's truly original insight into the governance realm. Reciprocity is essential because it describes an important set of civil norms on which political leaders can legitimate a claim to rule.

It is worth taking a few moments to rehearse the qualities that distinguish reciprocal relations from other types of political interaction. Reciprocity is "a continuing relationship . . . based fundamentally upon expectations of behavior, not immediately contingent, on the part of others" (Hyden, Chapter 1). Actors contribute to the welfare of others in the hope that, at some unspecified time in the future, they will receive some appropriate consideration in return. Because the currency of reciprocity is neither discrete nor equivalent, and the norms are unwritten, actors can rely only on one another's moral commitments to abide by the rules of the political game. Thus a reciprocal relationship is an implicit social covenant—as opposed to a written legal contract—that, if perceived to be broken, justifies noncompliance by the aggrieved party.

Nevertheless, as analysts, how would we recognize a productive reciprocity if we saw one? What precise performance criteria would constitute the fulfillment of a covenant? Presumably the participants in any political relationship could be asked whether they expected to receive benefits in return for their contributions. But the personal subjectivity and cultural relativity of responses, plus the nonequivalence of items of exchange, would make responses difficult to interpret and compare. There are therefore several methodological hurdles to be jumped before reciprocity can be made serviceable for purposes of operational research.

Moreover, there are conceptual difficulties in distinguishing reciprocity from other political relationships in the governance realm. We wish to cite two examples from African politics. First, with reference to the horizontal relations among political actors in society, what distinguishes reciprocity and exchange? Hyden (1990:256) has suggested that reciprocity is the predominant social logic in poor societies where, from year to year, each person must rely on others in order to guarantee survival. In the context of such a "moral economy" the basis of social organization is the community, and the boundary between individual and collective interests is blurred. The search for survival helps to explain why there is "a greater elasticity in the inclination to voluntarily cooperate with others" (Hyden 1990:259). We concur that mutual social obligation can provide a powerful incentive to collective action, especially in rural Africa. But we also note that such obligations appear to be increasingly challenged and undermined by market relations. Resources that were previously accessible to community members as a matter of right are now often exchanged for money. Does this mean that the covenants upon which communities are based are being violated and replaced by the secular norms of contract? Or are such covenants broad and flexible enough to embrace money as just another item of reciprocal consideration? We cannot offer a definitive answer to these questions but merely wish to note that reciprocal and exchange relations are often thoroughly interpenetrated in practice.

Second, with reference to vertical relations between citizens and state elites, what distinguishes reciprocity from authority? Contributors to this volume have noted that nationalist political leaders in Africa entered into a social compact with their followers at the time of political independence (see Bratton and van de Walle, Chapter 2). In return for political acclamation and quiescence, leaders promised to improve mass living standards. Yet state elites ultimately violated reciprocal norms by taking arbitrary decisions, by failing to deliver goods and services, and by diverting public resources to private ends. Citizens then felt justified and emboldened to exercise their rights of noncompliance: at first they disengaged by retreating into informal activities; latterly they reengaged in political dialog with the state—for example, through popular protests in African capital cities. Can we accurately characterize the nature of the African legitimacy crisis? Is it a decline in political authority, whose onset is marked by the citizen noncompliance with the substantive content of given policies? Or is it the breakdown of reciprocity reflected in the decay of institutional capacity to generate new forms of consensus about the basic rules in politics? Further work remains to be done in distinguishing reciprocity from other means of securing legitimacy.

THE CONCERNS OF CONTRIBUTORS

It is now time to turn to issues raised by other contributors to this book. How do their various analyses cut into the question of governance? What are the obstacles to regularized interactions between state and society? The state, as Thomas M. Callaghy (1984:421) observes, "can protect liberties or it can destroy them." How do contributors deal with this implicit challenge, directing our attention to new options for ensuring political participation, accountability, and responsiveness under conditions of dire economic scarcity? On the whole, these contributions are country-specific, yet analytic. Analytically, they help us to gain insights into four main aspects of regime change: the nature of social institutions; the reform of state institutions; the interactions between state and society; and the processes of governance, liberalization, and democracy. We will examine each of these aspects in turn.

The Nature of Social Institutions

Several contributors, including Janet MacGaffey and Aili Tripp, regard civil society as the source of impetus for governance reforms. These authors examine local social institutions that run the gamut from smuggling and trading networks in Zaire to vigilante groups and sports clubs in Tanzania. Because such institutions are numerous and relatively autonomous from the state, they potentially constitute a countervailing force. And while they serve ostensibly economic or social goals (from income generation to recreation), their impact is decidedly political. They provide alternative poles of association outside of the state and, filling gaps where the state has failed, deliver employment opportunities and social services to needy populations. Especially in the second economy, where many operations are illegal, citizens openly challenge the legitimacy of the state to regulate private behavior. Moreover, illegal activities also deprive the state of taxes and other revenues, thereby further reducing its capacity and hastening its demise.

MacGaffey raises at least two issues of direct relevance to the debates on governance. The first concerns the unwritten operating rules of the second economy, which, she argues, are known and subscribed to by all participants. She suggests that these rules informally codify "standardized equivalences" for transactions and ratify the obligations owed by both patrons and clients. At the same time, however, she stresses that illegal trading does not assure social equity, since the rich and powerful have greater opportunities to obtain and allocate resources. This implies that the second economy, as an unregulated market par excellence, may not promote fully reciprocal relations unless guided by a regime of corrective state laws. Second, MacGaffey considers that the net effect of alternative social action is a "hidden" or "silent" revolution. To be sure, this is a social—as opposed to political— revolution, marked by the emergence of an entrepreneurial class based on petty-commodity production and trade. Following Szelenyi's work on Hungary, she regards self-employment in small businesses as the preeminent source of countervailing power to the state-based bureaucratic bourgeoisie. To understand the potential for a change in governance practices in Zaire, however, one would have to know a great deal more about the political alignments of these new middle classes. How do they relate to the fragmented array of political parties within the anti-Mobutu opposition movement? Are they able to use their influence to bring about lasting changes in the way that power is exercised by national leaders?

Aili Mari Tripp usefully traces the origins of local voluntary organizations in Tanzania to popular efforts to win governance reforms from colonial governments. In the postcolonial era the state attempted to crowd out independent associations, but revolving credit clubs and neighborhood security groups survived to provide basic services in neglected areas. Tripp notes the importance of trust among members; for example, in handling money or apprehending criminals in a situation where the police are regarded as corrupt. But how, one might ask, can trust in face-to-face groups be converted to political accountability in larger organizations? Moreover, do strong local voluntary organizations increase or decrease demands on the state? Tripp argues that civic organizations absorb popular demands for services that otherwise would have been directed at state agencies and thereby help the state to avert a crisis of political legitimacy. But she also contends—and here the evidence is less compelling—that professional and business interests were instrumental in Tanzania in getting the state to reduce regulations and encourage private initiatives. Interestingly, she sees a role for the political party in interest representation, even in a single-party state, citing numerous examples where local party leaders aid constituents to resist official policies that undermine people's survival. Along these lines, we feel that more work needs to be done to understand how voluntary associations can be aggregated to influence policy and obtain power, and how official institutions may be adapted to accommodate, even promote, governance reforms.

The Reform of State Institutions

Because much of the inspiration for political reform comes from within Africa, it is misleading to view governance as the imposition of alien notions of democracy by external donors. Rather, governance involves the reconciliation of institutions and state practices with domestic public values and aspirations (Rothchild & Ravenhill, forthcoming; Legum 1990:1–2). To the extent that these become aligned, the possibilities for responsive government and creative statecraft are greatly enhanced.

Such institutions as parliaments, political parties and election systems, trade unions, cooperatives, interest groups, ethnic and religious associations, and so forth are important because they offer the public poles around which to mobilize for the articulation of demands or arenas in which group representatives can participate in the political process (Wanyande 1988:74–77; Ademolekun 1990:81–83). Institutions establish mechanisms and channels for making societal claims on other groups and on the state. As such, they create indispensable opportunities for overcoming social isolation and for facilitating regularized patterns of state-society relations.

When discussing the role of formal election systems in contemporary Senegal, Crawford Young and Babacar Kante offer important insights into the process of instituting accountability in an African setting. Despite the backdrop of a difficult economic environment, Senegal's former President Léopold Sedar Senghor, searching for new options in the political arena, nonetheless permitted the establishment of a limited multiparty system. Calls for further liberalization became insistent, and in April 1981 the National Assembly approved proposals for the removal of restrictions on the number of political parties. In the 1983 elections that followed, President Diouf won over 83 percent of the presidential vote, and his Parti Socialiste (PS) secured nearly 80 percent of the votes cast for National Assembly candidates (Hayward 1987:261).

As Young and Kante suggest, the 1988 elections were to prove a better test of the recent Senegalese experiment with multiparty elections. In seeking a renewed mandate for continued rule, President Diouf was now challenged by established political parties on the basis of a full term in office. Nevertheless, after extensive campaigning by both PS and opposition parties, Diouf and his ruling party emerged with a somewhat lower but a still very convincing victory. The opposition, contesting the validity of the election results, reacted bitterly. Violence erupted in Dakar, followed by the declaration of a state of emergency. In light of the high level of tensions that emerged immediately after the elections, Young and Kante's nuanced conclusions on the implications of this constitutional experiment for the unfolding process of governance are important. For them, the flaws in the electoral system should not be allowed to obscure the gains in terms of participation and state accountability. In that sense, the elections, for all their imperfections, appear to represent useful structures that promoted a learning experience for the future.

In Rwanda, with President Juvenal Habyarimana's cautious experimentation with a policy of decentralization, the commune has emerged as an increasingly important institution for rural mobilization and participation, and for the negotiation of assistance from international donor agencies. As Catharine Newbury explains, the former centralizing thrusts of the regimes of Grégoire Kayibanda and his successor, Habyarimana, eased a little in the mid-1980s. The Rwandan government continued to appoint burgomasters, assumed responsibility for the salaries of key officials employed by the commune, and provided a substantial share of their developmental budgets; even so, Habyarimana prudently decided to allow these local government agencies an increased scope to secure additional revenues, administer development projects, and enter into direct relations with donor agencies. Obviously it is too early to determine the effect of these decentralization reforms on public participation and development. Nevertheless, the government's preferences for hierarchy and top-down decisionmaking are likely to prove difficult to reconcile with a more thoroughgoing structure of local autonomy over the long term.

Finally, the chapter by Donald Williams on consociational practices in Nigeria gives further insights into the process of developing formal and informal rules of the game to enhance constructive social relations. Because of its assumed ability to promote accommodative practices among state and societal representatives, the consociational democracy model may act as both a "unifying force" and a means of "preserv[ing] societal diversity" in Nigerian circumstances (see Chapter 5). The consociational democracy model, as developed by Arend Lijphart, has four main aspects: a grand coalition including the political leaders from all major societal segments; protection of minority interests by means of a mutual veto rule; utilization of the proportionality principle in the formation of coalitions, appointment of civil servants, and allocation of resources; and the preservation of a high degree of segmental autonomy in the management of their own affairs (Lijphart 1977:25, 1981, 1985a). Building upon an elite's willingness to cooperate in avoiding divisive conflicts in socially and culturally fragmented societies and in achieving certain objectives of mutual interest, the consociational democracy model seeks to reconcile open, public participation with elite cooperation in the management of governmental affairs. The majority rule principle is replaced by an inclusive norm that emphasizes the participation of political leaders within the ruling cartel. With the general public kept largely distant from the day-to-day conduct of public business, their political representatives engage in a process of adjustments, accommodations, and negotiations with each other to determine the nature of public policies (Rothchild 1986:66–69).

Although consociational arrangements may have some usefulness when applied to small, unified, and relatively affluent Western democracies (Belgium, Austria, and, until recently, the Netherlands), we wonder whether it is transferable to Nigeria, and more generally to Africa. Williams most appropriately examines some of the consociational practices that were in evidence during Nigeria's Second Republic: pragmatism in such areas as inclusive coalitions; the application of a regional and ethnic balance in the recruitment of elite representatives into party, legislative, and bureaucratic positions; and the use of the proportionality rule in distributing scarce state-controlled resources. He is careful to point out that evidence of consociational practices is not tantamount to the operation of a consociational democracy system of governance (Ekeh 1989:20–21). Moreover, he comments in passing that such practices have surfaced in several other African states with one-party systems, raising questions as to why Williams and other writers restrict their analysis of consociational experiments to democratic regimes alone.

Certainly a number of conditions in postcolonial Nigeria and Africa challenge the relevance of the consociational democracy model under current African circumstances. These conditions include the determination of the leaders in these new states to stress the legitimacy of communitywide values and purposes as against contending sectional and subunit claims; the intensity of interethnic competition for scarce public resources; the large size and diversity of some of the most promising African candidates for experimentation with consociational democracy (Nigeria, Sudan, Zaire). Moreover, the heterogeneity of the African ethnic, religious, and regional groupings requires a complicated, even laborious, bargaining process, both within the group as well as with other groupings in the community at large. And the informal understandings and norms of relationship worked out among elite representatives at the time of independence have proved difficult to transfer to new leaders when a change of power occurs. Given the power of central leaderships, it is also difficult to guarantee that the true representatives for sectional interests will emerge. Williams carries this analysis further, contending that in Nigeria "there was apparently little concern for grand coalitional arrangements or the formalities of law when extremely high stakes were on the line in the possession of elected offices" (see Chapter 5). There is much reason to doubt the appropriateness of a full-blown consociational solution in current circumstances. If leaders in certain developed societies are prepared to make the subunit the basis for participation in political life, many African leaders have misgivings about accepting such a reality, fearing that it will increase the polarization of the society. The consequence is to create suspicion about consociational solutions even while making use of a number of consociational practices to facilitate reciprocity and political exchange.

The Interactions Between State and Society

We agree with Hyden's (1990:255) emphasis on the important place of reciprocity in the study of state-society relations. However, as indicated above, we feel the focus should be expanded to take even greater account of the role of political exchange, both in its tacit and direct forms. "In practice," as Warren Ilchman and Norman Uphoff (1969:94) note, "exchanges seldom occur in isolated, explicit, or barter situations." They involve political and social as well as economic values. Not surprisingly, therefore, much insight can be gained by analyzing such processes as coalition formation and the allocation of public resources in light of political exchange concepts. We regard power in relational, not in absolute, terms; even so, we recognize that most patron-client ties and a good number of political exchange relations are in fact asymmetrical. To what extent have these patterns of interaction become routinized? Are there regularities and predictable patterns of relations that have become manifest under weak state conditions? And if reciprocities and exchanges fail to materialize in one sphere, have they nonetheless become evident in another?

Pearl T. Robinson focuses on the efforts of the military regimes in Burkina Faso and Niger to consolidate power at the political center while at the same time structuring the participation of citizens at the local level. The military regime, she argues, bolsters its legitimacy by fostering the adoption of corporatist-style patterns of organization and representation. The effect is to play down class and sectional cleavages and to emphasize the inclusion of the populace in the affairs of state. But how far does this effort at top-down administered participation at the grassroots level go in assuring the objectives of mobilizing a consensus in support of the regime and in incorporating the citizenry in the affairs of state? There is, after all, a great difference between public acceptance and public acquiescence. Moreover, as Robinson's data on Niger make apparent, many people in the rural areas had little knowledge of the workings of the conseils de développements in their areas, and ethnic claims remained evident despite the government's inclusive politics. Clearly, unless the new corporatist-style institutions can gain validity over time in the eyes of the public, the solution to the "legitimacy crisis" may prove elusive for these regimes.

John Holm and Patrick Molutsi arrive at ambiguous conclusions about the dynamics of state-society interactions in Botswana. On one hand, they note the emergence of alternative centers of power in the form of opposition-controlled local councils, private newspapers, interest groups, and educated and entrepreneurial classes. But they also question the liberalizing impact of these forces, noting that they are poorly organized, narrowly supported, and unable to gain the attention of bureaucrats. It is difficult to determine from their account whether nonstate actors have played any role in forming or sustaining Botswana's status as an exceptional African democracy. Yet their analysis suggests a line of inquiry worth pursuing: as in Eastern Europe, democratization initiatives emanate from the intelligentsia, the church, and the organized working class rather than from an entrepreneurial bourgeoisie. Do the African cases therefore call into question Barrington Moore's law of "no bourgeoisie, no democracy"? Or does the eclectic class composition of African democracy movements impair political liberalization initiatives, making them inevitably fragile, premature, and subject to reversal?

Naomi Chazan makes a case for an interactive model of governance based on the mutually conditioning effects of political action in state and social arenas. In her view, the "second coming" of Ghana's Jerry Rawlings in 1981 did not presage the continuation of top-down populist revolution; instead, the power of the hegemonic Ghanaian state was disaggregated and then reconstructed from below in a qualitatively new form. Chazan cites numerous strands of evidence for this argument: IMF–sponsored privatization measures reduced the reach of the state into the economy; the state elite supplemented its populist rhetoric with norms of political accountability and administrative efficiency; associational life blossomed to fill some of the gaps left in the wake of the retreating state; and the social base of the ruling coalition shifted from urban to rural areas. Such adjustments apparently amounted to regime change that, although incomplete, helped to legitimize the state. Moreover, the consolidation of stateness was predicated on the assertion of political spaces by autonomous actors in society, especially students, trade unionists, small-scale entrepreneurs, and district assemblies. Chazan concludes that state and civil society stand or fall together: the organization of social interests to engage state elites in negotiation on the rules of political behavior is a prerequisite for the emergence of governance.

Governance, Liberalization, and Democracy

Introducing a more generalized and comparative examination of the processes of reform and liberalization in contemporary Africa, Bratton and van de Walle give insight into the recent weakening of a number of authoritarian regimes in Africa and the halting, but discernible, movement toward increased pluralism and political competition. For a variety of reasons—a backdrop of economic malaise; indignation over internal repression, corruption, and austerity; resentment over the state's unresponsiveness to popular demands; the Eastern European demonstration effect; and various donor pressures for political reform—the issue of governance has surged into full public view. In part, the desire for greater openness and accountability is buttressed by a new awareness of the linkages between economic development and democratic practices. "There cannot be a transition to a market logic," writes Achille

Mbembe, (1989:129), "if, alongside structural adjustment programs, no attempt is made to reduce the weight of authoritarian institutions on society (the one-party system, censorship, state violence, limited civil liberties, intellectual ossification, and cultural stagnation)." Political liberalization, then, is perceived as not only contributing to a people's yearnings for participation, representativeness, equality, and accountability, but also to their ability to deal more effectively with the economic problems facing them.

Reflecting the interactional dynamics of state-society relations, Bratton and van de Walle focus more on the processes involved in political liberalization in Africa than on the operation of democratic systems. This seems logical in light of the limited, albeit significant, response made by the various African state elites to the demands of opposition leaders and groups. In the authors' words, a "partial liberalization of authoritarian regimes" occurred in 1990 that "[did] not amount to a transition to democracy" (see Chapter 2). A loose alliance of regime opponents, largely urban and middle class, emerged and demanded the opening up of the regime to new forms of participation and competition, both within the dominant political party and, in some cases, between legitimate and recognized parties. By Bratton and van de Walle's count, twenty-one out of thirty-one authoritarian regimes responded to these demands by November 1990, conceding some form of liberalization in their respective lands. In eight countries, moreover, provision was made for multiparty elections, although the ruling elites remained careful to keep tight control over the electoral process itself.

If the forces for change had proved sufficient to open the window to new political thinking and in some cases experimentation with liberalization, why are Bratton and van de Walle so cautious about the prospects, in the short term at least, of full-blown democratic practices in Africa? They point to three constraints in the present domestic and international environments: the continuing economic hardships; the limited impact of the external diffusion effect; and the ruling elite's organizational advantages and superior access to political and economic resources. At least two other explanations might be added to this list. First, the uncertainty that political and social conflict can be bounded and regularized, and consequently that multiparty democracy will lead to overpoliticization and a damaging "winner-take-all philosophy" (Mugaju 1988:86). Second is the related fear in Africa that multiparty politics will undermine political stability. A number of African leaders express a concern that parties will mobilize around ethnic symbols and identities, leading to intense conflicts and an unwillingness to practice the politics of reconciliation. Viewing ethnic politics as zero-sum encounters, these leaders incline, for the time being at least, toward the continuance of some form of single-party governance (Rothchild 1985:71–96; Diamond, Linz & Lipset 1988:12). In this light, it is not surprising that some African intellectuals have cautioned against premature moves toward "unbridled democracy" (Mugyenyi 1988:187). Arguing that Africa's societies lack social cohesion, Meddi Mugyenyi contends that "open democratic politics can be divisive and destabilizing." This leads him to put forward a case for the adoption of an alternative, hybrid form of governance, one he refers to as "minimalist democracy."

If the events of 1990 mark an important new opening in the transition toward more-democratic systems in Africa, Kenya's experience with what Joel Barkan (see Chapter 8) describes as "the deinstitutionalization of governance" is a sobering commentary on the brittle nature of the democratizing process, one that suggests that it is not helpful to underestimate the impediments to change. As Barkan indicates, the regime of President Jomo Kenyatta was able to establish an effective system of governance in a relatively brief period of time, but its successor, the Moi regime, dismantled much of the system with equal speed, transforming a stable patron-client system into one of personal rule. Not only did the informal rules governing cabinet appointments lose their predictability, but members of the inner court found themselves with diminished political autonomy and cut off from their constituency bases. The president, determined to undercut the autonomy of national institutions and associations, diminished the independence of the parliament, the judiciary, and the civil service, and placed additional restrictions on the activities of the country's various autonomous associations. Clearly, as Barkan warns, governance remains a fragile process that depends on the restraint of the ruler and the tolerance of the ruled.

CONCLUSION: A RESEARCH AGENDA

We conclude this book by suggesting a few avenues along which research on governance might usefully be pursued. We are guided by several observations: that definitional questions remain to be resolved; that governance would best be approached by studying interactions between state and social actors; and that greater effort is needed to explicate the policy dimensions of governance.

We think that the prospects for governance rest in the first instance on the condition of institutions—meaning both norms and structures—in civil society. Much research remains to be done on the normative underpinnings of governance in different societies. In Africa, we need to know whether values of reciprocal social obligation have survived the onslaught of modernization, and, if so, how they are expressed within large-scale political institutions. Does the secularization and monetization of social relationships permanently marginalize certain communities from participation in politics? Or do universal values provide a glue for new forms of organization and a justification for asserting the rights of all persons? We contend that the notion of "good government" increasingly embodies core universal values, even though colored by cultural emphases and interpretations in different world areas. Within this core is the notion of the political accountability of leaders to followers. Governance research should therefore probe how members of social organizations seek to hold their own leaders accountable and how they effect leadership transitions.

Although the institutions discussed by the various contributors (such as competitive elections, party primaries, and district assemblies) may be important indicators of liberalization, a sustained process of governance requires us to look at the organizing principles that structure the relationships between state and society over time. In this respect, we regard the choice of regimes as critical in terms of achieving effective governance. Regimes, which structure the basis for group encounters, can be described as the pattern of behavior accepted by state and societal elites as the legitimate formula for exercising political power. We regard three broad regimes types as pertinent to an analysis of governance in contemporary Africa: populist regimes; elite hegemonic exchange regimes; and polyarchical regimes.

First, a number of African leaders, despairing over their conditions of poverty and dependency, experimented in the 1980s with various homegrown populist regimes in an effort to achieve broad, popular involvement in the reconstruction of their societies (Rothchild & Gyimah-Boadi 1989:221–224, 241–244). Rejecting individualism, acquisitiveness, and neocolonial linkages, these radical leaders searched for authentic African paths to political and economic development. They sought to transform their societies to eliminate the exploitative features of past regimes (corruption, nepotism, class inequality, external domination) and to establish new, egalitarian and cohesive social orders. As Robinson (see Chapter 7) suggests, the popular character of such regimes arises from the full participation of the populace in the political process. The regimes in Ghana and Burkina Faso sought to give meaning to this value on public involvement by stressing the importance of wide citizen participation in the public tribunals and decisionmaking committees of government.

However, the inclusion of the populace often involved, in practice, curtailment of activities by privileged classes identified with the old social order. And this change in opportunities brought with it a sharp counterreaction on the part of middle-class interests. In both Ghana and Burkina Faso, albeit at different stages in their revolutions, the populist governments felt compelled to rein in zealous attempts at social transformation in an effort to conciliate their middle-class opponents. Although experience with radical populism in Africa remains limited, we expect the continent's grave economic difficulties to give rise to additional populist experiments in the future. These undertakings are likely to vary significantly in terms of their ability to transform economic structures and social relations as well as in their capacity to withstand domestic and international pressures for a shift toward a pragmatic orientation.

Nevertheless, where leaders with a populist bent have strategically important resources at their disposal (as in Libya) or where they have a dependable and well-placed coalition of supporters, they may be in a position to resist the forces pushing for a turn to the right and to endure over an extended time period.

Second, because autocracies may make only hesitant concessions to the demands for liberalization, they may seek to reconcile central control with reciprocity and political exchange. The results would not be democracy, but a hybrid form of elite-dominated hegemonic exchange. Single-party control is joined with certain practices associated with consociational democracy, including government by grand coalition and the principles of proportionality and segmental autonomy. Such mixed systems may well become more common in the period ahead, offering possibilities for liberalization without full democratization. Representing accommodations by the ruling elite to political reality, such regimes are often unstable, tending to be transitional phenomena in the African context. Given the pressures in Africa as elsewhere for equality and participation, elite networks that perpetuate the power and privileges of the ruling class are likely to remain suspect, raising serious doubts about the legitimacy and staying power of such regime forms. Hence we anticipate that these regimes, with their encapsulated relationships of reciprocity and political exchange within a dominant elite culture, will remain acceptable to the public for relatively limited time periods only.

And finally, majoritarian polyarchies are distinct from populist and elite hegemonic exchange regimes in their openness to competition for positions of government. More prepared to allow rivals to enter into contests for political power at the polls, leaders in polyarchies are inclined to accept a considerable degree of accountability and control by the public. Although polyarchic systems are distinguishable in their electoral practices and operating styles, they tend to be alike in their basic commitments to majority participation, partisan competition, and a broad inclusiveness in the decisionmaking process.

In recent times the African experience with two- or multiparty electoral systems has been limited to countries that are small in size and/or population and not highly fragmented in terms of ethnic or religious identity groups— Senegal, Botswana, Mauritius, Gambia, and Namibia. The failure of power-sharing constitutions in other African countries—such as Ghana, Nigeria, Uganda, and Zimbabwe—raises questions about the generalizability of this regime type. Given the uncertainty over organizing principles of state, the weakness of state regulatory capacity, economic scarcity, and the intensity of group competition over available state-controlled resources, we do not expect the current trend toward liberalization in Africa to result in full-blown democratic systems in the larger and more pluralistic countries in the near future. At this juncture more research is essential on the relationship between social norms and institutions of governance, and on the way that these institutions promote recurrent patterns of relations among the leaders and constituents in the various societies. We accept the point that a steady and more abundant flow of reciprocities and political exchanges increases the likelihood of economic development; what we need to learn about in greater depth, however, is the nature of the institutional arrangements appropriate to contemporary Africa and able to promote these ongoing interactions.

The nature of regime type and accompanying institutions has important implications for the dynamics of the interplay between state and society. Whereas democracies are inclined to accept and work with autonomously organized interest groups, autocracies, and most particularly their corporatist variants, are prone to push their own definitions of the legitimate interest groups on society. The consequences of this are significant, especially in Africa where the state tends to be weak and unable to impose its regulations effectively throughout its territory. Whereas the democratic regime may find itself with limited alternatives to negotiating with powerful, entrenched interest groups (including groups based upon regional, ethnic, or religious identities), the autocratic regime attempts to insist on its own definition of social reality, affirming the legitimacy of some interest groups and associations while banning and suppressing others regarded as objectionable.

The implications of this for societal stability, and hence the ability to achieve the tasks of government, deserve considerably more study than they have received. Certainly the willingness of the polyarchic (and for that matter the hegemonic exchange) regime to build upon elite reciprocities and political exchanges involves an implicit recognition that political stability requires an accommodation with the configurations of group power on the ground. Hence the democratically inclined state bargains with powerful, autonomous collective interests out of political necessity. By contrast, seeking to transform its own political reality to conform to a predetermined plan, the autocratic state bows grudgingly, if at all, to the need to accommodate regional, ethnic, and religious claims.

The question that must be confronted by those concerned with governance is the impact that these various regime types have on regularized patterns of state-society relations in the African context. Is the single-party system justified at times as a means of maintaining national unity and, if so, under what circumstances? When do autocratic regimes contribute to political instability and possibly their own undoing? What interest group claims can be rechanneled along legitimate lines, and what types of demands are most likely to lead to protest and violence if suppressed? Can regime change lead to a bargaining culture that encourages the settlement of reasonable group demands through negotiation, not fiat? Other questions could be raised as well, but the point must be obvious by now: there is a clear need for systematic study relating regime to state-society interactions that give us a fuller insight into which factors are most likely to produce constructive and self-fulfilling relations.

In brief, we regard governance as a timely concept because it encourages analysis of efforts to restore political legitimacy to governments that have lost it. Governance is particularly relevant to former colonial peoples who, in the rapid rush to decolonization and the crystalization of postcolonial authoritarianism, have rarely enjoyed the opportunity to legislate a form of government rightfully their own. It is an affirmation of a people's right to self-determination, to participate fully in political affairs, and to have their rulers accountable to them for their actions. Clearly more research is needed at this time in order to gain a comprehensive picture of the interrelations of state and society. A stronger state may paradoxically be necessary to achieve economic and social development, yet this stronger state is not a larger state determined on spending scarce resources on itself, but rather a more responsive state. And such an outcome, with its emphasis on a more regular flow of reciprocities and exchanges among state and societal interests, is at the core of the current scholarly concern with governance in Africa.

Bibliography

Abrahams, Ray
  1987   "Sungusungu: Village Vigilante Groups in Tanzania." *African Affairs*
          86, no. 343:179–196.
Adamolekun, Ladipo
  1990   "Institutional Perspectives on Africa's Development Crisis." In
          Carter Center, "African Governance in the 1990s." Atlanta: Carter
          Center.
———, and Bamidele Ayo
  1989   "The Evolution of the Nigerian Federal Administration System."
          Publius 19 (Winter):157–176.
Adamu, Haroun, and Alaba Ogunsanwo
  1983   *Nigeria: The Making of the Presidential System 1979 General
          Elections.* Kano: Triumph Publishing.
*African Charter for Popular Participation in Development and Transfor-
          mation*
  1990   International Conference on Popular Participation in the Recovery
          and Development Process in Africa. Arusha, Tanzania.
Agyeman-Duah, Baffour
  1987   "Ghana, 1982–86: The Politics of the P.N.D.C." *Journal of Modern
          African Studies* 25, no. 4:613–642.
Ahiakpor, James C. W.
  1985   "The Success and Failure of Dependency Theory: The Experience of
          Ghana." *International Organization* 39, no. 3:535–552.
Ake, Claude
  1990   "The Case for Democracy." In Carter Center, "African Governance in
          the 1990s." Atlanta: Carter Center.
Allen, Chris
  1986   "Staying Put: Handy Hints for Heads of State." Paper presented at the
          Symposium on Authority and Legitimacy in Africa, University of
          Stirling, Scotland, May.
———, et al.
  1989   *Benin, the Congo, Burkina Faso: Economics, Politics and Society.*
          London: Frances Pinter.
Almond, Gabriel A., and James S. Coleman, eds.
  1960   *The Politics of Developing Areas.* Princeton, NJ: Princeton
          University Press.

Almond, Gabriel A., and G. Bingham Powell, Jr.
   1966   *Comparative Politics: A Developmental Approach.* Boston: Little,
           Brown.
Almond, Gabriel A., and Sidney Verba
   1963   *The Civic Culture.* Boston: Little Brown.
Amnesty International
   1987   *Kenya: Torture, Political Detention and Unfair Trials.* London:
           Amnesty International Publications.
Amonoo, Ben
   1981   *Ghana 1957–1966: The Politics of Institutional Dualism.* London:
           George Allen and Unwin.
Andriamirado, Sennen
   1990   "Le feu dans la région des Grands Lacs?" *Jeune Afrique* no. 1562
           (December 5–11):28.
An-na'im, Abdullahi A., and Francis M. Deng, eds.
   1990   *Human Rights in Africa: Cross-Cultural Perspectives.* Washington,
           DC: Brookings Institution.
Anyang'Nyong'o, Peter, ed.
   1987   *Popular Struggles for Democracy in Africa.* London: Zed Press.
Apter, Andrew
   1987   "Things Fell Apart? Yoruba Responses to the 1983 Elections in Ondo
           State, Nigeria." *Journal of Modern African Studies* 25, no. 3:489–
           503.
Arendt, Hannah
   1958   *The Human Condition.* Chicago: University of Chicago Press.
Arrow, Kenneth J.
   1963   *Social Choice and Individual Values.* New Haven, CT: Yale University
           Press.
Austin, Dennis
   1985   "The Ghana Armed Forces and Ghanaian Society." *Third World
           Quarterly* 7, no. 1:97–111.
Awonoor, Kofi
   1984   *The Ghana Revolution: Background Account from a Personal
           Perspective.* Bronx, NY: Oasis Publishers.
Axelrod, Robert, and Robert O. Keohane
   1985   "Achieving Cooperation under Anarchy: Strategies and Institutions."
           World Politics 38, no. 1:226–254.
Ayee, Joseph R. A.
   1988   "The Provisional National Defence Council's 'Blue Book' on District
           Political Authority and the Future of Local Government in Ghana."
           The Journal of Management Studies 4:25–39.
Ayeni, Victor, and Dele Olowu
   1988   "The Politics of Revenue Allocation and Inter-Governmental
           Relations." In *Nigeria's Second Republic: Presidentialism, Politics
           and Administration in a Developing State*, ed. V. Ayeni and Kayode
           Soremekun. Lagos: Daily Times Press.
Ayo, Bamidele
   1988   "Social Policy." In *Nigeria's Second Republic: Presidentalism,
           Politics and Administration in a Developing State*, ed. V. Ayeni and
           K. Soremekun. Lagos: Daily Times Press.
Ayoade, John A.
   1978   "Federalism in Africa: Some Chequered Fortunes." *Plural Societies* 9
           (Spring):3–17.

1986   "Ethnic Management in the 1979 Nigerian Constitution." *Publius* 16
        (Spring):73–90.
———, and Rotimi T. Suberu
1990   "Federalism." *Quarterly Journal of Administration* 24 (April):152–
        165.
Azarya, Victor
1988   "Reordering State-Society Relations: Incorporation and Disengage-
        ment." In *The Precarious Balance: State and Society in Africa*, ed. D.
        Rothchild and N. Chazan. Boulder, CO: Westview Press.
———, and Naomi Chazan
1987   "Disengagement from the State in Africa: Reflections on the
        Experience of Ghana and Guinea." *Comparative Studies in Society
        and History* 19, no. 1:106–131.
Babalakin, Justice Bolarinwa
1986   *Commission of Inquiry into the Affairs of the Federal Electoral
        Commission, FEDECO (1979–83)*. Lagos: Government Printer.
Bach, Daniel C.
1989   "Unité nationale et société plurale au Nigeria: les mécanismes
        boomerang du fédéralisme." *Afrique Contemporaine* 150:5–
        27.
Baerhrel, Claude, Tshimanga Nsata, Nsungani Ndengo, Pierre Yves Bellon, and
        Christian Monnier
1985   *Transports informels à Kinshasa*. Kinshasa: Bureau d'Études,
        d'Aménagement et d'Urbanisme (BEAU).
Bagirameshi, Jean, Cléophas Bahizina, and Michel Barnaud
1986   "Pour une nouvelle pratique de la vulgarisation agricole au Rwanda."
        Revue Tiers Monde 27, no. 106:419–437.
Baldwin, David A.
1978   "Power and Social Exchange." *American Political Science Review* 72,
        no. 4 (December):1229–1242.
Bamishaiye, A.
1976   "Ethnic Politics as an Instrument of Unequal Socio-Economic
        Development in Nigeria's First Republic." In *Ethnic Relations in
        Nigeria*, ed. A. O. Sanda. Ibadan: Caxton Press.
Bamouni, Paulin Babou
1986   *Burkina Faso: processus de la révolution*. Paris: L'Harmattan.
Barkan, Joel D.
1976   "Further Reassessment of 'Conventional Wisdom': Political
        Knowledge and Voting Behavior in Rural Kenya." *American Political
        Science Review* 70, no. 2:452–455.
Forthcoming "Resurrecting Modernization Theory and the Emergence of Civil
        Society in Kenya and Nigeria." In *Political Development and the New
        Realism in Sub-Saharan Africa*, eds. David E. Apter and Carl G.
        Rosberg. Berkeley: University of California, forthcoming.
Barkan, Joel D., with Michael Chege
1989   "Decentralising the State: District Focus and the Politics of
        Reallocation in Kenya." *Journal of Modern African Studies* 27, no.
        2:431–453.
Barkan, Joel D., and Frank Holmquist
1989   "Peasant-State Relations and the Social Base of Self-Help in Kenya."
        World Politics 41, no. 2 (January):359–380.
Barkan, Joel D., and John J. Okumu
1978   "Semi-Competitive Elections, Clitentelism, and Political

Recruitment in a No-Party State." In *Elections Without Choice*, ed. Guy Hermet, Richard Rose, and Alain Rouquié. London: Macmillan.

Barrows, Walter
1976   *Grassroots Politics in an African State*. New York: Africana Publishers.

Barry, Boubacar
1988   *La Sénégambie du XVe au XIXe siècle: traite négrière, Islam et conquête coloniale*. Paris: L'Harmattan.

Bart, A.
1982   "La presse au Rwanda." Vol. 1: "Production, diffusion et lecture de la presse depuis le début du siècle." Doctoral diss., Université de Bordeaux III.

Bart, F.
1980   "Le café dans l'agriculture rwandaise: l'exemple de Kidahire (Runyinya)." *Cahiers d'Outre-Mer* 33, no. 132:301–317.

Bates, Robert H.
1981   *Markets and States in Tropical Africa: The Political Basis of Agricultural Policies*. Berkeley: University of California Press.

Baulin, Jacques
1986   *Conseiller du Président Diori*. Paris: Éditions Eurafor.

Bayart, Jean-François
1983   "Les sociétés africaines face à l'Etat." *Pouvoirs* 25:23–39.
1985   *L'État au Cameroun*. 2d ed. Paris: Presses de la Fondation Nationale de Sciences Politiques.
1986   "Civil Society in Africa." In *Political Domination in Africa*, ed. P. Chabal. Cambridge: Cambridge University Press.
1989   *L'État en Afrique: La politique du ventre*. Paris: Fayard.

Beckett, Paul A., and James O'Connell
1977   *Education and Power in Nigeria: A Study of University Students*. London: Hodder and Stoughton.

Bentsi-Enchill, Nii K.
1989   "The Storm of June 4." *West Africa* 3747:952–953.

Berg-Schlosser, Dirk
1985   "Elements of Consociational Democracy in Kenya." *European Journal of Political Research* 13 (March):95–109.

Bézy, Fernand
1990   *Rwanda. Bilan socio-économique d'un régime (1962–1989)*. Louvain: Institut d'Etude des Pays en Développement, Université Catholique de Louvain.

———, Jean-Philippe Peemans, and Jean-Marie Wautelet
1981   *Accumulation et Sous-Développement au Zaire, 1960–1980*. Louvain-la-Neuve: Presse Universitaire de Louvain.

Biaya, T. K.
1985   "La 'Cuistrerie' de Mbuji Mayi (Zaire)." *Génève Afrique* 23, no. 1:62–85.

Bienen, Henry
1970   *Tanzania: Party Transformation and Economic Development*. Princeton, NJ: Princeton University Press.

———, and Nicolas van de Walle
1989.   "Power and Time in Africa." *American Political Science Review* 83, no. 1 (March):19–34.

Biloa, Marie-Roger
    1990   "Rwanda. La Force de la discrétion: institutions, le président et les
            autres." *Jeune Afrique* no. 1526 (April 2):36–38.
Binder, Leonard et al.
    1971   *Crises and Sequences in Political Development*. Princeton, NJ:
            Princeton University Press.
Bing, Adotey
    1984   "Popular Participation vs People's Power: Notes on Politics and
            Power Struggles in Ghana." *Review of African Political Economy*
            31:91–104.
Blades, Derek W.
    1982   "The Hidden Economy and the National Accounts." *OECD Economic
            Outlook*, Occasional Studies, no. 2. Paris: OECD.
Blau, Peter M.
    1964   *Exchange and Power in Social Life*. New York: Wiley.
Bollen, Kenneth A.
    1980   "Issues in the Comparative Measurement of Political Democracy."
            American Sociological Review 45, no. 3 (June):370–390.
Botswana, MFDP (Ministry of Finance and Development Planning)
    1985   National Development Plan 1985–1991. Gaborone: Government
            Printer.
Boulle, L. J.
    1984   *South Africa and the Consociational Option: A Constitutional
            Analysis*. Cape Town: Juta.
Bratton, Michael
    1989a   "Beyond the State: Civil Society and Associational Life in Africa."
            World Politics 41, no. 3 (April):407–430.
    1989b   "The Politics of Government-NGO Relations in Africa." *World
            Development* 17, no. 4:569–587.
    Forthcoming "Peasant-State Relations in Post-Colonial Africa: Patterns of
            Engagement and Disengagement." In *State Power and Social Forces:
            Struggles and Accommodation*, ed. A. Kohli, J. Migdal and V.
            Shue.
Brent, Stephen
    1990   "Aiding Africa." *Foreign Policy* 80 (Fall):121–140.
Brydon, Lynne
    1985   "Ghanaian Responses to the Nigerian Expulsion of 1983." *African
            Affairs* 84, no. 337:561–575.
Burns, Tom, and G. M. Stalker
    1962   *The Management of Innovation*. London: Tavistock Publications.
Busia, K. A.
    1967   *Africa in Search of Democracy*. London: Routledge and Kegan
            Paul.
Callaghy, Thomas M.
    1984   *The State-Society Struggle: Zaire in Comparative Perspective*. New
            York: Columbia University Press.
    1987a   "Culture and Politics in Zaire." Washington, DC: Department of
            State, Bureau of Intelligence and Research.
    1987b   "The State as Lame Leviathan: The Patrimonial Administrative State
            in Africa." In *The African State in Transition*, ed. Zaki Ergas.
            London: Macmillan.
    1990   "Lost Between State and Market: The Politics of Economic

Adjustment in Ghana, Zambia and Nigeria." In *The Politics of Economic Adjustment in Developing Nations*, ed. Joan Nelson. Princeton, NJ: Princeton University Press.

Cardoso, Fernando H.
1979   "On the Characterization of Authoritarian Regimes in Latin America." In *The New Authoritarianism in Latin America*, ed. David Collier. Princeton, NJ: Princeton University Press.

Carter Center of Emory University
1989a   "Beyond Autocracy in Africa." Working Papers for the Inaugural Seminar of the Governance in Africa Program. Atlanta: Carter Center.
1989b   *Perestroika Without Glasnost in Africa*. Conference Report Series vol. 2, no. 1. Atlanta: Carter Center.
1990   "African Governance in the 1990s." Working Papers from the Second Annual Seminar of the African Governance Program. Atlanta: Carter Center.

Catlin, George E. G.
1930   *A Study of the Principles of Politics*. New York: Macmillan.

Chabal, Patrick, ed.
1986   *Political Domination in Africa*. London: Cambridge University Press.

Chazan, Naomi
1982   "The New Politics of Participation in Tropical Africa." *Comparative Politics* 14, no. 2:169–189.
1983   *An Anatomy of Ghanaian Politics: Managing Political Recession 1969–82*. Boulder, CO: Westview Press.
1986   "The Anomalies of Continuity: Perspectives on Ghanaian Elections Since Independence." In *Elections in Independent Africa*, ed. F. Hayward. Boulder, CO: Westview Press.
1987   "Politics and the State in Ghana: A Third Decade Assessment." Paper presented at the Conference on West African States Since 1976, School of Oriental and African Studies, London.
1988a   "Citizenship, the State and Social Relations in Ghana: Patterns and Trends." Paper presented at the Annual Meeting of the African Studies Association, Chicago, October 28–31.
1988b   "Ghana: Problems of Governance and the Emergence of Civil Society." In *Democracy in Developing Countries. Vol. 2: Africa*, ed. L. Diamond, J. Linz, and S. M. Lipset. Boulder, CO: Lynne Rienner Publishers.
1989   "Planning Democracy in Africa: A Comparative Perspective on Ghana and Nigeria." *Policy Sciences* 22:325–357.
1990   "Engaging the State: Associational Life in Africa." Paper presented at the Workshop on State Power and Social Forces: Domination and Transformation in the Third World, University of Texas Austin, February.
————, R. Mortimer, John Ravenhill, and Donald Rothchild, eds.
1988   *Politics and Society in Contemporary Africa*. Boulder, CO: Lynne Rienner Publishers.

Chazan, Naomi, and Donald Rothchild
1989   "Corporatism and Political Transactions: Some Ruminations on the Ghanaian Experience." In *Corporatism in Africa: Comparative Analysis and Practice*, ed. Julius Nyang'oro and Timothy M. Shaw. Boulder, CO: Westview Press.

Chilton, Stephen
    1988   *Defining Political Development*. Boulder, CO: Lynne Rienner
            Publishers.
Chipman, John
    1989   *French Power in Africa*. London: Blackwell.
Chrétien, Jean-Pierre
    1985   "Hutu et Tutsi au Rwanda et au Burundi." In *Au coeur de l'ethnie:
            ethnies, tribalisme et état en Afrique*, ed. Jean-Loup Amselle and
            Elikia M'bokolo. Paris: Éditions la Découverte.
Clark, Gracia
    1984   "Pools, Clients and Partners: Relations of Capital and Risk Control
            Between Kumasi Market Women." Paper presented at the Annual
            Meeting of the African Studies Association, Los Angeles, Decem-
            ber.
    1988   "Price Control of Local Foodstuffs in Kumasi, Ghana." In *Traders vs.
            the State: Anthropological Approaches to Unofficial Economies*, ed.
            G. Clark. Boulder, CO: Westview Press.
Cohen, Dennis L., and John Daniel
    1982   *Political Economy of Africa: Selected Readings*. London: Longman.
Colclough, Christopher, and Stephen McCarthy
    1980   *The Political Economy of Botswana: A Study of Growth and
            Distribution*. Oxford: Oxford University Press.
Coleman, James S.
    1988   "Social Capital in the Creation of Human Capital." *American Journal
            of Sociology* 94 (supplement):S95–S120.
Collier, David, ed.
    1979   *The New Authoritarianism in Latin America*. Princeton, NJ: Princeton
            University Press.
Collier, Ruth Berins
    1982   *Regimes in Tropical Africa: Changing Forms of Supremacy 1945–
            75*. Berkeley: University of California Press.
Commission Nationale de mise en place de la Société de Développement
    1983   *Recueil de discours du Lieutenant-Colonel Moumani Djermakoye
            Adamou, Président de la Commission Nationale de mise en place de la
            Société de Développement*. Niamey: Imprimerie Nationale du
            Niger.
Committee for the Defence of the Revolution
    1986   *Guidelines*. Accra: Government Printer.
Cooper, Frederick
    1981   "Africa and the World Economy." *African Studies Review* 24, nos. 2–
            3:1–86.
Coulon, Christian
    1981   *Le marabout et le prince (Islam et pouvoir au Sénégal)*. Paris: Éditions
            A. Pedone.
    1988   "Senegal: The Development and Fragility of Semidemocracy." In
            Democracy in Developing Countries. Vol. 2: Africa, ed. Larry
            Diamond, Juan Linz, and S. Martin Lipset. Boulder, CO: Lynne
            Rienner Publishers.
Coulson, Andrew
    1982   *Tanzania: A Political Economy*. Oxford: Clarendon Press.
Crisp, Jeff
    1984   *The Story of an African Working Class: Ghanaian Miners' Struggles*.
            London: Zed Press.

Crook, Richard
    1987, "Legitimacy, Authority and the Transfer of Power in Ghana." *Political Studies* 35, no. 4 (December):552–572.
    1989   "Patrimonialism, Administrative Effectiveness and Economic Development in Cote d'Ivoire." *African Affairs* 88, no. 351:205–228.

Cros, Marie France
    1989   "Rwanda: la république à trente ans. Une révolution inachevée?" *La Libre Belgique* (October 31–November 1).
    1990a   "La démocratie n'est pas le multipartisme; mais nous voulons la démocratie." Interview with President Juvenal Habyarimana. *La Libre Belgique* (May 25).
    1990b   "Régionalisme: un peu, beaucoup, passionnément." *La Libre Belgique* (May 25).
    1990c   "Rwanda: heurts entre étudiants et policiers." *La Libre Belgique* (June 5).
    1990d   "Démocratie: le Rwanda se refait une beauté." *La Libre Belgique* (August 10).
    1990e   "La justice du Rwanda juge des journalistes." *La Libre Belgique* (September 20).

Daalder, Hans
    1971   "On Building Consociational Nations." *International Social Science Journal* 32, no. 2:355–370.

Daddieh, Cyril Koffie
    1987.   "Economic Development and the Informal Sector in Ghana Reconsidered: Notes Towards a Reconceptualization." Unpublished manuscript.

Dagra, Mamadou
    1985   "La démocratie participative au Niger." *Bulletin CND* 16 (September):12–16.

Dahl, Robert A.
    1956   *A Preface to Democratic Theory.* Chicago: Chicago University Press.
    1971   *Polyarchy: Participation and Opposition.* New Haven, CT: Yale University Press.

DAI (Development Alternatives, Inc.)
    1986   *The Rwanda Social and Institutional Profile.* 3 vols. Washington, DC: Development Alternatives, Inc.

De Soto, Hernando
    1989   *The Other Path: The Invisible Revolution in the Third World.* New York: Harper and Row.

Decraene, Philippe
    1973   "Rwanda: L'armée au pouvoir." *Revue Française d'Etudes Politiques Africaines* no. 91 (July):19–20.
    1974   "Le 'coup' rwandais du 5 juillet 1973 et ses suites." *Revue Française d'Études Politiques Africaines* 99 (April):66–86.

Delis, Philippe, and Christian Girard
    1985   "Gestion foncière populaire par la construction en dur à Kinshasa." *Les Annales de la Recherche Urbain* (Kinshasa).

Diagne, Ndeye Madjiguene
    1986   "Le régime juridique des élections au Senegal depuis l'ouverture démocratique de 1976." Mémoire de D.E.A., Faculté des Sciences Juridiques et Économiques, Université de Dakar, Senegal.

Diamond, Larry
1982   "Cleavage, Conflict, and Anxiety in the Second Nigerian Republic."
        Journal of Modern African Studies 20, no. 4 (December):629–668.
1983   "Social Change and Political Conflict in Nigeria's Second Republic."
        In *The Political Economy of Nigeria*, ed. I. W. Zartman. New York:
        Praeger.
1987   "Class Formation in the Swollen African State." *Journal of Modern
        African Studies* 25, no. 4 (December):567–596.
1988   *Class, Ethnicity, and Democracy in Nigeria: The Failure of the First
        Republic.* Syracuse, NY: Syracuse University Press.
———, Juan Linz, and S. Martin Lipset, eds.
1988a   *Democracy in Developing Countries. Vol. 2: Africa.* Boulder, CO:
        Lynne Rienner Publishers.
1988b   *Democracy in Developing Countries. Vol. 1: Persistence, Failure,
        and Renewal.* Boulder, CO: Lynne Rienner Publishers.
Donnelly, Jack
1982   "Human Rights and Human Dignity: An Analytic Critique of Non-
        Western Conceptions of Human Rights." *American Political Science
        Review* 76, no. 2 (June):303–316.
Donnet, Michel
1989   "Théologie et libération." *Dialogue* no. 135:41–66.
Dudley, Billy J.
1973   *Instability and Political Order: Politics and Crisis in Nigeria.* Ibadan:
        Ibadan University Press.
Dunn, John
1986   "The Politics of Representation and Good Government in Post-
        Colonial Africa." In *Political Domination in Africa*, ed. P. Chabal.
        London: Cambridge University Press.
Easton, David
1965   *A Systems Analysis of Political Life.* New York: Wiley.
ECA (United Nations Economic Commission for Africa)
1989   *African Alternative Framework to Structural Adjustment Programmes
        for Socio-Economic Recovery and Transformation.* E/ECA/CM/15/6/
        Rev 3. Addis Ababa, Ethiopia.
EIU (Economist Intelligence Unit)
1987   *Country Profile: Ghana.* London: Economist Intelligence Unit.
1988   *Country Profile 1988–89. Zaire, Rwanda, Burundi.* London:
        Economist Intelligence Unit.
1989a   *Country Profile 1989–90. Zaire, Rwanda, Burundi.* London:
        Economist Intelligence Unit.
1989b   *Country Report. Zaire, Rwanda, Burundi.* No. 3. London: Economist
        Intelligence Unit.
Ekeh, Peter
1975   "Colonialism and the Two Publics in Africa: A Theoretical
        Statement." *Comparative Studies in History and Society* 17, no.
        1:91–112.
1989   "The Structure and Meaning of Federal Character in the Nigerian
        Constitution." In *Federal Character and Federalism in Nigeria*, ed. P.
        Ekeh and E. Osaghae. Ibadan: Heinemann.
Ekwa bis Isal, S. J.
1986   "La PME 'informelle', pivot indispensable de l'édifice social et
        économique du Zaire." *Zaire Afrique* 207:391–395.

Elaigwu, J. Isawa
1988   "Nigerian Federalism Under Civilian and Military Regimes." *Publius*
        18 (Winter):173–188.
———, and Victor A. Olorunsola
1983   "Federalism and the Politics of Compromise." In *State Versus Ethnic
        Claims: African Policy Dilemmas*, ed. Donald Rothchild and V. A.
        Olorunsola. Boulder, CO: Westview Press.
Elazar, Daniel J.
1985   "Federalism and Consociational Regimes." *Publius* 15 (Spring):17–
        35.
Elster, Jon
1989   *The Cement of Society: A Study of Social Order.* New York:
        Cambridge University Press.
Ephson, Ben
1989   "People Are Watching." *West Africa* 3747:952.
Epstein, A. L.
1958   *Politics in an Urban African Community.* Manchester, Eng.:
        University of Manchester Press.
Etzioni, Amitai
1988   *The Moral Dimension: Toward a New Economics.* New York: Free
        Press.
Les Evêques du Rwanda
1990   "Lettre pastorale sur la justice (extraits)." *Dialogue* 141 (July–
        August):3–18.
Ewusi, Kodwo
1986   *Statistical Tables on the Economy of Ghana, 1950–85.* Legon:
        Institute for Statistical, Social and Economic Research,
Fall, Ibrahima
1977   *Sous-développement et démocratie multipartisane: l'expérience
        sénégalaise.* Dakar: Nouvelles Éditions Africaines.
Falola, Toyin, and Julius Ihonvbere
1985   *The Rise and Fall of Nigeria's Second Republic.* London: Zed Press.
Fatton, Robert, Jr.
1988   "The State of African Studies and Studies of the African State: The
        Theoretical Softness of the 'Soft State'." Paper presented at the
        Annual Meeting of the African Studies Association, Chicago,
        October 28–31.
1990   "Liberal Democracy in Africa." *Political Science Quarterly* 105
        (Fall):455–474.
Fieldhouse, D. K.
1986   *Black Africa 1945–1980: Economic Decolonization and Arrested
        Development.* London: Allen and Unwin.
Fishman, Robert M.
1990   "Rethinking State and Regime: Southern Europe in Transition to
        Democracy." *World Politics* 42, no. 3 (April):422–440.
Flouriot, Jean
1986   "Transport et écoulement des produits vivriers en Afrique
        subsaharienne: approvisionnement des grandes villes et problèmes
        de transport au Zaire." Unpublished manuscript.
Foltz, William J.
1973   "Political Opposition in Single Party States of Tropical Africa." In
        Regimes and Oppositions, ed. Robert A. Dahl. New Haven, CT: Yale
        University Press.

Ford Foundation
1990   *Annual Report, 1989*. New York: Ford Foundation.
Forrest, Joshua B.
1988   "The Quest for State 'Hardness' in Africa." *Comparative Politics* 20, no. 4:423–442.
Forrest, Tom
1985   "The Political Economy of Civil Rule and the Economic Crisis in Nigeria (1979–84)." *Review of African Political Economy* (May):4–26.
Forsythe, David P., ed.
1989   *Human Rights and Development: International Views*. London: Macmillan.
Gastil, Raymond D.
1989   *Freedom in the World 1988–89*. New York: Freedom House.
Gboyega, Alex
1984   "The Federal Character or the Attempt to Create Representative Bureaucracies in Nigeria." *International Review of Administrative Sciences* 50, no. 1:17–24.
1985   "Intergovernmental Relations in Nigeria: Local Government and the 1979 Constitution." *Public Administration and Development* 5, no. 2:281–290.
Geiger, Susan
1982   "Umoja wa Wanawake wa Tanzania and the Needs of the Rural Poor." *African Studies Review* 25, no. 2/3:45–65.
Gerschenkron, Alexander
1962   *Economic Backwardness in Historical Perspective*. Cambridge, MA: Harvard University Press.
Gershuny, J. I., and R. E. Pahl
1980   "Britain in the Decade of the Three Economies." *New Society* 51, no. 900:7–9.
Gerth, H. H. and C. Wright Mills
1946   *From Max Weber: Essays in Sociology*. New York: Oxford University Press.
Ghana
1982   *PNDCL 42: Provisional National Defence Council (Establishment) Proclamation (Supplementary and Consequential Provisions) Law*. Accra: Government Printer.
1983a   *Economic Recovery Programme, 1984–1986*. Accra: Government Printer.
1983b   *Summary of the PNDC's Budget Statement and Economic Policy for 1983*. Accra: Government Printer.
1984   *1984 Population Census of Ghana: Preliminary Report*. Accra: Central Bureau of Statistics.
1987a   *District Political Authority and Modalities for District Level Elections* (July). Accra: Ghana Publishing Corporation.
1987b   *National Programme for Economic Development (Revised)* (July). Accra: Ghana Publishing Corporation.
N.d.a   "Decentralisation in Ghana." Accra: Information Services Department.
N.d.b   "The Search for True Democracy in Ghana." Accra: Information Services Department.
Gitonga, Afrifa K.
1988   "The Meaning and Foundations of Democracy." In *Democratic Theory*

and Practice, ed. Walter O. Oyugi, E. S. Atieno Odhiambo, Michael Chege, and A. Gitonga. Portsmouth, NH: Heinemann.

Godding, Jean-Pierre

1984 "Foreign Aid as an Obstacle to Development: The Case of Rwanda's Rural Development Projects." In *International Perspectives on Rural Development*, ed. Michael Lipton et al. Lewes: University of Sussex Institute of Development Studies.

1987 "Les grands projets de développement rural et le développement des communes." In *Les projets de développement rural: réussites, échecs et stratégies nouvelles*, ed. Augustin Nkundabashaka and Joachim Voss. Butare: Université Nationale du Rwanda.

1989 "Grand projets et développement communal." *Dialogue* no. 134 (May–June):3–15.

Gordon, David F.

1986 *Decolonization and the State in Kenya*. Boulder, CO: Westview Press.

Gran, Guy

1990 "Policy and Strategy Issues in Participatory Rural Development in Africa." Paper presented at the Workshop on Planning and Implementation Techniques for Participatory Rural Development in Africa, organized by the Economic Commission for Africa and the Food and Agriculture Organization, Addis Ababa, Ethiopia.

Grant, Sandy, and Brian Egner

1989 "The Private Press and Democracy." In *Democracy in Botswana*, ed. J. D. Holm and P. P. Molutsi. Gaborone and Athens, OH: Macmillan Botswana and Ohio University Press.

Guba, Egon G.

1985 "The Context of Emergent Paradigm Research." In *Organizational Theory and Inquiry: The Paradigm Revolution*, ed. Y. S. Lincoln. Beverly Hills, CA: Sage Publications.

Guichaoua, André

1986. "Isolement et méconnaissance." *Revue Tiers-Monde* 27, no. 134 (May–June):245–252.

1989 *Destins paysans et politiques agraires en Afrique centrale*. Vol. 1: *L'ordre paysan des hautes terres centrales du Burundi et du Rwanda*. Paris: Éditions Harmattan.

Gyimah-Boadi, E.

1989 "Economic Recovery and Politics in the PNDC's Ghana." Paper presented at the Inter-Faculty Lecture, University of Ghana, Legon, August.

———, and Donald Rothchild

1982 "Rawlings, Populism and the Civil Liberties Tradition in Ghana." *Issue: A Journal of Opinion* 12, no. 3/4:64–69.

Habermas, Jürgen

1971 *Knowledge and Human Interests*. Boston: Beacon Press.

1973 *Legitimation Crisis*. Boston: Beacon Press.

1979 *Communications and the Evolution of Society*. Trans. Thomas McCarthy. Boston: Beacon Press.

Habyarimana, Juvenal

1988 "Discours du Général-Major Habyarimana Juvenal, Président de la République et Président fondateur du M.R.N.D. à l'ouverture et à la clôture du séminaire national des bourgmestres, tenu à Kigali du 18 au 21 avril 1988." Kigali: Service de l'Information et des Archives Nationales, Présidence de la République Rwandaise.

Harbeson, John W.
1986 "Constitutions and Constitutionalism in Africa: A Tentative Theoretical Exploration." In *Democracy and Pluralism in Africa*, ed. Dov Ronen. Boulder, CO: Lynne Rienner Publishers.

Harroy, Jean-Paul
1984 *Rwanda: de la féodalité à la démocratie*. Brussels: Hayez.

Harvey, Charles, and Stephen R. Lewis
1990 *Public Choice and Development Performance in Botswana*. London: Macmillan.

Hayward, Fred M., ed.
1987 *Elections in Independent Africa*. Boulder, CO: Westview Press.

Heper, Metin
1986 "Extremely 'Strong State' and Democracy: The Turkish Case in Comparative and Historical Perspective." Paper presented at the Conference on Comparative Dynamics of Democratization, Israel Academy of Sciences, Jerusalem, December.

Herbst, Jeffrey
1990 "Migration, the Politics of Protest and State Consolidation in Africa." *African Affairs* 84, no. 235:183–204.

Hill, Stuart, and Donald Rothchild
1986 "The Contagion of Political Conflict in Africa and the World." *Journal of Conflict Resolution* 30, no. 4 (December):716–735

Hirschman, Albert O.
1970 *Exit, Voice and Loyalty: Responses to Decline in Firms, Organizations and States*. Cambridge, MA: Harvard University Press.
1981 *Essays in Trespassing: Economics to Politics and Beyond*. London: Cambridge University Press.
1984 *Getting Ahead Collectively: Grassroots Experiences in Latin America*. New York: Pergamon.

Hitchcock, Robert H.
1978 *Kalahari Cattle Posts*. Gaborone: Government Printer.

Hoben, Susan J.
1989 *School, Work and Equity: Educational Reform in Rwanda*. African Research Studies no. 16. Boston: Boston University African Studies Center.

Hodder-Williams, Richard
1984 *An Introduction to the Politics of Tropical Africa*. London: George Allen and Unwin.

Holm, John D.
1988 "Botswana: A Paternalistic Democracy." In *Democracy in Developing Countries. Vol. 2: Africa*, ed. L. Diamond, J. Linz, and S. M. Lipset. Boulder, CO: Lynne Rienner Publishers.
———, and Patrick P. Molutsi, eds.
1989 *Democracy in Botswana*. Gaborone and Athens, OH: Macmillan Botswana and Ohio University Press.

Holmquist, Frank
1980 "Defending Peasant Political Space in Independent Africa." *Canadian Journal of African Studies* 14, no. 1:157–167.
1984 "Self-Help: The State and Peasant Leeverage in Kenya." *Africa* 54:72–91.

Horowitz, Donald L.
1985 *Ethnic Groups in Conflict*. Berkeley: University of California Press.

1988 "Cause and Consequence in Public Policy Theory: The Malaysian System Transforming Itself." Working Paper, no. 32 (January). Duke University Program in International Political Economy, Durham, NC.

Hountondji, Paulin J.
1983 *African Philosophy: Myth and Reality.* Bloomington: Indiana University Press.

Houyoux, Joseph, Kinavwuidi Niwembo, and Okita Onya
1986 *Budgets des Ménages, Kinshasa, 1986.* Kinshasa: Bureau d'Études, d'Aménagement et d'Urbanisme.

Howard, Rhoda, E.
1986 *Human Rights in Commonwealth Africa.* Totowa, NJ: Rowman and Littlefield.

Hult, Karen M., and Charles Walcott
1990 *Governing Public Organizations: Politics, Structures and Institutional Design.* Pacific Grove, CA: Brooks/Cole.

Huntington, Samuel P.
1968 *Political Order in Changing Societies.* New Haven, CT: Yale University Press.

Hutchful, Eboe
1986 "New Elements in Militarism: Ethiopia, Ghana, and Burkina." *International Journal* 41 (Autumn):802–830.

Hyden, Goran
1980 *Beyond Ujamaa in Tanzania: Underdevelopment and an Uncaptured Peasantry.* Berkeley: University of California Press.
1983 *No Shortcuts to Progress: African Development Management in Perspective.* Berkeley: University of California Press.
1988 "Governance: A New Approach to Comparative Politics." Paper presented at the Annual Meeting of the African Studies Association, Chicago, October 28–31 .
1989 "Governance and Liberalization: Tanzania in Comparative Perspective." Paper presented at the Annual Meeting of the American Political Science Association, Atlanta, August 31–September 3 .
1990 "Reciprocity and Governance in Africa." In *The Failure of the Centralized State*, ed. J. Wunsch and D. Olowu. Boulder, CO: Westview Press.

Ihinmodu, I. I.
1982 "Problems of Revenue Mobilization in Kwara State: A Case Study of the Effects of Abolishing Poll/Community Taxes." Paper presented at the International Conference on the Evolution of Local Government in West Africa, Ile-Ife, Nigeria.

Ilchman, Warren, and Norman T. Uphoff
1969 *The Political Economy of Change.* Berkeley: University of California Press.

Iliffe, John
1979 *A Modern History of Tanganyika.* Cambridge: Cambridge University Press.

ILO (International Labour Organization)
1982 *Basic Needs in Danger: A Basic Needs Oriented Development Strategy for Tanzania.* Addis Ababa: International Labour Office, Jobs Skills Programme for Africa.

Itangishaka, Bernard
1988 "Pour la défense du revenu du paysan." *Dialogue* no. 130 (September–October):26–36.
Jackson, Robert H., and Carl G. Rosberg
1982 *Personal Rule in Black Africa.* Berkeley: University of California Press.
Jagannathan, N. Vijay
1987 *Informal Markets in Developing Countries.* London: Oxford University Press.
Jeffries, Richard
1982 "Ghana: Jerry Rawlings ou un populisme à deux coups." *Politique Africaine* 2, no. 8:8–20.
Jinadu, Adele
1985 "Federalism, the Consociational State, and Ethnic Conflict in Nigeria." *Publius* 15 (Spring):71–100.
Jonah, Kwesi
1987 "The IMF in Ghana's Political Economy." Paper presented at the Conference on the Post-Colonial State and National Development, University of Ghana, Legon, April.
1989 "Crisis and Response in Ghana." Working paper (April). University of West Indies Institute of Social and Economic Research, Kingston, Jamaica.
Joseph, Richard
1987 *Democracy and Prebendal Politics in Nigeria.* New York: Cambridge University Press.
1990 "Political Renewal in Sub-Saharan Africa: The Challenge of the 1990s." In Carter Center, "African Governance in the 1990s." Atlanta: Carter Center.
Kabeya, Charles
1987 "Évolution et rôle des syndicats au Burkina." *Presence Africaine* 142 (2d Trimester):130–147.
Kaïdi, Hamza
1990 "Rwanda: Economie. Quand le café ne paie plus." *Jeune Afrique* no. 1526 (April 2):42–43.
Kaniki, M. N. Y.
1974 "TANU: The Party of Independence and National Consolidation," in *Towards Ujamaa: Twenty Years of Tanu Leadership*, ed. Gabriel Ruhumbika. Dar es Salaam: East African Literature Bureau.
Kasfir, Nelson
1974 "Departicipation and Political Development in Black African Politics." *Studies in Comparative International Development* 9, no. 3:3–25.
1976a *The Shrinking Political Arena.* Berkeley: University of California Press.
1976b "Civilian Participation under Military Rule in Uganda and Sudan." In *Political Participation under Military Regimes*, ed. H. Bienen and D. Morell. Beverly Hills, CA: Sage Publications.
1983 "Relating Class to State in Africa." *Journal of Commonwealth and Comparative Politics* 21, no. 3:1–21.
1987 "Class, Political Domination and the African State." In *The African State in Transition*, ed. Zaki Ergas. London: Macmillan.

Keller, Edmond
    1988   *Revolutionary Ethiopia: From Empire to People's Republic.*
            Bloomington: Indiana University Press.
Kenya
    1970   *Kenya Population Census, 1969.* Vol. 1. Nairobi: Government
            Printer.
    1986   *Economic Management for Renewed Growth.* Nairobi: Government
            Printer.
    1990   "The Non-Governmental Organization Bill of 1990." Nairobi:
            Government Printer.
————. Office of the President
    1987   *District Focus for Rural Development.* Nairobi: Government Printer.
Khapoya, Vincent
    1991   *The African Experience: An Interdisciplinary Introduction to African
            Studies.* Englewood Cliffs, NJ: Prentice-Hall.
Kilson, Martin
    1987   "Anatomy of African Class Consciousness: Agrarian Populism in
            Ghana from 1915 to the 1940s and Beyond." In *Studies in Power and
            Class in Africa*, ed. I. L. Markovitz. London: Oxford University
            Press.
Kiser, Larry, and Elinor Ostrom
    1982   "The Three Worlds of Action: A Meta-Theoretical Synthesis of
            Institutional Approaches." In *Strategies of Political Inquiry*, ed. E.
            Ostrom. Beverly Hills, CA: Sage Publications.
Kleemeier, Lizz
    1984   "Domestic Policies vs. Poverty-Oriented Foreign Assistance in
            Tanzania." *The Journal of Development Studies* 20, no. 2:171–201.
Klingman, D.
    1980   "Temporal and Spatial Diffusion in the Comparative Analysis of
            Social Change." *American Political Science Review* 74, no. 1
            (March):123–137.
Konings, Piet
    1986   *The State and Rural Class Formation in Ghana.* London: KPI.
Kountché, Seyni
    1974   "Discours programme de Président du Conseil Militaire Suprême, chef
            de l'Etat." Niamey: Imprimerie Nationale.
    1979   "Résultats édifiants d'un Sursaut National." Niamey: Imprimerie
            Nationale.
Kulaba, Saitiel
    1989   "Local Government and the Management of Urban Services in
            Tanzania." In *African Cities in Crisis: Managing Rapid Urban
            Growth*, ed. R. E. Stren and R. R. White. Boulder, CO: Westview
            Press.
Kunz, Frank
    1990   "Liberalization in Africa: Some Preliminary Reflections." Paper
            presented at the Center for African Studies, University of Florida.
Lancaster, Carol
    1990   "Governance in Africa: Should Foreign Aid be Linked to Political
            Reform?" In Carter Center, "African Governance in the 1990s."
            Atlanta: Carter Center.
Lasswell, Harold, and Myres S. McDougal
    1943   "Legal Education and Public Policy." *Yale Law Journal* 52, no. 2
            (March):203–295.

Legum, Colin
1990   "What Is Behind the Demand for Multi-Party Democracy?" *Third World Reports*, O.C./2 (July 18):1–2.
———, ed.
1988   "Rwanda." In *Africa Contemporary Record 1986–87*. New York and London: Africana Publishing.
Lemarchand, René
1970   *Rwanda and Burundi*. London: Pall Mall.
1972   "Political Clientelism and Ethnicity in Tropical Africa." *American Political Science Review* 66, no. 1 (March):68–90.
1982   "The World Bank in Rwanda: The Case of the Office de Valorisation Agricole et Pastorale du Mutara (OVAPAM)." Bloomington: Indiana University African Studies Program.
1987   "The Dynamics of Factionalism in Contemporary Africa." In *The African State in Transition*, ed. Zaki Ergas. London: Macmillan.
1988   "The State, the Parallel Economy, and the Changing Structure of Patronage Systems." In *The Precarious Balance: State and Society in Africa*, ed. Donald Rothchild and Naomi Chazan. Boulder, CO: Westview Press.
Leslie, J.A.K.
1963   *A Survey of Dar es Salaam*. London: Oxford University Press.
Le Vine, Victor
1989   "Parapolitics: Notes for a Theory." Unpublished manuscript.
Leys, Colin
1974   *Underdevelopment in Kenya*. Berkeley, University of California Press.
Liebenow, Gus
1985   "The Military Factor in African Politics: A Twenty-Five Year Perspective." In *African Independence: The First Twenty-Five Years*, ed. G. M. Carter and P. O'Meara. Bloomington: Indiana University Press.
1986   *African Politics: Crises and Challenges*. Bloomington: Indiana University Press.
Lijphart, Arend
1977   *Democracy in Plural Societies: A Comprehensive Exploration*. New Haven, CT: Yale University Press.
1981   *Conflict and Coexistence in Belgium*. Berkeley: University of California Institute of International Studies.
1985a   "Non-Majoritarian Democracy: A Comparison of Federal and Consociational Theories." *Publius* 15 (Spring):3–15.
1985b   *Power-Sharing in South Africa*. Berkeley: University of California Institute of International Studies.
Lindblom, Charles E.
1977   *Politics and Markets*. New Haven, CT: Yale University Press.
Linden, Ian, and Jane Linden
1977   *Church and Revolution in Rwanda*. Manchester, Eng.: Manchester University Press.
Linz, Juan L., and Alfred Stepan, eds.
1978   *The Breakdown of Democratic Regimes*. 4 vols. Baltimore, MD: Johns Hopkins University Press.
Little, Peter D., and Michael Horowitz
1987   "Subsistence Crops *Are* Cash Crops: Some Comments with

Reference to Eastern Africa." *Human Organization* 46, no. 3:254–258.

1988   "Authors' Reply." *Human Organization* 47, no. 3:271–273.

Lofchie, Michael
1989   "Perestroika without Glasnost: Reflections on Structural Adjustment." In Carter Center, "Beyond Autocracy in Africa." Atlanta: Carter Center.

Lomnitz, Larissa Adler
1988   "Informal Exchange Networks in Formal Systems: A Theoretical Model." Universidad Nacional Autónoma de México. Unpublished manuscript.

———, and Claudio Lomnitz Adler
1989   "La representación simbólica del poder: política, ritual y símbolo en la compañía presidencial del Partido Revolucionario Institucional de México." Unpublished manuscript.

Lonsdale, John
1986   "Political Accountability in African History." In *Political Domination in Africa*, ed. Patrick Chabal. Cambridge: Cambridge University Press.

Lowenthal, Abraham
1986   "International Aspects of Democratization." In *Transitions from Authoritarian Rule: Comparative Perspectives*, ed. G. O'Donnell, P. C. Schmitter, and L. Whitehead. Baltimore, MD: Johns Hopkins University Press.

MacGaffey, Janet
1987   *Entrepreneurs and Parasites: The Struggle for Indigenous Capitalism in Zaire*. New York: Cambridge University Press.

———, Vwakyanakazi Mukohya, Rukarangira wa Nkera, Brooke Grundfest Schoepf, Makwala ma Mavumbu ye Beda, and Walu Engundu
1991   *The Real Economy of Zaire*. London and Philadelphia: James Currey and University of Pennsylvania Press.

Maclure, Robert A.
1988   "Intervention and Dependency: A Case Study of *Animation Rurale* in Burkina Faso." Ph.D. diss., Stanford University.

Magassouba, M.
1985   *L'Islam au Sénégal—demain les mollahs?* Paris: Karthala.

Makwala ma Mavambu ye Beda
1991   "The Trade in Food Crops, Manufactured Goods and Mineral Products in the Frontier Zone of Luozi, Lower Zaire." In J. MacGaffey et al., *The Real Economy of Zaire*. London and Philadelphia: James Currey and University of Pennsylvania Press.

Malloy, James M., ed.
1977   *Authoritarianism and Corporatism in Latin America*. Pittsburgh, PA: University of Pittsburgh Press.

Maquet, Jacques J., and Marcel d'Hertefelt
1959   *Élections en société féodale: une étude sur l'introduction du vote populaire au Ruanda-Urundi*. Brussels: Académie Royale des Sciences Coloniales.

March, James G., and Johan P. Olsen
1984   "The New Institutionalism: Organizational Factors in Political Life." *American Political Science Review* 78, no. 3 (September):734–749.

1989   *Rediscovering Institutions: The Organizational Basis of Politics*. New York: Free Press.

Marenin, Otwin
1987　"The Managerial State in Africa: A Conflict Coalition Perspective."
In *The African State in Transition*, ed. Zaki Ergas. London:
Macmillan.
1988　"The Nigerian State as Process and Manager: A Conceptualization."
Comparative Politics 20, no. 2 (January):215–232.
Marijsse, S.
1982　"Basic Needs, Income Distribution and the Political Economy of
Rwanda." Center for Development Studies Paper, no 82. Antwerp,
University of Antwerp.
Martin, Guy
1987　"Ideology and Praxis in Thomas Sankara's Populist Revolution of
August 4, 1983 in Burkina Faso." *Issue: A Journal of Opinion* 15:77–
90.
Mattera, Philip
1985　*Off-the-Books: The Rise of the Underground Economy*. New York: St.
Martin's Press.
Mbembe, Achille
1988　*Afriques indociles*. Paris: L'Harmattan.
1989　"Economic Liberalization and the Post-Colonial African State." In
Carter Center, "Beyond Autocracy in Africa." Atlanta: Carter Center.
Mbithi, Philip, and Rasmus Rasmusson
1977　*Self-Reliance in Kenya: The Case of Harambee*. Uppsala:
Scandinavian Institute of African Studies.
Mbugulize, Ephrem
1986　"Autosuffisance alimentaire: mythe ou réalité?." *Dialogue* no. 117
(July–August):5–15.
Melson, Robert, and Howard Wolpe, eds.
1971　*Nigeria: Modernization and the Politics of Communalism*. East
Lansing: Michigan State University Press.
Mensah, Kwaku
1989　"Equal Rights and Justice." *West Africa* 3725:21–22.
Mfizi, Christophe
1983　*Les lignes de faite du Rwanda Independant*. Kigali: Office Rwandais
d'Information.
Mgadla, P. T., and A. C. Campbell
1989　"Dikgotla, Dikgosi and the Protectorate Administration." In
Democracy in Botswana, ed. J. D. Holm and P. P. Molutsi. Gaborone
and Athens, OH:Macmillan Botswana and Ohio University Press.
Migdal, Joel
1988　*Strong Societies and Weak States: State-Society Relations and State
Capabilities in the Third World*. Princeton, NJ: Princeton University
Press.
Mikell, Gwendolyn
1989　"The State, Local Resources and Political Participation in Ghana."
Paper presented at the Annual Meeting of the African Studies
Association, Atlanta, October 31–November 3.
Miles, William
1988　*Elections in Nigeria: A Grassroots Perspective*. Boulder, CO: Lynne
Rienner Publishers.
Miller, Norman N.
1970　"The Rural African Party: Political Participation in Tanzania."
American Political Science Review 64, no. 2 (June):548–571.

Mlimuka, Aggrey K. L. J., and Palamagamba J. A. M. Kabudi
  1985   "The State and the Party." In *The State and the Working People in Tanzania*, ed. Issa G. Shivji. Dakar: Codesria.
Moi, Daniel arap
  1985   Speech delivered at Kenya Institute of Administration, Nairobi, March 6.
Molokomme, Athaliah
  1989   "Political Rights in Botswana: Regression or Development?" In *Democracy in Botswana*, ed. J. D. Holm and P. P. Molutsi. Gaborone and Athens, OH: Macmillan Botswana and Ohio University Press.
Molutsi, Patrick
  1991   "International Influences on Botswana's Democracy." Paper presented at a symposium on The Political Economy of Botswana, School of Advanced International Studies, Johns Hopkins University, Washington, DC, April.
———, and John D. Holm
  1990   "Developing Democracy When Civil Society Is Weak: The Case of Botswana." *African Affairs* 89 (July):323–340.
Moore, Barrington, Jr.
  1966   *Social Origins of Dictatorship and Democracy*. Boston: Beacon Press.
Moore, Sally F.
  1988   "Legitimation as a Process: The Expansion of Government and the Party in Tanzania." In *State Formation and Political Legitimacy*, ed. Ronald Cohen and J. D. Toland. New Brunswick, NJ: Transaction Books.
Morna, Colleen Lowe
  1990   "Pluralism: A Luxury No More." *Africa Report*, 35, no. 5 (November–December).
Mugaju, J. B.
  1988   "The Illusions of Democracy in Uganda, 1955–1966." In *Democratic Theory and Practice in Africa*, ed. Walter Oyugi, E. S. Atieno Odhiambo, Michael Chege, and Afrifa Gitonga. Portsmouth, NH: Heinemann.
Mugesera, Antoine
  1986   "Le prix des produits rwandaise." *Dialogue* no. 119 (November–December):30–43.
Mugyenyi, Meddi
  1988   "Development First, Democracy Second." In *Democratic Theory and Practice in Africa*, ed. Walter Oyugi, E. S. Atieno Odhiambo, Michael Chege, and Afrifa Gitonga. Portsmouth, NH: Heinemann.
Mukayiranga, Landrada
  1986   "Femmes et société rwandaise." *Dialogue* no. 115 (March–April):61–68.
Munyarugerero, François-Xavier
  1990a   "Rwanda: ou au multipartisme." *Jeune Afrique* no. 1560 (November 21–27):7.
  1990b   "Dérapages de moins en moins contrôlés." *Jeune Afrique* no. 1562 (December 5–11):29.
  1990c   "Rwanda: plus dur sera l'ajustement." *Jeune Afrique* no. 1562 (December 5–11):74–75.

Murego, Donat
1975   *La révolution rwandaise, 1959–60.* Louvain: Institut des Sciences Politiques et Sociales.
National Commission for Democracy
1991   *Evolving a True Democracy: Summary of NCD's Work Towards the Establishment of a New Democratic Order.* Accra: Ghana Publishing Corporation.
National Defence Committee
N.d.   *Guidelines for the Formation and Functioning of the People's Defence Committees.* Accra: Government Printer.
Ndegwa, Philip
1982   *Report and Recommendation of the Working Party.* Nairobi: Government Printer.
Nelson, Joan
1984   "The Political Capacity of Stabilization: Commitment, Capacity and Public Response." *World Development* 12, no. 10:983–1006.
Newbury, Catharine
1978   "Ethnicity in Rwanda: The Case of Kinyaga." *Africa* 48, no. 1:17–29.
1980   "Ubureetwa and Thangata: Catalysts to Peasant Political Consciousness in Rwanda and Malawi." *Canadian Journal of African Studies* 14, no. 1:97–112.
1983   "Colonialism, Ethnicity, and Rural Political Protest: Rwanda and Zanzibar in Comparative Perspective." *Comparative Politics* 15, no. 3:253–280.
1984   "Dead and Buried or Just Underground? The Privatization of the State in Zaire." *Canadian Journal of African Studies* 18, no. 1:112–115.
1986   "Survival Strategies in Rural Zaire: Realities of Coping with Crisis." In *The Crisis in Zaire: Myths and Realities,* ed. Nzongola Ntalaja. Trenton, NJ: Africa World Press.
1988   *The Cohesion of Oppression: Clientship and Ethnicity in Rwanda, 1860–1960.* New York: Columbia University Press.
Newbury, David
1986   "From 'Frontier to Boundary': Some Historical Roots of Peasant Strategies of Survival in Zaire." In *The Crisis in Zaire, Myths and Realities,* ed. Nzongola Ntalaja. Trenton, NJ: Africa World Press.
Ngcongco, Leonard D.
1989   "Tswana Political Tradition: How Democratic?" In *Democracy in Botswana,* ed. J. D.Holm and P. P. Molutsi. Gaborone and Athens, OH: Macmillan Botswana and Ohio University Press.
Ngom, Benoit S.
1989   *L'arbitrage d'une démocratie en Afrique: la Cour Suprême du Sénégal.* Paris: Éditions Presence Africaine.
Nicol, Davidson
1986   "African Pluralism and Democracy." In *Democracy and Pluralism in Africa,* ed. Dov Ronen. Boulder, CO: Lynne Rienner Publishers.
Nigeria
1978   *Constitution of the Federal Republic of Nigeria.* Lagos: Government Printer.
1980a   *Report of the Presidential Commission of Revenue Allocation.* Vol. 1. Lagos: Government Printer.

1980b *Fourth National Development Plan, 1981–85.* Lagos: Government Printer.
1989   *Constitution of the Federal Republic of Nigeria.* Lagos: Government Printer.
Nimbona, Gabriella
1988   "Groupements féminins et développement communal." *Dialogue* no. 131 (November–December):64–77.
Nimtz, August H., Jr.
1980   *Islam and Politics in East Africa: The Sufi Order in Tanzania.* Minneapolis: University of Minnesota Press.
Ninsin, Kwame A.
1987   "Ghanaian Politics after 1981: Revolution or Evolution." *Canadian Journal of African Studies* 21, no. 1:17–37.
1988   "Recognizing Left and Right in Ghanaian Politics: A Reply to Ahiakpor." *Canadian Journal of African Studies* 22, no. 1:137–139.
1990   "District Assemblies as a Solution to the Crisis of Governance in Ghana." In Carter Center, "African Governance in the 1990s." Atlanta: Carter Center.
———, and F. K. Drah, eds.
1987   *The Search for Democracy in Ghana.* Accra: Assempa Publishers.
Niskanen, William A.
1971   *Bureaucracy and Representative Government.* Chicago: Aldine-Atherton.
Niyibizi, Tite
1987   "Le Plan d'Action Communal." In *Les projets de développement rural: réussites, échecs et stratégies nouvelles,* ed. A. Nkundabashaka and J. Voss. Butare: Université Nationale du Rwanda.
Nkundabashaka, Augustin
1987   "Introduction et méthodologie du développement." In *Les projets de développement rural: réussites, échecs et stratégies nouvelles,* ed. A. Nkundabashaka and J. Voss. Butare, Université National du Rwanda.
Nnoli, Okwudiba
1978   *Ethnic Politics in Nigeria.* Enugu: Fourth Dimension Publishers.
Ntakirutimana, Jean-Damascène
1990   "Multipartisme: Leurre ou espoir?" *Dialogue* no. 144 (January–February):105–119.
Ntamahungiro, Joseph
1988   "Eloge du paysan rwandais." *Dialogue* no. 130 (September–October):5–16.
1989   "Flash sur les 3emes législatives." *Dialogue* no. 133 (March–April):4–13.
Ntazinda, Charles
1990   "Les grand problèmes de l'heure au Rwanda." *Dialogue* no. 144 (January–February):85–98.
Ntezimana, Emmanuel
1978   "*Kinyamateka, Temps nouveaux d'Afrique* et l'évolution socio-politique du Rwanda (1954–1959)." *Etudes Rwandaises,* special issue (March):1–29.
1990   "Principes essentiels et conditions préalables à la démocratie." *Dialogue* no. 144 (January–February):33–49.
Nwabueze, Ben O.
1985   *Nigeria's Presidential Constitution: The Second Experiment in Constitutional Democracy.* London: Longman.

Nwankwo, G. Onyekwere
  1984 "Management Problems of the Proliferation of Local Government in Nigeria." *Public Administration and Development* 4, no. 1:63–76.
Nyerere, Julius K.
  1973 *Freedom and Development.* Dar es Salaam: Oxford University Press.
Oakerson, Ronald
  1983 "Reciprocity: The Political Nexus." Paper prepared for the Workshop in Political Theory and Policy Analysis, Indiana University, Bloomington.
Obasanjo, Olusegun
  1987 *Africa in Perspective: Myths and Realities.* New York: Council on Foreign Relations.
O'Connell, James
  1970 "The Fragility of Stability: The Fall of the Nigerian Federal Government." In *Protest and Power in Black Africa*, ed. Robert I. Rotberg and Ali A. Mazrui. New York: Oxford University Press.
O'Donnell, Guillermo A.
  1973 *Modernization and Bureaucratic-Authoritarian States in South American Politics.* Berkeley: University of California Institute of International Studies.
————, Philippe Schmitter, and Laurence Whitehead, eds.
  1986 "Transitions from Authoritarian Rule: Tentative Conclusions About Uncertain Democracies." In *Transitions from Authoritarian Rule: Comparative Perspectives.* Baltimore, MD: Johns Hopkins University Press.
Okeke, Barbara
  1982 *4 June: A Revolution Betrayed.* Enugu: Ikenga Publishers.
Okpu, Ugbana
  1984 "Nigerian Political Parties and the Federal Character." *Journal of Ethnic Studies* 12 (Spring):119–126.
Okuridibo, Justice Anthony A.
  1987 *Report of the Judicial Commission of Inquiry into the Activities of the Federal Ministry of Works and Housing, 1979–1980.* Lagos: Government Printer.
Olorunsola, Victor A.
  1986 "Questions on Constitutionalism and Democracy: Nigeria and Africa." In *Democracy and Pluralism in Africa*, ed. Dov Ronen. Boulder, CO: Westview Press.
Olson, Mancur
  1965 *The Logic of Collective Action.* Cambridge, MA: Harvard University Press.
Olurode, Olayiwola
  1987 "Grassroots Politics, Political Factions, and Conflict in Nigeria: The Case of Iwo, 1976–83." *Rural Africana* 25/26 (Spring–Fall):113–124.
Omoruyi, Omo
  1990 "Federal Character and the Party System in the Second Republic." In *Federal Character and Federalism in Nigeria*, ed. Peter Ekeh and Eghosa E. Osaghae. London: Heinemann.
Onwordi, Ike
  1988 "The Compaoré Enigma." *West Africa* 3716: (October 31–November 6):2028.

Oquaye, Mike
1980   *Politics in Ghana, 1972–79.* Accra: Tornado Publications.
Osaghae, Eghosa E.
1988   "The Complexity of Nigeria's Federal Character and the Inadequacies of the Federal Character Principle." *Journal of Ethnic Studies* 16 (Fall):1–25.
Ostrom, Elinor
1990   *Crafting Irrigation Institutions: Social Capital and Development.* Decentralization: Finance and Management Project. Burlington, VT: Associates in Rural Development.
Otayek, René
1987   "Burkina Faso." *Politique Africaine* 28 (December):120–121.
Ouchi, William
1981   *Theory Z: How American Business Can Meet the Japanese Challenge.* Reading, MA: Addison-Wesley.
Oyovbaire, Samuel E.
1984   *Federalism in Nigeria: A Study of the Development of the Nigerian State.* New York: St. Martin's Press.
Pain, Marc
1984   *Kinshasa: la Ville et la Cité.* Paris: Éditions de l'ORSTOM.
Paul, James C. N.
1990   "Participatory Approaches to Human Rights in Sub-Saharan Africa." In *Human Rights in Africa: Cross-Cultural Perspectives,* ed. A. Ahmed Ab-Na'im and F. M. Deng. Washington, DC: Brookings Institution.
Peil, Margaret
1976   *Nigerian Politics: The People's View.* London: Cassell.
Pellow, Deborah, and Naomi Chazan
1986   *Ghana: Coping with Uncertainty.* Boulder, CO: Westview Press.
Peters, T. J., and R. H. Waterman
1982   *In Search of Excellence: Lessons from America's Best Run Companies.* New York: Harper and Row.
Picard, Louis A.
1987   *The Politics of Development in Botswana: A Model for Success?* Boulder, CO: Lynne Rienner Publishers.
Pinkney, Robert
1988   "Ghana: An Alternating Military/Party System." In *Political Parties in the Third World,* ed. V. Randall. London: Sage Publications.
Pollis, Adamantia, and Peter Schwab, eds.
1979   *Human Rights: Cultural and Ideological Perspectives.* New York: Praeger.
Posnansky, Merrick
1984   "Ghana: Hardship of a Village." *West Africa:*2161.
Post, Kenneth W. J., and Michael Vickers
1973   *Structure and Conflict in Nigeria 1960–1966.* Madison: University of Wisconsin Press.
Powell. G. Bingham, Jr.
1982   *Contemporary Democracies: Participation, Stability, and Violence.* Cambridge, MA: Harvard University Press.
Pradervand, Pierre
1989   *Listening to Africa: Developing Africa From the Grassroots.* New York: Praeger.

Pratt, Cranford
  1979   "Tanzania's Transition to Socialism: Reflections of a Democratic Socialist." In *Towards Socialism in Tanzania*, ed. B. Mwansasu and C. Pratt. Toronto: University of Toronto Press.
Press, Robert M.
  1990   "Rwandan Rebels Offer Cease-Fire, But Land, Ethnic Issues Simmer." *Christian Science Monitor*, October 24.
Price, Robert
  1984   "Neo-Colonialism and Ghana's Economic Decline: A Critical Assessment." *Canadian Journal of African Studies* 18, no. 1:163–193.
"Procès an rédacteurs du journal *Kinyamateka*."
  1990   *Dialogue* no. 143 (November–December):90–96.
Przeworski, Adam
  1986   "Some Problems in the Study of Transition to Democracy." In *Transitions from Authoritarian Rule*, ed. G. O'Donnell, P. Schmitter, and L. Whitehead. Baltimore, MD: Johns Hopkins University Press.
Pye, Lucian W.
  1990   "Political Science and the Crisis of Authoritarianism." *American Political Science Review* 84, no. 1 (March):3–21.
Rado, Emil
  1986   "Notes Towards a Political Economy of Ghana Today." *African Affairs* 18, no. 1:563–572.
Rae, Douglas
  1979. "The Egalitarian State: Notes on a System of Contradictory Ideals." *Daedalus* 108, no. 4:37–54.
Ranger, Terence O.
  1975   *Dance and Society in Eastern Central Africa: The Beni Ngoma 1890–1970*. London: Heinemann.
Rawlings, Jerry J.
  1983   "Discipline and Productivity: Radio and Television Broadcast, Sunday 28 August, 1983." Accra: Government Printer.
  N.d.   *A Revolutionary Journey: Selected Speeches of Flt-Lt Jerry J. Rawlings, Chairman of the PNDC, Dec 31, 1981–Dec. 31, 1982.* Vol. 1. Accra: Ghana Publishing Corporation.
Ray, Donald I.
  1986   *Ghana: Politics, Economics and Society.* London: Frances Pinter.
Reyntjens, Filip
  1980   "La nouvelle constitution rwandaise du 20 septembre 1978." *Penant* 90, no. 768:117–134.
  1984   "Les élections rwandaises du 26 décembre 1983: considérations juridiques et politiques." *Le Mois en Afrique* nos. 223–224:18–28.
  1985   *Pouvoir et droit au Rwanda. Droit public et évolution politique, 1916–1973.* Tervuren: Musée Royale de l'Afrique Centrale.
  1988   "Rwanda: Recent History." In *Africa South of the Sahara 1989.* London: Europa Publications.
  1989   "Cooptation politique à l'envers: les législatives de 1988 au Rwanda." *Politique Africaine* no. 34:121–126.
"The Right to Choose."
  1988   *Africa News* 30, no. 3 (August 8).

Robertson, Claire
 1983 "The Death of Makola and Other Tragedies." *Canadian Journal of African Studies* 17, no. 3:469–495.

Robins, Edward, and Valens Ndoreyaho
 1988 "Agricultural Policy and Practice in Rwanda: A Response to Little and Horowitz." *Human Organization* 47, no. 3:270–271.

Robinson, Pearl
 Forthcoming "Niger. Anatomy of a Neotraditional Corporatist State." *Comparative Politics.*

Robotham, Don
 1988 "The Ghana Problem." *Labour, Capital and Society* 21, no. 1:12–35.

Rochon, Thomas R., and Michael J. Mitchell
 1989 "Social Bases of the Transition to Democracy in Brazil." *Comparative Politics* 21, no. 3:307–322.

Rogers, S. G.
 1983 "Efforts Toward Women's Development in Tanzania: Gender Rhetoric vs Gender Realities." In *Women in Developing Countries: A Policy Focus*, ed. K. Staudt and J. Jaquette. New York: Haworth Press.

Ronen, Dov, ed.
 1986 *Democracy and Pluralism in Africa.* Boulder, CO: Lynne Rienner Publishers.

Rotberg, Robert I., and John Barrat, eds.
 1980 *Conflict and Compromise in South Africa.* Cape Town: David Philip.

Rothchild, Donald
 1985 "State-Ethnic Relations in Middle Africa." In *African Independence: The First Twenty-Five Years*, ed. Gwendolen Carter and Patrick O'Meara. Bloomington: Indiana University Press.

 1986a "Hegemonial Exchange: An Alternative Model for Managing Conflict in Middle Africa." In *Ethnicity, Politics and Development*, ed. D. L. Thompson and D. Ronen. Boulder, CO: Lynne Rienner Publishers.

 1986b "Interethnic Conflict and Policy Analysis in Africa." *Ethnic and Racial Studies* 9 (January):66–86.

 1987 "Hegemony and State Softness: Some Variations in Elite Responses." In *The African State in Transition*, ed. Zaki Ergas. London: Macmillan.

 ———, ed.
 1991 *Ghana: The Political Economy of Recovery.* Boulder, CO: Lynne Rienner Publishers.

Rothchild, Donald, and Naomi Chazan, eds.
 1988 *The Precarious Balance: State and Society in Africa.* Boulder, CO: Westview Press.

Rothchild, Donald, and Michael Foley
 1983 "The Implications of Scarcity for Governance in Africa." *International Political Science Review* 4, no. 3:311–326.

 1988 "African States and the Politics of Inclusive Coalitions." In *The Precarious Balance: State and Society in Africa*, ed. D. Rothchild and N. Chazan. Boulder, CO: Westview Press.

Rothchild, Donald, and E. Gyimah-Boadi
 1986 "Ghana's Economic Decline and Development Strategies." In *Africa in Economic Crisis*, ed. John Ravenhill. New York: Columbia University Press.

1989   "Populism in Ghana and Burkina Faso." *Current History* 88, no. 538:241–244.
Rothchild, Donald, and Victor A. Olorunsola, eds.
1983   *State Versus Ethnic Claims: African Policy Dilemmas.* Boulder, CO: Westview Press.
Rothchild, Donald, and John Ravenhill
1991   "Retreat from Globalism: U.S. Policy Toward Africa in the 1990s." In *Eagle In a New World: American Grand Strategy in the Post-Cold War Era*, ed. Kenneth A. Oye, Robert J. Lieber, and Donald Rothchild. New York: Harper Collins.
Rukarangira wa Nkera and Brooke Grundfest Schoepf
1991   "Unrecorded Trade in Southeast Shaba and Across Zaire's Southern Border." In J. MacGaffey et al., *The Real Economy of Zaire.* London and Philadelphia: James Currey and University of Pennsylvania Press.
Rumiya, Jean
1985   "Ruanda d'hier, Rwanda d'aujourd'hui." *Vivant Univers* no. 357 (May–June):2–8.
Runge, Carlise F.
1986   "Common Property and Collective Action in Economic Development." *World Development* 14, no. 5:623–635.
Russell, Diane
1989   "The Outlook for Liberalization in Zaire: Evidence from Kisangani's Rice Trade." Working Papers in African Studies, No. 139. Boston: Boston University.
Rustow, Dankwart A.
1970   "Transitions to Democracy: Toward a Dynamic Model." *Comparative Politics* 2, no. 3 (April):337–364.
Rwanda
1985   *Résultats de l'enquête national agricole 1984*, Vol. 1. Kigali: Ministère de l'Agriculture, de l'Élevage et des Forêts.
Samoff, Joel
1973   "Cell Leaders in Tanzania: A Review of Recent Research." *Taamuli* (Dar es Salaam) 4, no. 1:63–75.
1974   *Tanzania: Local Politics and the Structure of Power.* Madison: University of Wisconsin Press.
1979   "The Bureaucracy and the Bourgeoisie: Decentralization and Class Structure in Tanzania." *Comparative Studies in History and Society* 21, no. 1:30–62.
Sandbrook, Richard
1972   "Patrons, Clients, and Factions: New Dimensions of Conflict Analysis in Africa." *Canadian Journal of African Studies* 17 (December):531–552.
1985   *The Politics of Africa's Economic Stagnation.* Cambridge: Cambridge University Press.
1990   "Taming the African Leviathan: Political Reform and Economic Recovery." *World Policy Journal* 7, no. 4, (Fall):673–701.
———, and Robin Cohen
1975   *The Development of the African Working Class: Studies in Class Formation and Action.* London: Longman.
Sankara, Thomas
1987   *Thomas Sankara Speaks: The Burkina Faso Revolution 1983–87.* trans. by Samantha Anderson. New York: Pathfinder Press.

Sartori, Giovanni
    1987   *The Theory of Democracy Revisited.* Chatham, NJ: Chatham House
             Publications.
Saul, John S.
    1985   *A Difficult Road: The Transition to Socialism in Mozambique.* New
             York: Monthly Review Press.
Schapera, Irving
    1970   *A Handbook of Tswana Law and Custom.* London: Frank Cass.
Schatzberg, Michael G.
    1980   *Politics and Class in Zaire.* New York: Africana.
    1988   *The Dialectics of Oppression in Zaire.* Bloomington: Indiana
             University Press.
Schneidman, Whitney W.
    1991   "Conflict Resolution in Mozambique: A Status Report." *CSIS Africa
             Notes* 121 (February 28).
Schoepf, Brooke G., and Walu Engundu
    1991   "Women's Trade and Contributions to Household Budgets in
             Kinshasa." In J. MacGaffey et al., *The Real Economy of Zaire.*
             London and Philadelphia: James Currey and University of
             Pennsylvania Press.
Sharkansky, Ira
    1979   *Whither the State?* Chatham, NJ: Chatham House Publications.
Sibomana, René
    1988   "Défendre le paysan c'est reconnaître son existence." *Dialogue* no.
             130 (September–October):17–25.
Sidikou, Hamidou, and Robert Charlick
    1985   *Organisations locales dans le Départment de Niamey.* Niamey:
             USAID.
Skinner, Elliott P.
    1958   "Christianity and Islam among the Mossi." *American
             Anthropologist* 60 (December):1102–1119.
    1988   "Sankara and the Burkinabé Revolution: Charisma and Power, Local
             and External Dimensions." *Journal of Modern African Studies* 26, no.
             3 (September):437–455.
    1989   *The Mossi of Burkina Faso: Chiefs, Politicians and Soldiers.*
             Prospect Heights, IL: Waveland Press.
Sklar, Richard
    1979   "The Nature of Class Domination in Africa." *Journal of Modern
             African Studies* 17, no. 4 (December):531–552.
    1986   "Democracy in Africa." In *Governing in Black Africa*, eds. Marion E.
             Doro and Newell M. Stultz. New York: Africana.
    1987   "Developmental Democracy." *Comparative Studies in Society and
             History* 29, no. 4:686–714.
Smith, B. C., and G. S. Owojaiye
    1981   "Constitutional, Legal, and Political Problems of Local Government
             in Nigeria." *Public Administration and Development* 1, no. 2:211–
             224.
Smith, J. D.
    1985   "Market Motives in the Informal Economy." In *The Economics of the
             Shadow Economy*, ed. G. Gaertner and A. Wenig. Heidelberg:
             Springer Verlag.
Somolekae, Gloriah
    1989   "Do Batswana Think and Act as Democrats?" In *Democracy in*

Botswana, ed. J. D. Holm and P. P. Molutsi. Gaborone and Athens, OH: Macmillan Botswana and Ohio University Press.

Soyinka, Wole
1972 *The Man Died*. London: Rex Collings.

Steiner, Jurg
1981 "The Consociational Theory and Beyond." *Comparative Politics* 13, no. 3 (April):339–354.

Streeck, Wolfgang, and Philippe C. Schmitter, eds.
1985 *Private Interest Government*. Beverly Hills, CA: Sage Publications.

Swantz, Lloyd W.
1965 "Church, Mission, and State Relations in Pre and Post Independent Tanzania (1955–64)." NTIS, no. 19. Syracuse, NY: Program of Eastern African Studies, Syracuse University Maxwell Graduate School of Citizenship and Public Affairs.

Swantz, Marja-Liisa
1985 *Women in Development: A Creative Role Denied?* London: C. Hurst.
1988 "Self-Reliance by Default." In *Approaches That Work in Rural Development*, ed. J. Burbridge. Munich: K. G. Saur.

Sylla, Salifou
1983–1985 "Les leçons des élections sénégalaises du 27 février 1983." *Annales Africaines* (Université Cheik Anta Diop de Dakar, Senegal).

Szelenyi, Ivan, Robert Manchin, Pal Juhasz, Balint Magyar, and Bill Martin
1988 *Socialist Entrepreneurs: Embourgeoisement in Rural Hungary*. Madison: University of Wisconsin Press.

Thomas, Barbara P.
1985 *Politics, Participation and Poverty: Development Through Self-Help in Kenya*. Boulder, CO: Westview Press.

Thomas, Clive
1984 *The Rise of the Authoritarian State in Peripheral Societies*. New York: Monthly Review Press.

Thompson, Michael, Richard Ellis and Aaron Wildavsky
1990 *Cultural Theory*. Boulder, CO: Westview Press.

Throup, David
1987 "The Construction and Deconstruction of the Kenyatta State." In *The Political Economy of Kenya*, ed. Michael Schatzberg. New York: Praeger.

Tilly, Charles, ed.
1975 *The Formation of Nation-States in Western Europe*. Princeton, NJ: Princeton University Press.

Toh, K.
1984 "Recent Macroeconomic Developments in Niger: Country Situation, Policy and Outlook." Annex G. In USAID/Niger, *Agricultural Sector Development Grant*. Niamey: USAID.

Triaud, Jean-Louis
1982 "L'Islam et l'état en République du Niger." *Le Mois en Afrique* 194–195 (January–February):37.

Tripp, Aili M.
1988 "Defending the Right to Subsist: The State vs Urban Informal Economy in Tanzania." Paper presented at the Annual Meeting of the African Studies Association, Chicago, October 28–31.

1989a   "Women and the Changing Urban Household Economy in Tanzania."
         Journal of Modern African Studies 27, no. 4:601–624.
1989b   "The Informal Economy, Labour and the State in Tanzania." Paper
         presented at the Annual Meeting of the African Studies Association,
         Chicago, October 28–31.
1990   "The Urban Informal Economy and the State in Tanzania." Ph.D.
         diss., Northwestern University, Evanston, IL.

Tseayo, J. I.
1980   "The Emirate System and Tiv Reaction to 'Pagan' Status in Northern
         Nigeria." In *Nigeria: Economy and Society*, ed. Gavin Williams.
         London: Rex Collings.

Tshibanza, Monji
1986   "Le 'Phénomène Creuseurs' et ses paradoxes." *Zaire Afrique* 206:345.
———, and Tshimanga Mulangula
1985   "Matières précieuses et liberalisation." *Zaire Afrique* 96:344–345.

T-Vieta, Kojo
1989   "Ghana: Mixed Results." *West Africa*, 3757:510–511.

Ubonabenshi Ngango, Odette
1987   "Activités des femmes génératrices de revenus: Cas du Rwanda."
         Femmes et Développement (Gisenyi) 2 (December):7–10.
1989   "Femme rurale et développement du pays." *Dialogue* 133 (March–
         April):25–36.

"Uganda/Rwanda: Picking Up the Pieces."
1990   *Africa Confidential* 31, no. 23.

Ukwu, Ukwu I.
1980   "Federal Financing of Projects for National Development and
         Integration." Paper presented at the National Institute for Policy and
         Strategic Studies, Kuru, Nigeria.

UNDP (United Nations Development Programme)
1980   *Rural Women's Participation in Development.* Evaluation Study, no.
         3. New York: UNDP.

UNICEF (United Nations Children Fund)
N.d.   *Ghana: Adjustment Policies and Programmes to Protect Children and
         Other Vulnerable Groups.* Accra: UNICEF.

United States Committee for Refugees
1991   *Exile from Rwanda: Background to an Invasion.* Issue paper prepared
         by Catharine Watson. Washington, DC: U.S. Committee for
         Refugees.

Uphoff, Norman T.
1990   "Post-Newtonian Social Science: Organizing Farmers in Sri Lanka as
         an Impetus to the Revision of Theory." Paper presented at the Annual
         Meeting of the American Political Science Association, San
         Francisco, August 30–September 2.
1991   *Learning from Gal Oya: Possibilities for Participatory Development
         and Post-Newtonian Social Science.* Ithaca, NY: Cornell University
         Press.

USAID (United States Agency for International Development)
1990   *Democratization in Africa.* Background paper (October).
         Washington, DC: USAID, Africa Bureau.

van den Berghe, Pierre L.
1971   "Pluralism and the Polity: A Theoretical Explanation." In *Pluralism
         in Africa*, ed. Leo Kuper and M. G. Smith. Los Angeles: University of
         California Press.

Vidal, Claudine
   1973   "Rwanda: l'affrontement entre Hutus et Tutsis." *Revue Française d'Études Politiques Africaines* no. 88 (April):30–32.
   1985   "Situations ethniques au Rwanda." In *Au coeur de l'ethnie: ethnies, tribalisme et état en Afrique*, ed. Jean-Loup Amselle and Elikia M'bokolo. Paris, Editions la Découverte.
Voss, Joachim
   1987   "L'Amélioration de la culture du haricot sur la base d'un diagnostic des contraintes de production, des pratiques et des potentiels des agriculteurs." In *Les projets de développment rural: réussites, échecs et stratégies nouvelles*, ed. A. Nkundabashaka and J. Voss. Butare: Université Nationale du Rwanda.
Vwakyanakazi, Mukohya
   1982   "African Traders in Butembo, Eastern Zaire (1960–80): A Case Study of Informal Entrepreneurship in a Cultural Context of Central Africa." Ph.D. diss., University of Wisconsin, Madison.
   1991   "Import and Export in the Second Economy in North Kivu." In J. MacGaffey et al., *The Real Economy of Zaire*. London and Philadelphia: James Currey and University of Pennsylvania Press.
Wade, Abdoulaye
   1989   *Un destin pour l'Afrique*. Paris, Karthala.
Wallerstein, Immanuel
   1964   "Voluntary Associations." In *Political Parties and National Integration in Tropical Africa*, ed. J. S. Coleman and C. G. Rosberg. Berkeley: University of California Press.
Wanyande, Peter
   1988   "Democracy and the One-Party State." In *Democratic Theory and Practice*,ed. Walter O. Oyugi, E. S. Atieno Odhiambo, Michael Chege, and Afrifa Gitonga. Portsmouth, NH: Heinemann.
Wasserman, Gary
   1976   *Politics of Decolonization: Kenya Europeans and the Land Issue, 1960–65*. Cambridge: Cambridge University Press.
Watson, Catharine
   1989   "Rwanda: Relying on Equilibre." *Africa Report* 34, no. 1 (January–February):55.
Weber, Max
   1947   *The Theory of Social and Economic Organization*. New York: Free Press.
Weiner, Myron, and Samuel P. Huntington, eds.
   1987   *Understanding Political Development*. Boston: Little, Brown.
Welch, Claude E., and Robert I. Meltzer, eds.
   1984   *Human Rights and Development in Africa*. Albany: State University of New York Press.
Wiarda, Howard J., ed.
   1985   *New Directions in Comparative Politics*. Boulder, CO: Westview Press.
Williams, Robert
   1987   *Political Corruption in Africa*. Brookfield, VT: Gower Publishers.
Wilmsen, Edwin N.
   1989   *Land Filled with Flies: A Political Economy of the Kalahari*. Chicago: Chicago University Press.

Winans, Edgar V., and Angelique Haugerud
    1977   "Rural Self-Help in Kenya: The Harambee Movement." *Human Organization* 36:334–351.

Wiseman, John
    1986   "Urban Riots in West Africa." *Journal of Modern African Studies*, 24, no. 3:509–518.
    1990   *Democracy in Black Africa: Survival and Renewal.* New York: Paragon House Publishers.

Wolf, Eric
    1966   "Kinship, Friendship and Patron-Client Relations in Complex Societies." In *The Social Anthropology of Complex Societies*, ed. M. Banton. Cambridge: Cambridge University Press.

World Bank
    1986   *Ghana: Towards Structural Adjustment.* Washington DC: The World Bank.
    1989   *Sub-Saharan Africa: From Crisis to Sustainable Growth.* Washington, DC: The World Bank.

Wunsch, James S., and Dele Olowu, eds.
    1990   *The Failure of the Centralized State: Institutions and Self-Governance in Africa.* Boulder, CO: Westview Press.

Yeebo, Zaya
    1985   "Ghana: Defence Committees and the Class Struggle." *Review of African Political Economy* 32:64–72.

Young, Crawford
    1965   *Politics in the Congo.* Princeton, NJ: Princeton University Press.
    1985   "Ethnicity and the Colonial and Post-Colonial State in Africa." In *Ethnic Groups and the State*, ed. Paul R. Brass. Totowa, NJ: Barnes and Noble Books.
    1990   "A Look at Sub-Saharan Africa." In *Sea Changes: American Foreign Policy in a World Transformed*, ed. Nicholas X. Rizopolous. New York: Council on Foreign Relations.

———, and Thomas Turner
    1985   *The Rise and Decline of the Zairean State.* Madison: University of Wisconsin Press.

Zaire
    1985   *Conjuncture économique.* Vol. 24. Kinshasa: Département de l'Economie Nationale, Industrie et Commerce
    1987   *Conjuncture économique.* Vol. 26. Kinshasa: Département de l'Economie Nationale, Industrie et Commerce

Zolberg, Aristide
    1966   *Creating Political Order: The Party States of West Africa.* Chicago: University of Chicago Press.

About the Authors

JOEL D. BARKAN is professor in the Department of Political Science, University of Iowa, Iowa City, Iowa.

MICHAEL BRATTON is professor in the Department of Political Science, Michigan State University, East Lansing, Michigan.

NAOMI CHAZAN is professor of political science and director of the Harry S. Truman Institute for the Advancement of Peace, Hebrew University of Jerusalem, Mt. Scopus, Jerusalem, Israel.

JOHN D. HOLM is professor and chair of the Department of Political Science, Cleveland State University, Cleveland, Ohio.

GORAN HYDEN is professor of political science at the University of Florida, Gainesville, Florida.

BABACAR KANTE is director of the Legal Studies Unit, University of St. Louis, Senegal.

JANET MACGAFFEY is assistant Professor of Anthropology at Bucknell University, Lewisburg, Pennsylvania.

PATRICK P. MOLUTSI is a lecturer in the Department of Political and Administrative Studies, University of Botswana, Gaborone, Botswana.

CATHARINE NEWBURY is associate professor in the Department of Political Science, University of North Carolina at Chapel Hill, North Carolina.

PEARL T. ROBINSON is associate professor of political science at Tufts University, Medford, Massachusetts.

DONALD ROTHCHILD is professor of political science at the University of California at Davis, California.

AILI MARI TRIPP is assistant professor of political science and women's studies, University of Wisconsin, Madison, Wisconsin.

NICOLAS VAN DE WALLE is assistant professor in the Department of Political Science, Michigan State University, East Lansing, Michigan.

DONALD C. WILLIAMS is assistant professor in the Department of Political Science, Western New England College, Springfield, Massachusetts.

CRAWFORD YOUNG is a professor in the Department of Political Science, University of Wisconsin, Madison, Wisconsin.

Index

Abaluhya, 170
Abidjan, 48
Accommodation, 99, 106, 117; in Nigeria, 100–102, 103, 113–114
Accountability, 13(figs.), 14, 62, 75, 266, 268; trust and, 11, 12
Acheampong, I. K., 125
Action Group (AG), 100, 101
Adminstration, 71, 263–264; in Kenya, 183–184; in Rwanda, 205–207, 217(nn4, 7), 218(n11)
AFRC. *See* Armed Forces Revolutionary Council
African Association, 225
African Charter of Human and Peoples' Rights, 24
African Commercial Association, 224
African Governance Program, 6
African National Congress, 43
African Teachers Association, 226
AG. *See* Action Group
Agricultural extension service: in Rwanda, 207–208
Agricultural sector, 100, 129; in Botswana, 82, 90; in Rwanda, 193, 194, 202, 204–212, 213, 218(nn12, 14, 15, 16), 219(n21)
Ahmadiyya brotherhood, 227
Ahomadégbé, Justin-Tometin, 50
Aid, 80; foreign, 45, 93, 199, 200–201, 204, 258; political influence of, 47–48
Ajibade, Stephen, 109
Akan, 125
Akintola, Samuel, 101
Akuffo, Fred, 125
Algeria, 43
Alli, Ambrose, 111
Amin, Idi, 24
Amin, Samir, 161
Amnesty International, 150

Amnesty law, 70
Anambra (Nigeria), 111
And-Jef/Mouvement Révolutionnaire pour la Démocratie Nouvelle, 64
Anglicans, 227
Annan, D. F., 131, 132
Anti-erosion measures, 205
Apartheid, 4
APROSOMA. *See* Association pour la Promotion Sociale de la Masse
Armed Forces Revolutionary Council (AFRC), 125
Army. *See* Military
Arrests, 34, 35
Arusha Declaration, 228
Asians: in Botswana, 90–91
Assassinations, 34, 190(n7)
Assemblies of God, 227
Association of Businesswomen, 237
Association of Traditional Chiefs, 155
Association pour la Promotion Sociale de la Masse (APROSOMA), 196, 197
Associations, 61, 129, 155; in Kenya, 174–175, 185–187; political influence of, 238–241; in Tanzania, 223–228, 234–238, 242(n3). *See also* Organizations
Austerity measures, 40–41, 47, 53, 54, 213
Authoritarian regimes, 62, 76, 194, 278–279; continuity of, 38–39; end of, 27, 29; in Kenya, 175, 185
Authority, 12, 13(figs.), 14, 23, 60; political, 24–25; and power, 10, 11; vs. reciprocity, 271–272; social roots of, 266–267
Autocracy, vii, viii, 29, 60, 282, 283
Autonomy, 185, 204; in Nigeria,

110–113; political, 130, 138
Awolowo, Obafemi, 100, 101, 104, 105, 109, 110
Azikiwe, Nnamdi, 100, 104

Babangida, Ibrahim, 116
Bagamoyo (Tanzania), 224
Bakalagadi, 89, 95(n12)
Bakgatla, 87, 88
BAKWATA. *See* Baraza Kuu wa Islam wa Tanzania
Bamangwato, 88
Banda, 46
Bandi, Hastings, 39
Bangwaketse, 87, 88
Banques Populaires, 202
Baptists, 227
Baraza Kuu ya Waislamu wa Tanzania (BAKWATA), 227
Barre, Siad, 45
Bas Zaire, 254
Bateke, 50
Bathily, Abdoulaye, 70
Bayei, 89
BDP. *See* Botswana Democratic Party
Belgium, 196, 197
Bendel (Nigeria), 111
Benedictines, 224
Benin, 31, 47, 48, 117; constitutional reform in, 39, 43; multiparty elections in, 40, 51; protests in, 33, 44, 50
Beni societies, 225
Berlin Mission Society, 224
Berlin Wall, 3, 54(n4)
Biya, Paul, 35, 46
Black, Yondo, 35
BNF. *See* Botswana National Front
BOFESETE. *See* Botswana Federation of Secondary School Teachers
Bokassa, Emperor, 24
Bongo, Omar, 33, 38, 39, 48, 50, 52
Borno (Nigeria), 105, 110

About the Book

The question of "getting politics right" has taken on growing importance in Africa, as the continent's economic crisis continues unabated, and with political reforms occurring in the Soviet Union and Eastern Europe. In response to this situation, scholars are addressing how African countries are being governed and what the constraints and opportunities are for political reform. Their focus on governance marks a new departure in comparative politics, recognizing the potential significance of actors other than governments, notably the various associations that make up civil society.

This book is the first to systematically explore this new conceptual orientation. Nine case studies are introduced by a discussion of the meaning of "governance" and by an overview of events in 1990 that illustrate the movement away from authoritarianism. A concluding chapter points to where we are in the study of governance today, and where we may be heading.